Sufism and Early Islamic Piety

Sufism and Early Islamic Piety: Personal and Communal Dynamics offers a new story about the formative period of Sufism. Through a fresh reading of diverse Sufi and non-Sufi sources, Arin Shawkat Salamah-Qudsi reveals the complexity of personal and communal aspects of Sufi piety in the period between the ninth and thirteenth centuries. Her study also sheds light on the interrelationships and conflicts of early Sufis through emphasizing that early Sufism was neither a quietist nor a completely individual mode of piety. Salamah-Qudsi reveals how the early Sufis' commitment to the Islamic ideal of family life led to different creative arrangements among them in order to avoid contradictions with this ideal and the mystical ideal of solitary life. Her book enables a deeper understanding of the development of Sufism in light of the human concerns and motivations of its founders.

Arin Shawkat Salamah-Qudsi is a senior lecturer of Sufi and Islamic studies at the University of Haifa, Israel. Her research focuses on Medieval Sufi literature and doctrines, the role and position of women in early Sufism, Sufi autobiographies and Sufism and society in early medieval Islam. In 2011, Dr. Salamah-Qudsi obtained Ma'uf fellowship for Outstanding Arab Lecturers, the Council of Higher Education.

Sufism and Early Islamic Piety

Personal and Communal Dynamics

ARIN SHAWKAT SALAMAH-QUDSI
University of Haifa

CAMBRIDGE
UNIVERSITY PRESS

CAMBRIDGE
UNIVERSITY PRESS

University Printing House, Cambridge CB2 8BS, United Kingdom

One Liberty Plaza, 20th Floor, New York, NY 10006, USA

477 Williamstown Road, Port Melbourne, VIC 3207, Australia

314–321, 3rd Floor, Plot 3, Splendor Forum, Jasola District Centre, New Delhi – 110025, India

79 Anson Road, #06–04/06, Singapore 079906

Cambridge University Press is part of the University of Cambridge.

It furthers the University's mission by disseminating knowledge in the pursuit of education, learning, and research at the highest international levels of excellence.

www.cambridge.org
Information on this title: www.cambridge.org/9781108422710
DOI: 10.1017/9781108395014

First published 2019

Printed in the United States of America by Sheridan Books, Inc.

A catalogue record for this publication is available from the British Library.

Library of Congress Cataloging-in-Publication Data
NAMES: Salamah-Qudsi, Arin, 1978- author. | Shawkat, Arin
TITLE: Sufism and early Islamic piety : personal and communal dynamics / Arin Salamah-Qudsi, Arin Shawkat.
DESCRIPTION: Cambridge, United Kingdom : Cambridge University Press, 2018. | Includes bibliographical references and index.
IDENTIFIERS: LCCN 2018009860 | ISBN 9781108422710 (hardback)
SUBJECTS: LCSH: Sufis–Family relationships. | Sufis–Social conditions. | Sufism–History.
CLASSIFICATION: LCC BP189.2 .S257 2018 | DDC 297.409–dc23
LC record available at https://lccn.loc.gov/2018009860

ISBN 978-1-108-42271-0 Hardback

In loving memory of my father
Shawkat Salamah (1947–2008)

Contents

Preface

A well-established fashion among scholars of Sufism during recent decades is to mark the early phase of Sufism, before the fourth/tenth century, as a period of individualism, self-marginalization and a radical life of renunciation, while marking Sufism after that period with clear social and communal impact and formulations. Some important communal aspects of early Sufism, integrated with certain personal and interpersonal aspects in the lives of Sufi personalities, have been underestimated in earlier scholarship. My argument here is that the fabric of early Sufism, prior to the fourth/tenth century, included many more community-based elements than previously thought and that there were stronger communal tendencies in early Sufism than many scholars have shown. This project seeks to explore such tendencies.

The paradigmatic attempt of distinguishing early Sufism with individuality and later Sufism with communal tendencies should be replaced by a multifaceted viewpoint, according to which both individuality and communality are relevant to each phase in the development of Sufism. Early Sufism, thereby, should be treated as a crucible of various modes of personal and spiritual life, as well as of diverse human concerns, interpersonal relationships and conflicts.

It is true that the process of establishing the collective identity of the Sufis reached its peak by embodying the boundaries of Sufi activities and doctrinal systems in the framework of detailed manuals and compendia during the fourth/tenth century. Meanwhile, the earlier stage could also witness certain constituents of this identity. Different forms of connection, interaction and networks between early Sufi figures in undertaking certain kinds of ascetic exercises were not uncommon according to the available sources.

The established scholarly fondness of narrating the story of hostility between Sufi and non-Sufi parties – that could very often become fraught with ideological controversies, polemical interchanges and codes of persecution and violence – presupposes by its very essence the existence of such a coherent group of pious men in the early medieval Islamic landscapes called *ṣūfiyya*. As a result of this presupposition, *ṣūfiyya* became distinguished with clear collective features, and no room was given to detailed discussions of the individual cases of those personalities who acted within the boundaries of that group and had different ambitions, codes of behaviour, life choices and destinies.

Articulating the inter-Sufi confrontations and friction points could, more than the narrative of 'Sufi vs. anti-Sufi confrontation', help us establish our argument that early Sufism was, since its very beginnings, founded on personal differences beside certain communal activities that led to distinguishing the early Sufis as a group.

I am looking to make two basic assumptions here: The first is that more communal and collective operations could be traced to early Sufis, and those should be surveyed and examined, and the other is that the very feature of individuality in reference to early Sufism needs to be redefined. When we refer to individuality in Sufi studies, we directly think about the quietest mode of piety, which is believed to have been undertaken by the early Sufis of Iraq. I would suggest introducing other components to the concept of individuality in this context. In addition to particular individual modes of piety and the quietest undertakings, individuality also had to do with questions like how early Sufis were as family members and how they managed to work their interpersonal ties, which were sometimes fraught with controversies and conflicts in both their particular Sufi communities as well as in the wider Muslim society. Individuality in this sense should also be treated as a broad sphere of mutual influences and interactions. Individual aspects should be observed and analysed in their encounters with communal aspects, and vice versa, the communal aspects of early Sufis' lives should be also reconsidered through their interconnections with more individual aspects of life.

Early foundations of the dynamics of influence and interaction between the personal and the communal spheres of the early Sufis' lives are present in the available sources, as this study will show. Modes of operation within the boundaries of Sufis' communal lives could influence the familial engagements of those Sufis. Meanwhile, in certain cases, familial and personal aspects could leave their marks on the different forms of operation within Sufi communal commitments and engagements.

This study seeks to tell the story of early Sufis in the period between the third/ninth and seventh/thirteenth centuries, from a new perspective in the field: to place the personal and interpersonal narratives in the lives of those Sufis in the foreground, to examine their familial ties and engagements, and to provide insight into the communal dynamics and confrontations within early Sufi circles in their search for a compromise between the mystic's way of life on the one hand and the obligations of normative religion and of normative Sufi conduct and ethos on the other.

By 'personal and interpersonal narratives', I refer to early Sufi personalities within their families and to their forms of interaction with other family members, in particular women, mothers and maternal uncles. In addition, personal dynamics include issues like celibacy and marriage among early Sufis and the different forms of approaching those situations. The wish of the early Sufis to be committed to the Islamic ideal of family life led to different creative arrangements among them in order to avoid contradictions with both this ideal and the mystical ideal of seclusion and solitary life.

By 'communal dynamics', I refer to early Sufis' interactions with other Sufis and the different forms of engagement in Sufi communities. These interactions include tensions, conflicts and quarrels.

In addition to examining the personal and the communal domains of early Sufis' lives, each by itself, I intend to examine the intergraded dynamics between the two domains as they appear in the sources. The different forms of relationship between the personal lives of Sufi individuals and their wider communal lives under their Sufi communities are an additional focus of my work.

Studying Sufi personalities in their familial and close communal circles is essential for unveiling the hard core of the early Sufi movement and also central to understanding the nature of the evolution of this movement in its early phase as a whole.

TOPIC AND STRUCTURE

My intention is to explore Sufi writings of the period under investigation in light of the most recent results of scholarship in this field. Both Sufi and non-Sufi texts will be examined as instruments to reconstruct the individual fragments and interpersonal ties of early Sufis. My access to the primary sources is confined to works in Arabic and Persian. A survey of the different types of primary sources on which this study relied will be included in the **Introduction**. Among these, I would mention *ādāb* literature (Sufi rules of ethics), Sufi letters and correspondence, which I consider a good source for some personal ideas and fragments that were not included in the famous Sufi compendia and *magna opera*. In addition, Sufi hagiographies, autobiographies, introductory sections in Sufi writings, non-Sufi sources such as works of *adab*, chronicles, non-Sufi biographies, travel literature, anti-Sufi literature and both religious and polemic literature should also be consulted. In the underlying argument undertaken here, an attempt is presented to reconsider the scholarly value of hagiographic material as a literary basis able to embed certain social and interpersonal shifts in the actual lives of early Sufis.

The twentieth century witnessed the publication of significant monographs on prominent Sufi figures, in most of which the philological approach was undertaken. In addition, the growing interest among scholars in the history of Sufi orders has prompted an upsurge of collective monographs dedicated to particular Sufi *ṭarīqa*s, and more studies of this type have been undertaken by anthropologists. Such new studies are rarely accurate in the treatment they offer of the spiritual life of these personalities. Individual monographs imply, by their very definition, the crucial role of distinct Sufi personalities. The starting point in these types of monographs is the suggestion that particular Sufi individuals are interesting for their uniqueness and singularity, and therefore, they deserve, more than others, detailed studies of their lives and teachings.

My book covers several early Sufi individuals. A focus is put on how the disparate personal and interpersonal tendencies within the family or the community dynamics of these individuals contributed to shaping their distinctive spiritual worldviews, each of which played a fundamental role in creating the spiritual and practical ethos of early Sufis, and in consolidating their unique identity as a distinctive spiritual group.

THE STRUCTURE OF THE BOOK

I chose to divide the study into two parts, demonstrating two sets of narratives. **Part I** presents an analysis of the personal narratives, while **Part II** examines the communal narratives and different modes of operation that were undertaken by early Sufis in the framework of their lives within Sufi communities in particular and medieval Muslim societies in general. The **Introduction** will briefly introduce the general climate of the period under investigation and review the modern research literature and the expected innovation of the current study; present the working hypotheses, method and design; and, finally, survey in great detail the types of sources and suggested methods to benefit from them.

This will allow me to articulate my basic argument that early Sufism was founded on personal-individual differences in addition to certain communal activities, and that individuality in this domain should not be restricted to the quietest mode of piety that is believed to have been undertaken by the Sufis of the formative phase; rather, it should involve real personal domains, like how early Sufis acted as family members and the way they managed to work their interpersonal ties in their Sufi communities and wider Muslim society.

Beginning with the personal perspective, I suggest adding to its definition the family lives and their interconnections with the communal commitments of early Sufis. **Part I**, thereby, sheds light on a few cases of early Sufis whose lives reflect diversified forms of family life. **Chapter 1** focuses on the roles of early Sufis as family members, spouses and providers, while seeking to re-examine questions of celibacy and working for one's living among them. I gathered here many textual notions that reflect the attempts of certain Sufis to reconcile some ascetic practices like *siyāḥa* (roving in the deserts without taking provisions) with family duties and others that reflect different approaches towards the ascetic ideal of the priority of celibacy over marriage. The prominent premise behind **Chapter 2** is that the various dynamics to reconcile the demands of the increasingly established system of initiation into the Sufi community with family duties become more sophisticated when we approach female Sufis. I relied on Sufi and non-Sufi biographical collections to examine transformations in the Sufi approach towards women and to present an attempt to uncover, through the limited evidences offered by the sources, the different voices and options that these women had. Both **Chapters 3** and **4** present additional support for my argument that the development of early Sufism could, interestingly, be narrated and viewed from the perspective of Sufis' personal lives, along the line between one's own familial commitments and that of the system of affiliation to the Sufi life, which over time gathered clear communal-collective characteristics. **Chapter 3** offers stories of certain mothers who were Sufis themselves as well as mothers of Sufi figures, while **Chapter 4** focuses on maternal uncles who played fundamental roles in the Sufi careers of their nephews. Studying nephew–maternal uncle relationships in early Sufi spheres, despite the problematic nature of the available material, could shed light on additional points of conjunction between the personal and the communal aspects of life on both sides. When the Sufi master is the maternal uncle, the boundaries between the family space and the Sufi space, where the devotee gets his spiritual guidance, dissolve to become one integrative unit.

Examining the diversified forms of communication that were adopted by certain Sufis with their counterparts in the framework of Sufi communal lives is the topic of **Part II**. It is here where the personal-individual tendencies of the early Sufis meet the communal ethos that continued to be established throughout the first centuries of the development of Sufism. In **Chapter 5**, I seek to present what I call the lenient approaches of certain Sufis who introduced the idea of exempting new initiates from strict codes of behaviour and spiritual practice as a measure of facilitating broader and more solid recruitment. While this approach was not common in the early part of the considered period, it succeeded in the course of the sixth/twelfth century in becoming one of the major traits of the Sufi practical system and actual communal life of the Sufis of Islam. In addition to Abū al-Qāsim al-Junayd al-Baghdādī (d. 298/910–911) and his lenient approach, this chapter discusses Sufi personalities who managed to gain positions of renown and fame within their communities ('consensually acclaimed Sufis', as I called them) such as Abū Saʿīd al-Kharrāz (d. 286/899 or a few years earlier) and Abū Ḥafṣ al-Ḥaddād (d. c. 265/878–879). In **Chapter 6**, a detailed discussion of the fourth/tenth century's interesting figure Muḥammad b. ʿAbd al-Jabbār al-Niffarī (d. c. 354/965) is presented. Niffarī's marginalized case reflects a unique mode of medieval spirituality that essentially differs from what can be seen as the Sufi mainstream, which was anchored in the institution of *taṣawwuf*. Beside the representatives of the Sufi ethos on the one hand and those who chose to detach themselves completely from the communal life of institutionalized *taṣawwuf* on the other, **Chapter 7** examines individual tendencies and personal views that generated controversies and poignant conflicts among the Sufis themselves.

While it is considered to be one of the neglected facets of the relationships between the mystic as an individual and his wider community, the critical custom of companionship with youth (*ṣuḥbat al-aḥdāth*) is the topic of **Chapter 8**. Examining this topic could enrich our understanding of the diverse ways in which Sufis, particularly those whose names were associated with *ṣuḥbat al-aḥdāth*, as well as Sufi authors, used to accommodate certain personal patterns of behaviour with a general system of thought and norms constituting the collective Sufi identity. Particular controversial figures like Yūsuf b. al-Ḥusayn al-Rāzī are the main focus of my discussion here.

NOTE ON TRANSLITERATION, TRANSLATION AND DATES

Transliteration of Arabic and Persian in this book follows the system of transliteration adopted in *International Journal of Middle East Studies (IJMES)*. Wherever the proper nouns and concepts that appear are common in English, they are introduced without transliteration, such as 'Sufi' and 'Sufism'.

The English translations of Arabic and Persian citations are the author's unless otherwise stated. Dates include the *Hijrī* year followed by the Christian year.

Acknowledgements

My infinite gratitude goes to Professor Reuven Snir at the University of Haifa, who was my supervisor and who continued to provide me with his trustworthy advice after I finished my Ph.D. I owe Professor Snir a debt that cannot be repaid for his endless support and sincere encouragement.

I also want to thank Beatrice Rehl, Publisher, Religious Studies, at Cambridge University Press, whose guidance accompanied this project from the early stage of writing the primary proposal through that of completing the chapters and submitting the manuscript for review, to working on the manuscript and completing its very last version. I am also thankful to the anonymous reviewers who read the manuscript and provided insightful comments that were very helpful in improving the discussions in each chapter and in arriving at the ideal form of presenting the general arguments of the book as a whole.

And last, I would like to thank my dear family: my mother Amina, my husband Salam, and my children Hasan, Duna and Amir. This work could never have seen light of day without their endless support, patience and constant encouragement.

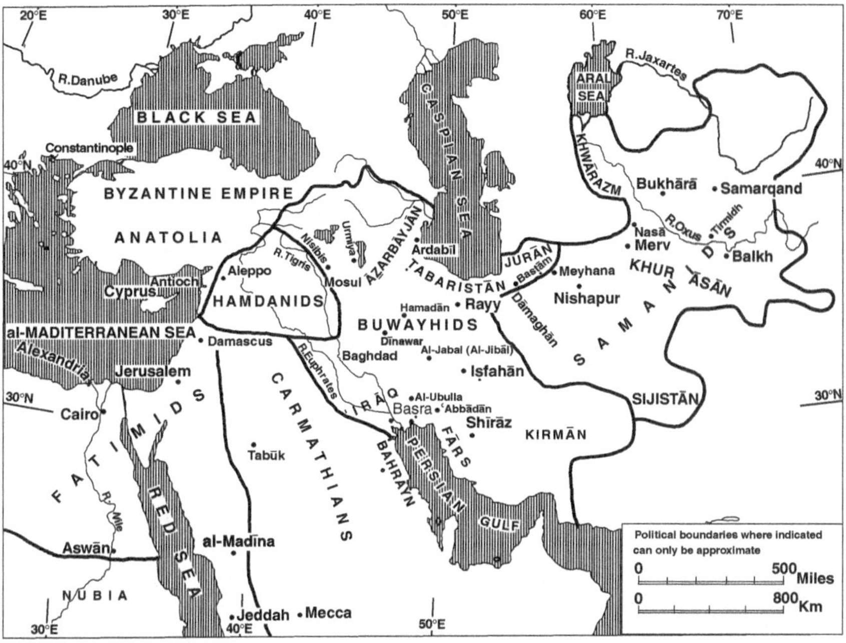

Map 1 The central Islamic lands in the late fourth/tenth century.
Source: *The Cambridge History of Islam*, vol. IA: The Central Islamic Lands from Pre-Islamic Times to the First World War, ed. by P. M. Holt, Ann K. S. Lambton and Bernard Lewis (Cambridge: Cambridge University Press, first published in 1970), 155.

Introduction

SCENE AND BACKGROUND

According to an anecdote narrated by Abū Naṣr al-Sarrāj al-Ṭūsī (d. 378/988) and repeated in later biographies, Abū Ḥamza al-Ṣūfī (d. 269/882–883 or 289/902), one of the earliest Sufi figures who comes to mind when we speak of ecstatic situations and utterances (*shaṭaḥāt*),[1] came to visit al-Ḥārith al-Muḥāsibī (d. 243/857) at his house. When Abū Ḥamza heard the rooster crowing, he started whooping: 'At Your service, My Lord' (*labbayka yā sayyidī*). Allegedly, his guest's strange behaviour made al-Muḥāsibī very nervous, so he took a knife and threatened to kill Abū Ḥamza if the latter did not repent for his behaviour: 'If you do not repent for this behaviour, then I will slay you', he told him. Abū Ḥamza's reply was confusing. He told al-Muḥāsibī that if he, al Muḥāsibī, was incapable of contemplating the sincere motivations behind this ecstatic

[1] There is a common confusion in relation to this character. Some sources refer to him as Abū Ḥamza al-Baghdādī, while others mention him as Abū Ḥamza al-Khurāsānī or simply as Abū Ḥamza al-Ṣūfī. Most probably, the references are made to the same character that was a contemporary of Junayd and one of the famous Sufis of Baghdad, though he was originally from Khurāsān. [See his biography in Abū ʿAbd al-Raḥmān al-Sulamī, *Ṭabaqāt al-ṣūfiyya*, ed. by Johannes Pedersen (Leiden: Brill, 1960), 328–331; Abū al-Qāsim ʿAbd al-Karīm al-Qushayrī, *al-Risāla al-qushayriyya* (Cairo: al-Bābī al-Ḥalabī, 1940), 26.] Interestingly, Persian hagiographies provide us with two separate biographies of two so-called different figures of the late third/ninth century who had close contacts with the circle of Junayd: Abū Ḥamza al-Khurāsānī and Abū Ḥamza al-Baghdādī [see ʿAbd Allāh Anṣārī Haravī, *Ṭabaqāt al-ṣūfiyya*, ed. by Akram Shifāʾī (Tehran: N.p., n.d.), 46–47 (www.sufi.ir/books/download/farsi/khajeh-abdollah/tabaghat-sofieh.pdf, accessed 11 January 2017); ʿAbd al-Raḥmān Jāmī, *Nafaḥāt al-uns*, ed. by Mahdī Pūr (Tehran: Intishārāt-i Kitābfurūshī-i Maḥmūdī, 1918), 70–71].

behaviour, then he should not allow himself to enjoy the life of wealth he was living. In other words, if al-Muḥāsibī allowed himself to enjoy a wealthy lifestyle, it was a proof that he had reached a high spiritual rank where wealth would not harm his renunciation, and therefore, he should be able to recognize the reasons for and nature of the state of intoxication underlying Abū Ḥamza's behaviour.[2]

This interesting anecdote might illustrate how the solidarity of the highly esteemed group of *ṣūfiyya*, the mystics of Baghdad, could have been challenged. Abū Ḥamza himself was one of the companions of Abū al-Qāsim al-Junayd, the great master of Baghdad (d. 298/910-911). He allegedly criticized the wealthy lifestyle of one of the pillars of this group, al-Ḥārith al-Muḥāsibī. The anecdote also illustrates how Abū Ḥamza, an intoxicated personality of a passionate yet controversial mode of piety, was able to integrate into the general fabric of what became known in the history of early Sufism as the School of Baghdad.

According to the available sources, Abū Ḥamza committed himself to a life of hard renunciatory practices, and he would frequently roam alone as well as with other Sufi figures. His biographical account in Abū ʿAbd al-Raḥmān al-Sulamī's (d. 412/1021) *Ṭabaqāt al-ṣūfiyya* is fraught with statements in which he calls for a life of seclusion and constant roving. Interestingly, Sulamī chose to end this account with the following anecdote:

One day, Abū Ḥamza heard one of his companions criticising another for not refraining from showing his ecstatic state in the presence of non-Sufi associates (*iẓhār wajdihi wa-ghalabat al-ḥāl ʿalayhi wa-iẓhār sirrihi fī majlis fīhi baʿḍ al-aḍdāḍ*). Abū Ḥamza, at that time, said to the critic: 'Leave behind your critique, since ecstasy (*wajd*) overwhelms the conciseness and removes the ability to differentiate between things. It turns all places into one single place, and all essences into one single essence. The one who becomes overwhelmed by ecstasy should not be blamed at all.'[3]

The case of Abū Ḥamza is not uncommon in the history of early Sufism. As the sources document, the unity of the Baghdadi group of *ṣūfiyya* could have been unavoidably disrupted by certain voices of controversy. As for the above anecdote of Abū Ḥamza with al-Ḥārith al-Muḥāsibī, it is

[2] See Abū Naṣr al-Sarrāj al-Ṭūsī, *Ṣuḥuf min kitāb al-lumaʿ*, ed. by A. J. Arberry (London: Luzac, 1947), 6–7. The anecdote appears also in Shams al-Dīn Muḥammad b. Aḥmad al-Dhahabī, *Siyar aʿlām al-nubalāʾ*, ed. by Shuʿayb al-Arnāʾūṭ and others (Beirut: Dār al-Risāla, 1982–1988), vol. 13, 167 (the biography of Abū Ḥamza al-Baghdādī).

[3] See Sulamī, *Ṭabaqāt*, 330–331.

interesting to note that, regardless of the historical authenticity or lack thereof in such texts, the reference to it in Sarrāj's work is very significant. Even if the anecdote comes from Sarrāj or from one of his contemporaries' imaginative work during the course of the fourth/tenth century, we should ask how such stories help portray the general boundaries of the Sufi ethos or establish the perception of key topics, such as wealth and poverty and sobriety and intoxication, in accordance with this ethos.

It seems most likely that, in al-Sarrāj's eyes, this anecdote was not going to defame the group of *ṣūfiyya* or destabilize the solidarity between them during the particular historical context of his time. It appears as though Sarrāj was convinced that the interpersonal controversy between Abū Ḥamza and al-Muḥāsibī and the mutual criticism was a legitimate feature of early Sufi life and that this was not enough in itself to hurt the desired ideal of solidarity. This is the most outspoken message of Sarrāj's discourse, as I perceive it.

From another perspective, this anecdote as well as similar material provided by Sufi works around Sarrāj's time leaves a strong impression that portraying the group of *ṣūfiyya* at harmony and solidarity was due to particular agendas, those of the group's leaders and of Sufi authors who supported them and were willing to disseminate such agendas.[4]

Early Sufis during the period under investigation succeeded in consolidating their identity as men of a distinct spiritual identity. They enjoyed a great degree of public veneration, being the most outspoken and undisputable representatives of Islamic piety in times that had witnessed the increasing distrust in the office of the Abbasid *khalīfa* and the latter's eventual loss of his religious authority in favour of the group of *ḥadīth* scholars, the *ahl al-ḥadīth*.[5] Many of the early Sufis were, in fact, scholars of *ḥadīth*, and this, beside other dynamics, advanced their increasing power and authority, led to their integration into the general fabric of the honoured group of *ahl al-ḥadīth*, and qualified them for a high position of public admiration since the early Abbasid era. *Ahl al-ḥadīth*, both Sufi and non-Sufi, had succeeded in the course of early medieval

[4] On this title and its reference to the particular group of the Baghdadi Sufis, see Ahmet T. Karamustafa, *Sufism: The Formative Period* (Berkeley and Los Angeles: University of California Press, 2007), 1–37; Christopher Melchert, 'Origins and Early Sufism', in *The Cambridge Companion to Sufism*, ed. by Lloyd Ridgeon (New York: Cambridge University Press, 2015), 13–14.

[5] See a detailed discussion of the shifts that occurred in the office of *khalīfa* in Patricia Crone and Martin Hinds, *God's Caliph: Religious Authority in the First Centuries of Islam* (Cambridge: Cambridge University Press, 1986), 80–96.

Islam in inheriting the religious-spiritual authority which had been almost exclusively embedded into the ultimate institution of *khilāfa*.[6] Many Sufis sought to integrate their practice as *ḥadīth* transmitters into their distinctive Sufi training, encouraging a broad basis of public recognition for their unique integrative agenda. In the course of time, however, these Sufi *ḥadīth* scholars began to outline the distinguishing features of their agenda, namely the combination of the knowledge of the prophetic tradition with the inward spiritual conception of that tradition, which differed from the outward agenda of the non-Sufi *ḥadīth* scholars. Even though these attempts were not always undertaken openly, many of them could be deduced from the sources. The detailed comparisons between the terms *ʿilm* (*ḥadīth* science) and *maʿrifa* (Sufi knowledge) and the celebration of the desired position of *ʿārifūn* versus what could be seen as the inferior positions of *ʿulamāʾ* and *qurrāʾ* (lit. the reciters of the *Qurʾān*) in Sufi writings of this historical phase provide one such example. It is interesting to note that the group of *qurrāʾ* in particular appears frequently in some early Sufi sources with very negative connotations. Its members claimed to be the true heirs of the Prophet and the ultimate protectors of his message while they were, in fact, as Abū Ṭālib al-Makkī (d. 386/996) puts it, nothing but hypocrites. 'The most hypocritical people in the Muslim community are its *qurrāʾ*' (*akthar munāfiqī ummatī qurrāʾuhā*), declares Makkī while describing this situation.[7] A similar criticism of those who memorized the *Qurʾān* without being able to cleanse their inner selves of hypocrisy and utilitarianism is noted in other Sufi sources.[8]

[6] D. G. Tor relies on the above-mentioned work of Crone and Hinds to examine the transition from what he calls a 'Caliphal Sunna' towards a 'prophetic Sunna' and the rise of the group of *ahl al-ḥadīth* in which many of the early ascetics (*zuhhād*), not yet the *ṣūfiyya*, were embedded. A special reference to al-Fuḍayl b. ʿIyāḍ (d. 187/803) and his relationships with the Abbasid ruler as well as his powerful impact upon him is presented here. See D. G. Tor, 'God's Cleric: al-Fuḍayl b. ʿIyāḍ and the Transition from Caliphal to Prophetic Sunna', in *Islamic Cultures, Islamic Contexts: Essays in Honor of Professor Patricia Crone*, ed. by Behnam Sadeghi, Asad Ahmed, Adam Silverstein and Robert Hoyland (Leiden and Boston: Brill, 2015), 195–228.

[7] Abū Ṭālib al-Makkī, *Qūt al-qulūb fī muʿāmalat al-maḥbūb wa-waṣf ṭarīq al-murīd ilā maqām al-tawḥīd* (Cairo: al-Bābī al-Ḥalabī, 1961), vol. 1, 97.

[8] See e.g., Abū Naṣr al-Sarrāj al-Ṭūsī, *Kitāb al-lumaʿ fī al-taṣawwuf*, ed. by Reynold A. Nicholson (Leiden: Brill, 1914), 266: 'Blot out your name from the list of *qurrāʾ*.' Cf. the introduction of the fourth/tenth century work, *Adab al-mulūk*, where the anonymous author asserts that the group of *qurrāʾ* in his days instead of being completely occupied with a thorough study of the holy texts went on to utilize their position for the sake of fulfilling material interests [see an anonymous author, *Adab*

The legacy of sayings and anecdotes and of complete compositions attributed to early Sufi personalities all document an identity that started to come into being and was clearly recognized in the general scene of Sufi activity and thinking. Even in this early phase, this identity was collective. Early Sufis were undoubtedly aware of their unique method of reaching God which distinguished them from 'normative' members of the Muslim community. The existence of different individual modes of piety did not contradict the emergence of that collective identity. Certain circles of power, which were fully controlled by charismatic Sufis in Iraq and Persia, sought to forcefully grab those on the edges of this diversity and to reunite individual intentions and aspirations, at least on the level of the idealized reality portrayed in Sufi works. The most influential circle of this kind was that of the incontrovertible Junayd. The main target of Junayd and his circle, the Baghdadi *ṣūfiyya*, was to constitute an overwhelming framework that could embed all appearances of individual identity by blurring their distinction and uniqueness as far as this was possible. The *ṣūfiyya* was not in fact the ultimate face of early Sufism in the period under investigation here. Various attempts to destabilize this position were documented in the sources. In certain cases, these attempts took the form of direct criticism against the high ethos imposed by the renowned leaders of the group. In other cases, such attempts were undertaken by means of adopting a lifestyle that set its members apart from that ethos, as in the case of Ruwaym b. Aḥmad (d. 303/915), or even through total self-exclusion from the centralized Baghdadi institution, as in the case of Niffarī.

It was remarkable that Junayd and his conformist circle of companions appeared to avoid attempts of marginalization. Instead of ignoring and separating Sufi figures with different yet problematic agendas, Junayd preferred to adopt procedures of integration for the sake of protecting *taṣawwuf*'s reputation for respect and dignity. If we follow Junayd's agenda throughout his teachings and writings, we come across his desired formula of establishing an individual identity that fully corresponds with a collective one instead of conflicting with it. This intended formula did not always seem to be successful.

Attempts to challenge the Baghdadi-centric ideal of communal solidarity were frequent. In some cases, challenging this formula took the form of disagreeing with the criteria based on which Junayd imposed his collective

al-mulūk, ed. by Bernd Radtke (Beirut: Beiruter Texte und Studien Herausgegeben vom Orient-Istitut der Deutschen Morgenländischen Gesellschaft in Kommission bei Franz Steiner Verlag Stuttgart, 1991), 4].

identity, while in other cases the individual identity dominated the lives and work of certain figures and led them to totally reject the very formula of Junayd with all its criteria and potential outcomes.

This book seeks to examine how the pragmatic leaders of *ṣūfiyya* tended to stretch the boundaries of the high Sufi ethos that they had created so that those boundaries could be able to embrace as many as possible of the individual modes of piety of those days. What were the different strategies that these leaders employed for the purpose of establishing a centralized Baghdadi-based system of *taṣawwuf* with a well-defined theoretical, ethical and practical agenda? As the following chapters will show, this pragmatism manifested itself in sophisticated processes of absorbing controversial personalities and trends for the purpose of bringing them under one broad and multicoloured umbrella. Such processes relied primarily on a lengthy interpretative campaign for what was considered problematic and shocking from the texts and sayings attributed to certain Sufi personalities. In order to present a harmonious reconciliatory image of *taṣawwuf*, the leaders of *ṣūfiyya* went on to promote the doctrinal basis of concepts such as *fanāʾ* (annihilation), *ghayba* (spiritual absence) and *shaṭḥ* (ecstatic utterance). I argue, for instance, that the doctrinal basis of the last concept, *shaṭḥ*, is the ultimate product of the *ṣūfiyya* and their leaders' mentality. Only this group could really provide brilliant interpretations of the emotionally intensive states of intoxication and passion. The detailed treatment of *shaṭḥ* and *shaṭaḥāt* in Sarrāj's *Lumaʿ* is one example of such work. It is here that the controversial behaviour of certain Sufis managed to gain moral and religious justification, even if these Sufis themselves were not supposed to agree with such intellectual discussions of their forms of behaviour.

The most prominent objective of *ṣūfiyya* 's life work, as I see it, was to impose the Baghdadi umbrella over as many people as possible. A close reading between the lines of the available sources, nevertheless, guarantees unveiling the actual controversies among all who lost their uniqueness and individuality under the common umbrella. Abū ʿAbd al-Raḥmān al-Sulamī during the late fourth/tenth century provided the biography of Ibn Yazdānyār, the Sufi of northwestern Persia, even though Ibn Yazdānyār himself was one of the early figures who challenged the ideal of Sufi solidarity. Sarrāj devotes a separate section to him in which he criticizes him and reveals what he considers Ibn Yazdānyār's attempts to defame the Sufis of Baghdad. In the meantime, we find that another Sufi author of the late fourth/tenth century, ʿAbd al-Malik al-Kharkūshī (d. 407/1016), relies heavily on Ibn Yazdānyār's detailed discussion of the concept of *ḥayāʾ*

(modesty) and its various categories in his *Tahdhīb al-asrār*.[9] Like other Sufi authors, Kharkūshī refers to Ibn Yazdānyār on many occasions in his work. The case of Ibn Yazdānyār, as will be thoroughly examined later, demonstrates the interesting mechanism behind some particularly daring attempts to bypass the homogeneous image of the *ṣūfiyya* as well as the sophisticated strategies of the representatives of *ṣūfiyya* themselves to confront such attempts. Apart from Sarrāj who chose to defame Ibn Yazdānyār, there was a sort of a general consensus among the majority of Sufi authors to keep this personality within the walls of *taṣawwuf*.

The centralization of the Baghdadi-based mode of piety, with the powerful and pragmatic personality of Junayd and his circle of Sufi companions and novices, left its marks on diverse aspects of the family lives and interpersonal ties of early Sufis. The attempts of certain figures to release themselves from the chains imposed by the creators of the high Sufi ethos according to which all members of *ṣūfiyya* should live and work were not restricted to the religious-spiritual arenas, but these attempts began to appear also in personal domains of life. In order to challenge the agenda of Junayd, his contemporary, Ruwaym b. Aḥmad, for instance, appears in the sources as very eager to proclaim his paternal feelings towards his daughter in the presence of his Sufi companions who had a different perception of familial emotions and personal forms of expressing them in Sufi spheres. For Ruwaym, the mystic's involvement in courtly affairs was not expected by any means to harm his pure state of *tawakkul* (the principle of maintaining trust in God). This latter notion provided the theoretical basis for two alleged contradictory procedures most probably undertaken by the *ṣūfiyya* then: disseminating a criticism of Ruwaym's involvement in the Sulṭān's affairs, yet investing sufficient effort for the sake of keeping his individual piety inside the Sufi consensual ethos. The different patterns of the attempts led by certain Sufi figures to disengage themselves from the authority of *ṣūfiyya* 's unifying ethos attracted our interest from various perspectives in this book. Such attempts and counter-attempts to bring back those who dared to rebel against the desired consensus of the Sufis constitute the fascinating story told in this book.

Early Sufis had active social lives, and they led sophisticated interpersonal relationships more than what has been suggested. In the course of time, the social engagements of early Sufis took place around particular centres of power and authority in Syria, Iraq and Persia. Internal power

[9] See ʿAbd al-Malik b. Muḥammad al-Naysābūrī al-Kharkūshī, *Tahdhīb al-asrār*, ed. by Bassām Bārūd (Abū Ẓabī: al-Majmaʿ al-Thaqāfī, 1999), 440–445.

struggles among certain Sufi figures, those that the authors of Sufi compendia did not feel free to discuss, seemed to be one of the inevitable outcomes of this sophisticated social fabric. Behind the praiseworthy principles that early Sufis usually celebrated, such as companionship (*ṣuḥba*), brotherhood (*ukhuwwa*) and altruism (*īthār*, *futuwwa*), emotions of mutual envy and rancour appeared not uncommon. I would argue that the frequency of works entirely dedicated to *ṣuḥba* and its rules and ethics in the early history of Sufism is a clear evidence, somehow, of a pragmatic need that early Sufi authors felt for such material in light of a reality fraught with tension among their contemporaries, those who were expected to act in perfect brotherhood and cultivate their virtuous relationships springing from their shared spiritual aspirations and destiny. Once we develop an understanding of these relationships, albeit partly and selectively as far as our sources allow, we shall obtain a clearer picture of the ways and dynamics according to which Sufi doctrinal systems developed and branched out in the period under consideration. Going into the personal-social and day-to-day lives of those who contributed to the work of consolidating the various Sufi theories should help explain how such theories were, in fact, products of particular social environments. In order to properly understand the Sufi concept of *ṣuḥba*, we need to examine the nature and structures of the social ties and the personal interests of the Sufis in the particular context of the term's genesis rather than approach *ṣuḥba* as a mere theoretical term isolated from any possible body of human needs and contextual necessities. Such necessities likely stood behind the shifts that occurred in the content and clues of the term *ṣuḥba*.

Early Sufis, similar to other men of letters in medieval Islam, conducted lives that were not completely free of personal conflicts that could potentially escalate into mutual defamation and calumny. Such situations contained the very human essence of actual living Sufi figures while literary Sufi heroes, with whom Sufi oeuvres were filled, were portrayed as perfectly harmonious and generally compatible. It would be worthwhile to inquire into the reasons underlying the appearance of a consistent Sufi ethos and the identity of those with an interest in guaranteeing this ethos, as well as their motivations and strategies.

This book presents an attempt to reread known sources with human concerns in mind. It is an attempt to again contemplate the relationships between the Sufi text and its cultural–social and communal contexts. At its very core, this method involved the act of re-examining the possible meeting points between the linguistic indicator and the contextual-human-personal meaning when approaching texts dominated by theoretical agendas and literary contents. Examining this method throughout the various chapters of the book provides an example that might be useful for other endeavours to investigate the social lives of non-Sufi groups who, like the Sufis, have left us a rich legacy of writings.

RECENT SCHOLARSHIP AND THE CONTRIBUTION OF THE CURRENT BOOK

The main reason that motivated me to undertake the writing of this book is the crucial need I felt for a new scholarly work to thoroughly investigate the private lives of early Sufis as well as the relationships within their circles and communities in the period between the third/ninth and seventh/thirteenth centuries. Recent scholarship into early Sufism lacks attempts to reveal some of the hidden facets of early Sufis' everyday lives, their emotions, concerns, interpersonal relationships and conflicts. It does not attempt to expose the sophisticated dynamics between the personal spheres of the early Sufis' family lives and engagements and the communal spheres involving their engagement in Muslim societies in general and in the activities of the Sufi communities in particular.

To reconstruct the early stage of development, I usually consulted the compelling work of Ahmet Karamustafa, *Sufism: The Formative Period* (2007). This book adopts an uncompromising historical approach while integrating early developments into a clear and homogeneous narrative of the emergence of Sufism. Karamustafa's work puts the focus on what he terms 'Baghdad Sufism' as a special mode of Iraqi piety whose major characteristics are clearly presented. His narrative is centred around the theme of how between the third/ninth and sixth/twelfth centuries, Sufism became a self-conscious mode of piety, developed a distinctive system of doctrines and practices that came to be enhanced by an influential body of literary tradition, and eventually occupied the forefront of both early medieval Islamic intellectual life and actual social-religious life. Karamustafa's work is of enormous importance for our understanding of the socio-historical scope of the emergence of Sufism and its development in one of the most ambiguous phases in the history of this movement.

Modern scholarship on early Sufism is typically shaped by two major arguments. The first involves the strict dichotomy between what are seen as 'a-social' trends in the early period of Sufism and what can be considered as socially active Sufism. This argument regards early Sufism as a-social, very quiet and 'genuine' pattern of Sufism, while considering later Sufism in the period that followed the fifth/eleventh century as 'social' and 'popular'. The second argument concerns the way in which multifarious developments of Sufism were described as a part of 'huge' and influential historical shifts in the world of Islam. The latter argument is best demonstrated in the scholarly trend to classify early Sufism in various stages and the attempts to draw upon shared theoretical and practical features of each stage. I argue that the first argument is imprecise and says little about the actual life and interpersonal relations of the early Sufis in the individual and communal realms, while the second needs to be combined with a scholarly endeavour to shed significant new light on individual arenas and interpersonal ties among early Sufis.

In recent years, an increasing number of studies have adopted a new scholarly attitude, placing the Sufi movement in Islam in different cultural and social spheres. The articles in John Curry and Erik Ohlanders' work, *Sufism and Society* (2012), keenly illustrate the different types of sources that scholars are turning to for the history of Sufism and the new viewpoints they suggest when incorporating long-ignored sources such as hagiographies and court records. The main challenge facing the contributors of *Sufism and Society* was how to reread the existing sources and interpret the various narrative voices and strategies used by their authors in order to reconstruct the varied activities of the Sufis in the period with which most of the articles in the volume are concerned, that is, 1200–1800 CE. Although the period between the fourth/tenth and seventh/thirteenth centuries is given some attention, the period that follows the seventh/thirteenth century and lasts until the premodern era has caught the interest of most of the contributors. This is the period that saw the consolidation of the sheikh–disciple relationship into the basic manifestation of the Sufi institution, which may help explain why for modern scholarship it forms one of the 'most attractive' periods in the history of the Sufi movement in Islam. A major strength of *Sufism and Society* for our purposes here is the critical attention it pays to hagiographical material, reclaiming its historical power as a legitimate source for social and historical study. In my book, therefore, hagiographical sources, long deemed a-historical and therefore without sociopolitical implications, will be treated, in additional to other types of material, in the same light as the recent positive approach.

Sufism and Society brings to the surface the sociopolitical contexts of Sufi activities at different points of time and place by providing us with new research tools that cover a broader spectrum. I will take these benefits, as I focus on the third/ninth to the seventh/thirteenth century, and seek to reappraise the diverse religious projects of the Sufi actors of this period as creators of unique individual identities.

Kenneth Avery's monograph, *Shiblī: His Life and Thought in the Sufi Tradition* (2014), presents a new attempt to reconsider Sufi hagiographies and to examine them again in light of the most recent results of scholarship in this field. While adopting Jawid Mojaddedi's suggestion to consider the functions of Sufi accounts rather than their historicity, Avery approaches the narrative structures and styles of the anecdotal segments, which are the building blocks of the hagiographical body of writing. For scholars of the formative period of Sufism, these types of sources are simply the only option, and therefore, the methodological notes made by Avery to explain the scholarly value of hagiographical material despite its historically inauthentic features are very insightful. His monograph presents us with a pioneering attempt to use a better and fresher method, derived from the existing hagiographies, to reconstruct Abū Bakr al-Shiblī's (d. 334/946) image and spirituality through the different phases of Sufism. I agree with Avery's suggestion that the image of a particular Sufi figure as portrayed by his near-contemporaries can provide a means that is more useful in examining his unique piety than exploring his real life, and I also agree that the idealized images of the hagiographies' heroes contain very little historical truth. However, I would argue that, in certain cases, whenever particular unique stories occur, certain historical conclusions could be construed (see 'Working Hypothesis, Method and Sources' hereinafter).

The growing interest among scholars in the history of Sufi orders has prompted an upsurge of collective monographs dedicated to particular Sufi *ṭarīqa*s, and more studies of this type have been undertaken by anthropologists. Such new studies are rarely accurate in their treatment of the spiritual life of these personalities.

Philological methods are still capable of providing a sufficient basis for investigating new arenas in Sufi studies when combined with socio-historical methods. One interesting example of this philological method relates to early Sufi theories on *waqt* that is the mystic moment. The different meanings of the term *waqt* in early Sufi teachings have already attracted the interest of scholars like Louis Massignon, Richard Gramlich, Gerhard Böwering and, most recently, Kenneth Avery.[10] Generally

[10] Since ancient Arabic lexicons neither provide a precise meaning of the word *waqt* nor do they determine its exact duration in comparison with other words in Arabic that indicate time, these scholars rely on early Sufi compendia in order to present their own understanding of the term. Böwering, for instance, agrees with Richard Gramlich, who shows that in the circles of Persian Sufis of the classical period the term *waqt* was interchangeable with *ḥāl* (state). *Waqt* could also carry the same content of *ān*, as Böwering states. See Gerhard Böwering, 'Ideas of Time in Persian Sufism', *Iran*, vol. 30

speaking, *waqt* refers to a transitory state of experiencing revelations and spiritual observations. Sufi authors, such as Sarrāj, Abū al-Qāsim al-Qushayrī (d. 465/1073) and ʿAlī b. ʿUthmān Jullābī Hujwīrī (d. between 465/1072 and 469/1077), emphasized that 'the Sufi is the son of his present moment' (*al-ṣūfī ibn waqtihi*).[11] Living the mystic moment is attained through total separation from both past and future. In addition to the common meaning of the phrase '*ibn waqtihi*', I suggest that early Sufis were also aware of the unbreakable ties between the mystic's individual life and engagements, on the one hand, and the actual life of his extended community, on the other. Phrases like '*yanfarid bi-ḥālihi wa-waqtihi*' ('he is singled out by his individual mystic state and *waqt*')[12] and 'he was the one of his *waqt*' appear in Sulamī's *Ṭabaqāt al-ṣūfiyya*.[13] Basically, both statements could be seen as proof of the interchangeability between *waqt* and the mystic state (*ḥāl*) in early Sufi writings. In addition to the reference to *ḥāl*, *waqt* could refer in certain cases to the unique position that a mystic would hold among his fellows and the way they would treat him and relate to his spiritual position. In his treatment of the term, Avery points to several places in Sufi works where the term *waqt* is used in a 'non-mystical sense'.[14] This is often true when we refer to the plural form *awqāt* (times). However, in many occasions where Sulamī uses *waqt* without the word *ḥāl* following or preceding it, such as when he describes someone saying that he 'in his *waqt* was unique in his method' (*fī waqtihi kāna wāḥidan fī ṭarīqatihi*),[15] we get a strong impression that the term refers to an elevated 'status' or 'position' that this man enjoyed in the eyes of the Sufis of his time.

(1992), 83. Cf. Richard Gramlich, *Die Schiitischen Derwischorden Persiens: Zweiter Teil: Glaube und Lehre* (Wiesbaden: Franz Steiner, 1976), 352. See also Louis Massignon, 'Le Temps dans la Pensée Islamique', in *Opera Minora: Texte Recuellis, Classes et Presentes avec une Bibliographie par Y. Moubarac* (Beirut: Dār al-Maʿārif, 1963), vol. 2, 606–612; also Kenneth Avery, *A Psychology of Early Sufi Samāʿ: Listening and Altered States* (London and New York: Routledge Curzon, 2004), 74–83.

[11] See Sarrāj, *Lumaʿ*, 396; Qushayrī, *Risāla*, 33; Abū al-Ḥasan ʿAlī b. ʿUthmān al-Jullābī al-Hujwīrī, *Kashf al-maḥjūb*, ed. by Valentin Zukovsky (Leningrad: Maṭbaʿat-i Dār al-ʿUlūm-i Ittiḥād-i Jamāhīr-i Shūravī-yi Sūsyālīstī, 1926), 480–484. See also Najm al-Dīn al-Kubrā, *Fawāʾiḥ al-jamāl wa-fawātiḥ al-jalāl*, ed. by Fritz Meier (Wiesbaden: F. Steiner, 1957), Arabic text, 50. See also ʿAbd Allāh Anṣārī's chapter on *waqt* where he identifies three levels of meanings, the highest of which relates to the state of preoccupation of God (*istighrāq rasm al-waqt fī wujūd al-Ḥaqq*). [See ʿAbd Allāh Anṣārī Haravī, *Manāzil al-sāʾirīn* (Beirut: Dār al-Kutub al-ʿIlmiyya, 1988), 102.]

[12] See Sulamī, *Ṭabaqāt*, 476, 495.

[13] See e.g., ibid., 175, 283, 340, 476.

[14] See Avery, *Psychology*, 76–77.

[15] Sulamī, *Ṭabaqāt*, 175.

A similar usage of the term appears in Qushayrī's *Risāla* and Jullābī Hujwīrī's *Khashf al-maḥjūb*.[16] This usage might be in a 'non-mystical sense' as Avery calls it, but I would suggest keeping in mind its importance when we deal with Sufi communal lives and the ways early Sufis evaluated other Sufis' spiritual position. Interestingly, the two meanings of *waqt* – the personal, as a synonym of a spiritual state, and the communal, as a venerable spiritual position among fellows – could appear together in particular occasions where both terms *waqt* and *ḥāl* appear in the same statement. The above-mentioned *yanfarid bi-ḥālihi wa-waqtiḥi* is one example.[17] The early commentator of Abū Bakr al-Kalābādhī's (d. 380/990) *Kitāb al-ta'arruf li-madhhab ahl al-taṣawwuf*, Abū Ibrāhīm Ismā'īl b. Muḥammad al-Mustamlī al-Bukhārī (d. 434/1043), describes the true Sufis as those who 'do not choose their times'. The word *waqt* here implies *ḥāl* since God alone is capable of granting the Sufis their 'times', that is, most probably, their unique states of grace.[18]

Individual monographs imply, by their very nature, the crucial role of distinct Sufi personalities. The starting point in this type of monograph is the suggestion that particular Sufi heroes are interesting for their uniqueness and singularity, and therefore, they deserve, more than others, detailed studies of their lives and teachings.

In the framework of my book, several early Sufi heroes will be treated. A focus will be put on how the disparate personal and interpersonal tendencies of these figures shaped their distinctive spiritual worldviews, each playing a fundamental role in creating the spiritual and practical ethos of early Sufis. My argument is that the fabric of early Sufism prior to the eighth/fourteenth century included more community-based elements than previously thought. The paradigmatic attempt to distinguish early Sufism with individuality and later Sufism with communal tendencies should be replaced by a multifaceted viewpoint according to which both individuality and communality are relevant to each phase in the development of Sufism. Early Sufism, thereby, should be treated as a crucible of various modes of personal and spiritual life, as well as of diverse human

[16] See e.g., Qushayrī, *Risāla*, 27 (the biography of Shiblī), 28 (the biography of 'Abd Allāh b. Munāzil). Cf. Jullābī Hujwīrī, *Kashf al-maḥjūb*, 538. On the latter reference to Hujwīrī, see also Avery, *Psychology*, 77–78.

[17] See also Abū al-Ma'ālī 'Abd Allāh b. Muḥammad 'Ayn al-Quḍāt Hamadhānī, *Tamhīdāt*, ed. by 'Afīf 'Usayrān (Tehran: Kitābkhānih-yi Manūchihrī, 1341 *Shamsī*/1962), 35; Anṣārī Haravī, *Ṭabaqāt al-ṣūfiyya*, 68.

[18] Mustamlī Bukhārī, *Sharḥ kitāb al-ta'arruf li-madhhab al-taṣawwuf* (Tehran: Chāpkhānih-yi Dānishgāh-i Tehrān, 1346 *Shamsī*), vol. 1, 174.

concerns, interpersonal relationships and conflicts. When we refer to individuality in Sufi studies, we immediately think about the quietest mode of piety, which is believed to have been undertaken by the early Sufis of Iraq. Individuality, I argue, has also to do with questions such as how early Sufis conducted themselves as family members and how they managed to deal with their interpersonal ties, which were sometimes fraught with controversy and conflict, both in their particular Sufi communities as well as in the wider Muslim society. During the past few years, as I began to outline my preliminary conceptions of certain angles of this topic, I turned my attention towards the roles of mothers in early Sufism. At the same time, I made a very brief statement in reference to the interesting position of maternal uncles in the lives of early Sufi personalities.[19] It is here that I attempt to further develop this statement by integrating the issues of mothers and maternal uncles into a broader discussion of the personal and communal dynamics of early Sufism.

WORKING HYPOTHESIS, METHOD AND SOURCES

According to the basic hypothesis in the book, the early phase of Sufism witnessed the appearance of a common ethos that was set to differentiate the Sufis from other religious groups in the Islamic landscape. This ethos was not explicitly formulated in any written source, and it should be sought out and reconstructed through using the available data and cross-checking the findings over different sources. This phase witnessed more communal traits and practices of the Sufis than previously suggested. Such traits and practices could reflect this ethos. The available texts of this period do not allow sufficient room for individual voices, which is why those voices could not be easily distinguished. Nonetheless, the paucity, or sometimes even the absence, of such voices does not mean that they were lacking in the cultural scene of Sufism. In anthropology, for instance, the assumption that a 'mere lack of mention of traits in ethnographic reports had been assumed to mean that such traits were lacking in the cultures' began to be challenged in the last decade. Forrest Clements argues that 'negative evidence', or the lack of a mention of data, is equally as important as 'positive data'.[20] Certain scholarly approaches in anthropological

[19] See A. Salamah-Qudsi, 'A Lightning Trigger or a Stumbling Block: Mother Images and Roles in Classical Sufism', *Oriens*, vol. 39, no. 2 (2011), 199–226.

[20] Forrest Clements, 'Use of Cluster Analysis with Anthropological Data', *American Anthropologist*, vol. 56, no. 2 (2009), 181.

studies adopt a cluster analysis method to reconstruct the common traits of different ethnographic groups by means of illustrating the relationships between one common cluster and the individual elements that split from that cluster through tree diagrams. This method is identified in this discipline as a 'divisive top down' approach according to which 'all objects initially belong to one cluster. Then the cluster is divided into sub-clusters, which are successively divided into their own sub-clusters'.[21] In spite of the ontological differences between this discipline and its sources of data, on one hand, and the textual research undertaken here, on the other, it is still insightful to benefit from the general model implied in cluster analysis methods to rethink the early Sufi ethos and the individual attempts of certain personalities to release themselves from it. The word 'cluster' here, it should be noted, does not refer to one group of objects but, rather, to a group of common traits and values that the early charismatic masters of Baghdad tried to set together and impose upon everyone who wanted to become initiated along the Sufi path as much as the circumstances in their times allowed them to do. The common traits and values were embedded into texts, personalities, manners and modes of piety. From a general perspective, those traits and values appear as one homogeneous cluster; however, inside the cluster, many 'grapes' differ in fact in their size and shape. It is not always easy for the observer to pay attention to those differences between the grapes since the pretty and fresh view of the cluster as a whole attracts the eyes more. When this ethos began to lose its authority and influence, several sub-clusters began to split away. 'Sub-clusters' in this context might imply the distinctive modes of piety that started to challenge the unity and solidarity of the mother-cluster. I would argue that Sufi sources of the fourth/tenth century had already recorded the appearance of such attempts. The authors of Sufi sources invested great effort to revive the early solid ethos, as well as to celebrate its validity and essentiality. Their insistence to 'polish' the unifying features of *taṣawwuf* could not succeed in abolishing the very existence of disparate trends.

In the course of the twentieth century, a debate was introduced by Anglo-American psychologists who claimed that the study of individual lives (idiographic studies) should be effectively used side-by-side with the 'nomothetic approach', which is based on the search for general principles

[21] See Lior Rokach and Oded Maimon, 'A Survery of Clustering Algorithms', in *Data Mining and Knowledge Discovery Handbook*, ed. by Lior Rokach and Oded Maimon (New York: Springer, 2005), 278.

or laws across individuals. The idiographic discipline is essentially concerned with what is particular to the individual case. It is concerned more with individualized traits and the identification of central themes within an individual life.[22] The descriptive study of individuals in their particular socio-historical context can enrich our knowledge of the early phase of Sufism beside the scholarly approach in which general or even abstract processes of development control the variability of cases and spiritual experiences.

Each of the individual trends that began to be documented in the sources, albeit rarely and unfrequently in the course of the period under consideration here, preserves certain aspects of that ethos, while differing from others. There is a crucial need, therefore, to start distinguishing such individual trends as well as their dynamic relationships and connections with that common Sufi ethos. From another perspective, each Sufi work could be also treated as a sub-cluster where many components of that original cluster-ethos as well as of previous Sufi works, which are also sub-clusters by themselves, meet together. This method can enrich our understanding of Sufi texts and enable us to examine some of their features and stylistics. The repetition of certain anecdotal structures and the frequency of certain frames of expression in reference to different names are examples of such features.

As previously noted, Sufi hagiographies constitute the main body of our sources. To be satisfied with the precept that these have nothing to provide for any scholarly endeavour on early Sufism means that we, as scholars, should reconcile ourselves to the inefficiency of all attempts to investigate early Sufism. The first working hypothesis here suggests that certain historical and interpersonal conclusions could be deduced from hagiographical material. This type of source was not entirely divorced from its cultural context. Some of the anecdotes and sayings that frequently appear in Sufi hagiographies are ascribed to different personalities. In many cases, such anecdotes take the form of what we might call a typical-paradigmatic structure which is repeated in different biographies of different Sufi figures. One example of such a typical-paradigmatic structure in the narratives of Sufi hagiographies could be as follows: A particular Sufi figure commits a fault in the presence of a great Sufi master. A fault of this kind could be, for instance, a forbidden gaze at a

[22] On the idiographic-nomothetic debate in psychology, see e.g., W. McKinley Runyan, 'Idiographic Goals and Methods in the Study of Lives', *Journal of Personality*, vol. 51, no. 3 (1983), 413–415.

beautiful woman. This master who witnessed this incident warns his fellow of the upcoming punishment. At the end of this recurrent narrative structure, this punishment comes, and the Sufi becomes certain that he had to avoid making even the slightest mistake. The readers of such an episode could not be sure of the identity of the two personalities since they appear with different names on different occasions in Sufi hagiographies. However, what should be perceived as certain here is the very idea that Sufis, very often, disagreed on how Sufi theories should be practised in day-to-day life and that certain Sufi personalities acted as sponsors to their companions and as guardians of what could be seen as the ultimate Sufi ethos.

Authors of Sufi hagiographies chose different ways to shape the biographical accounts of early Sufi personalities. The general outlines and points of emphasis in the biography of the same Sufi figure provided by different authors could illustrate the diverse personal choices of the authors as well as the different relationship dynamics each had with his environment. If we read Sufi hagiographies carefully, we come across several expressions that recur in specific biographies. One example of such is found in the biographical accounts of Ruwaym b. Aḥmad. Ruwaym is repeatedly quoted as urging his fellows to avoid becoming preoccupied with the 'nonsense trifles of the Sufis'. This idea of avoiding the nonsense trifles of the Sufis (*tark al-ishtighāl bi-turrahāt al-ṣūfiyya*) appears frequently in the sources referring to Ruwaym as part of different sayings ascribed to him. Should we consider this reiterative form of expression as a typical call for the general ethic codes that Ruwaym wanted his Sufi contemporaries to adopt, or should we inquire into some implied personal indications that involve certain aspects of Ruwaym's life and relationships with which this expression was loaded? I would consider the latter more feasible.

Very often, Sufi hagiographies would embed segments of original letters and pieces of correspondence between early Sufi figures (*mukātabāt al-ṣūfiyya*). The importance of Sufi correspondence has already been pointed out by Sarrāj in his *Kitāb al-lumaʿ*. In some early compilations, fragments of Sufis' correspondence were gathered and presented in separate sections, such as those in Sarrāj's *Lumaʿ* and Kharkūshī' *Tahdhīb al-asrār*. Sufi correspondence is a good source of some of the ideas that were not included in the famous Sufi compendia and *magna opera*. If the latter were originally designed to address the general concerns of the Sufis as a community, Sufi letters were able to express more personal and interpersonal emotions and interest. This component of the hagiographical material sheds light on many interesting aspects of the lives of early Sufis. Even when typical expressions recur in the main body of letters ascribed to one Sufi figure, particular characteristics of each letter that appear to attach it to its unique context of interpersonal relationships and attitudes should be sought. Such were Junayd's letters (*Rasāʾil*) to different addressees in his days. As well as the expressions common to all of the letters, each letter relates to one aspect of Junayd's diverse networks of relationships which came to be manifested through diverse discourse and rhetoric.

Moving from hagiographies to autobiographic material, it should be noted that the early legacy of Sufism includes only very few works of this type. The works of al-Ḥakīm al-Tirmidhī (d. circa 300/912) and Rūzbihān Baqlī (d. 606/1209) are the most outspoken in this regard. Additionally, certain autobiographical sections are also included in the famous Sufi compilations and manuals. At the very rationale of the composition of Sufi autobiographical material lies the assumption that the act of unveiling the self and revealing its human fears and aspirations in public is recognized and accepted. The very existence of Sufi autobiographies is an interesting indicator of a social context in which certain Sufi personalities successfully created a literary tunnel through which they could preserve communication within their Sufi communities. Treating this material with the latter perception in mind provides us with an additional key aspect of the Sufis' personal lives and interpersonal engagements. It provides us with an important basis for tracing the ways in which the authors of these works chose to express different individual experiences and forms of self-consciousness in different socio-historical contexts.

Treating *ādāb* literature (Sufi rules of ethics) requires a fresh methodological approach in order to consider the contents as echoes of changing patterns in comprehending actual realities. When one author of *ādāb* work chooses to focus on a principle such as brotherhood (*ukhuwwa*) and uses available techniques to emphasize the high ethical value of *ukhuwwa* and chivalry (*futuwwa*), then we should be able to conclude that this emphasis is an echo of a reality that was not exactly free of mutual rancour and envy between figures usually expected to have acted as perfect brothers. This interpretation is not always true, we should state. Meanwhile, a shift from the iconic perception of the early Sufis, the one that portrays them in absolute perfect terms, towards a more realistic image as far as the available sources allow, is necessary today.

Beside *ādāb* literature, I would point out the significance of introductions to Sufi works, generally known as *muqaddima* (pl. *muqaddimāt*) or *maṭla*ʿ (pl. *maṭāli*ʿ) in Arabic sources, and *dībāchih* in Persian sources. The introductory sections in early Sufi works present interesting portraits of the different ways of authors to approach their realities and react to them. One common theme in the introductions of both Sarrāj and Qushayrī, for instance, is the confutation of the anti-Sufi voices that frequently accused the Sufis of heresy and abandonment of religious duties. Each, meanwhile, has his own perspective. Sarrāj refers to those who attached themselves to the Sufis (*al-mutashabbihūn bi-ahl al-taṣawwuf*) and composed many works on Sufi doctrines on behalf of the Sufis. Their statements and behaviour were manipulated by certain people who sought to defame the Sufis as a group. Based on Sarrāj's introduction, the main problem of the *ṣūfiyya* in his day was external. It related primarily to the dynamics that operated outside the Sufi community and could be utilized against its true members.

Different from Sarrāj, Qushayrī clearly presents a sort of self-critique, and concentrates on forms of depravity inside the Sufi community. Differences between the respective historical contexts of the two texts could not be ignored. Qushayrī states that he wrote his work in 437 of *hijra* and that he addressed it to the community of *ṣūfiyya* around the lands of Islam (*jamāʿat al-ṣūfiyya bi-buldān al-Islām*).[23] After praising the Sufis for being the spiritual elite of the Muslim community, he provides us with severe criticism against particular customs that have appeared among them. He explicitly states that the majority of true Sufi masters are no longer alive and that what really exists in his day was nothing but the traces of those masters. Qushayrī was not able to ignore a reality that witnessed the appearance of certain antinomian customs; however, he did not intend to provide a broader description of that reality which was expected to mislead the readers and confirm the negative image of *taṣawwuf*. Instead, he chose to allude very briefly to these customs and invest his efforts in defending the true pattern of *taṣawwuf* through different rhetorical, structural and thematic strategies. The *Risāla* ends with a piece of counsel that Qushayrī dedicated to the Sufi novices in his days (*al-waṣiyya li-l-murīdīn*). The text of the *waṣiyya* turns into a message addressed by Qushayrī directly to his contemporary Sufis. It is where all the components of Qushayrī's agenda meet in one terse but forceful textual unit. Sarrāj's discourse, on the other hand, leaves some doubt that he was entirely involved in the pressing issues of the Sufi practical system of

[23] Qushayrī, *Risāla*, 2.

training and guidance in his days, and his reference to the imitators of the Sufis (*al-mutashabbihūn bi-l-ṣūfiyya*) demonstrates an attempt to remove depravity from the *ṣūfiyya* and to place the responsibility for it on others!

In his introduction, Hujwīrī introduces some autobiographical data. He points, for instance, to one phenomenon from which he himself suffered: Some who claimed to be Sufis in his days used to ascribe to themselves works on Sufi doctrines where the names of their authors were not clearly indicated or simply deleted. Two of Hujwīrī's own works were plagiarized as such. The very existence of this phenomenon implies the prestigious position that authors of Sufi manuals could then enjoy. Like Qushayrī, Hujwīrī comes to the conclusion that true *taṣawwuf* became obliterated (*mundaris*) and that many claimants ascribed themselves to it and tried to utilize it for their own benefits. Hujwīrī went on to say that some had even tried to destroy some of his own works or, occasionally, to take parts of them and pass them off as their own in order to attract novices.[24]

Najm al-Dīn al-Rāzī Dāya (d. 654/1256) opens his *Mirṣād al-ʿibād* with a long *dībāchih* in which he discusses in great detail the reasons that motivated him to compose his work in Persian as well as the rationale behind the structure that he chose. Dāya's introduction contains interesting data dealing with the religious, social and political circumstances of his time. It also reveals the author's pragmatic agenda to defend *taṣawwuf* and his own perspective on the ways Sufi life integrates into the general fabric of Islam, as well as into one cosmic order where three phases of man's creation and life constitute the main structural body of the work.

Sufi introductions are, in fact, sources for the diverse personal perspectives of their authors. Sometimes, the last sections in Sufi works should be combined with the introductory sections in order to arrive at the completed structure on which each author established his own perspective and agenda. The aforementioned case of Qushayrī's *waṣiyya* is one example. Even though the current study does not thoroughly discuss introductions, we must point out the significance of studying introductions and concluding sections in early Sufi works in the future.

General works of *adab* refer occasionally to Sufis. An early work, al-Muḥsin al-Tanūkhī's (d. 383/993) *Nishwār al-muḥāḍara,* dated from the fourth/tenth century provides us with certain aspects of the anti-Sufi approach. Anecdotes about certain Sufi personalities served as one of

[24] See Jullābī Hujwīrī, *Kashf al-maḥjūb*, 1–7.

the most effective strategies in the hands of the authors of such works to defame major Sufi principles and practices. The principle of *ṣuḥba* (companionship), for instance, was among Sufi doctrines that survived a long process of slander and pungent criticism, according to early works of *adab*. A detailed reference to Tanūkhī's defamation of the renowned Sufi master of Shīrāz, Abū ʿAbd Allāh Ibn Khafīf (d. 371/982), for instance, will be included in our discussions of *ṣuḥba* and its implications in early Sufism. Abū Ḥayyān al-Tawḥīdī's (d. ca. 414/1023) works, including his *al-Ishārāt al-ilāhiyya*, a collection of personal prayers and intimate conversations, provide interesting viewpoints of a distinguished Muslim author on Sufis and the fourth/tenth century institution of *taṣawwuf*. Throughout the following chapters, other works of *adab*, in addition to chronicles, non-Sufi biographies and polemic literature, will be cross-referenced with the rich variety of Sufi sources.

PART I

PERSONAL NARRATIVES

Early Sufis and Family Ties

1

Celibacy, Marriage and Familial Commitments among Early Sufis

On one occasion in Ibn Khamīs al-Mawṣilī's (d. 552/(1157 *Manāqib al-abrār*, Ibrāhīm b. Isḥāq al-Ḥarbī (d. 285/898), a famous ascetic and *ḥadīth* transmitter from third/ninth century Baghdad,[1] relates that:

A truly pious man keeps his grief inside himself and does not cause grief to his children. I suffered from migraines for forty-five years, and I did not tell anyone about that. I spent thirty years on two loaves of bread. If my mother and sister brought food to me I ate, but if they did not I stayed hungry until the following night. I spent thirty years of my life on a single loaf of bread for each day and night. If my wife or one of my daughters brought food to me I took it and ate, and if they did not I stayed hungry and thirsty until the following night [...]. When my daughter became sick, my wife left me behind and spent a whole month with her. During that month I ate what cost one *dirham* and two and a half *dāniqs*.[2]

Referring to early Sufis as family members was not part of the general biographical tradition of medieval Islam. If we seek to put the focus on the roles of early Sufis as family members, spouses and providers, while seeking to re-examine questions of celibacy, marriage and familial commitments among them, we need to retrieve data from the existing

[1] See e.g., Sulamī, *Ṭabaqāt*, 40 (he appears to have transmitted a statement of Bishr b. al-Ḥārith. In another place, Abū ʿAlī al-Rūdhbārī mentions him as his master of *ḥadīth* ('my master in *ḥadīth* is Ibrāhīm al-Ḥarbī': Ibid., 369). See his biography in Abū ʿAbd Allāh Shams al-Dīn al-Dhahabī, *Tadhkirat al-ḥuffāẓ* (Beirut: Dār al-Kutub al-ʿIlmiyya, n.d.), vol. 2, 584–586).

[2] Al-Ḥusayn b. Naṣr Ibn Khamīs al-Mawṣilī, *Manāqib al-abrār wa-maḥāsin al-akhyār fī ṭabaqāt al-ṣūfiyya*, ed. by Saʿīd ʿAbd al-Fattāḥ (Beirut: Dār al-Kutub al-ʿIlmiyya, 2006), vol. 2, 244.

biographical material which has come to us mainly in the form of structured units of sayings and episodes with very few references to personal backgrounds and family ties. It is here, in this particular domain, that questions of how early Sufis were as family members and how they managed to handle their interpersonal ties come to the surface. Such issues should be raised and examined. What I will present here is an attempt to look into some aspects of early Sufis' personal lives, despite the scarcity of data, as well as questioning the possible modes of interaction between the familial involvements of those Sufis and their forms of commitment to the ethical-practical system that stimulated the activities and interrelationships of Sufi communities. As this chapter will show, the necessity that early Sufis encountered to maintain the socio-religious ideals of family life and normative marital ties and to integrate them with the Sufi call to practise a devotional life of absolute solitude and freedom from all sorts of engagements motivated, among other dynamics, the appearance of the Sufi discussions of issues such as *tawakkul* (absolute trust in God), working for one's living (*kasb*) and the possible ways to identify the boundaries and practical conditions of the Sufi's perfect life with God. Since no scholarly attempt of this type has yet been tackled, this chapter seeks to lay the foundations for further research in the future.

The ascetic ideal of the priority of celibacy over marriage among early *zuhhād*, and the strong echo it left on the teachings of early Sufi figures should be reconsidered. How can we explain the massive number of statements and anecdotes preserved in Sufi sources in which an extremely frigid approach towards one's wife and children is repeatedly documented? How should we treat the shocking behaviour of someone such as al-Fuḍayl b. ʿIyāḍ (d. 187/803) who, for instance, laughed for the first time in his life when his son died,[3] and what do sayings that disparage women and familial commitments reveal about the 'real' status of celibacy in the lives of those Sufis?

CELIBACY AND MARRIAGE

Complaints and utterances against one's familial ties and duties that prevent the sincere ascetic or mystic from practising a perfect devotional life with God are not indicative of the actual lives of those who said them.

[3] See Abū Nuʿaym al-Iṣfahānī, *Ḥilyat al-awliyāʾ wa-ṭabaqāt al-aṣfiyāʾ*, ed. by Muṣṭafā ʿAbd al-Qādir ʿAṭā (Beirut: Dār al-Kutub al-ʿIlmiyya, 1997), vol. 8, 103.

Al-Ḥasan al-Baṣrī (d. 110/728) was quoted to have said 'If God wishes to help His servant; He puts his children to death.'[4] According to early biographies, al-Ḥasan had at least two sons and a daughter whom he refused to marry off to a rich person.[5] On one occasion in Makkī's *Qūt al-qulūb*, Al-Ḥasan is quoted to have slandered his son, ʿAbd Allāh, because he used to drive out his father's companions who frequently visited him and caused him to spend long stretches of time associating with them. When news of this behaviour reached al-Ḥasan, he said to his son: 'Leave them alone Oh miscreant! (*daʿhum yā lukaʿ*); I prefer their company to yours; they love me for God's sake, while you want me for the sake of this earthly world!'[6] This anecdote originated in Ibn Saʿd's *al-Ṭabaqāt al-kubrā*. ʿAbd Allāh appeared there to tell the companions that his father was not able to eat or drink due to their lengthy visits.[7]

Early biographers frequently refer to al-Ḥasan's mother who was, most probably, a servant of Umm Salama, the Prophet's wife. This piece of data was significant in establishing al-Ḥasan's sanctified image in the history of the early *zuhd* tradition.[8]

The early renunciant Mālik b. Dīnār (d. 123/741, 129/747, 130/748 or 131/749)[9] was alleged to have prayed to God not to grant him wealth or children.[10] When he was asked whether he wished to get married, as Abū Nuʿaym al-Iṣfahānī tells, he replied: 'If I were allowed, I would divorce myself.'[11] In fact, however, Mālik did get married at least once in his lifetime. Iṣfahānī went on to relate that Mālik once bought his wife some perfume that cost him one *dirham* and that he spent twenty years afterwards reproaching himself for it.[12] Sayings that imply an emotional coldness towards one's children are frequent in *zuhd* literature as well as in early Sufi sources.[13] The biography of Sufyān al-Thawrī

4 See e.g., ʿAbd al-Wahhāb al-Shaʿrānī, *al-Ṭabaqāt al-kubrā* (Cairo: al-Maṭbaʿa al-Azhariyya, 1925), vol. 1, 25.

5 See Muḥammad b. Saʿd, *Kitāb al-ṭabaqāt al-kabīr*, ed. by ʿAlī Muḥammad ʿUmar (Cairo: Maktabat al-Khānjī, 2001), vol. 9, 173. See also Suleiman Ali Mourad, *Early Islam between Myth and History: al-Ḥasan al-Baṣrī (d. 110H/728CE) and the Formation of His Legacy in Classical Islamic Scholarship* (Leiden and Boston: Brill, 2006), 25.

6 Makkī, *Qūt*, vol. 2, 455–456.

7 See Ibn Saʿd, *Ṭabaqāt*, vol. 9, 170.

8 See ibid., 157. Cf. the separate biography of al-Ḥasan's mother in ibid. vol. 10, 442. See also Dhahabī, *Siyar*, vol. 4, 564.

9 In addition to his biography in early medieval biographies, see Richard Gramlich, *Alte Vorbilder des Sufitums* (Wiesbaden: Otto Harrassowitz Verlag, 1996), vol. 1, 59–121.

10 See Shaʿrānī, *Ṭabaqāt*, vol. 1, 32.

11 Iṣfahānī, *Ḥilyat al-awliyāʾ*, vol. 2, 414.

12 See ibid., 366.

13 See e.g., Qushayrī, *Risāla*, 84, lines 29–30; ibid., 10, lines 5–7. Among *zuhd* writings, see e.g., al-Muʿāfā b. ʿImrān, *Kitāb al-zuhd*, ed. by ʿĀmir Ṣabrī (Beirut: Dār al-Bashāʾir

(d. 161/777–778), for instance, is full of sayings in which Sufyān celebrates solitude and celibacy though he himself was married. Being destined for marriage in the cases of the majority of ascetics whom we know about opened the door to the literary tradition of expressing coldness towards one's children. When Sufyān's son was injured and had his broken limbs set in plaster, his father was quoted as having wished that he had died instead. According to the story, it was not long before the son, in fact, died.[14]

The picture that early sources present leaves a strong impression that renunciants and Sufis were both conscious of the necessity to justify certain customs that some of them undertook to a broad audience of Muslims. According to available statements and anecdotes, genuine devotional life was very frequently conditioned by solitude and loneliness, and apathy towards wives and children was highly celebrated. This body of statements in favour of celibacy is considered by Tor Andrae as a manifestation of 'isolated voices' that 'drew attention to themselves all the more since they ran counter to general opinion. For the majority even among those who practised a stricter piety kept firmly to the view that it was a duty of all the faithful to marry.'[15] Andrae points out that in only two cases we are able to be absolutely certain that the mystics remained celibate throughout their lives: Ibrāhīm b. Adham (d. between 160/776 and 166/783) and Abū Yazīd al-Basṭāmī (d. 234/848 or 261/875).[16] Regarding the first, the claim that he abandoned marriage due to a personal choice, even though he himself did not reject marriage in principle, was also raised.[17] While referring to the scholarly and historical values of the negative statements against marriage, women and raising children, Andrae indicates that those statements were not 'meant to be taken too seriously', but a type of 'pious snobbery'.[18] Andrae's work, which appeared in its original Swedish in 1947, was a pioneer work in this field. It presents the

al-Islāmiyya, 1999), 186, no. 14; ibid., 188, no. 19; ibid., 192, no. 25. Makkī, for example, describes one's children as the 'divine punishment of his desire of the licit deeds in the religious law' (*'uqūbat shahwat al-ḥalāl*) (Makkī, *Qūt*, vol. 2, 491).

14 See Iṣfahānī, *Ḥilyat al-awliyā'*, vol. 7, 78–79.

15 Tor Andrae, *In the Garden of Myrtles: Studies in Early Islamic Mysticism*, trans. from the Swedish by Birgitta Sharpe (Albany: State University of New York Press, 1987), 45.

16 It seems most probably that in addition to those two figures, Abū Sulaymān al-Dārānī (d. 215/830) remained celibate for his entire live. See e.g., Avner Giladi, 'Sex, Marriage and the Family in al-Ghazālī's Thought: Some Preliminary Notes', in *Islam and Rationality: The Impact of al-Ghazālī, Papers Collected on His 900th Anniversary*, ed. by Georges Tamer (Leiden and Boston: Brill, 2015), vol. 1, 173–174.

17 See Andrae, *Garden of Myrtles*, 46–47.

18 See ibid., 49.

earliest attempt in modern scholarship of Sufism to investigate the attitudes of early Sufis towards marriage and family commitments in view of the huge demands that devotional life imposed upon them. As for the suggestion that the majority of early Sufis were married, I find myself arguing that this piece of data does not, in essence, contradict the most probable situation in which many of those personalities, who got married at a particular point in their devotional careers, practised a sort of a temporary celibacy for certain periods of time. Beginning spiritual careers as celibate was believed to be very beneficial for all novices regardless of the degree of their willingness and devotional backgrounds. Celibacy of this type was not intended by the Sufis to challenge the tradition of marriage, as this was advocated by the Prophet and his successors.[19] However, when temporary celibacy became combined with the fashion of abandoning work for a livelihood as a way to prove total dependence on God for one's physical and spiritual needs, the conflict between Sufi celibates and traditionalists became unavoidable. I would argue here that practising temporary celibacy by the Sufis could provoke only a little criticism against them. The attitude towards abandoning work for profit (*tark al-kasb*), however, was different. *Tark al-kasb*, or as it was also known in the sources in reference to the early group of *karrāmiyya* as *taḥrīm al-makāsib* ('the prohibition against working for profit'), or *inkār al-makāsib* ('the denial of working for profit') was, most likely, more than a marginal theoretical principle in early medieval Islamic landscapes. The antipathy to certain kinds of economic livelihood found a major parallel in Muḥammad b. Karrām's (d. 255/869) way of thinking as the works of

[19] The discussion of celibacy in early Islam involves the early debate around Islam's approach towards *rahbāniyya* (monasticism) with all customs it implies: sexual abstinence, solitude and constant roving. The first foundations of the question of *rahbāniyya* and its impact on the early renunciants are found in early works of *ḥadīth* in relation to the famous tradition attributed to the Prophet Muḥammad ('*lā rahbāniyya fī al-Islām*', there is no monasticism in Islam) and *Qur'ān* commentaries in relation to verse 27 of *Sūra* 57. Ignaz Goldziher set the pillars for treating Islam's approach towards monasticism in modern scholarship. [See Ignaz Goldziher, *Die Richtungen der Islamischen Koranauslegung* (Leiden: Brill, 1920), 154–155; idem, *Muhammedanische Studien* (Halle A. S.: Max Niemeyer, 1890), zwiter Theil, 394–396. See also Ignaz Goldziher, *Introduction to Islamic Theology and Law*, trans. by Andras and Ruth Hamori with an introduction and additional notes by Bernard Lewis (Princeton, N.J.: Princeton University Press, 1981), 122–123 and footnotes 21–23.] A detailed analysis of the hermeneutical traditions that treat Christian monasticism and the ways it was conceived and evaluated in early Islam is provided in: Sara Sviri, '*Wa-Rahbānīyatan Ibtada'ūhā*: An Analysis of Traditions Concerning the Origin and Evaluation of Christian Monasticism', *Jerusalem Studies in Arabic and Islam*, 13 (1990), 195–208.

Joseph van Ess and Margaret Malamud have shown in light of newly discovered materials written by the followers of the group.[20] It is interesting to note that *karrāmiyya* had been ignored by Sufi authors though more and more scholars have recently been paying attention to the strong impact that the teachings of Ibn Karrām left on the general engagements of early Sufis in terms of practical systems and organizational patterns.[21]

In the course of the third/ninth century, Islamic landscapes were already witnessing discussions on the problematic nature of gaining one's livelihood and its conflict with the principle of absolute trust in God (*tawakkul*). In the eastern territories of the Muslim empire, such discussions came to be highly influenced by *karrāmiyya* 's tendency to practise a rigid mode of renunciatory life in which abandoning work was an integral part. Abū al-Ḥusayn Muḥammad b. Aḥmad al-Malaṭī (d. 377/988) refers to the *ʿabdakiyya* among other sects that flourished until his time and were considered by traditionalists as heretics (*zanādiqa*). The followers of *ʿabdakiyya*, according to Malaṭī, claimed that, if the great masters of justice (*aʾimmat al-ʿadl*) passed away, worldly existence would become all unlawful (*ḥarām muḥarram*), and this is why it is absolutely prohibited to acquire anything of this world, except for food.[22] M. Malamud points to the most common inquiries that arose among *karrāmī* and non-*karrāmī* ascetics in that period, all of which found their appearance in the writings of early Sufis: How could *kasb* be reconciled with a life of

[20] See Joseph van Ess, *Ungenützte Texte zur Karrāmiyya: Eine Materialsammlung* (Heidelberg: C. Winter-Universitaetsverlag, 1980); Margaret Malamud, 'The Politics of Heresy in Medieval Khurāsān: The Karrāmiyya in Nishapur', *Iranian Studies*, vol. 27, no. 1/4, Religion and Society in Islamic Iran during the Pre-Modern Era (1994), 37–51; Aron Zysow, 'Karrāmiya', *Encyclopaedia Iranica*, vol. xv, fasc. 6, 590–601. On the different meanings of *kasb* in medieval Islam, see e.g., Cl. Cahen and L. Gardet, 'Kasb', *Encyclopaedia of Islam*, second edition, ed. by P. Bearman, Th. Bianquis, C. E. Bosworth, E. van Donzel, and W. P. Heinrichs, consulted online on 1 October 2017 http://dx.doi.org/10.1163/1573-3912_islam_COM_0457. On *kasb* 's connotations among early Sufis, see L. Massignon, *The Passion of al-Ḥallāj, Mystic and Martyr of Islam*, trans. from the French with a biographical foreword by Herbert Mason (Princeton, N.J.: Princeton University Press, 1982), vol. 3, 227.

[21] A. Karamustafa argues that the different trends of *malāmatiyya* that appeared and developed in Khurāsān may have been aligned against the *karrāmiyya* whose ostentatious piety and prohibition of working for a living was opposed to the inward-looking religiosity of the *malāmatiyya*. Karamustafa goes on to assert that, while this does not necessarily entail hostility between the two parties, 'it certainly signals an oppositional stance' (see Karamustafa, *Sufism*, 60–61).

[22] See Abū al-Ḥusayn Muḥammad b. Aḥmad al-Malaṭī, *al-Tanbīh wa-l-radd ʿalā ahl al-ahwāʾ wa-l-bidaʿ*, ed. by Muḥammad al-Kawtharī (Baghdad and Beirut: Maktabat al-Muthannā and Maktabat al-Maʿārif, 1968), 93.

total renunciation? Was voluntary poverty seen as better than earning a living? I would add the following question: Did the Muslim renunciant need to reconcile the very basis of his religious life that is his total trust in God with the well-established fashion of earning one's living and supporting families and children with the complete body of *Qur'ān*ic verses and prophetic traditions supporting it?

The principle of *tark al-kasb* was very influential in the general scene of early Sufism. It left its marks also on those Sufis who decided to earn a living in all territories of Islam. Abū ʿAbd al-Raḥmān al-Sulamī refers to the fourth/tenth century Sufi of Nishapur Abū ʿAmr al-Zajjājī (d. 348/959) who urged one of his companions to get married since the observance of the prophetic tradition of marriage would open the doors of livelihood (*rizq*) for him.[23] Marriage could hardly be experienced without earning one's living. Recent research of the nature of marital relationships during medieval Islam has drawn on different types of early sources to show that the institution of Islamic medieval marriage was, in fact 'fluid' with high rates of divorce and an increasing number of single women, who could, as those sources tell, support themselves independently.[24] The issue of large dowries that had been imposed upon men was implied by the fourth/tenth century Sufi author Abū Ṭālib al-Makkī in the chapter which he devotes to marriage. Makkī devotes one of the longest chapters of his *Qūt* to marriage and celibacy. One of the major themes that caught the special interest of the author was the economic difficulty that young men had to face before marriage. Starting with paying large dowries for women who were not slaves (*ḥarā'ir*), contrary to slave women (*imā'*) who could be taken as wives without paying a normative-large dowry, and having to endure the inflexible demands of family commitments and livelihood, Makkī's text presents a reality in which poor young Sufis preferred to remain celibate for long periods of their lives or to marry slave women.[25] The first solution seemed to Makkī acceptable particularly in light of the fact that it was becoming more and more difficult in his days to earn money and support families without being involved in acts which were not considered acceptable.

Early Sufi sources imply that, among those who married, there was a group of Sufis who worked to gain their livelihood normatively and another group whose members, apparently, chose to abandon *kasb* and

[23] See Abū ʿAbd al-Raḥmān al-Sulamī, *Jawāmiʿ ādāb al-ṣūfiyya and ʿuyūb al-nafs wa-mudāwātuhā*, ed. by Etan Kohlberg (Jerusalem: Jerusalem Academic Press, 1976), 27.

[24] See Chapter 2.

[25] See Makkī, *Qūt*, vol. 2, 492–493.

to turn their families into recipients for people's alms and acts of charity. Sufi authors, such as Makkī and Sarrāj, refer to this phenomenon and criticize it severely.[26] One of the few personalities in early Sufism who most probably stayed celibate for their entire lives, Ibrāhīm b. Adham, appears in Kharkūshī's *Tahdhīb al-asrār* to have emphasized the high rank of those who earn money and provide their children. Ibrāhīm urges the pious of his days to work as heroes (*'alayka bi-'amal al-abṭāl*) for their children's sustenance (*nafaqa 'alā al-'iyāl*).[27] This is most probably a fabricated statement that those who rejected *tark al-kasb* attributed to early venerated figures like Ibrāhīm b. Adham as part of their campaign against the custom. The criticism that was addressed to Ruwaym b. Aḥmad by his contemporary Sufi 'brothers' was, most probably, motivated by his involvement in the governmental system by accepting an appointment to the position of the deputy of the *qāḍī* and not due to his unique teachings on *tawakkul* and family life.[28] All of those dynamics led many Sufis in the course of time to undertake celibacy for longer periods of time. The infrequent references in the sources to those who 'at their death were still celibate' should not be understood as evidence of the infrequency of celibacy. Temporary celibacy became increasingly practised, and it also motivated a paralleled theoretical support in Sufi literature. Increasingly explicit references to marriage and the essential paradox that it imposed with one's devotional engagements could be heard. Besides, Sufi literature mentions the paradox from another interesting angle: Many early Sufi personalities tried, through various strategies, to reconcile marriage with a private devotional life.

The structure of Sarrāj's chapter on 'the rules of ethics of married Sufis and those who had children' ('*Bāb fī ādāb al-muta'ahhilīn wa-man lahu walad*') leaves a strong impression that temporary celibacy was common in Sarrāj's day. On one occasion, interestingly, Sarrāj indicates that true Sufis do not agree to live at their wives' expense in cases where women were rich: '*Laysa min ādābihim an yatazawwajū dhawāt al-yasār wa-yadkhulū fī rifq nisā'ihim.*'[29] A true Sufi should preferably marry a poor woman; however, in the event that a rich woman wanted to marry him (*raghibat fīhi imra'a ghaniyya*) he should distance himself completely from her wealth and properties. The latter notion, as emphasized by Sarrāj, implies an early reality in which rich women looked for spiritual

[26] See Sarrāj, *Luma'*, 200; Makkī, *Qūt*, vol. 2, 29–33.
[27] Kharkūshī, *Tahdhīb al-asrār*, 299.
[28] See the detailed reference to him in Chapter 7.
[29] Sarrāj, *Luma'*, 200.

benediction (*baraka*) and thereby initiated marriage to Sufi figures. ʿAbd al-Malik al-Kharkūshī draws one's attention also to the necessity of a Sufi to avoid a situation in which he would marry a woman who is wealthier than himself. It is interesting to note, rather, that none of Kharkūshī's references to the Sufis' manners in marriage and marital relationships refers to particular names of Sufi personalities. In fact, such references take a general literary form since the author seemed to be interested in those sayings more than in the persons who stood behind them. However, in the cases in which he refers to famous traditionalists, renunciants and some of the Prophet's companions, he was eager to mention the names.[30] According to one interesting episode in Kharkūshī's work, an anonymous Sufi married a woman whom he used to serve. When she wanted to go to the bathroom, this Sufi even used to go before her with the water in his hands.[31]

Referring again to Makkī, it should be noted that his long aforementioned chapter on marriage and celibacy differs essentially from a similar chapter by Sarrāj.[32] The focus of Makkī's discussion was, undoubtedly, the choice between marriage and celibacy at different stages of the mystic's life and in accordance with personal preferences and spiritual capacities. At the end of his chapter, Makkī summarizes his detailed discussion by drawing one's attention to three basic categories of the Sufis: At the bottom of his hierarchy were those who chose marriage due to their weakness and inability to protect themselves from adultery; then there were those who could patiently bear the situation of solitude and remained celibate and at the top of the hierarchy were the 'strong' Sufis who married and despite that could patiently manage their conjugal lives, control them and keep any adverse effects away from their devotional lives with God.[33] According to his *Sīra*, the renowned Sufi master of Shīrāz, Abū ʿAbd Allāh b. Khafīf got married 400 times during his lifetime since women always wanted to get his spiritual *baraka* by being married to him.[34] The Persian mystic of Shīrāz, Rūzbihān Baqlī, indicates in his visionary autobiography, *Kashf al-asrār*, that he bought an orchard

[30] See Kharkūshī, *Tahdhīb al-asrār*, 417–428. [31] See ibid., 418.

[32] For a detailed comparison between Makkī's *Qūt* and Sarrāj's *Lumaʿ* in respect to their different structural arrangements, approaches and aims, see Saeko Yazaki, *Islamic Mysticism and Abū Ṭālib al-Makkī: The Role of the Heart* (London and New York: Routledge, 2013), 86–89.

[33] See Makkī, *Qūt*, vol. 2, 528–529.

[34] See Abū al-Ḥasan ʿAlī b. Muḥammad al-Daylamī, *Sīrat al-shaykh al-kabīr Abī ʿAbd Allāh Muḥammad ibn Khafīf al-Shīrāzī*, trans. from the Persian into Arabic (after the

in the region of Fās, and when his beloved wife died, he grieved for her and decided to leave Fās forever.[35] With respect to the later period, Nūr al-Dīn ʿAbd al-Raḥmān Jāmī (d. 898/1492) relates that Najm al-Dīn Kubrā (d. 618/1221), on the night of his marriage to a young slave, asked all his disciples to take a break from all their ascetic austerities as to be in agreement with his situation (*shumā nīz dar muvāfiqat-i mā tark-i riyāzat kunīd*) in enjoying a legal pleasure (*lizzat-i mashrūʿ*).[36] The chapter of Sarrāj, on the other hand, prefers to focus on married Sufis and some of the doctrines that were known among them in this regard, although some statements in favour of celibacy were also provided. In order to justify the tendency towards temporary celibacy among his fellow Sufis, Makkī did not, according to his text, refrain from referring to the Prophet's wives who were according to him inclined to *ghiwāya* (temptation) and *taswīl* (seduction). Makkī is referring here to two famous traditions, the first of which appears in *ḥadīth* literature, while the other has a *Qurʾān*ic origin to emphasize one of the approaches towards women who were known in his days: If the 'mothers of believers', the Prophet's wives as those were identified in the history of Islam, could not be saved from falling under the influence of their lower souls (*hawā*), then what could we expect from normal women?[37] Junayd appears in Makkī's chapter beside another key figure among the renunciants of the first generation of Islam, ʿAbd Allāh b. ʿUmar (d. 74/693). Both are alleged to have celebrated sexual intercourse: 'I need \sexual intercourse in the same way as I need food', says Junayd while ʿAbd Allāh b. ʿUmar appears to have preferred sexual intercourse over food as a way to break a day of fasting.[38] I assume that notions of this type were presented by the authors to create a balance with the huge body of views in favour of celibacy in early compositions on

original Arabic had been lost) by Ibrāhīm al-Dusūqī Shatā (Cairo: al-Hayʾa al-ʿĀmma li-Shuʾūn al-Maṭābiʿ al-Amīriyya, 1977), 270.

35 See Rūzbihān Baqlī, *The Unveiling of Secrets Kashf al-Asrār: The Visionary Autobiography of Rūzbihān al-Baqlī (1128–1209 A.D.)*, ed. by Firoozeh Papan-Matin in collaboration with Michael Fishbein (Leiden: Brill, 2006), the Arabic text, 53, section 109; 65–66, section 131.

36 See Jāmī, *Nafaḥāt al-uns*, 431.

37 See ibid., 491. According to one tradition in *ḥadīth* literature, the Prophet is said to have asked his followers during his last moments to appoint Abū Bakr as an *imām* who would lead the Muslims in prayers. ʿĀʾisha, the Prophet's wife and Abū Bakr's daughter, was said to have tried to change her husband's mind, telling him that her father was a weak-tempered man that could not endure the hard requirements of this position. The other reference in Makkī's text is found in verse 4 of *Sūra* 66.

38 See ibid., 495.

zuhd as well as the active tendencies to practise celibacy in the reality of early Sufis. Those tendencies, as the following discussion will show, were more common than we have long believed.

References to Junayd's family ties are very rare in the sources. During his childhood he apparently lived with his mother, very close to the house of his maternal uncle Sarī al-Saqaṭī (d. 253/867). No definite data are available to tell us when exactly Junayd's father died. We know also that he had a maternal cousin who was also known as a pious renunciant, Ibrāhīm b. al-Sarī al-Saqaṭī. Both Iṣfahānī and, later on, Ibn al-Mulaqqin refer to him very briefly.[39] Junayd's relationships with his cousin are not referred to. In Sarī al-Saqaṭī's biography in Qushayrī's *Risāla*, a short reference to Sarī's daughter is provided.[40] Based on other textual evidence, we come to know that Junayd had very close relationships with one of his paternal uncles who was wealthier than Junayd's father. Subkī, in his *Ṭabaqāt al-shāfiʿiyya*, narrates that once Junayd met al-Ḥārith al-Muḥāsibī who appeared to be starving; Junayd invited him to eat and went into his paternal uncle's house to bring some food since in Junayd's words: 'My paternal uncle's house was more spacious that ours, and it could include food of superior quality none of which our house could provide' (*bayt ʿammī wa-kāna awsaʿ min baytinā lā yakhlū min aṭʿima fākhira lā yakūn mithluhā fī baytinā*).[41]

Though the sources are silent with regard to Junayd's marital life as they are, indeed, with regard to all early Sufis, some fragments and short episodes that are scattered throughout Sufi and non-Sufi sources in different contexts and for reasons other than identifying Junayd's personal background deserve our attention. On one occasion of his *Risāla*, Qushayrī mentions an episode that introduces Shiblī and his unique form of ecstatic piety in order to introduce his definitions of two religious elements, *ghayba* (spiritual absence) and *ḥuḍūr* (presence with God): 'Junayd was sitting in the company of his wife when Shiblī entered the place. When the woman wanted to cover her head Junayd asked her to calm down and remain seated since Shiblī at that moment was not able to identify her. Junayd started talking with Shiblī until the latter began to cry. Then Junayd asked his wife to cover her head since Shiblī was waking

39 See Iṣfahānī, *Ḥilyat al-awliyāʾ*, vol. 10, 324; Abū Ḥafṣ ʿUmar b. ʿAlī Ibn al-Mulaqqin, *Ṭabaqāt al-awliyāʾ*, ed. by Nūr al-Dīn Sharība (Beirut: Dār al-Maʿrifa, 1986), 165.

40 See Qushayrī, *Risāla*, 11.

41 Tāj al-Dīn al-Subkī, *Ṭabaqāt al-shāfiʿiyya al-kubrā*, ed. by ʿAbd al-Fattāḥ al-Ḥilū and Maḥmūd al-Ṭanāḥī (Cairo: Dār Iḥyāʾ al-Kutub al-ʿArabiyya, n.d.), vol. 2, 276. The same anecdote appears in Ibn al-Mulaqqin, *Ṭabaqāt al-awliyāʾ*, 176.

up from his loss of spiritual consciousness (*afāq al-Shiblī min ghaybatihi*).'[42] A more detailed version of the episode appears prior to Qushayrī's work in Abū Nuʿaym al-Iṣfahānī's *Ḥilyat al-awliyāʾ* and with the same structure in the work of the late eighth/fourteenth century biographer Ibn al-Mulaqqin.[43] What we are certain about here is that the narrators of this episode sought to shed light on the ecstatic character of Shiblī. For Qushayrī, in particular, the story seemed really informative for his discussion of the state of spiritual absence. In terms of mere rhetorical techniques, neither Junayd nor his wife were the focus of the story, and their involvement in it might have served the narrators to present the character of Shiblī. It might be assumed, then, that the components of the story were invented and overstated in favour of Shiblī and his unique mode of piety, especially the reference to Junayd's wife whom Shiblī came upon unexpectedly while bareheaded in the company of her husband. It is important to note, meanwhile, that the story as narrated in the early work of Iṣfahānī, even if not completely historically authenticated, provides us with some important data: Iṣfahānī, who lived in the late fourth/tenth century and died in the early part of the fifth/eleventh century, portrays the boundaries of *taṣawwuf* as they were perceived in his day. The reference to Junayd and his wife, even if this was not designated originally to serve Junayd's image, indicates that, in Iṣfahānī's days at least, certain Sufis could ensure their spiritual positions as great masters despite the fact that they led normal marital lives. Even if the tendency to practise celibacy was also common at that time, great masters like Junayd were still able to remain married. If we take for granted that this incident really took place, and I do not find a convincing reason for considering it automatically as being fabricated, then it would be interesting to pay attention to the way in which Junayd talked to his wife to calm her following the insane behaviour of his companion.

Turning back to Shiblī, it would be worthy to indicate that few sources mention some of his sons. Iṣfahānī, for instance, relates that he had a son who was called Ghālib and that this son died during his father's lifetime. Another son who was called Yūnus transmitted *ḥadīth* from his father according to Samʿānī.[44] Abū al-Ḥasan al-Daylamī, the famous author of

[42] Qushayrī, *Risāla*, 40.
[43] See Isfahānī, *Ḥilyat al-awliyā'*, vol. 10, 394; Ibn al-Mulaqqin, *Ṭabaqāt al-awliyā'*, 211.
[44] See ʿAbd al-Karīm b. Muḥammad al-Samʿānī, *Kitāb al-ansāb*, ed. by ʿAbd al-Raḥmān al-Yamānī (Ḥaydarābād al-Dukn, India: Maṭbaʿat Dāʾirat al-Maʿārif al-ʿUthmāniyya, 1977), vol. 8, 54.

Sīrat al-shaykh Abī ʿAbd Allāh ibn Khafīf al-Shīrāzī, points out that for one year the people of Baghdad suffered from a severe drought, and everyone in the city had to 'withdraw into his own corner'. It was told that 'Shiblī practised during that year unlimited austerities due to the large number of children that he had' (*zāwal al-Shiblī fī tilka al-sana riyāḍāt lā ḥadd lahā bi-sabab kathrat al-ʿiyāl*).[45]

Another interesting figure whose life demonstrates an interesting form of relationship between the Sufi's personal domains and the demands of his piety is Bishr b. al-Ḥārith, who is known in Sufi literature as Bishr al-Ḥāfī (Bishr the 'barefoot', d. c. 227/841). If we discuss celibacy in early Sufism, the name of Bishr comes immediately to mind. It appears that, beside his renunciatory life, Bishr occupied himself also with compiling books, and Ibn al-Nadīm refers to one of his works on *zuhd*.[46] Makkī indicates that Bishr was undervalued by many of his contemporaries due to abandoning marriage.[47] He was quoted by Sulamī to have said: 'You will not be able to taste the sweetness of worship until you build a great wall of iron between you and your earthly desires.'[48] Sarrāj points to one of Bishr's statements in which he emphasizes his fear of supporting a wife,[49] while alluding on other occasions to his renunciatory mode of life.[50] References to Bishr's character in *Taʾrīkh baghdād* portray him as an unmarried man who lived close to his sister's house and as one whose sister and nephews sustained him with food and other necessities for his existence. On one occasion in Makkī's *Qūt al-qulūb*, it is indicated that Bishr used to stay overnight at his sister's house (the sister's name is not mentioned) after her husband died.[51] Bishr's relationship with his maternal uncle, ʿAlī b. Khashram, will receive a detailed reference in Chapter 4. Bishr, according to al-Khaṭīb al-Baghdādī, used to leave his house every day, lock the door and leave the key with one of his neighbours for fear that he might lose it. In the evenings, when he returned home, he would take back the key and enter his house.[52] Bishr's elder sister, Muḍgha bint al-Ḥārith, died before him, and he grieved over her as Ibn Khillikān

[45] See Daylamī, *Sīra*, 168.

[46] See Ibn al-Nadīm, *al-Fihrist* (Beirut: Dār al-Maʿrifa, n.d.), 261. See also, David Stewart, 'The Structure of the *Fihrist*: Ibn al-Nadīm as Historian of Islamic Legal and Theological Schools', *International Journal of Middle East Studies*, vol. 39, no. 3 (2007), 382.

[47] See Makkī, *Qūt*, vol. 2, 490, 492. [48] Sulamī, *Ṭabaqāt al-ṣūfiyya*, 35–36.

[49] See Sarrāj, *Lumaʿ*, 200. [50] See ibid., 207. [51] See Makkī, *Qūt*, vol. 2, 571.

[52] See Aḥmad b. ʿAlī al-Khaṭīb al-Baghdādī, *Taʾrīkh baghdād*, ed. by Bashshār Maʿrūf (Beirut: Dār al-Gharb al-Islāmī, 2001), vol. 7, 556.

relates. This sister used to spin and support her renunciant brother.[53] It is not clear enough in the sources whether Muḍgha was the same sister whose son, Abū Ḥafṣ, is mentioned in Baghdādī's work as a narrator of anecdotes about his pious uncle. It appears that Bishr himself joined his provider, his sister, in spinning. On one occasion in *Luma*ʿ Sarrāj mentions that Bishr used to work with spinning wheels (*wa-kāna Bishr yaʿmal fī al-maghāzil*). It seems probable that he earned sufficiently from that work until one of his Sufi contemporaries, Isḥāq al-Mughāzilī, sent him a letter blaming him for seeking worldly profits instead of practising a totally devotional life. Sarrāj narrates that the letter left a deep impact on Bishr and caused him to completely abandon that profession.[54]

Comparisons between Bishr and his contemporary Aḥmad b. Ḥanbal (241/855) appear frequently in the sources. In Makkī's *Qūt*, for instance, it was Bishr himself who is quoted as presenting the following comparison: 'Aḥmad was proven superior to me by three things: The first is his search for lawful deeds (*ḥalāl*) in favour of himself as well as in favour of others, while my search for lawful deeds is in favour of myself only; and the second thing is his frequent commitment to marriage (*ittisāʿuhu fī al-nikāḥ*) as opposed to my limited commitment to it (*ḍīqī ʿanhu*). The last point is that Aḥmad was appointed to be the leader of his community, while I used to seek solitude.'[55] Michael Cooperson has shown how Muslim biographers drew upon the two different narratives of those two figures in order to establish the theoretical basis for the existence of diversified styles of piety in early medieval Muslim community. It was the same legacy of the Prophet Muḥammad that provided the foundation for the appearance of the various modes of piety in approaching religious knowledge and praxis.[56]

Early sources present a consensus in reference to Bishr's celibacy. In *Taʾrīkh baghdād*, Ibn Ḥanbal expresses his sorrow that Bishr did not succeed in getting married.[57] It is interesting to note, further, that Ibn Ḥanbal himself, according to his biography, got married at a late stage in his life, most probably after the age of forty. His successor, Ibn Taymiyya

[53] See Aḥmad b. Muḥammad Shams al-Dīn Ibn Khillikān, *Wafayāt al-aʿyān wa-anbāʾ abnāʾ al-zamān*, ed. by Iḥsān ʿAbbās (Beirut: Dār Ṣādir, 1968–1972), vol. 1, 276.

[54] See Sarrāj, *Luma*ʿ, 195.

[55] Makkī, *Qūt*, vol. 2, 496.

[56] See Michael Cooperson, 'Ibn Ḥanbal and Bishr al-Ḥāfī: A Case Study in Biographical Traditions', *Studia Islamica*, 86 (1997), 75.

[57] See Baghdādī, *Taʾrīkh baghdād*, vol. 7, 553. See also Christopher Melchert, 'Early Renunciants as *Ḥadīth* Transmitters', *The Muslim World*, 92 (2002), 412.

(d. 728/1328), nonetheless, did not marry at all.[58] Celibacy during medieval Islam was not as uncommon as we tend to believe today. In reality, it was not a serious reason for criticizing someone over making a choice that contradicts the prophetic tradition. According to one story provided by Ibn Baṭṭūṭa (d. 779/1377), practising celibacy was accompanied with public boasting and a kind of an impudence over the Prophet and his commitment to marriage. Ibn Baṭṭūṭa tells that a Sufi who was known as *shaykh al-mashāyikh* lived with his disciple on a mountain close to the city of ʿIntāb (southeast Anatolia). People used to visit him and ask his *baraka*. This man kept celibate for his entire life, and he was heard to have said: 'The Prophet Muḥammad could not bear patiently living without women, while I myself can.' As a result of this daring statement, this man was executed along with his disciple.[59]

Celibacy was practised more than we think it was, and the custom crossed the boundaries of renunciation and *taṣawwuf*. The early renowned grammarian of Baṣra Abū ʿAbd al-Raḥmān Yūnus b. Ḥabīb (d. 182/798), as Ibn Khillikān mentions, did not marry.[60] The early traditionalist and *ḥadīth* transmitter, Ḥusayn b. ʿAlī al-Juʿfī (d. 203/818), as Dhahabī indicates, never got married.[61] The expression 'he did not marry nor did he take a concubine' (*mā tazawwaj wa-lā tasarrā*) frequently appears in early biographical works such as those of Baghdādī, Dhahabī and Ibn Khillikān. Dhahabī, for instance, relates that the ḥanbalite traditionalist and grammarian, ʿAbd Allāh b. Aḥmad known as Ibn al-Khashshāb (d. 567/1172), 'did not marry nor took a concubine' and that he was always dirty with a dirty black turban on his head.[62]

Al-Fuḍayl b. ʿIyāḍ had a pious son, ʿAlī, to whom Abū al-Faraj Ibn al-Jawzī (d. 597/1200) devotes a separate biography in his *Ṣifat al-ṣafwa*.[63] Kharkūshī, earlier, refers to ʿAlī's pious character on one occasion of his *Tahdhīb al-asrār*.[64]

58 See e.g., Caterina Bori, 'A New Source for the Biography of Ibn Taymiyya', *Bulletin of the School of Oriental and African Studies*, vol. 67, no. 3 (2004), 321–348.

59 Ibn Baṭṭūṭa, *Riḥlat Ibn Baṭṭūṭa, tuḥfat al-nuẓẓār fī gharāʾib al-amṣār wa-ʿajāʾib al-asfār*, ed. by Muḥammad al-ʿAryān and Muṣṭafā al-Qaṣṣāṣ (Beirut: Dār Iḥyāʾ al-ʿUlūm, 1987), 664.

60 Ibn Khillikān, *Wafayāt al-aʿyān*, vol. 7, 245.

61 See Dhahabī, *Siyar*, vol. 9, 400.

62 See ibid., vol. 20, 526.

63 See Jamāl al-Dīn Abū al-Faraj Ibn al-Jawzī, *Ṣifat al-ṣafwa* (Ḥaydarābād al-Dukn, India: Maṭbaʿat Dāʾirat al-Maʿārif al-ʿUthmāniyya, 1936–1937), vol. 2, 140.

64 See Kharkūshī, *Tahdhīb al-asrār*, 310.

It is worth noting that Sufi figures that completely or temporarily chose not to marry could, in many cases, enjoy firm family ties with other family members: brothers, sisters and uncles. For them, a celibate life did not necessarily mean that they were committing themselves to a pattern of absolute seclusion and individuality. Those Sufis were, in fact, socially involved even when they called for a pure life of total seclusion. This social involvement is documented in two aspects: in their activities and associations with other renunciants at their time and in their personal ties within their own families. From another perspective, the very nature of involvement in the Sufi mode of life in the course of the third/ninth and fourth/tenth centuries brought about situations in which brothers and sisters, fathers and children, husbands and wives associated with one another within the frameworks of *taṣawwuf*. This was the case of the early mystic of Balkh Aḥmad b. Abī al-Ḥawārī (d. 230/845) whose father and brother and son were all Sufis, as Jāmī indicates.[65] Abū Sulaymān al-Dārānī's (d. 215/830) Sufi brother was also mentioned by Jāmī in addition to his famous Sufi sisters. Those who chose not to marry among the early Sufis could, in many cases, enjoy firm ties with other family members who were very often engaged in various forms of *taṣawwuf*. Al-Khuldiyya was Jaʿfar al-Khuldī's (d. 348/959) daughter who played a particular role in transmitting the body of sayings and teachings of her father's great master, Junayd.[66] It is to say that *taṣawwuf* succeeded in breaking out of the family boundaries of early Sufi personalities, that is many brothers and sisters, fathers and children, mothers and daughters could share the same way of life by becoming initiated into Sufi training. The dynamic interrelationships of each Sufi within his own family circle when the latter includes additional forms of engagement into *taṣawwuf* parallel to his own form are highly interesting. One example of this sort of relationship will be presented and analysed over the course of Chapter 4 which seeks to shed light on the relationship between certain Sufi figures and their maternal uncles. The aforementioned relationship between Bishr b. al-Ḥārith and his sister, Muḍgha, provides another example. Sarī al-Saqaṭī's relationship with his sister is also very interesting and will be referred to in the following section.

As I pointed out earlier, the tendency to lead a celibate life among early Sufis, at least temporarily and for specific periods of time, was not uncommon. During the course of the late sixth/twelfth century, the Sufi

[65] See Jāmī, *Nafaḥāt al-uns*, 65. [66] See Baghdādī, *Taʾrīkh baghdād*, vol. 16, 634.

doctrinal system started devoting more attention to what I like to call a 'theoretical cluster' that was not exactly unknown earlier. By 'theoretical cluster' I refer to a group of theories that appeared in the earliest Sufi compendia, such as Sarrāj's *Luma'* and Makkī's *Qūt*; however, they succeeded in gaining a strong and influential position that enabled them to affect the whole fabric of Sufi thinking only in later stages. The idea that a Sufi who had reached a high spiritual rank was allowed to enjoy several luxuries that he was not allowed at the beginning of his religious way of life is very interesting. Early foundations of this theory appear in Sarrāj's *Luma'* and other Sufi sources. Abū al-'Abbās b. 'Aṭā' (d. 309/922 or 311/923), for instance, used to wear silk and carry a rosary made of pearls.[67] Notwithstanding, a long time passed until those foundations became one of the pillars that constituted the doctrinal system of the late sixth/twelfth century Sufi master, Abū Ḥafṣ al-Suhrawardī (d. 632/1234), and, more particularly, his elaborate theoretical system on sheikh-status (*mashyakha*). According to Suhrawardī, a Sufi master is one who succeeds in achieving the final destination of the Sufi path (*muntahī*) and, thereby, enjoys a high degree of freedom and authority; this is indicated in Suhrawardī's maxim, *si'a / sa'a mujāza li-l-muntahī* (all deeds and luxuries that are permitted to the *muntahī*). Those who have attained the *intihā'* state are thus allowed to do what was forbidden to them at the start of their spiritual journey.[68] If we add to this theoretical pillar the late Sufi theory on the principle of renunciation (*zuhd*), we can see a sort of a theoretical cluster in which each of its components covers one aspect of the way in which later Sufis conceived their spiritual life and practices. Again, it was Suhrawardī who treated three stages of renunciation while making an influential statement according to which the 'third stage of renunciation' (*al-zuhd al-thālith*) is the most celebrated. Early Sufis were concerned with renouncing the world and a 'renunciation of renunciation' (*al-zuhd fī al-zuhd*). While *zuhd* in its original meaning implies replacing worldly goals with higher goals for whose sake the aspirant renounces all others, the stage of *al-zuhd fī al-zuhd* presupposes that the renunciant may be renouncing the world from (partly) secret motives such as a desire for approval or attention or self-conceit. Through *al-zuhd fī*

[67] See Louis Massignon, *Recueil de Textes Inédits* (Paris: P. Geuthner, 1929), 57. Cf. the anecdote of Abū Sa'īd b. Abī al-Khayr (d. 440/1049) in Jullābī Hujwīrī, *Kashf al-maḥjūb*, 207.

[68] See Abū Ḥafṣ 'Umar al-Suhrawardī, *'Awārif al-ma'ārif*, in Abū Ḥāmid al-Ghazālī, *Iḥyā' 'ulūm al-dīn* (Cairo: al-Bābī al-Ḥalabī, 1967), vol. 5, 157–158.

al-zuhd, the Sufi defeats such motives and indeed loses his own free will so that he is no longer conscious of being a renunciant. To these two stages of *zuhd*, Suhrawardī adds a third in which the Sufi recovers his free will after having lost it entirely at the second level. However, his will is now no longer controlled by his human desires since it has become totally divine.[69] The practical effect of this theory is that the *muntahī* may possess money without being condemned for violating an important condition of *zuhd* and he may get married several times and to more than one woman at once. Having many wives and enjoying good food and expensive clothes, as well as possessing property, became, according to this theoretical cluster, a facet of the divine states of grace at the end of the path.[70] The final stage that allows possessing property became, in the course of time, a major characteristic of the Sufi sheikhs of the Suhrawardī order, the most outspoken of whom is Bahā᾽ al-Dīn Zakariyyā Multānī (d. 661/1262), the direct successor of Abū Ḥafṣ al-Suhrawardī himself.[71]

When the Sufi becomes *muntahī*, marriage ceases to be an obstacle blocking his spiritual advancement, and it is considered a privilege or a luxury that he is allowed to enjoy: 'Sufis are allowed to enjoy freedom and ease in marriage for the sake of granting their lower souls their worldly pleasures [...] those permitted pleasures are not expected to harm their souls nor do they weaken their spiritual aspirations.'[72] Suhrawardī did not refrain from insisting that marriage is not the ideal situation at the beginning of one's career. If a novice Sufi got married, however, his companions in the Sufi path should assist him and behave with him leniently since he is considered weak and immature.[73] I would argue that

[69] See ibid., 332.

[70] On early claims against such 'exaggerations' of the Sufi shaykhs in marriage, see e.g., Makkī, *Qūt*, vol. 2, 403.

[71] On the critical attitude of Zakariyyā's contemporaries among the followers of the Chishṭiyya order in India against the wealth of the Suhrawardī centres, see for example: Simon Digby, 'The Sufi Shaikh as a Source of Authority in Mediaeval India', in *Islam et Société en Asie du Sud*, ed. by Marc Gaborieau (Paris: Editions de l'École des Hautes Études en Sciences Sociales, 1986), 64. On the attitude of the Suhrawardī order towards the state and the tradition of living decently and well, see Khaliq Ahmad Nizami, 'Muslim Mystic Ideology and Contribution to Indian Culture', in *Sufism and Society in Medieval India*, ed. by Raziuddin Aquil (New Delhi: Oxford University Press, 2010), 14–19; Cf. Tanvir Anjum, *Chishtī Sufis in the Sultanate of Delhi 1190–1400: From Restrained Indifference to Calculated Defiance* (Karachi: Oxford University Press, 2011), 11–114.

[72] See Suhrawardī, *'Awārif*, 150–151.

[73] See ibid., 147. In one unpublished treatise by Suhrawardī, he indicates that, in his day, it is better for the novice to remain celibate if he does not need to be worried about adultery

Suhrawardī's major contribution to the discussions of marriage and celibacy in classical Sufism lies in his influential attempt to strengthen the pillars of what can be seen as a sanctification of the institution of marriage, a theory that was designated to replace the early rigid approach towards sex, marriage and women by means of considering all those as luxuries that identify elevated spiritual ranks.

Discussing marriage as one aspect of the *si'a mujāza* theory, which is in itself the basis of the whole matrix of Sufi thinking on the celebrated state of *intihā'* and *shaykh*-status, comes as a response to a reality that witnessed situations of permanent celibacy among the Sufis in Suhrawardī's time and before it. It is Sarrāj who provides us with a critical voice against a group of Sufis who cut off their genitals in order to be 'protected' from the earthly desires of their lower souls (*jabbū anfusahum wa-ẓannū annahum idhā qaṭa'ū dhālika salimū min āfāt al-shahwa al-nafsāniyya*). On the same occasion, Sarrāj criticizes other renunciatory customs that were common among certain groups of Sufis in his day such as the custom of eating grass and avoiding drinking water, or the custom of wandering in the deserts without undertaking provisions (*siyāḥa*) as a way to prove one's absolute trust in God (*tawakkul*), or practising a gradual reduction of the amount of food eaten until one faints, a habit which was well known among young Sufis (*jamā'a min al-aḥdāth*).[74]

Yūsuf b. Yaḥyā al-Tādilī known as Ibn al-Zayyāt (d. 617/1220), the author of a famous biographical work on pious North African men and Sufis dating from the sixth/twelfth century, refers frequently to Sufis, both male and female, who remained celibate for their entire lives.[75]

Meanwhile, it should also be noted that what I called the sanctification of the institution of marriage during the course of the sixth/twelfth and seventh/thirteenth centuries was not only a response for tendencies to practise celibacy among Sufis but also a response to a reality in which certain Sufis adopted polygamous lives or got married and divorced very frequently.[76]

After Suhrawardī, the question of maintaining celibacy or being married, together with other issues in the personal lives of Sufi novices, were moved

(*fī hādhā al-zamān al-awlā li-l-murīd tark al-tazawwuj idhā lam yakhaf al-'anat*). (idem., *al-ajwiba al-Suhrawardiyya*, MS. Jagiellońska, 3476, fol. 18b).

[74] See Sarrāj, *Luma'*, 417–418.

[75] See Abū Ya'qūb Yūsuf b. Yaḥyā al-Tādilī known as Ibn al-Zayyāt, *al-Tashawwuf ilā rijāl al-taṣawwuf wa-akhbār Abī al-'Abbās al-Sabtī*, ed. by Aḥmad al-Tawfīq (Casa Blanca: Manshūrāt Kulliyyat al-Ādāb, 1997), 94, 109, 136, 161, 233, 255.

[76] See e.g., Makkī, *Qūt*, vol. 2, 495.

into the hands of the authoritative Sufi masters. Jāmī, during the eighth/fourteenth century, exalted celibacy as the ideal form of Sufi life in spite of the fact that he himself got married at least twice during his lifetime. Hamid Algar notes that, after losing his first wife, Jāmī postponed remarriage until the age of fifty.[77] The Egyptian mystic and scholar ʿAbd al-Wahhāb al-Shaʿrānī (d. 973/1565) indicates that, if the man who began his journey along the Sufi path was married, he was not required to divorce his wife; however, if he was celibate at the time of his initiation into the Sufi path, then he should not get married without a clear permission from his master.[78]

BROTHERS AND SISTERS

The following short passage appears in the biography of Maymūna, the maternal sister of Ibrāhīm al-Khawwāṣ (d. 291/903–904) in Ibn al-Jawzī's *Ṣifat al-ṣafwa*:

> She committed herself to the same devotional life of her brother Ibrāhīm in renunciation and piety and *tawakkul* (*kānat tasluk maslak akhīhā Ibrāhīm fī al-zuhd wa-l-taqallul wa-l-waraʿ wa-l-tawakkul*). Aḥmad b. Sālim said: Someone knocked on the door of Ibrāhīm al-Khawwāṣ. Ibrāhīm's sister asked the visitor who was knocking: 'Whom do you seek?' The visitor answered: [I seek] Ibrāhīm al-Khawwāṣ. Then, the woman said: 'He has gone out.' The visitor asked: 'When will he return?' The woman answered: 'Would that person whose soul is in the hands of others be able to know when he will return?'[79]

Stories about brothers and sisters who shared devotional lives appear very frequently in the sources. In several cases, brothers and sisters were documented to have lived together and supported each other financially. Sarī al-Saqaṭī had a sister who worked in spinning and supported her Sufi brother. Kharkūshī indicates that when Sarī abandoned the trade his sister started providing him with money for his existence. When she was late once and slow in providing him with the money, Sarī asked her: 'Why are you late?' (*lima abṭaʾti?*). She answered that this was because her textile could not be sold that day since people believed that it was not good enough.[80] Kharkūshī goes on to say that, as a result, Sarī decided to

77 See Hamid Algar, *Jami* (New Delhi: Oxford University Press, 2013), 120–122.

78 See ʿAbd al-Wahhāb b. Aḥmad al-Shaʿrānī, *al-Anwār al-qudsiyya fī bayān qawāʿid al-ṣūfiyya* (Beirut: Dār Ṣādir, 1999), 170.

79 Ibn al-Jawzī, *Ṣifat al-ṣafwa*, vol. 2, 296.

80 The word that appears in this context is *mukhallaṭ*, which indicates that the textile's outward is sufficient while its inward is not.

abstain from eating any food that his sister had bought since the money that had been earned to buy it had become suspect, possibly earned illegally, in his eyes. It was told, furthermore, that once, when his sister came to visit him at his place after this event, she was frightened to discover that her pious brother had an old lady as a housekeeper in his place instead of her. Sarī's sister became aggrieved and went to Aḥmad b. Ḥanbal in order to complain about her brother (*ightammat ukhtuhu li-dhālik wa-atat Aḥmad b. Ḥanbal fa-shakat ilayhi akhāhā*). When Aḥmad spoke to Sarī on this matter, the latter said to him: 'When I abstained from eating her food, God subjected the whole world to me in order to serve me and help me maintain my subsistence.'[81] Sarī was suggesting that he could replace his sister's services with those of another woman.

The aforementioned biography of Maymūna, the sister of Ibrāhīm al-Khawwāṣ, leaves the impression that not only did she share a devotional life with her brother but also lived with him in the same house. An earlier version of her biography appears in Baghdādī's *Taʾrīkh baghdād*.[82] Al-Ḥawāriyya, the sister of Abū Saʿīd al-Kharrāz, was also mentioned by Baghdādī. According to the biography of al-Ḥawāriyya in *Taʾrīkh baghdād*, she was a disciple of her renowned brother, as well as being a Sufi guide herself, for other pious women. One of her female disciples was Fāṭima bint Aḥmad al-Sāmiriyya who became a famous authority on *ḥadīth* among male transmitters.[83]

Ibn al-Jawzī refers to the two pious sons of Muḥammad b. Abī al-Ward, Muḥammad and Aḥmad, who both underwent Sufi training under Abū ʿAlī al-Rūdhbārī (d. 322/934).[84] The relationship between Bishr b. al-Ḥārith and his sister and nephews are interesting in this regard as I previously mentioned. More textual evidence leaves a strong impression that Bishr lived in his sister's house or very close to it. On one occasion in Ibn al-Jawzī's *Ṣifat al-ṣafwa*, Bishr's maternal nephew, ʿUmar, tells the following anecdote:

> I heard my maternal uncle saying to my mother: 'I have a strong pain in my abdomen and my loins.' My mother said to him: 'Allow me to prepare a soup for you with some flour to help your body recover.' Bishr then said to her: 'Woe unto you! I am afraid that God will ask me: From where did you get this flour? and

[81] See Kharkūshī, *Tahdhīb al-asrār*, 367.
[82] See Baghdādī, *Taʾrīkh baghdād*, vol. 16, 626–627.
[83] See ibid., vol. 16, 627. See Fāṭima's biography in ibid., 634.
[84] See Ibn al-Jawzī, *Ṣifat al-ṣafwa*, vol. 2, 222–224.

I will not be able to answer Him.' My mother cried and Bishr cried with her, and I cried with them.[85]

Another anecdote about Bishr was narrated by his nephew, ʿUmar, on the same occasion:

My mother noticed one night that Bishr was starving, and as a result, his breathing was weak. She, thereby, said to him: 'Oh my brother! I wish that your mother had not given birth to me since my heart is broken by your miserable situation.' Then I heard him [Bishr!] say to her: 'Me too, I wish that your mother had not given birth to me, and if she had, I wish that she had not given me her breast for nursing.' ʿUmar goes to tell that his mother used to cry for her brother for days and nights! (*wa-kānat ummī tabkī ʿalayhi al-layl wa-l-nahār*).[86]

It is interesting to note that references to familial data appear in the cases of particular Sufi figures more than others. The case of the early Sufi of Baghdad Maʿrūf a-Karkhī (d. 200/815–816) could be presented as an example here. The allusion to his conversion to Islam in Sufi biographies seemed to have necessitated a reference to his Christian parents who converted to Islam after their son's running away from home. In his biography in Qushayrī's *Risāla*, this piece of data involved his mother and father,[87] while in Ibn al-Jawzī's *Ṣifat al-ṣafwa*, the story of his influence on his family to convert to Islam involved only his mother.[88] References both to Maʿrūf's brother, ʿĪsā, and to his maternal nephew are also provided by Ibn al-Jawzī. ʿĪsā is the narrator of the story of Maʿrūf with his teacher in the Christian *kuttāb* (elementary school) who beat him severely for his refusal to repeat the Christian formula of Trinity. ʿĪsā narrates another story about his brother during his last moments, according to which Maʿrūf explains his doctrine on fasting and the necessity to observe this habit with sincerity. Maʿrūf relates that he used to fast frequently throughout his life; however, when he was invited for a meal he preferred to break his fast and not tell anybody that he was fasting. This is one of the techniques that early Sufis practised in order to avoid public praise and, thereby, to prevent their lower souls from enjoying the self-esteem resulting from practising ascetic austerities. Maʿrūf's nephew appears on one occasion in Ibn al-Jawzī's biographical account. He reports that one day he said to his maternal uncle: 'Oh my uncle! I notice you responding to everyone who just calls you.' Maʿrūf, then, commented: 'Oh my dear son! Your maternal uncle is nobody other than a guest that decides to stop wherever

[85] Ibn al-Jawzī, *Ṣifat al-ṣafwa*, vol. 2, 186. [86] Ibid. [87] See Qushayrī, *Risāla*, 10.
[88] See Ibn al-Jawzī, *Ṣifat al-ṣafwa*, vol. 2, 179–180.

he finds himself.'[89] Dhahabī mentions another family member of Maʿrūf in the latter's biography, his paternal nephew, Jusham b. ʿĪsā al-Karkhī.[90] Such references give the impression that the Sufi's relatives appear in the sources basically in order to establish the piety of the Sufi himself. There was little interest among the authors of those sources to relate to the personal background of the Sufi's familial life. Allusions to familial ties appear more in biographies of pious females as I will show in Chapter 2.[91] References of this type would have played a more fundamental role in the process of establishing images of spiritual women even though they are, mostly, brief and, thereby, could provide a better basis for studying the personal aspects of those female personalities.

INTERGRADED DYNAMICS BETWEEN PERSONAL-FAMILIAL AND COMMUNAL-PRACTICAL DOMAINS

Early Sufi sources provide a massive number of statements and anecdotes in which an extremely frigid approach towards one's wife, children and all familial ties is celebrated. One aspect of this body of textual evidence relates to such allusions in which one's familial members are portrayed as obstacles in the path of his spiritual progress. Jāmī tells, for instance, that ʿAmr b. ʿUthmān al-Makkī (d. 291/903–904 or 296/909) used to associate with a youth and that the youth's father attempted to prevent his son from this association until a miracle occurred to that youth which proved to the father that the relationship between his son and Makkī was chaste so that he desisted from his former attitude.[92] As previously mentioned, al-Ḥasan al-Baṣrī's son used to drive his father's companions away

[89] See ibid., 180. [90] See Dhahabī, *Siyar*, vol. 9, 340.

[91] Ahmet Karamustafa, more recently, wrote a chapter on the 'Ghazālī brothers', in which he tries to shed light on the relationships between Abū Ḥāmid al-Ghazālī (d. 505/1111) and his younger brother, Aḥmad al-Ghazālī (d. 517/1123 or 520/1126). Karamustafa suggests that, although we do not have reliable information on the nature of the fraternal bond between the two, the two brothers 'may have been personally close to one another or that at the very least they kept in touch and fended for each other when either of them needed help'. Aḥmad, according to the sources, was the temporary substitute of his brother when the latter left his prestigious professional appointment at the Niẓāmiyya *madrasa* in Baghdad. Abū Ḥāmid's turn to Sufism after his crisis brought him closer to Aḥmad. [See Ahmet Karamustafa, 'The Ghazālī Brothers and Their Institutions', in *Ötekilerin Peşinde: Ahmet Yaşar Ocak'a Armağan* (Festschrift in Honor of Ahmet Yaşar Ocak), ed. by Mehmet Öz and Fatih Yeşil (Istanbul: Timaş Yayınları, 2015), 265–275.]

[92] See Jāmī, *Nafaḥāt al-uns*, 84–85.

because they used to stay with him for a long time and distract him from his family and children.[93]

Beside such references in which the conflict between a Sufi career and family duties are emphasized, there are several anecdotes that reflect an attempt made by individual Sufis to reconcile renunciatory practices with family duties. One of the most significant renunciatory customs among early Sufis was the custom of *siyāḥa*. This term indicates the custom of wandering alone in the deserts without provisions, undertaken by some early renunciants and Sufis. The writings of al-Ḥārith al-Muḥāsibī dating from the mid third/ninth century illustrate the importance of God's lovers' 'escape to places of seclusion' (*al-firār ilā mawāṭin al-khalawāt*) as a sign of their pure intimacy with the divine beloved.[94] The latter idea was very common in the writings of early Muslim renunciants such as ʿAbd Allāh b. al-Mubārak (d. 181/797).[95] During the course of the fourth/tenth century, a Sufi source by an anonymous author, *Adab al-mulūk*, refers to the custom of *siyāḥa* in chapter 21, which was entitled '*Bāb siyāḥat al-ṣūfiyya* '. It is here that the reader comes across an implied attempt to defend the Sufi custom of 'entering the deserts without taking along provisions because of a total trust in God' (*al-dukhūl fī l-bawādī ʿalā ḥukm al-tawakkul bi-l-tajrīd*).[96] Allusions to this Sufi custom also appear in the works of *adab* going back to the fourth/tenth century.[97]

[93] Makkī, *Qūt*, vol. 2, 455–456. On the preference of Sufi companions to one's family, see e.g., Abū ʿAbd al-Raḥmān al-Sulamī, *Kitāb al-arbaʿīn fī al-taṣawwuf* (Ḥaydarābād al-Dukn, India: Maṭbaʿat Dāʾirat al-Maʿārif al-ʿUthmāniyya, 1950), 11; Makkī, *Qūt*, vol. 2, 455–456; Suhrawardī, *ʿAwārif*, 253.

[94] See al-Ḥārith al-Muḥāsibī, *Risāla fī l-maḥabba*, in Iṣfahānī, *Ḥilyat al-awliyāʾ*, vol. 10, 111.

[95] See e.g., ʿAbd Allāh b. al-Mubārak, *Kitāb al-zuhd wa-l-raqāʾiq*, ed. by Ḥabīb al-Raḥmān al-Aʿẓamī (Mālkūn, India: Majlis Iḥyāʾ al-Maʿārif, 1971), 289–292. On Ibn al-Mubārak's *Kitāb al-zuhd*, its structure and themes, see Feryal Salem, *The Emergence of Early Sufi Piety and Sunnī Scholasticism: ʿAbdallāh b. al-Mubārak and the Formation of Sunnī Identity in the Second Islamic Century* (Leiden and Boston: Brill, 2016), 114–129.

[96] Anonymous author, *Adab al-mulūk*, 58–60.

[97] Abū Ḥayyān al-Tawḥīdī for instance, refers to a Khurāsānian group of Sufis who, because of political circumstances that occurred in Nishapur during the Samanid rule and the unsafe situation on the roads in that period, were not able to leave the Sufi centre (*duwayrat al-ṣūfiyya*) to perform *siyāḥa* (*lā qudra lanā ʿalā l-siyāḥa li-insidād al-ṭuruq*). Those Sufis were said to be starving and raving (*nahdhī wa-l-jūʿ yaʿmal ʿamalahu*) while blockaded in that *duwayra* [see e.g., Abū Ḥayyān al-Tawḥīdī, *Kitāb al-imtāʿ wa-l-muʾānasa*, ed. by Muḥammad al-Fāḍilī (Algeria: Dār al-Abḥāth, 2007), 349]. The literature of *adab*, which goes back to the fourth/tenth century, provides us with sarcastic anecdotes concerning groups of Sufis who used to make *siyāḥa*. See e.g., al-Muḥsin b. ʿAlī al-Tanūkhī, *Nishwār al-muḥāḍara wa-akhbār al-mudhākara*, ed. by

Ibn al-Zayyāt notes an interesting aspect in the biographical account of Abū al-ʿAbbās Aḥmad b. ʿAbd al-Raḥmān known as al-Ḥarmal (d. 612/1215). Ibn al-Zayyāt relates that this pious man wandered among the territories of *aʿājim*, being committed to the principle of *tawakkul* and that he used to 'enter the desert accompanied by his wife and children without taking any provisions' (*fa-kāna yadkhul al-ṣaḥrāʾ bi-ahlihi wa-awlādihi ʿalā al-tajarrud*).[98]

In other cases, the Sufi's relatives appear to be close followers of his teachings, and references to them in the sources contribute to his sanctified image. The aforementioned pious son of al-Fuḍayl b. ʿIyāḍ used to accompany his father in prayers. Kharkūshī relates that one day, ʿAlī, whose pious character was frequently celebrated in the sources, fainted when he was listening to his father reciting the *Qurʾān*.[99] According to Ibn al-Mulaqqin, ʿAlī died before his father as a result of a heightened ecstatic state.[100] The case of the early figure al-Ḥakīm al-Tirmidhī is also informative in this regard. Tirmidhī left us a unique autobiographical text, *Badʾ* (or *Buduww*) *shaʾn Abī ʿAbd Allāh al-Ḥakīm al-Tirmidhī* (*The Beginning of the Career of al-Ḥakīm al-Tirmidhī*) in which he refers very frequently to his wife. Tirmidhī attributes the most powerful of his mystic visions to others, including several male companions as well as to his wife. Throughout the text, his wife appears to describe some visions: She was able to see in her dreams everything relating to her husband's spiritual position. It is worth noting that the voice of Tirmidhī's wife sometimes appears louder than that of Tirmidhī himself.[101]

Married Sufis appear in the biographical sources to have practised seclusion for particular periods of time despite their family commitments.

ʿAbbūd al-Shāljī (Beirut: Dār Ṣādir, 1995), vol. 3, 119. Al-Muqaddasī (d. 380/991), the author of *Aḥsan al-taqāsīm fī maʿrifat al-aqālīm*, refers to the custom known in his day among some renunciants of entering the Arabian desert to perform pilgrimage without taking any food (*al-ḥajj ʿalā l-tawakkul wa-l-khurūj bi-lā zād*) [see Muḥammad b. Aḥmad al-Muqaddasī, *Aḥsan al-taqāsīm fī maʿrifat al-aqālīm* (Beirut: Dār Iḥyāʾ al-Turāth al-ʿArabī, 1987), 208]. On *siyāḥa* in early Sufi literature and life, see: A. Salamah-Qudsi, 'Crossing the Desert: *Siyāḥa* and *Safar* as Key Concepts in Early Sufi Literature and Life', *Journal of Sufi Studies*, 2 (2013), 129–147.

98 Ibn al-Zayyāt, *Tashawwuf*, 432.

99 See Kharkūshī, *Tahdhīb al-asrār*, 338.

100 See Ibn al-Mulaqqin, *Ṭabaqāt al-awliyāʾ*, 270–271.

101 See A. Salamah-Qudsi, 'The Will to Be Unveiled: Sufi Autobiographies in Classical Sufism', *Al-Masaq: Islam and the Medieval Mediterranean*, vol. 24, no. 2 (2012), 199–207.

Abū ʿUbayd al-Busrī[102] used to ask his wife to let him spend the whole month of Ramaḍān alone in his room. In his biography in Jāmī's *Nafaḥāt al-uns*, two references to his son are provided.[103] Ruwaym used to eat cooked plants for dinner and to spend every night in his own room (*yadhhab ilā miḥrābihi*) as Daylamī asserts.[104] Others practised seclusion very often in separate rooms that they reserved for this purpose. The sister of Yūsuf b. al-Ḥusayn (d. 304/916–917) mentions that her brother had a separate room in which he used to engage himself in demanding devotional practices overnight (*lahu bayt yataʿabbad fīhi*).[105] Mosques and public Sufi lodges, as well as the homes of companions, could accommodate those who had long solitary periods or those who intensively travelled in search of Sufi masters.[106] Abū Aḥmad al-Faḍl b. Muḥammad (d. 377/987), the disciple of Ibn Khafīf, used to practise a life of seclusion on the roof of his master's *ribāṭ*.[107] It appears most probable that Sufis who committed themselves to *siyāḥa* used to leave their families behind for particular periods of time. The huge body of anecdotes about such journeys in early sources supports this assumption. Abū ʿAlī al-Wārijī, as Ibn Khafīf relates, moved to Shīrāz and gained an administrative position there. He used to sit with Ibn Khafīf every evening, and once he told Ibn Khafīf that he practised wandering in the mountains of *Lukkām*[108] until his mother grew old and his debts accumulated until they became unbearable so that he was obliged to abandon his *siyāḥa* and to take off his Sufi cloak (*khirqa*) and to start working for his livelihood.[109]

[102] See his biography in Qushayrī, *Risāla*, 23–24; Muḥammad b. Mukarram Ibn Manẓūr, *Mukhtaṣar taʾrīkh dimashq*, ed. by several scholars (Damascus: Dār al-Fikr, 1984–1988), vol. 22, 88–93.

[103] See Jāmī, *Nafaḥāt al-uns*, 112–113. The reference to his custom of seclusion during Ramaḍān was originally provided by Sarrāj in: Sarrāj, *Lumaʿ*, 163.

[104] See Daylamī, *Sīra*, 153.

[105] See Kharkūshī, *Tahdhīb al-asrār*, 473.

[106] Nathan Hofer refers to the different roles that the networks of *khānqāh*s played in Ayyubid and Mamluk Egypt. Through a detailed examination of the Saʿīd al-Suʿadāʾ *khānqāh* of Cairo, Hoffer argues that the collective action of that *khānqāh* 'constituted the production and popularization of a culture of Sufism on a large scale in Cairo'. [Nathan Hofer, *The Popularisation of Sufism in Ayyubid and Mamluk Egypt, 1173–1325* (The Tun: Edinburgh University Press, 2015), 68–80.] Such Sufi lodges were not always isolated spaces that served those who sought solitary devotions as Hofer asserts in reference to Ayyubid and Mamluk Egypt (see ibid., 69), but they acted, rather, as active centres for the Sufis' communal lives and connectivities prior to that period and in other different Muslim territories.

[107] See Daylami, *Sīra*, 268.

[108] A mountain in the coast of Syria close to Anṭākia. See Yāqūt b. ʿAbd Allāh al-Ḥamawī, *Muʿjam al-buldān* (Beirut: Dār Ṣādir, 1977), vol. 5, 22.

[109] See Daylamī, *Sīra*, 301.

It is reasonable to suggest that the majority of early Sufis were able to find the formula for integrating family duties and a life of renunciation. Even when some of them committed themselves to *siyāḥa* in solitude or in groups, they most probably did so during their celibate lives or, if they were married, for limited periods of time. Both Ibrāhīm al-Khawwāṣ and Abū Bakr al-Kattānī (d. 322/933) were the most outspoken figures in relevance with *siyāḥa*. According to one anecdote in Qushayrī's *Risāla*, Kattānī asked for his mother's permission before going out on a pilgrimage. After a while, he returned home where his mother had been sitting, waiting for him.[110] The available data in Sufi and non-Sufi sources support the assumption that Ibrāhīm al-Khawwāṣ remained celibate for his whole life. Abū al-Ḥusayn al-Nūrī (d. 295/907–908), as Qushayrī indicates, used to leave his house every day and to take some bread with him. His wife and family believed that he ate the bread during his stay in the marketplace while the men of the marketplace believed that he ate at home.[111] An earlier reference to him is provided in the fourth/tenth century work, *Adab al-mulūk*. The author of this work indicates that Nūrī was among the early Sufis who lived in some ruins in the region of *Sawād* in southern Iraq and that it occurred that the great master of Baghdad Junayd sought Nūrī for one whole week and was not able to find him. Nūrī, as the text reads, died in a ruined site (*māt ākhir ʿumrihi fī khirba*).[112] If we combine the references provided by Qushayrī and the anonymous author of *Adab al-mulūk*, then we find a pious mode of life through which Nūrī and other Sufis of his time attempted to integrate the austere habits of renunciation with family commitments. No satisfactory textual basis is available to help us adequately reconstruct the nature or the extent of the involvement of those Sufis in their day-to-day lives with their families.

The case of Ruwaym b. Aḥmad, which will be examined in detail in Chapter 7, is quite unusual. The critical voices of his Sufi contemporaries against his engagement in family life were, most probably, motivated by his involvement in the state administrative system and his wealthy life. As I mentioned at the beginning of this chapter, early Sufis praised the principle of *tark al-kasb* which left its marks on both parties: Those Sufis who rejected paid work as well as those who made the decision to earn their living. Ruwaym, who chose to support his family by attaching himself to the position of the deputy of the *qāḍī*, gave rise to a

110 See Qushayrī, *Risāla*, 144. 111 See ibid., 21–22.
112 See anonymous author, *Adab al-mulūk*, 32.

controversial approach towards his mode of life in the circles of his Sufi contemporaries. It appears that Ruwaym's fellow Sufis made use of his celebration of his family commitments as well as his interpretation of the principle of *tawakkul*, according to which family life and worldly wealth and *kasb* do not contradict *taṣawwuf*, as a cover for their opposition of his political attachments. The dynamic of Ruwaym's relationships with the circle of Baghdadi Sufis and their influential leader, Junayd, is an interesting topic that deserves further research.

2

Female Sufis

A PARTICULAR FEMALE PIETY?

The various dynamics among early Sufis to reconcile the demands of the increasingly established system of initiation into the Sufi community with family duties and family ties become more sophisticated when we approach female Sufis. Reading the history of 'her story' through 'her' own eyes seems almost impossible. All Sufi biographies of this period were written by male authors. A long time passed until Sufism started to witness female figures whose pious lives and Sufi attachments became increasingly authenticated by a wider range of self-documentation and authorship.

One of those female authors was ʿĀʾisha al-Bāʿūniyya (d. 923/1517). Besides being an important manual for Sufi initiates in general, her *Kitāb al-muntakhab fī uṣūl al-rutab fī ʿilm al-taṣawwuf* (*Selections on the Principles of the Stations in the Science of Sufism*)[1] and her other writings provide interesting insights into the roles of women in Sufi public spheres. Though her case is not directly relevant to my discussion here, it is still important to raise questions such as: To whom did ʿĀʾisha address her works? How does her discourse differ from parallel Sufi works produced by male authors in her day or earlier? What can the autobiographical information that she presents say about her unique mode of piety and about her patterns of bridging the personal and communal spheres? The

[1] See ʿĀʾisha al-Bāʿūniyya, *al-Muntakhab fī uṣūl al-rutab fī ʿilm al-ṭaṣawwuf* (*The Principles of Sufism*), ed. and trans. by Emil Homerin (New York and London: New York University Press, 2014).

will to share aspects of her Sufi life with readers can, in itself, say something in this concern. The general fabric of her *Principles* is largely drawn from a long history of male authorship on Sufi ethos and practicum in a way that it might be difficult or even unnecessary to point out that its author is a woman. In proper historical terms, it is still of little value to identify a 'spirituality particular to women', as Laury Silvers puts it. Meanwhile, Silvers agrees to name 'certain types of bodies, experiences, and articulations female' while referring to intersecting socio-historical narratives.[2]

Leaving aside her poetry, the poetic and fiery style of prose that she invested in writings on Sufi conduct provides different elements of ʿĀʾisha's female identity. Locating sincerity (*ikhlāṣ*) as the second principle after repentance (*tawba*), for instance, might have been intended to emphasize equality between man and woman in the way to God. One of ʿĀʾisha's strategies to assert this point was to quote the well-known *ḥadīth*: 'God looks neither at your bodies nor at your images, but He looks at your hearts.'[3] While she frequently quotes from Qushayrī, her tone differs essentially from that of the great Sufi author of the fifth/eleventh century. Sufi conduct implied in ʿĀʾisha's work is carried out through an emotional-personal language and intensive poetical metaphors. Poetical abilities are clearly shown in her prose writings, as seen in the following example:

> You, the pretender of love, where are your wasting away and your anguish? Where are your burning passions and your dismay? Where are your longings and your yearning? Where are your cravings and your groaning? Where are your grief and your sighing?[4]

At the very end of her work, ʿĀʾisha prays for the sake of her offspring, family and loved ones. From a philological point of view, this form of ending differs from the conventional formulaic endings known from earlier Sufi writings. Qushayrī, for instance, chooses to end his testament (*waṣiyya*) with his invocation for the sake of Sufi novices in general.

[2] Laury Silvers, 'Early Pious, Mystic Sufi Women', in *The Cambridge Companion to Sufism*, 29.

[3] This *ḥadīth* is mentioned in *Ṣaḥīḥ Muslim* as ʿĀʾisha asserts. Bāʿūniyya, *Principles of Sufism*, 42. See also Abū al-Ḥusayn Muslim b. al-Ḥajjāj, *Ṣaḥīḥ Muslim*, ed. by Muḥammad Fuʾād ʿAbd al-Bāqī (Cairo and Beirut: Dār Iḥyāʾ al-Kutub al-ʿArabiyya and Dār al-Kutub al-ʿIlmiyya, 1991), vol. 4, 1987.

[4] Bāʿūniyya, *Principles of Sufism*, 152.

Earlier, Sarrāj, Makkī and Kalabādhī chose to end their works with the conventional formulae of thanking God and asking for His acceptance and contentment.

As for her audience, it seems difficult to suppose that ʿĀʾisha al-Bāʿūniyya intended to address such a composition to her normative disciples, be they men or women. The linguistic style and implied doctrines required readers with a high level of religious education. Her fourfold division of the Sufi path, which differs from the standard division into *maqāmāt* (stations) and *aḥwāl* (states) known in former Sufi manuals (such as those of Sarrāj, Qushayrī and others), calls to mind a similar division made by Shaqīq b. Ibrāhīm al-Balkhī (d. 194/809–810) from an earlier stage.[5]

In modern scholarship, various terms come into use regarding the position of women in early Sufism: 'Sufi women', 'female Sufis/mystics' and more general conceptions such as 'female piety' and 'the feminine in mystical Islam'. The latter, in particular, refers not only to the women's different modes of involvement in Sufi life and theory but also to a wide range of cosmological doctrines according to which women and femininity were symbolically conceived in the description of God–man–cosmos' primordial relationships. Both terms, 'female Sufis' and 'Sufi women', have no male equivalents unless we come across gender-oriented discussions. It could be suggested that each one of the two, hypothetically, has its own focus. The first, most likely, emphasizes the Sufi identity of women, while the second emphasizes their female identity. Where should we put the focus while treating 'female Sufis'/'Sufi women' during the early stage of Sufism? This is indeed a hypothetical question because in its very basis it implies a total and an earlier separation between the so-called female domain and the general Sufi communal domain. *Separation* is not the correct term here. Obviously, different forms of intervention and attachments between those two domains are found and, hence, should be sought.

While forms of intervention between the two domains among male Sufis occupied our interest in the previous chapter, a careful reading of classical and medieval sources is needed to reconstruct the social and religious status of women in their different family attachments and social strata.

[5] See Shaqīq al-Balkhī, *Ādāb al-ʿibādāt*, in *Nuṣūṣ ṣūfiyya ghayr manshūra*, ed. by Paul Nwyia (Beirut: Dār al-Mashriq, 1973), 17–22. See the biography of Shaqīq e.g., in Sulamī, *Ṭabaqāt*, 54–59; Gramlich, *Alte Vorbilder*, vol. 2, 13–62.

BETWEEN PRAISE AND DISPARAGEMENT: TRANSFORMATIONS IN THE SUFI APPROACH TOWARDS WOMEN

Statements on dispraising women (*dhamm al-nisāʾ*) in *zuhd* literature and early Sufi writings should be considered very cautiously. The most important approach that needs to be avoided is referring to such literary references as direct manifestations of reality. Deception and temptation by women had a destructive impact on pious men, as many authors of early medieval Islam very frequently claim. Al-Ḥasan al-Baṣrī, the renowned *zāhid* of Baṣra, states that: 'The man who obeys his wife in everything she likes, no sooner does he enter into morning until God throws him to hellfire.'[6] The famous jurist Muḥammad b. Idrīs al-Shāfiʿī (d. 204/820) is quoted as saying: 'There are three types of people who are expected to humiliate you when you dignify them, and to dignify you when you humiliate them: a woman, a servant and a *nabaṭī*.'[7] The Prophet himself is quoted as having said: 'A time will come when man's destruction (*halāk*) will be caused by his wife, parents and children. All of those rebuke him with poverty and, thus, leading him to do [illegal] things that bring about a total destruction of his religion.'[8]

I would prefer here to use expressions such as 'fear' or 'disparagement of women' instead of 'the hatred of women' or 'misogyny'. The general attitude of dislike for women in works of *zuhd* and early Sufi writings appears not to have been addressed to women because they are women, as the sociological definition of misogyny implies. It was, rather, a theoretical way to counter sexual activity, family ties and other social attachments that were all believed to distract men from a complete devotional life. Extolling one's coldness towards women was only one aspect of extolling a general detachment from society as a whole. This is the reason why disparaging women was commonly related to a public coldness for one's children. A type of heroism or spiritual perfection was celebrated through an emotional coldness or even through a declaration of great

6 Makkī, *Qūt*, vol. 2, 490.

7 Ibid., 521. *Nabaṭī* is one of the *nabaṭ* or the *nabīṭ*, people who settled in the region of *Sawād* in southern Iraq and relied on agriculture for their living. Arabic lexicons and *adab* collections leave the impression that *nabaṭī*s' way of life was usually negatively regarded in the eyes of Arabs because it involves pursuit of wealth and collecting properties. See e.g., Ibn Manẓūr, *Lisān al-ʿarab* (Beirut: Dār Ṣādir, 1994), vol. 7, 411–412.

8 Makkī, *Qūt*, vol. 2, 492.

happiness when one's child dies. Many sayings attributed to the first *zuhhād* of Iraq include themes as such as these.[9] However, this view, which sometimes contained a clear misogynistic character, should be correlated with the socio-cultural shifts that occurred in Muslim societies in the period following that of Islamic conquests in the first two centuries of Islam. It has been noted by several scholars that, due to the expansion of Islam and the continuous process of urbanization, 'the position of urban Muslim women deteriorated considerably'.[10] As a result, the claims of men's superiority over women were asserted by *ḥadīth* reporters and *Qur'ān* commentators despite the fact that the holy text itself supplied a basis both for women's superiority and women's inferiority with respect to men.

As I have already indicated, celebrating the high spiritual status of celibate novices in the fourth/tenth century Sufi collections had little to do with social norms and actual behaviour of the Sufis themselves. On the theoretical level, celebrating celibacy and the disparagement of women had undergone remarkable changes in the course of the fourth/tenth and fifth/eleventh centuries and afterwards, as Sufi sources show. The disparagement and the praise of women are both documented in the various sources of each stage. However, I argue that a thorough reading of sources composed in the course of the early consecutive stages of Sufism reveals a probable transformation in the general framework of Sufis' attitude towards women. One aspect of the negative attitude and the common tendency to disparage women as part of affirming one's piety and absolute devotion, which was apparently tinged with strong ascetic impacts, was gradually replaced by a more sympathetic approach or even, in certain cases, by one in favour of women.

A major factor that contributed to highlighting women's spirituality within Sufism is the increasingly active fashion in associating Sufi spheres undertaken by Sufi women. A special role in this process, as I will show, is related to pious mothers.

Yossef Rapoport maintained that the ideal principle of marriage in Islam had only little to do with the high rates of divorce that frequently

9 See e.g., Iṣfahānī, *Ḥilyat al-awliyā'*, vol. 6, 210 (the biography of Riyāḥ b. ʿAmr al-Qaysī); Makkī, *Qūt*, vol. 2, 529; Jullābī Hujwīrī, *Kashf al-maḥjūb*, 84.

10 See Avner Giladi, *Muslim Midwives: The Craft of Birthing in the Premodern Middle East* (New York: Cambridge University Press, 2015), 27. See also Leila Ahmed, 'Early Islam and the Position of Women: The Problem of Interpretation' in *Women in Middle Eastern History: Shifting Boundaries in Sex and Gender*, ed. by Keddie and Baron (New Haven: Yale University Press, 1991), 58–59.

took place in medieval Islamic societies. This means that the institution of marriage was quite flexible and that women very often were expected to become single. This might have contributed to strengthening the women's bonds with their children, and, consequently, to consolidating the impact they could have on their lives and religious practices.[11] Sufi mothers became increasingly revered in Sufi writings and, as in the case of Ibn ʿArabī (d. 638/1240), they became an expression of sanctified femininity, and their ways of bridging family bonds with deeply religious lives played a fundamental role in shaping the general veneration of women in later Sufi works.

In addition to being naturally a part of the whole socio-cultural reality of medieval societies, Sufis contributed, in their own domain, to strengthening the fluid character of the institution of marriage. According to one of the theoretical pillars of the Sufi system of thought in the period following the great Sufi compendia of the fourth/tenth century, women, marriage and the fulfillment of one's sexual desire became accepted elements of the group of 'luxuries' permitted to a Sufi who succeeded in achieving the final destination of the Sufi path, the *muntahī*, as Sufi authors designated him. The idea of allowing the masters of the path as well as those who succeeded in getting close to them in spiritual terms to enjoy again what beginners were recommended to avoid – this idea was not unknown in early Sufi writings. However, in later Sufi manuals, like in Suhrawardī's *ʿAwārif al-maʿārif*, it gained a central position in the Sufi doctrinal system. *Muntahī* was given permission to enjoy various acts of relaxation and ease (*rukhaṣ*), such as having many wives and enslaved women and possessing property.[12]

Those 'dispensations' (*rukhaṣ*)[13] are considered clear 'proofs' of God's ultimate state of grace. The total state of renunciation of worldly and

[11] See Yossef Rapoport, *Marriage, Money and Divorce in Medieval Islamic Society* (New York: Cambridge University Press, 2005), 38–44.

[12] See A. Salamah-Qudsi, 'The Everlasting Sufi: Achieving the Final Destination of the Path (*Intihāʾ*) in the Sufi Teachings of ʿUmar al-Suhrawardī (d. 632/1234)', *Journal of Islamic Studies*, vol. 22, no. 3 (2011), 320–322.

[13] The literal meaning of '*rukhṣa*' in the single form indicates ease and relaxation. In Islamic law, it refers to conditional lenience in applying an Islamic law, an exemption from the original behaviour code that becomes permissible in specific circumstances. See, for example, ʿAlī b. Muḥammad al-Jurjānī, *Kitāb al-taʿrīfāt* (Beirut: Maktabat Lubnān, 1969), 225. In Sufi literature, the term contradicts the strict prescriptions of *zuhd*. The word *ʿazīma*, therefore, has been used for such a state in which the Sufi must observe these prescriptions and not slide to the lower degree of indulgence. According to ʿAmmār al-Bidlīsī (d. between 590/1194 and 604/1207), Sufi states differ in their weakness and

social affairs in the *zuhd* doctrine of early Sufi writings had been modified into a more sophisticated doctrine, according to which the highest degree of *zuhd* could, unexpectedly, be accompanied by owing money without being condemned.[14] This might be paradoxical for those who were not capable of experiencing the elevated state of *intihāʾ*.

This idea seems to have reflected an actual reality among the Sufis. Many of the latter, in all likelihood, continued to marry many times in their lives, as I pointed out in the previous chapter. The above-mentioned theory on *siʿa mujāza* was nothing but a doctrinal confirmation of that reality. Both the mirrored reality and the mirroring theories contributed, among other general dynamics in medieval Islamic societies, to the deterioration of wifehood and the superiority given to motherhood with a positive and even sanctifying approach towards it.

The development of theories about the symbolic feminine element in spiritual life should also be combined with or seen as a mirror of the change which occurred in the Sufi theoretical approach towards women. The feminine symbol of wisdom and the position of *nafs* in cosmological doctrines of what was conceived in the writings of the sixth/twelfth century as 'the primordial intercourse and mutual passion between the female soul and the male spirit' (*al-tazāwuj/al-taʿāshuq al-aṣlī*) are examples of this approach.[15] Works such as those of Ibn ʿArabī and Bahāʾ

strength in that weak states are characterized by indulgences, strong states by certainty and complete trust in God. Hence for the Sufi of the second type, difficulty and ease are equal as are divine presence (*wajd*) and loss (*faqd*), spiritual voyaging (*safar*) and settling (*ḥaḍar*). [See ʿAmmār al-Bidlīsī, *Ṣawm al-qalb*, in *Zwei Mystische Schriften des ʿAmmār Al-Bidlīsī*, ed. by Edward Badeen (Beirut: Orient Institut in Kommission bei Franz Steiner Verlag Stuttgart, 1999), 52–53.] Abū Ḥafṣ al-Suhrawardī indicates that marriage, for the beginner Sufi, is a 'sliding' from the high state of *ʿazīma*, an obligation of his state, and a salient condition for his sincerity as a beginner in the path, towards the lower state of *rukhṣa* (see Suhrawardī, *ʿAwārif*, 147). On the terms *rukhṣa* and *ʿazīma* in Sufi literature see e.g., Abū al-Najīb al-Suhrawardī, *Ādāb al-murīdīn*, ed. by Menahem Milson (Jerusalem: Institute of Asian and African Studies, Hebrew University of Jerusalem, 1977), 80–99; Carlo A. Nallino, *Raccolta di Scritti Editi e Inediti, a Cura di Maria Nallino* (Roma: Istituto per l'Oriente, 1940), vol. 2: *l'Islām: Dogmatica, Ṣūfismo, Confraternite*, 227, 271; A. J. Wensinck, *Concordance et Indices de la Tradition Musulmane* (Leiden: Brill, 1992), entries '*rukhṣa*' and '*rukhaṣ*.'

14 On the concept of *zuhd thālith*, see e.g., Salamah-Qudsi, *Everlasting Sufi*, 321–322.

15 According to Suhrawardī, *al-tazāwuj/al-taʿāshuq al-aṣlī* is a combination of the Holy Spirit (*rūḥ qudsī*, which can be seen as the theoretical equivalent of Muslim philosophers' concept of *ʿillat al-ʿilal*), which is equivalent to masculinity, and the spiritual soul (*nafs rūḥāniyya*) emanating from the 'masculine' spirit, which is equivalent to femininity. The *rūḥ qudsī* is a father who, after bestowing part of his being on the animal soul which was thus transformed into the spiritual soul, became attracted to that spirit. From that

al-Dīn Walad (d. 628/1231) are the most outspoken among the positive and symbolic images of femininity.

A vital shift in the fashions of women associating with Sufi activities can be perceived from the Sufi sources. This shift might have synchronized with that theoretical change in the Sufi approach towards women and femininity in Sufi compositions. This shift does not refer to the number of pious women in medieval Islamic landscapes but more to the changing fashions and modes of activism that those women undertook within Sufi spheres. In the following discussion, I will examine in greater detail how Sufi women succeeded in the course of time in consolidating their forms of association with Sufi institutions as well as directing their spiritual activities to a way that could ensure a wider degree of involvement. In addition to the wish to understand women's different ways of practising Sufism, an attempt will be presented to reconstruct some aspects of the social ties of those Sufi women relying on available textual evidence and recent scholarly innovations. By doing so, a clearer portrayal of the Sufi element in the complete fabric of the Islamic social scene can hopefully, be attained. Throughout this discussion, our focus will be directed to the dynamics between the devotional life of those pious women and their social engagements in both circles: their close families and the whole Sufi community. While examining the biographical accounts of married Sufi women, I hope to bring to the fore some interesting insights into the probable nature of their marital lives and the ways in which they perceived celibacy.

THE FIRST FLASHES OF DATA: SULAMĪ'S *DHIKR AL-NISWA*

Before examining the data gathered in Sulamī's unique work, *Dhikr al-niswa al-muta'abbidāt al-ṣūfiyyāt*, it is important to make a note concerning the author's motivations and intended audience. There is no available biography specializing in pious women's biographies prior to Sulamī. This work was, most probably, composed originally as a separate work and not as an appendix to the author's most influential work *Ṭabaqāt*

passion, the heart (*qalb*) is born. A partial copy of this spiritual intercourse went beyond *'ālam al-amr* (the invisible world = *malakūt*) into the *'ālam al-khalq* (the material phenomenal world = *mulk*) and became a part of every human being. On this theory, see Suhrawardī, *untitled treatise*, MS. Jagiellońska, fols. 40a–40b; idem, *'Awārif*, 165, 308–309.

al-ṣūfiyya.[16] What were Sulamī's motivations in composing *Dhikr al-niswa*? To whom did he intend to address it? Did Sulamī's personal life include anything that could have caused him to act differently from other authors who were completely committed to a long tradition of not writing on women? In his detailed discussion of Sulamī's *Ṭabaqāt*, Jawid Mojaddedi suggests that Sulamī 'was immersed in Sufism to an extent that he took an interest even in the more contentious aspects of the tradition'.[17] Sulamī, as noted by Mojaddedi, seems to have been attracted, as an author, to contentious topics such as Sufi *samāʿ*, *malāmatiyya* and Sufi exegesis of the *Qurʾān*. Mojaddedi draws our attention to the fact that the longest biographical account in Sulamī's *Ṭabaqāt* is that of Abū Bakr al-Shiblī, one of the most controversial Sufis during Sufism's formative phase.[18]

Sulamī's interest in such topics is supported by an early anecdote quoted originally by Qushayrī. According to this anecdote, Qushayrī himself was commanded by his master, Abū ʿAlī al-Daqqāq (d. 405/1014–1015), to visit Sulamī's place and take, without his permission, a copy of a work that included poems of none other than al-Ḥusayn b. Manṣūr al-Ḥallāj (executed 309/922). Sulamī, who is said to have been endowed with supernatural faculties to prophesy actions and thoughts, succeeded in convincing Qushayrī to abandon his plan. At the end of the anecdote, Sulamī gave Qushayrī his copy of Ḥallāj's work and asked him to tell his master, Daqqāq, that he himself used to quote verses from this work into his own writings.[19] Sulamī was accused by many later traditionalists of fabricating *ḥadīth* traditions among those which he largely quotes in his works and with spreading unacceptable esoteric doctrines in his Sufi exegesis, *Ḥaqāʾiq al-tafsīr*.[20] Meanwhile, it seems that, in the eyes

16 See Abū ʿAbd ar-Raḥmān as-Sulamī, *Early Sufi Women: Dhikr an-niswa al-mutaʿabbidāt aṣ-ṣūfiyyāt*, ed. and trans. by Rkia Elaroui-Cornell (Louisville: Fons Vitae, 1999), *introduction*, 44–45.

17 Jawid A. Mojaddedi, *The Biographical Tradition in Sufism: The Ṭabaqāt Genre from al-Sulamī to Jāmī* (Richmond, Surrey: Curzon Press, 2001), 10 and footnote 12.

18 See ibid., 15. On Shiblī's controversial character, see Kenneth Avery, *Shiblī: His Life and Thought in the Sufi Tradition* (Albany: State University of New York Press, 2014), 109–112.

19 See Qushayrī, *Risāla*, 117–118.

20 See Dhahabī, *Siyar*, vol. 17, 252; ʿAbd al-Raḥmān Ibn al-Jawzī, *Talbīs Iblīs*, ed. by ʿIṣām al-Ḥarastānī and Muḥammad al-Zughlī (Beirut: al-Maktab al-Islāmī, 1994), 215; Jalāl al-Dīn ʿAbd al-Raḥmān al-Suyūṭī, *Ṭabaqāt al-mufassirīn*, ed. by ʿAlī Muḥammad ʿUmar (Cairo: Maktabat Wahba, 1976), 98.

of his fellow citizens of Nishapur, Sulamī was highly admired, as was asserted by his biographer, al-Khaṭīb al-Baghdādī.[21]

As for his personal life, Sulamī took his *nisba*[22] from the Arab tribe of *Sulaym* through his maternal grandfather, Ismāʿīl b. Nujayd al-Sulamī (d. 365/976).[23] It was cited that his father and mother were Sufis and that he received his earliest Sufi training from them until the time when his father died. He then went along the path with his maternal grandfather's guidance. The latter left his grandson a large legacy, and that is why Sulamī was able to travel widely and to write books and even to build a small *duwayra* (Sufi lodge) for the Sufis of Nishapur. In this *duwayra*, Sulamī was later buried. Though we lack a detailed portrait of his personal life, it would be possible to argue that Sulamī's parents, both his father and mother, had a strong influence on his spirituality. This is in addition to the direct Sufi guidance he obtained from his grandfather. Dhahabī reports several ideas of Sulamī himself that, apparently, were derived from an early biographical work of Muhammad b. ʿAlī al-Khashshāb, Sulamī's close disciple, who later became a highly regarded *ḥadīth* transmitter of Nishapur.[24] In one of them, Sulamī is quoted to have said that when his grandfather died, he left behind large areas of land and that he had no heirs except for his daughter, Sulamī's mother. The following is the passage quoted from Sulamī:

> An imperious man was in charge of this legacy. Thanks to God's protection, this man was not able to seize anything from the legacy, and he conveyed it all to me. When Abū al-Qāsim al-Naṣrabādhī [d. 367/977–978] started undertaking preparations to pilgrimage, I asked my mother's permission to perform a pilgrimage, I sold one *sahm* [a specific/ space of land!], and then left [intending to leave for Mecca!] in the year 366. My mother said to me: 'If you wish to betake yourself to God's holy place, then you should protect yourself totally from any possible state

[21] See Baghdādī, *Taʾrīkh baghdād*, vol. 3, 43. Cf. Jean-Jacques Thibon, *L'oeuvre d'Abū ʿAbd al-Raḥmān al-Sulamī (325/937–412/1021) et la Formation du Soufisme* (Damas: Institut Français du Proche-Orient, 2009), 23–24.

[22] *Nisba* is one of the cultural codes of pre-modern Arab societies. It expresses the relation of the individual to a group, a place, a concept or a profession. See Jacqueline Sublet, 'Nisba', *Encyclopaedia of Islam*, second edition, consulted online on 7 August 2016 http://dx.doi.org/10.1163/1573-3912_islam_COM_0866.

[23] Sulamī himself mentions this *nisba* in his *Ṭabaqāt* (see Sulamī, *Ṭabaqāt*, 476). See also Samʿānī, *Ansāb*, vol. 7, 183; S. Sh. Kh. Hussaini, 'Abū ʿAbd-Al-Raḥmān Solamī', *Encyclopædia Iranica*, I/3, 249–250; an updated version is available online at www.iranicaonline.org/articles/abu-abd-al-rahman-solami-mohammad-b (last updated: 19 July 2011).

[24] He died, according to Dhahabī, in 456. See his biography in Dhahabī, *Siyar*, vol. 18, 150–152.

in which your two guardian angels (*ḥāfiẓāk*) register [in the book of men's actions according to the Muslim faith!] anything that may cause you shame on the day after.'[25]

Asking one's mother's permission before leaving to go on a *ḥajj* was a well-documented norm in medieval Islamic biographies. It seems most probable that the permission that Sulamī asked for, according to the above-mentioned passage, refers particularly to the need to sell the inherited land in order to get money for his long journey. When his grandfather died, Sulamī was aged between thirty-two and forty.[26] It would be possible to suggest that his mother remained highhanded regarding her father's properties and that her son always needed her permission to make use of those properties. One could not avoid combining the guidelines of Sulamī's personal life and his implied project in *Dhikr al-niswa*. Was that project somehow inspired by the 'maternal' part of his author's life? A proposed reference to this inquiry will be given after the following attempt to present the available data in the work of *Dhikr al-niswa*. Sulamī's *Dhikr al-niswa al-mutaʿabbidāt al-ṣūfiyyāt* includes eighty-two biographical accounts of early pious women.[27] Sulamī's women are identified as slaves, married women and widows, as well as mothers and sisters of male Sufis. Like other Sufi hagiographies, Sulamī's accounts are collections of sayings and anecdotes attributed to the women involved. In the table that appears in the Appendix, I present a survey of Sulamī's accounts based on the ways in which he introduces each woman. His choice to introduce each woman appears at the start of her biography. Introducing the biographies under a specific criterion helps identify Sulamī's preference to put the focus on one particular aspect of the data. When he begins the account by stating that one woman was the wife of a particular Sufi and later refers to the masters she associated with, the biographical focus is to be perceived as her marital relationship.

Before referring to the data presented in the table, I would like to make the following points:

25 Ibid., vol. 17, 249.

26 Ibn Nujayd died in 365 or 366. Sulamī was born in 325 or, according to other accounts cited by Dhahabī, in 330.

27 It should be noted that three biographies appear in two versions in Sulamī's work so that the total number of the female personalities is not eighty-two but seventy-nine (biography no. 22 is a version of biography no. 2; biography no. 39 is a version of 12 and biography no. 40 is a version of biography no. 13).

1. In few biographical accounts in Sulamī's work (which are not included in any of the categories listed in the table), no particular places, forms of association and social-religious ties with any of the women's contemporaries are mentioned.[28] Interestingly, except for the case of Dhakkāra, all those women are described to have sworn themselves to the service of male Sufis in their days. In two of those accounts, the pious woman is described as being committed to help the poor (*muta ʿahhida li-l-fuqarāʾ*).[29]
2. In two accounts, Sulamī introduces women only as daughters. I do not refer here to the general identification of a woman as 'the daughter of', which is the female equivalent of the title *ibn* in classical biographies, but to particular places where women are identified only as daughters. The first such account is that of ʿĀʾisha the daughter of the renowned mystic of Nishapur, Abū ʿUthmān al-Ḥīrī (d. 298/910), while the other is that of her daughter, Umm Aḥmad bint ʿĀʾisha. The latter, thus, is introduced as the daughter of her famous previously mentioned mother.[30] In the case of Ziyāda bint al-Khaṭṭāb, Sulamī introduces her as a mother of Ismīʿīl b. Ibrāhīm al-Quhistānī, as well as the daughter of al-Khaṭṭāb, who was Abū Yazīd al-Basṭāmī's greatest companion.[31]
3. In one case only, that of Umm al-Aswad bint Zayd al-Baṣriyya, Sulamī begins the very short account by stating that Muʿādha al-ʿAdawiyya was Umm al-Aswad's wet nurse.[32]
4. Women who are introduced by Sulamī with reference to the places where they lived are described usually at the beginning of their accounts with general statements, such as '*min mutaʿabbidāt al-niswān*',[33] or '*min al-mutaʿabbidāt al-mujtahidāt al-ʿārifāt*',[34] or '*min arbāb al-mujāhadāt*'.[35]
5. In one case only, that of Fāṭima who was nicknamed Zaytūna, the woman is said to have served different Sufi masters: Abū Ḥamza, Junayd and Nūrī.[36]
6. Except for two cases, Sulamī does not mention dates of death in his *Dhikr al-niswa*. The two cases are that of Fakhrawayh (d. 313/925 according to al-Sulamī)[37] and that of ʿĀʾisha (d. 346/957 according to him), the daughter of the well-known Abū ʿUthmān al-Ḥīrī of

[28] See the biographical accounts of Dhakkāra (ibid., 183); Hawra (ibid., 223) and Āmina al-Marjiyya (ibid., 255) and Fāṭima al-Khānqahiyya (ibid., 257).
[29] Ibid., 255, 257. [30] Ibid., 219. [31] Ibid., 231. [32] Ibid., 105; repeated in 167.
[33] Ibid., 111. [34] Ibid., 119. [35] Ibid., 131. [36] Ibid., 159. [37] Ibid., 179.

Nishapur.[38] Both women had close ties with Ibn Nujayd since Fakhrawayh was the woman whom he married (although she was not Sulamī's grandmother), and the other, ʿĀʾisha, was his master's daughter. Sulamī himself associated with ʿĀʾisha's daughter, Umm Aḥmad, since he directly quotes her sayings in her mother's account.

7. Though it became common in later biographies, like that of Shams al-Dīn al-Sakhāwī (d. 902/1497), we do not come across the expression 'she was under' (*kānat taḥt*) instead of 'she was a wife of' except for only one place.[39]
8. The name of Umm al-Ḥusayn al-Qurashiyya appears in several accounts in addition to her separate account.[40] As for male figures, the name of the renowned Sufi of Nishapur, Abū al-Qāsim al-Naṣrābādhī (d. 367/977–978), appears frequently in Sulamī's work. Both figures deserve a closer examination in the following discussion.

The data in the table show that in a large number of the cases (twenty-two cases) women are attributed to spatial spaces only.[41] Of those twenty-two cases, eight are attributed to Iraq, Baghdad or Baṣra, while four are attributed to Syria or Damascus. Remarkably, Egypt is totally absent from the scope of Sulamī's work. Furthermore, our survey leaves no doubt that Sulamī seems very eager to portray many women on the basis of their association with the male masters of their days. He does so in nineteen cases. Highlighting the involvement of women in the religious scene of their time was crucial in Sulamī's eyes. While watching Nūrī eating with his dirty hands, his aforementioned female disciple, Zaytūna, said: 'Oh Lord! How filthy are Your friends!' Nūrī, later, succeeded in saving her from an accusation of robbery and blamed her for her insulting statement. At first sight, this anecdote serves to celebrate the supernatural capacities of Nūrī more than to praise Zaytūna's sincere *tawba*. However, for Sulamī, the anecdote was an excellent way to establish Zaytūna's piety by combining it with the dramatic story of *tawba*. It was a well-known strategy in early Sufi works to portray the 'starting points' of many key

[38] Ibid., 185. [39] Ibid., 217. [40] Ibid., 241, 243, 247.

[41] The cases in which Sulamī refers to places in addition to other distinguishing features of his female personalities exceed, indeed, twenty-two. The data in the table relates to the occasions where Sulamī chooses to introduce women by spatial spaces only. See a similar reference to the spatial coverage of Sulamī's *Dhikr al-niswa* and a detailed survey of this work in: Thibon, *L'oeuvre d'Abū ʿAbd al-Raḥmān al-Sulamī*, 330–339.

figures in highly dramatic terms. Dramatic beginnings that took place by means of shocking triggers were the most effective way of affirming the sanctity of mystics.[42]

Asserting women's associations with pious males was an additional strategy to celebrate their piety. Only in one case of his work does Sulamī refer to a woman who was the formal teacher, *ustādh* in the original text, of another woman. That was the case of Ḥukayma al-Dimashqiyya, who was the *ustādh* of the famous Rābiʿa bint Ismāʿīl. Rkia Cornell explains this unfamiliar use of the grammatical masculine form as Sulamī's way of indicating that this woman succeeded in attaining the status of the 'men', the *rijāl* which, according to early Sufi tradition, implies the highest spiritual degree that a Sufi, male or female, could achieve. In most of the references to women who were known as teachers in the Sufi path, male disciples or associates are mentioned.

The word '*khidma*' (service) appears frequently in reference to women who are described by Sulamī as practising chivalry (*futuwwa*). This frequency provides a strong impression that, among the different conceptions that constituted the hard core of early Sufi theory, *futuwwa* in particular was the most celebrated in the eyes of women.[43] The deep wish

[42] See Gerhard Böwering, 'Early Sufism between Persecution and Heresy', in *Islamic Mysticism Contested: Thirteen Centuries of Controversies and Polemics*, ed. by Frederick de Jong and Bernd Radtke (Leiden: Brill, 1999), 45–54.

[43] The word *futuwwa* here designates the quality of altruism and unquestioning loyalty to fellow members of the particular group. This individual-ethical content of the term enjoyed a seminal role in early Sufi ethical writings and manuals. See e.g., Qushayrī, *Risāla*, 113–115; Sulamī, *Risālat al-malāmatiyya*, in Abū al-ʿAlāʾ ʿAfīfī, *al-Malāmatiyya wa-l-ṣūfiyya wa-ahl al-futuwwa* (Cairo: Dār Iḥyāʾ al-Kutub al-ʿArabiyya, 1945), 117–120. The rise of the social and organizational implications of the term took place in Iraq and Persia during the Umayyid and ʿAbbāsid eras. Many urban associations of youth (*fityān* in Arabic and *javānmardī* in its Persian equivalent) practised different forms of *futuwwa* in several centres of the Muslim world. While the theoretical-ethical implications of *futuwwa* could be witnessed in the early context of Sufism, its organizational structures succeeded to influence later Sufi practices. Scholars differed in their attempts to explain the motivations and dynamics that brought about the appearance of various forms of the *futuwwa* organizations. The works of Lloyd Ridgeon investigate elaborately the origins and developments of *futuwwa* groups in medieval Islam with a special focus on Sufi-*futuwwat* in Iran. See e.g., Lloyd Ridgeon, 'Javanmardi: Origins and Development until the 13th Century and its Connection to Sufism', *Annals of Japan Association for Middle East Studies*, vol. 21, no. 2 (2006), 49–74; idem, *Jawanmardi: A Sufi Code of Honour* (Edinburgh: Edinburgh University Press, 2011), the *introduction*, 1–22. For a detailed study of *futuwwa* that includes an investigation of its forms during the modern era, see idem, *Morals and Mysticism in Persian Sufism: A History of Sufi-futuwwat in Iran* (London and New York: Routledge, 2010). A detailed reference to Sulamī's *Risālat al-futuwwa* is provided in ibid., 35–45.

to practise it in daily life and behaviour affected their religious-social relationships and teachings. *Khidma* involves the financial support granted by certain rich women to their fellow male Sufis as a means to practise *futuwwa*. *Khidma* seems to be a very ambiguous word in early Sufism. Both the verbal form *khadama* (served) and its nominal equivalent *khādim* (servant) were common in Arabic works of *adab*. In Sufi contexts, this word could signify the relationship between the Sufi master and his advanced disciple. Over the course of time, *khādim* could also indicate the one who claimed to belong himself to the Sufi community by supporting its members financially and guaranteeing their living without necessarily being an active part of their religious life and rituals.[44] It would be possible to suggest, then, that the latter meaning of *khidma* is referred to in the two biographical accounts of Fāṭima al-Khānqahiyya and Āmina al-Marjiyya. In both cases, the woman is described as *muta'ahhidat al-fuqarā'*, and no additional references to her religious life and interrelationships with other pious people are mentioned.

It is remarkable that those women who are basically portrayed by Sulamī in an abstract manner, that is their ascriptions to specific locations and personalities are not provided, share the same characteristic of practising *futuwwa* and supporting poor Sufis.[45] It is possible to suggest that those women became interested more than others in 'serving' the Sufis in the field and that they were less interested in associating with Sufi masters for studying or teaching Sufi theories. They might have sought spiritual blessing (*baraka*) by means of serving Sufi males in their households without committing themselves to more solid relationships that develop around the aspiration for Sufi instruction and teachings. This might be the case of 'Amra of Farghāna.[46]

There is no evidence supported by Sulamī of any formal associations of female *futuwwa* parallel to that known among male *fityān*. Cornell argues that through Sulamī's use of the term *niswān*, he feminizes the term *fityān* and signifies a subcategory of *niswa*, that is the practitioners of female chivalry whose 'own corporate identity' is asserted.[47] The etymological

[44] See A. Salamah-Qudsi, 'The Idea of *Tashabbuh* in Sufi Communities and Literature of the Late 6th/12th and Early 7th/13th Century in Baghdad', *Revista al-Qantara*, XXXII, 1 (January–June 2011), 189–195.

[45] Ridgeon refers to the large number of females who were either practitioners of *futuwwa* or had an opinion about it in Sulamī's work, and indicates that this was a result of Sulamī consideration of *futuwwa* as an essential component of Sufism. See Ridgeon, *Morals and Mysticism*, 34.

[46] See Sulamī, *Dhikr*, 191.

[47] See ibid., Cornell's *introduction*, 66–67.

explanations given for Sulamī's use of the three terms *nisā'*, *niswa* and *niswān* to express 'enhancement' on three levels of the meaning is well-established in the text of *Dhikr*. While Laury Silvers agrees with Cornell on this point, she does not make any reference to the conventional traits of women who are said to have practised female *futuwwa*.[48]

What seems most probable is that Sulamī did not attempt to consolidate the separate identity of his women through the system of *futuwwa*. He sought, rather, to stress women's integration into the general fabric of medieval religiosity through emphasizing their active roles in *khidma*, which indicates women's impressive financial service that helped support Sufi communities with a vibrant backing through the effective system of *arfāq* (the plural form of *rifq*; donations and alms).[49] The above-mentioned Fāṭima al-Khānqahiyya is quoted to have defined true *futuwwa* as follows: '*Futuwwa* is to maintain service to others without discrimination.' This definition might illustrate women's will to integrate into the general Sufi sphere and not to restrict themselves to any distinctive female milieu. The same Fāṭima, for instance, was introduced by Sulamī as 'one of the *fityān* in her age', while another woman, Amat al-ʿAzīz, was introduced as 'one of the greatest women who practised *futuwwa* at her time (*kānat min aftā waqtihā fī al-niswān*).[50] Many of those women who practised *futuwwa* and service seem to have associated with the great master of Nishapur and one of the prominent founders of *futuwwa* and *malāmatiyya* doctrines there, Abū ʿUthmān al-Ḥīrī. One of those was ʿĀʾisha of Merv. She was even invited by Abū ʿUthmān to stay with him in his house, as Sulamī tells at the beginning of her account. When *fityān* were visiting her place, she used to serve them.[51] The latter notion indicates that male Sufis used to apply to certain pious women, basically those who were known for their willingness to support Sufis, and ask them to fulfill all their daily needs. Fāṭima bint Aḥmad b. Hāniʾ of Nishapur associated with Abū ʿUthmān al-Ḥīrī and even spent much of her money on him and his companions.[52] Fakhrawayh bint ʿAlī, the wife of Sulamī's grandfather Ibn Nujayd, was known for her deep *futuwwa* that could, even, be equated with that of Abū ʿUthmān himself, in her husband's view.[53]

[48] See Silvers, *Early Pious Mystic Sufi Women*, 36, 49.

[49] See Ibn Manẓūr, *Lisān al-ʿarab*, vol. 10, 118.

[50] Sulamī, *Dhikr*, 223. Cornell's translation of this sentence fits with her assumption of the existence of a 'female chivalry' among Sulamī's women: 'She was one of the most altruistic practitioners of female chivalry in her day' (Ibid., 222).

[51] Ibid., 197. [52] Ibid., 199. [53] Ibid., 177.

In order to assert the ideal of *futuwwa*, Sulamī mentions the story of Abū ʿAbd Allāh al-Rūdhbārī (d. 367/977), who came to the house of his female disciple, Qusayma, and when he found that the door was locked, he asked his companions to break the lock, enter the house and to take everything in it! When Qusayma arrived, her husband told her what had happened, but instead of getting angry, she followed her master to his gathering and gave him the robe that she was wearing as a proof of her sincere *futuwwa*.[54]

Sufi literature frequently describes rich women who used to donate food, alms, presents and money to poor Sufis. The famous tradition according to which Sufis were warned against accepting women's support (*arfāq*) is, most probably, a response to the degree of popularity that this custom had reached in early medieval Islamic societies. In many cases, great Sufi masters rejected donations from women, causing the latter to severely reprehend them. Regarding this point in particular, the reader of early Sufi literature would come across a common structure of the story: A woman sends a donation to a renowned male colleague; the latter refuses to accept it, commenting that 'lowness and humbleness are in accepting women's donations'. The woman sends her colleague a severe critical response or only makes a severe comment before the messenger. The main aim in this response was to highlight the negative motives behind her colleague's refusal, that is his wish to seek glory and praise from the people or even his weak spiritual state that kept him from seeing a human source of subsistence instead of seeing the divine will to bestow wealth upon him.

The last biographical account in *Dhikr al-niswa* refers to ʿĀʾisha bint Aḥmad al-Ṭawīl of Merv, who was ʿAbd al-Wāḥid al-Sayyārī's (d. 375/985) wife. This woman, according to Sulamī, 'spent more than five thousand *dirhams* on the Sufis of her time'. When she was told that a particular Sufi refused to accept her gift, she replied in the same way that other women do on similar occasions: 'When the slave seeks glory in his servitude, his foolishness is revealed.'[55] The core of this story in reference to several women is frequently celebrated by Sulamī. It might be possible, then, to assume that there was one original-actual story related to a particular female figure and that the framework of this story later became used by Sufi authors in their references to other pious women as one of their techniques to establish women's piety. Interestingly, in the biography of ʿĀʾisha bint

[54] Ibid., 211. [55] Ibid., 259, the English translation of Cornell, 258.

Aḥmad al-Ṭawīl, another story is presented by Sulamī. Rkia Cornell translates the story as follows:

> I was informed that a professional invoker said to her: 'Do this and that and an unveiling of divine secrets will be granted to you.' She said: 'Concealment is more appropriate for women than unveiling, for women are not to be exposed.'[56]

I would suggest interpreting the statement about that 'invoker' in a different way. It seems most probable that this man referred to the pious woman and asked her to act in a particular way in order to ensure the state of unveiling, *kashf*, while his request implied an erotic intimation. This might explain why the woman replied as told in the story.

While Sulamī devotes a separate biography to ʿĀʾisha in his *Dhikr*, her renowned husband, ʿAbd al-Wāḥid b. ʿAlī al-Sayyārī (d. 375/985–986), is not granted such an account in Sulamī's *Ṭabaqāt al-ṣūfiyya*. In the text of *Ṭabaqāt*, meanwhile, Sulamī frequently mentions Sayyārī's name as a transmitter of many anecdotes and sayings. ʿAbd al-Wāḥid al-Sayyārī was a disciple of Sulamī's grandfather, Abū ʿAmr b. Nujayd, as Sayyārī is quoted to have said in the biography of Ibn Nujayd: 'I asked Ibn Nujayd when I left him to advise me.'[57] He was the nephew on his mother's side of Abū al-ʿAbbās al-Qāsim b. al-Qāsim al-Sayyārī (d. 342/953–954), the famous Sufi of Merv.[58] The following narrative appears several times in Sulamī's work: A pious woman sends a gift to one of her male acquaintances; the latter rejects it, and the woman responds with an insulting comment on the man's behaviour. This narrative does not pass without notice among certain great Sufi masters. The story of Fāṭima al-Naysābūriyya with Dhū al-Nūn al-Miṣrī (d. 245/860) is a good example. Fāṭima was considered 'one of the greatest female gnostics of her time'. When she once sent Dhū al-Nūn a gift, he sent it back and said: 'In accepting women's *arfāq* there is humiliation and weakness.'[59] It might be possible that Fāṭima asked her messenger to tell the great Egyptian master that: 'There is no Sufi in this world lowlier than the one who sees the [earthy!] cause [behind the gift instead of seeing the true cause, that is God, Who stands behind all actions and all causes!].'[60]

[56] Ibid. [57] Sulamī, *Ṭabaqāt*, 479.

[58] The famed maternal uncle, Abū al-ʿAbbās al-Sayyārī, was Abū Bakr al-Wāsiṭī's (d. ca. 320/928) associate, who was Junayd's associate. It is worth noting here that Hujwīrī devotes to what he entitles '*al-Sayyāriyya*' a separate section in his detailed discussion of the Sufi sects. See Jullābī Hujwīrī, *Kashf al-maḥjūb*, 323–333.

[59] Sulamī, *Dhikr*, 143.

[60] Ibid. The English translation suggested by R. Cornell here does not express the deep nuances of Fāṭima's reply. Cornell's translation reads: 'There is no Sufi in this world more lowly than one who doubts another's motives.' The translator feels unsatisfied with the

The stories of ʿĀʾisha of Merv and Fāṭima of Nishapur (d. 232/846) might leave the impression that male Sufis used to sharply reject sources for subsistence, particularly those offered by rich women. Nonetheless, we should keep in mind that this rejection might not have been gender oriented. It might be seen as a part of a wider approach that was very common among early Sufis, as shown in the sources. Satisfaction with a determined source for subsistence (*istināma ilā maʿlūm*) in general terms was considered as one of the epidemics (*āfāt*) with which the mystic might become 'afflicted' since it calls into question the idea of absolute trust in God.[61] The word *arfāq* could also indicate a wide range of donations, presents, alms, food and money that the Sufis used to receive from their supporters, both male and female. Sarrāj quotes the following statement of Abū ʿAbd Allāh al-Naṣībī: 'I travelled for thirty years and during this period I used not to sew my patched frock, or to enter any place that I knew offers *rifq*. '[62] It sounds more interesting or perhaps more 'dramatic' to understand the rejection of both Dhū al-Nūn al-Miṣrī and the anonymous male Sufi in the biography of ʿĀʾisha of Merv in a gender-oriented way. However, I would suggest that this behaviour originates in the above-mentioned critical approach towards 'satisfaction with a determined source for subsistence' even when the phrasing of Dhū al-Nūn's statement takes the form of 'the gifts of Sufi women'.

Unlike earlier Sufi manuals in which wives were portrayed as one of the major 'enemies' that the Sufi male had to challenge or, even worse, as a 'substitute for hellfire',[63] wives in Sulamī's work were portrayed in a far more respectful tone. Wives were often said to have willingly taken upon themselves to support their families when their husbands decided to devote themselves to the Sufi path. In other cases, rich wives were able to financially support all the companions of their husbands in Sufi communities, as has been recorded about Rābiʿa bint Ismāʿīl, the wife of

translation and that is why she explains Fāṭima's statement in the footnote as follows: 'This means that the person who rejects such a gift is needlessly suspicious or lacking in thankfulness' (Ibid., 142).

[61] See Qushayrī, *Risāla*, 202.

[62] Sarrāj, *Lumaʿ*, 190. Cf. Kharkūshī, *Tahdhīb al-asrār*, 267. Interestingly, the same statement is quoted later by Qushayrī. However, the word *rifq* is replaced there by *rafīq* (companion). See Qushayrī, *Risāla*, 144, lines 15–17.

[63] See e.g., Makkī, *Qūt*, vol. 2, 490–492. Sarrāj reports that a group of Sufis during his lifetime were said to have tried cutting off their genitals in order to 'protect' themselves from sexual desire (Sarrāj, *Lumaʿ*, 418).

Aḥmad b. Abī al-Ḥawārī.[64] According to certain anecdotes, it was Rābiʿa herself who initiated her marriage to Ibn Abī al-Ḥawārī in order to 'serve' him and his Sufi companions by bestowing on them the property she had inherited from her first husband. Woman's initiation of marriage to a renowned Sufi figure was not rare in Sufi tradition.[65] However, in several cases, such offers were rejected.[66] Sources tell that, after her marriage, Rābiʿa bint Ismāʿīl had no interest in sexual intercourse and eventually asked her husband to marry another woman. She adhered to wifely duties such as cooking meat for her husband while encouraging him to satisfy his other wives sexually.[67]

Our impression is that portraits of wives of famous Sufis in Sulamī's *Dhikr* were not designed to reveal an additional realm of their spouses' spirituality but rather an attempt to shed light on the unique way of life and thinking of Sufi women themselves.[68] Even though some would claim that this was also a technique for praising male spirituality, exalting pious wives above their Sufi husbands for their knowledge and spiritual capacities, as shown in many biographies of Sulamī, could be taken as evidence of the seminal role that wives actually played in early Sufism in spite of their inferiority in general legal terms. It is interesting to note that Muslim biographers very often used the expression '*taḥt*' (lit. below) to indicate the status of a married woman.[69] However, in Sufi contexts, such as Sulamī's *Dhikr* and Ibn al-Jawzī's sections on pious women in his *Ṣifat al-ṣafwa*, the term primarily used is *zawja*.[70]

General biographies of medieval Muslim women provide us with data about wives who gained a certain degree of freedom while creating their

64 Sulamī, *Dhikr*, 139. Cf. Ibn Khamīs, *Manāqib al-abrār*, vo. 1, 153 (on the sister of Sarī al-Saqaṭī, d. 257/870).

65 See e.g., Jullābī Hujwīrī, *Kashf al-maḥjūb*, 149; Jāmī, *Nafaḥāt al-uns*, 101.

66 See e.g., Jāmī, *Nafaḥāt al-uns*, 101, 331.

67 See Makkī, *Qūt*, vol. 2, 507.

68 See e.g., Sulamī, *Dhikr*, 163, 169, 187, 201, 207.

69 See e.g., Yaḥyā b. Sharaf al-Dīn al-Nawawī, *Riyāḍ al-ṣāliḥīn min kalām sayyid al-mursalīn* (Cairo: Maktabat Maṣr, 1995), 102; ʿAlī b. al-Ḥasan Ibn ʿAsākir, *Taʾrīkh madīnat dimashq: tarājim al-nisāʾ*, ed. by Sukayna al-Shihābī (Damascus: Dār al-Fikr, 1981), 33, 42, 43, 524. Cf. W. Robertson Smith's reference to the common expression that a wife is under (*taḥt*) her husband in: W. Robertson Smith, *Kinship and Marriage in Early Arabia*, new edition with additional notes by the author and by Ignaz Goldziher (Oosterhout N.B.: Anthropological Publications, 1966), 161.

70 Cf. Sakhāwī's use of the verbs *tazawwajat* or *tazawwajahā* when he turns to pious women, in: Shams al-Dīn Muḥammad b. ʿAbd al-Raḥmān al-Sakhāwī, *al-Ḍawʾ al-lāmiʿ li-ahl al-qarn al-tāsiʿ* (Beirut: Dār Maktabat al-Ḥayā, n.d.), vol. 12, 11 (in the biography of a woman named Uns bint ʿAbd al-Karīm b. Aḥmad); ibid., 16. However, in few cases, Sakhāwī uses the word '*taḥt*' for pious women too. See, e.g., ibid., 20.

own religious careers. In Sakhāwī's *Mu'jam al-nisā'*, for instance, there is a description of a woman who used to perform the pilgrimage not only in the company of her husband but also of many other men. Her husband, who did not like her behaviour, eventually divorced her.[71] Even if this story is not historically accurate, when combined with other Sufi-oriented anecdotes, it might reveal another type of highly challenging wifehood for Sufi males. It is a type that does not appear among Sulamī's ideal pious women. In one variation of the well-known story of the encounter of Umm 'Alī Fāṭima, the wife of Aḥmad b. Khiḍrūya (d. 240/854–855), with Abū Yazīd al-Basṭāmī, which seems to have been written in Basṭāmī's favour, this woman promised to exempt her husband from a serious part of her dowry (in case they divorced) if he took her to Basṭāmī's place, where she could remove her veil while talking to him. The additional part of this story, that, when Basṭāmī one day noticed Fāṭima's hand was stained with henna, they could no longer meet, did not appear in this source.[72] Fāṭima's wish to exempt her husband from her dowry, in my view, did not concern her intention to marry Basṭāmī, even though the early text of Iṣfahānī clearly indicates this.[73] Whether this was so or not, Fāṭima's behaviour may symbolize a certain degree of independence that Sufi wives could enjoy, sometimes at the expense of their husbands' pride and self-esteem. Such independence seems to have originated, partly, in the women's own wealth and well-established economic backgrounds. This was also the case of Fāṭima and her husband, Ibn Khiḍrūya. None of the different versions of this anecdote was mentioned by Sulamī.[74]

The renowned mystic of Nishapur and Sulamī's influential master, Abū al-Qāsim al-Naṣrābādhī, is mentioned five times in Sulamī's *Dhikr*, where references are made to his association with five of the author's pious women. In four cases, Naṣrābādhī was referred to as the spiritual teacher of Sulamī's women, while in one case only the great master was subjected

[71] See Sakhāwī, *al-Ḍaw' al-lāmi'*, vol. 12, 2. The Arabic statement is still ambiguous; one cannot be sure whether the second sentence *wa-lam yartaḍi amrahā fa-fāraqahā* is a result of the first *wa-ḥajjat ma'ahu wa-ma' ghayrihi*.

[72] See Abū al-Faḍl Muḥammad b. 'Alī al-Sahlajī, *al-Nūr min kalimāt Abī Ṭayfūr*, in 'Abd al-Raḥmān Badawī, *Shaṭaḥāt al-ṣūfiyya* (Kuwait: Wikālat al-maṭbū'āt, 1976), 170. Cornell wrongly indicates that this variation originated in Iṣfahānī's *Ḥilyat al-awliyā'*. This part is found in Jullābī Hujwīrī, *Kashf al-maḥjūb*, 150. See also Iṣfahānī, *Ḥilyat al-awliyā'*, vol. 10, 43; Farīd-al-Dīn 'Aṭṭār, *Tadhkirat al-awliyā'*, ed. by R. A. Nicholson (Leiden: Brill, 1905), vol. 1, 288–289. See also a detailed survey of the sources describing Umm 'Alī, known also by her surname 'Mahdī-yi 'Alīya' in: Gramlich, *Alte Vorbilder*, vol. 2, 99–102.

[73] See Iṣfahānī, *Ḥilyat al-awliyā'*, vol. 10, 43.

[74] See e.g., Sulamī, *Dhikr*, 169.

to a severe criticism or even a humiliating approach from his female disciple, Umm al-Ḥusayn al-Qurashiyya of Nasā. The latter seems to have acted as one of Sulamī's direct transmitters of women's sayings and stories. She was his link with the world of female piety in his time and prior to it. In order to establish al-Qurashiyya's deep spirituality, Sulamī did not refrain from stating that she humiliated Naṣrābādhī for his ugly morals that contradicted his fine words. In the same biography of hers, al-Qurashiyya insolently replies to him.[75]

Interestingly, Naṣrābādhī's biography in Sulamī's *Ṭabaqāt* includes the following passage:

> When Naṣrābādhī was told that certain Sufis associate with women (*yujālis al-niswān*) and claim that they are protected [from adultery!] while looking at them, he said: 'As long as the shapes (*al-ashbāḥ*) exist, divine orders and prohibitions are valid.'[76]

This saying was provided by Sulamī, and repeated later by Qushayrī, because of the last part that conforms to Islamic law.[77] The reference to 'the ghosts' is ambiguous and calls to mind the belief in the primordial essence of the soul of which Naṣrābādhī was accused according to Dhahabī.[78] Naṣrābādhī might have used this belief to accentuate the need to conform to the divine prohibition against associating with women. While Naṣrābādhī might have intended to emphasize that this prohibition was permanent, his personal career included relationships with several women. He, like other Sufi figures of his time, was surrounded by pious women. The story behind the above-mentioned incident sounds paradoxical with his relationships within the Sufi communal life. Unexpectedly, Naṣrābādhī acted as the Sufi master who was consulted concerning his association with women. As we will see later, it was Yūsuf b. al-Ḥusayn who was said to forbid his contemporaries from associating with beardless men and gazing at them while he himself admitted that he was not able to avoid this. This way of establishing ideas throughout textual polarities is typical in early Sufi writings. Jaroslav Stetkevych discusses what he calls the 'cognitive paradoxes' that operate within the polarity

[75] Ibid., 224. [76] Sulamī, *Ṭabaqāt*, 513; Qushayrī, *Risāla*, 32.

[77] On the system of selecting the Sufi figures and their sayings in Qushayrī's *Risāla*, see Jawid Mojaddedi, 'Legitimizing Sufism in al-Qushayri's *Risāla*', *Studia Islamica*, 90 (2000), 37–50.

[78] See Dhahabī, *Siyar*, vol. 16, 264–265.

known in different scriptural texts among which is the *Qur'ān*.[79] The paradoxes addressed here are theoretical.[80] While Sufi writings accommodate this type of cognitive paradox when forming allegorical notions and rituals, they could also accept another type of paradox which could be set in the conjunction between the actual behaviour and the theoretical-cognitive aspects. This could be best witnessed in the process of writing about Sufi figures and their interrelationships. Returning to the case of Naṣrābādhī, it might be possible to assume that, since he was known as 'the master of women', it was very useful for Sulamī to make use of his character to establish women's powerful piety even at the expense of Naṣrābādhī's fame as a great Sufi master. It might be suggested, rather, that what motivated Sulamī to do so was the idea that those who seek to read about Naṣrābādhī's great piety among the male Sufis of his days would definitely not care about such incidental negative references made to his character in Sulamī's short work on female piety.

From another perspective, the stories about Sufi males who used to visit pious women, sometimes for the sake of food and other comforts of their existence, were not uncommon in early Sufi literature. In the late fourth/tenth century, Muḥammad b. Ṭāhir, known as Ibn al-Qaysarānī (d. 507/1113), defended the custom of Sufi visiting *niswān* known among his contemporaries. Certain *ḥadīth* traditions were called to mind to condone Ibn al-Qaysarānī's daring approach.[81]

To summarize the survey of Sulamī's *Dhikr*, it is worth noting that this work contributes to portrayals of pious women in terms of absolute devotion and sanctity while ignoring information on their personal lives and family bonds. Of the eighty-two accounts of Sulamī's *Dhikr*, fifteen were devoted to women who were basically identified as the wives of famous Sufis, while four were of women clearly identified as mothers of well-known figures. In seven cases, women were introduced as sisters. Ignoring family bonds and social activities while stressing sanctity was a very common strategy in hagiographies. This strategy is shown in

[79] See J. W. Wright Jr. 'Masculine Allusion and Structure of Satire in Early 'Abbāsid Poetry', in *Homoeroticism in Classical Arabic Literature*, ed. by J. W. Wright Jr. and Everett Rowson (New York: Columbia University Press, 1997), 3–4.

[80] J. W. Wright Jr. refers to different groups that made use of such cognitive paradoxes, such as the *mu'tazila*, who, by doing so, aimed at escaping 'the anthropomorphist entrapment of literal readings of revelation'. The *shī'a*, the *ismā'īlīs* and the Sufis also adopted different cognitive paradoxes, each for his own purposes. See ibid., 4.

[81] See Muḥammad b. Ṭāhir al-Maqdisī known as Ibn al-Qaysarānī, *Ṣafwat al-taṣawwuf*, ed. by Ghāda al-Muqaddim 'Udra (Beirut: Dār al-Muntakhab, 1995), 406–407.

Sulamī's *Ṭabaqāt* as well. On only a few occasions in his *Dhikr*, Sulamī refers to women's unhappiness in being occupied with housework and mothers' duties. Nusiyya bint Salmān, the wife of Yūsuf b. Asbāṭ al-Shaybānī (d. 199/814–815), is quoted by Sulamī to have said after she gave birth to a son: 'Oh, Lord! You do not see me as someone worthy of Your worship, so for this, You have preoccupied me with a child.'[82]

Similar anecdotes about male Sufis are more prevalent in Sulamī's *Ṭabaqāt*, as well as in other Sufi works of the later period. Sufi literature provides many stories about pious males who praised themselves for their emotional coldness towards their children, and, on the other hand, stories about Sufis who could break a fast day by having sexual intercourse, thus giving an example by their own behaviour to all those who might think that Sufi life contradicted normal family life. These two contrasting codes of behaviour are firmly rooted in early Sufi literature when referring to men. As for women, however, an 'iconic' pattern of female piety is created. This piety is explicitly subjected to a high theoretical and literary ethos according to which women's sincere worship is the basic and primarily the only theme to be asserted in a hagiography, while no conflicts between the individual spiritual realm and social-family commitments and duties are mentioned. Meanwhile, due to the infrequency of those notions in which women's coldness towards family members is celebrated, it seems most probable to suggest an authenticated historical value.

I would argue here that, in general, the writing on pious women after the days of Sulamī could, notably, enjoy a great deal of freedom from the above-mentioned literary-theoretical ethos and of what I have called the 'iconic' image of the pious female. In both *Ṣifat al-ṣafwa* of Ibn al-Jawzī and *Kitāb al-Tashawwuf ilā rijāl al-taṣawwuf* of Ibn al-Zayyāt al-Tādilī, both from the sixth/twelfth century, many are the stories about women whose lives demonstrate different ways of challenging that iconic image. Ibn al-Zayyāt, for instance, mentions a woman who, until her death, was celibate.[83] Celibacy among women in the early period of Sulamī was rarely indicated. In the following section, I will examine the changes in

[82] Sulamī, *Dhikr*, 93. Cf. similar stories about Christian female mystics who thanked God when their husbands and children died in David Herlihy, *Medieval Households* (Cambridge, Mass.: Harvard University Press, 1985), 115 and endnote 12, 208. However, in some of these Christian parallels, this attitude seems to have been a reaction to a miserable family life in which cruel mistreatment by husbands or other close relatives was involved (see ibid., 115).

[83] See later in this chapter.

portraying women's piety after the fourth/tenth century, as well as the different dynamics that enabled female Sufis to manage their lives of worship together with their family and other social duties.

FEMALE MYSTICS IN LATER BIOGRAPHICAL COLLECTIONS

As I have shown, Sulamī's work displays a high ethos of uncompromising female piety that depicts an iconic image of women who had succeeded in managing a deep spirituality with a sincere commitment to mothering and wifehood. Few are the cases where a challenge of this iconic image is revealed. Later hagiographical material, I argue, suggests a slightly different picture. An increasing number of anecdotes about women paying tributes to their children's death, for instance, are introduced to this genre. Muʿādha al-ʿAdawiyya is described by Ibn al-Jawzī to have asked those women who visited her to console her when her husband's son was killed to congratulate her, instead![84] Manfūsa bint Zayd al-Fawāris praises her endurance after her son was killed, stating that enduring the loss of her son is better than the fear of losing him.[85]

Abū Nuʿaym al-Iṣfahānī chose not to refer to any pious women of his day. Instead, he refers in much detail to women of the two early centuries of Islam. Later on, Ibn al-Jawzī criticizes Iṣfahānī's work by referring in detail to its defects and shortages. Apart from those, Ibn al-Jawzī calls our attention to the fact that, except for rare occasions, Iṣfahānī had no interest in pious women.

In his introduction to *Ṣifat al-ṣafwa*, Ibn al-Jawzī indicates that writing about pious women might be a useful way to instruct those men who failed to do what ought to be done in their religious lives: 'It is known that referring to women who were pious in spite of the inadequacy of femininity (*maʿ quṣūr al-unūthiyya*) might encourage men who neglected their religious duties. Sufyān al-Thawrī did not refrain from consulting Rābiʿa and benefitting from her spiritual guidance.'[86] Ibn al-Jawzī's work provides us with more anecdotes about women's patterns of involvement in the family's circle. The personal nature of those women as well as of their spirituality is conveyed in great detail. Ḥafṣa bint Sīrīn used to ask her son, al-Hudhayl, to leave her and go back to his wife since he used to spend much time with her.[87] Another woman, Umm al-Ḥuraysh, 'was

[84] See Ibn al-Jawzī, *Ṣifat al-ṣafwa*, vol. 4, 14.
[85] See ibid., 350.
[86] Ibid., Ibn al-Jawzī's *introduction*, vol. 1, 6.
[87] See ibid., vol. 4, 16.

afflicted with a husband who was a soldier' (*ubtuliyat bi-zawj min al-jund*). In Islamic hagiographies, soldiers, as other figures of authority, were viewed in a negative light. Their images automatically implied utilization, exploitation and the pursuit of money. That is why this woman refused to eat from her husband's plate. When, one day, he obliged her to share a meal with him, she pretended to eat while she was, in fact, throwing away her morsels of food.[88] Hunayda used to wake up her husband and her sons and servants to perform night prayers.[89] Shaʿwāna, whose biography in Sulamī's *Dhikr* was limited to two short informative paragraphs and two statements only, is honoured with a detailed biography in Ibn al-Jawzī's work. The latter refers in detail to Shaʿwāna's relationships with many pious figures of her time, such as al-Fuḍayl b. ʿIyāḍ, Yaḥyā b. Bisṭām and others. The last anecdote in her biography, interestingly, refers to her and her husband. It states that she joins her husband in his visit to Mecca and practised circumambulation together with him.[90]

In one biography, that of al-Māwardiyya of Baṣra (d. 466/1073), Ibn al-Jawzī quotes the following notion from Abū al-Ḥasan Muḥammad b. Hilāl b. al-Muḥassin known as Ghars al-Niʿma (d. 480/1087), the author of *ʿUyūn al-tawārīkh*: 'She used to write and read and preach to women.'[91] While preaching was a common activity undertaken by pious women at that time, the reference made here to the custom of writing is interesting in itself. This uncommon reference might imply that writing was rarely known among pious women because worship occupied most of their time. This communal activity of al-Māwardiyya leaves the impression that, as well as the cases where women used to seek the spiritual assembles of the famous men of their days, there were cases in which women, usually old, held such assemblies of their own, and some even could provide their female students with short treatises on spiritual instruction.

Ibn al-Jawzī's work does not refer to women who abandoned the institution of marriage. Ibn al-Zayyāt's *Kitāb al-tashawwuf* refers only once to a women who at the time of her death was celibate. This woman was the sister of the Tunisian pious ʿAbd al-ʿAzīz al-Tūnusī, and she died while she was still a virgin and was buried beside her brother.[92] Of the 279 biographical accounts in Ibn al-Zayyāt's work, only seven are devoted to female pious figures: Four are mentioned by name, and three

[88] See ibid., vol. 4, 26. [89] See ibid., vol. 4, 353. [90] See ibid., vol. 4, 38–39.
[91] Ibid., vol. 4, 32. [92] See Ibn al-Zayyāt, *Tashawwuf*, 94.

are anonymous.[93] The longest biography is that of the Moroccan Munya bint Maymūn (d. 595/1198). She tells a story about one miracle that occurred when she was on her way back from a visit to her son's place. She was able to reach her home which was far from her son's home within the short time needed to complete the call to the evening prayer. Another miracle happened when she unwillingly accepted an invitation addressed to her by a famous merchant. The story relates that the food asked her not to touch it since it was completely illicit![94] Pious males who maintained celibacy until they died were many in *Kitāb al-tashawwuf*.[95]

As for Islamic piety in North Africa during the late sixth/twelfth century, we come across another hagiographical work composed prior to Ibn al-Zayyāt's *Tashawwuf*, *al-Mustafād fī manāqib al-ʿubbād* of Muḥammad b. ʿAbd al-Karīm al-Tamīmī of Fās (d. 603/1206 or 604/1207). In Tamīmī's work, no single biography of a pious woman is found. Few references to wives of certain pious men are made so as to celebrate the spirituality of those men. Ibn Harān, who was fond of Sufi wandering (*siyāḥa*), used not to touch his wife for long periods. One day he told her that he would die within five days, and that is what happened.[96] The custom of *siyāḥa* involved leaving one's family and wife for lengthy periods of seclusion and devotion. Abū al-Faḍl al-ʿAbbās b. Aḥmad left his wife and children in Fās and went to Mecca; later he went to Syria for *jihād* and died there.[97] In the long biography of Ibn al-ʿAbbās b. Rushayd, it is interesting that his mother is portrayed in a negative way. It is reported that 'in his youth, he intended to leave Fās in order to perform *ḥajj*; however, his mother prevented him'. When, during her dream, she heard a voice calling her to permit her son to leave Fās for Mecca, she asked him to leave her all his property and money as a condition for her granting him permission! According to the anecdote, presented at the beginning of this biography, the young man left everything that he inherited to his mother, worked for several days in domestic service, and with the money that he earned, he succeeded in leaving the city of Fās. One of the pious men of Fās told him before he left that he would meet one of the true friends of God in Alexandria and a pious woman (*imraʾa ṣāliḥa*) in Mecca. The narrator relates that the young man met an

93 See ibid., 94, 265, 316, 331, 385, 387, 388.
94 See ibid., 318.
95 See e.g., ibid., 109, 136, 161.
96 See Abū ʿAbd Allāh Muḥammad b. ʿAbd al-Karīm al-Tamīmī al-Fāsī, *al-Mustafād fī manāqib al-ʿubbād bi-madīnat Fās wa-mā yalīhā min al-bilād*, ed. by Muḥammad al-Sharīf (Taṭwān: Kulliyyat al-Ādāb wa-l-ʿUlūm al-Insāniyya, 2002), vol. 2, 160.
97 See ibid., vol. 2, 87.

anonymous woman while circling the *ka'ba*. On his way back from *al-Madīna* to Mecca, he met another unnamed woman with her little son. This woman accompanied Abū al-ʿAbbās, prayed with him and encouraged him to keep walking and to ignore the fact that his companions had left him behind. On reaching Mecca, Abū al-ʿAbbās was unable to find this woman or to meet her again.[98]

The reference made to the mother in the above-mentioned biography raises many questions concerning the roles of mothers in early Sufi spheres. Little has been done to examine this topic in the recent scholarship of Sufism. Scrutinizing the roles of Sufi women as mothers helps shed much light on the dynamics between the individual-private aspects of life and the communal realm in which one's involvement in an increasingly authoritative Sufi institution could impose particular demands and conditions. This discussion will be the focus of Chapter 3.

It is worth noting that *al-Mustafād* is one of the Sufi hagiographies that pays more attention to the familial framework of the lives of the pious. It seems that more than other hagiographies, both by North African authors and authors of the eastern territories of Islam, Tamīmī's work refers frequently to the pious men's close circles of relationships with their wives and children while establishing their elevated ranks of devotion and sanctity. Abū al-ʿAbbās Aḥmad b. Lubb of Salā used to wear woollen clothes that only his wife had made for him.[99] During a period of famine, Ḥajjāj b. Yūsuf al-Kundurī used to feed his wife before going to sleep while he stayed hungry all night.[100] In addition to wives, we also come across anecdotes in which other family members are involved. The author of *al-Mustafād* starts the biography of Ibn Ḥirizhim, for instance, with a reference to his dispute with his brother on inheritance. This dispute and the greed involved in the dispute serve as the trigger that pushed Ibn Ḥirizhim to renounce his share of the inheritance in favour of his brother.[101]

Non-Sufi biographies are full of references to 'impudent' and 'dissolute' wives who were usually mentioned together with sharp warnings of God's punishment and curse.[102] One married woman, whose biography was interesting enough to be mentioned by Sakhāwī, was attracted to another man beside her husband, and eventually it was she who drove her

98 See ibid., vol. 2, 118–120. 99 See ibid., vol. 2, 144. 100 See ibid., 111–112.
101 See ibid., 16–17.
102 See e.g., Nawawī, *Riyāḍ al-ṣāliḥīn*, 92; ʿAlāʾ al-Dīn al-Muttaqī al-Hindī, *Kanz al-ʿummāl fī sunan al-aqwāl wa-l-afʿāl* (Ḥaydarābād al-Dukn, India: Dār al-Maʿārif al-ʿUthmāniyya, 1945–1974), vol. 21, 238–239. See also ibid., 202–207.

husband away.[103] In another incident mentioned in Sakhāwī's book, a highly educated woman named Bayram, who was also a preacher, after getting married, 'her situation changed due to her association with her husband' (*taghayyar ḥāluhā bi-mukhālaṭatihi*).[104] Even though the author provides no explanation for this remark, it is possible that wifely duties prevented this woman from full-time involvement in the active practice of her career. As I previously pointed out, the fluid nature of medieval marital ties that contributed to weaken the degree of dependence and mutual commitment that the spouses could feel towards each other in general terms had to be combined with another shift in Sufi spheres: the process of institutionalizing the Sufi community and praxis in the fifth/eleventh and sixth/twelfth centuries, which might have contributed to further weakening of the normative degree of dependence in the institution of marriage when the Sufi disciple became required to spend most of his time in the company of his sheik and his companions.

SUFI WOMEN IN WORKS OF *ADAB*

References to pious women occasionally appear in works of *adab*. The first author of *adab* to be mentioned here is ʿAmr b. Baḥr al-Jāḥiz (d. 255/869). He was the earliest author to mention Rābiʿa al-Qaysiyya. He refers to her in his *Kitāb al-ḥayawān* and *al-Bayān wa-l-tabyīn*.[105] In the latter, Jāḥiẓ mentions Rābiʿa among other famous pious women the most famous of whom was Muʿādha al-ʿAdawiyya, whom al-Jāḥiẓ introduces twice in his work as 'the wife of Ṣila b. Ashyam', in addition to Umm al-Dardāʾ, al-Baljāʾ of the *khawārij*, the *shīʿī* Laylā al-Nāʿiṭiyya and others.[106] In one appearance of Rābiʿa, Jāḥiẓ praises her refusal to ask for the assistance of people in spite of the fact that many of the people she knew encouraged her to do so.[107] In Tanūkhī's *Nishwār al-muḥāḍara*, a detailed reference is made to one anonymous young woman of Baghdad who suffered for more than fifteen years from a physical disability that prevented her from moving. It was reported that one night this woman saw in her dream the Prophet Muḥammad who prayed for her to recover.

[103] See Sakhāwī, *al-ḍawʾ al-lāmiʿ*, vol. 12, 64.
[104] Ibid., 15 (in the biography of Bayram bint Aḥmad b. Muḥammad).
[105] See ʿAmr b. Baḥr al-Jāḥiẓ, *Kitāb al-ḥayawān*, ed. by ʿAbd al-Salām Hārūn (Cairo: al-Bābī al-Ḥalabī, 1938), vol. 1, 170; vol. 5, 589; idem, *al-Bayān wa-l-tabyīn*, ed. by ʿAbd al-Salām Hārūn (Cairo: Maktabat al-Khānjī, 1968), vol. 1, 364.
[106] See Jāḥiẓ, *al-Bayān wa-l-tabyīn*, vol. 1, 365.
[107] See ibid., vol. 3, 127.

When she woke up, she was able to move and walk again. The narrator commented at the end of the story: 'I used to see her [later!] walking and visiting our children, and she is still healthy. She is the most pious woman I had ever heard about at this time. She does not do anything except pray and fast and make a living legally. She is still unmarried (*ʿātiq*).'[108] The use of the term *ʿātiq* here comes to designate that, though she was ready for marriage, this young woman, at least until the time of the narration of the story, had maintained celibacy

In two places in the section devoted to *dhikr al-nisāʾ* in Baghdādī's *Taʾrīkh baghdād*, pious women are reported to have encouraged their men not to sit on a carpet since they should not make any barrier between their bodies and the earth in which they will later be buried.[109] Baghdādī indicates that Fāṭima bint ʿAbd al-Raḥmān (d. 312/924) was known as *al-ṣūfiyya* since she 'used to wear wool' (*aqāmat talbas al-ṣūf*).[110] This title, most probably, has nothing to do with the contemporary circle of Baghdadi Sufis known as the *ṣūfiyya*.

Abū Ḥayyān al-Tawḥīdī mentions Rābiʿa three times in his *Baṣāʾir*. The first reference is related to Rābiʿa's famous reply to those who asked her whether she loved the Prophet Muḥammad: 'I love him. However, my love to God preoccupied me and took my attention away from the love of His creatures.' Tawḥīdī follows this anecdote with his comment: 'This statement is abstruse for interpretation. Turning tragacanth and picking up sand are both easier than understanding this statement (*kharṭ al-qatād dūnah wa-laqṭ al-raml ashal minhu*). I reported it as I heard it.'[111]

[108] See Tanūkhī, *Nishwār al-muḥāḍara*, vol. 2, 267.
[109] See Baghdādī, *Taʾrīkh baghdād*, vol. 16, 582, 601. [110] Ibid., vol. 16, 630.
[111] ʿAlī b. Muḥammad Abū Ḥayyān al-Tawḥīdī, *al-Baṣāʾir wa-l-dhakhāʾir*, ed. by Widād al-Qāḍī (Beirut: Dār Ṣādir, 1988), vol. 1, 150.

3

Maternal Narratives

Female Sufis as Mothers

Mothers who were Sufis themselves as well as mothers of Sufi figures provide us with different narratives of the harmony or even the disharmony between diversified maternal identities and Sufi devotional life. This topic, I suggest, should be viewed from three aspects:

1. The first aspect refers to those women who were Sufis in their own right. Although we have no means of knowing how they perceived their religiosity and the place it could occupy in their daily lives as mothers, it is still useful to examine the way or, more precisely, the different ways of those mothers to integrate their Sufi practices with their mothering duties and responsibilities, all of which can be raised from the glimpses of data implied in the early sources, both Sufi and non-Sufi.
2. The second aspect refers to those sons or daughters who initiated the Sufi path and, as the sources tell us, had to reconcile their spiritual careers with their family engagements or, more particularly, with compelling parental commitments. Here, the stories are narrated from the perspective of the offspring and, therefore, differ essentially from the references made by Sufi mothers, as the following discussion will show.
3. The third aspect involves different circle of maternal ties: maternal uncles who played fundamental roles in the Sufi lives of their

This chapter relies partially on my preliminary paper on Sufi mothers: A. Salamah-Qudsi, 'A Lightning Trigger or a Stumbling Block: Mother Images and Roles in Classical Sufism', *Oriens*, 39 (2011), 199–226. New and expanded insights were added to the current chapter.

nephews. In this circle of relationships, the dynamics between the personal and the Sufi-communal domains were very salient since in many cases those uncles acted as spiritual guides for their nephews.

MOTHERS AND SUFISM: SOME WORDS OF INTRODUCTION

Motherhood is a social system of relationships. In the culture of Islam, as in similar 'ortho-praxis' cultures, all physical and gynaecological processes that shape motherhood are concerns of the whole society.[1] Veneration of mothers in Islamic societies can be seen as a result of the many dynamics, one of which is the repression of women into their maternal role.[2] In general terms, ethical and legal discussions of topics such as giving birth and fertility are widespread in medieval sources. Maternal respect and filial piety are also frequently shown in works of *adab* and *belles lettres*. Textual references to these concerns are, generally, given by the offspring.

Motherhood in Sufi context is, notably, a twofold system of relationship: The first refers to the relationship between Sufi or non-Sufi mothers and their offspring while the other refers to the relationship between mothers and offspring, on one hand, and the wider framework of life within the Sufi community, on the other. Motherhood here is not a physical or medical concern but a complete fabric of different social, religious and spiritual patterns of relationships and commitments. References to mothers in the Sufi spheres from the offspring's point of view are demonstrated. From the mothers' point of view, however, there is scarcely any available material that might support sentimental and actual considerations of the mothers themselves.[3]

1 See Giladi, *Muslim Midwives*, 24.

2 See ibid., 25; Cf. Abdelwahab Bouhdiba, *Sexuality in Islam*, trans. from the French by Alan Sheridan (London: Routledge & Kegan Paul, 1985), 214; Salamah-Qudsi, *Lightning Trigger*, 202.

3 One could agree with Fatima Mernissi's remark that 'early Muslim historians gave considerable exposure to women in their writings', and that 'they did not, as might be expected, talk about them only as the mothers and daughters of powerful men' [Fatima Mernissi, 'Women in Muslim History: Traditional Perspectives and New Strategies', in *Women and Islam: Critical Concepts in Sociology*, ed. by Haideh Moghissi (London: Routledge, 2005), vol. 1, 37]. In my view, however, being 'active participants and fully involved partners in historical events' (ibid.) as history books, genealogies and chronicles have revealed, does not mean that mothers and daughters had really been identified in their literary appearances in the frameworks of their actual motherhood or daughterhood.

The neglect of mothers in Sufi literature does not differ from their general neglect in Islamic and non-Islamic cultures. The possibility of exploring this topic in the Sufi context is very limited. To reconstruct some parts of the portrait, we should extract the available data from the sources and use them to propose a possible method of synthesis. The results of this method, I should confess, will be limited; however, they will still be important and interesting in filling some gaps in this completely hidden arena. One of the problematic results of the lack of material in this regard is the fact that this lack could easily bring about informative gaps to be filled by dominant cultural evaluations in harmony with well-known ideas. In Sufi spheres, hence, scholars such as Annemarie Schimmel usually consider mothers as the uncompromising impetus for their children in the choice they make to undertake the devotional life. This image harmonizes perfectly with the image of mothers in medieval Islam in general terms: Mothers are undoubtedly agents of God's call to procreate,[4] and they are, in the eyes of medieval Muslim scholars, completely responsible for the birth of pious generations of Muslims. Healthy wombs could bring the birth of healthy foetuses who would be pious Muslims in the future. An additional reference to this idea will be made later.

In light of the increasing amount of scholarship on gender and feminism in recent decades, motherhood has gained more attention in various research projects. One research attempt in the last decade sought to 'de-essentialise' modern mothering, that is 'to address maternities in a variety of different contexts' after a long period in which motherhood had been 'seen within an essentialist and narrow frame'.[5] Taking this view into account when we deal with mothers in Islam would be of crucial significance.

The chapter on the 'Kingdom of the Mothers' by Abdelwahab Bouhdiba (1985), though it seems not to be entirely devoid of generalizations, is very interesting, and some of the suggestions put forward there have inspired our current discussion.[6] It is very important to make use of the author's extensive treatment of the exemplary virtues of the mother–child relationship over the virtues of wife–husband relationship in Muslim societies. Bouhdiba notes that 'children therefore very often constitute the only factor of stability. They alone give the *ṣilat al-raḥim* [the tie of the

[4] See Kathryn Kueny, *Conceiving Identities: Maternity in Medieval Muslim Discourse and Practice* (Albany, N.Y.: State University of New York Press, 2013), 19–49.

[5] Robyn Longhurst, *Maternities: Gender, Bodies and Space* (New York: Routledge, 2008), 1–15, 146.

[6] See Bouhdiba, *Sexuality in Islam*, 212–230. Cf. Giladi's note on Bouhdiba's contribution in: Giladi, *Muslim Midwives*, 25.

womb which binds a mother and her child!] its true meaning and value especially as custody of the children is almost always given to the mother.'[7] The author, in addition, refers to the long history of misery and endurance of the Muslim mothers while attempting to understand why 'so many Muslim mothers are possessive even to an abusive degree'. This dynamic, in his view, leads a mother to 'transfer all her affections to her children'.[8] Bouhdiba's psychological analysis of the mother-child relationship, which in the Muslim context is treated in terms of abuse and imprisonment 'in the shades of our mothers', might be summed up in the author's call to attack this image of mothers and to dispose of the extreme and pathological respect for them in order to fly with our own wings.[9]

It is remarkable that, in Sufi environments, the wives of famous Sufis gained more attention than mothers. This is partly due to the powerful institution of marriage in which wifehood in Sufi hagiographies helps the authors of those works consolidate the saintly characteristics of male mystics. Wives are mentioned when this sheds additional light on their husbands' careers while mothers, according to a well-known view, were usually surrounded by a strong tradition of sanctification that acted as a bar against any literary references.

The case of mothers in Sufi spheres cannot be excluded from the general portrait of maternity in medieval Muslim realities and thinking. The images of medieval Muslim mothers were subordinated to defining and regulating systems generated almost completely by male scholarly elites. The perfect and ideal mother, according to medieval sources, is first of all the one who is capable of giving birth and, second, of giving birth to pious offspring (*dhurriyya ṣāliḥa*).

In the Sufi domain, what rises from the hagiographical material is an attempt to portray the ideal-perfect mother as the one who is capable of reconciling her maternal duties, being responsible for guiding her offspring to the pious way of life, and her own spiritual life and Sufi practices. Relying upon diverse types of sources going back to medieval Islam (works of medicine, zoology, philosophy, theology, travelogues, works of sexual mores and literature), Kathryn Kueny concludes that female piety in medieval Islam was combined in the eyes of Muslim scholars with healthy wombs capable of bearing foetuses as many times as possible. Based on this idea, only healthy wombs can beget righteous

[7] Bouhdiba, *Sexuality in Islam*, 215. [8] Ibid. [9] See ibid., 227.

believers who will be true worshippers of God. If a woman's morality and piety are suspect, then her womb becomes flawed, and it stops performing its reproductive duty and brings 'monsters' to this world. 'Mother as Monster' was the title that Kueny chose to treat this aspect of maternity in medieval Muslim discourse, while giving Eve as the prototype the original example of this type.[10]

In addition to being a worthy and fascinating topic, as Annemarie Schimmel has already pointed out,[11] studying the role of the mothers in the biographies of the Sufis should be carried out through establishing a text-based argument of the nature of relationships between mothers and offspring in Sufi spheres. Those relationships, I argue, could serve as an additional interesting domain for exploring the question of personal-communal dynamics in early Sufism and reconstructing certain aspects of Sufi social life.

SUFI MOTHERS

As previously mentioned, Annemarie Schimmel was the first to call attention to the influence of pious mothers upon their Sufi sons.[12] In her *Meine Seele ist eine Frau*, Schimmel portrays, in much detail, the importance of mothers in Islamic culture. Underlying Schimmel's remarks is the general assumption that mothers in Sufi contexts contributed to the formation of their sons' spiritual leadership.

In Muslim devotional contexts, when the pious female was a mother, she was often distinguished by a high spiritual sense, even blaming herself when her mothering duties appear to distract her from worshipping God. The story of Nusiyya bint Salmān has already been mentioned. Another woman, 'Uthāma, blamed herself for asking her son whether he had prayed, thereby diverting her mind from God.[13] In biographies of male Sufis, their mothers were often portrayed in an aura of glory. According to the material available in Sufi literature, for Sufi mothers being Sufis in their own right does not seem to contradict their duties as mothers nor does it affect their sincere and boundless support for their Sufi sons.

[10] See Kueny, *Conceiving Identities*, 163–164.

[11] See Annemarie Schimmel, *Mystical Dimensions of Islam* (Chapel Hill: University of North Carolina Press, 1975), 430.

[12] See Annemarie Schimmel, 'Women in Mystical Islam', in *Women and Islam*, ed. by Aziza al-Hibri (Oxford: Pergamon Press, 1982), 149–150.

[13] See Sulamī, *Dhikr*, 111.

As the table we sketched in the Appendix shows, of the eighty-two accounts of Sulamī's *Dhikr al-niswa*, only four were of women clearly identified as mothers of well-known figures. In one of those accounts, that of Umm ʿAbd Allāh, her son, Ismāʿīl b. ʿAyyāsh, who appears as a transmitter of his mother, was also considered one of the greatest *ḥadīth* transmitters of his time.[14] In the biographical accounts of both Fāṭima bint Aḥmad, the mother of Abū ʿAbd Allāh al-Rūdhbārī, and Umm al-Ḥusayn bint Aḥmad b. Ḥamdān, the mother of Abū Bishr al-Ḥalāwī, Sulamī introduces the women with the names of their sons at the beginning of the biographies. In the account of Ziyāda bint al-Khaṭṭāb al-Ṭazariyya, the name of her son, Ismāʿīl b. Ibrāhīm al-Quhistānī, was not mentioned in the title. In all four accounts, no reference was made by the author to the nature of relationship that those mothers had with their sons. Meanwhile, the case of Fāṭima bint Aḥmad is interesting here: She was introduced by Sulamī as one of the greatest *niswān* and *ʿārifāt* (female Sufis who had achieved the sublime rank of knowledge of God) of her day. This woman was quoted by Sulamī as saying that her son, Abū ʿAbd Allāh al-Rūdhbārī, 'is not a Sufi, instead, he is a righteous man (*rajul ṣāliḥ*)', yet she adds: 'But my brother Abū ʿAlī was a Sufi.'[15] Before trying to understand this statement, we should make several notes on the two figures, her brother and her son: Early Sufi biographies combine Abū ʿAlī al-Rūdhbārī with the two great masters of the third/ninth century, Junayd and the Syrian Abū ʿAbd Allāh Aḥmad b. Yaḥyā b. al-Jallāʾ (d. 306/918–919). Al-Khaṭīb al-Baghdādī indicates that Abū ʿAlī left several compositions on *taṣawwuf* and that he was the leader of the Sufis in Egypt.[16] As for his nephew, Abū ʿAbd Allāh, Sufi biographers refer to his deep sympathy for the poor as well as to his sincere desire to help them.[17] He was also mentioned by Sulamī in the biographical account of Qusayma, the wife of Abū Yaʿqūb al-Tinnīsī. Qusayma's story with Abū ʿAbd Allāh al-Rūdhbārī was mentioned in Chapter 2 in the discussion of female *futuwwa*. This story implies the high position that Abū ʿAbd Allāh enjoyed among his disciples. Non-Sufi biographers, such as Baghdādī and Dhahabī, referred to him as a transmitter of *ḥadīth* while quoting statements of those who suspected him of fabricating *ḥadīth*.[18]

[14] See Sulamī, *Dhikr*, 101. [15] Ibid., 214–215.

[16] See Baghdādī, *Taʾrīkh baghdād*, vol. 2, 180.

[17] See Sulamī, *Ṭabaqāt*, 527 (*maḥabba li-l-fuqarāʾ wa-mayl ilayhim*); Cf. Qushayrī, *Risāla*, 33 (*wa-kān min muḥibbī hādhihi al-ṭāʾifa*).

[18] See Dhahabī, *Siyar*, vol. 16, 228; Baghdādī, *Taʾrīkh baghdād*, vol. 5, 552.

The comparison implied in the statement of Fāṭima bint Aḥmad leaves no doubt that this woman preferred the spiritual state of her brother while depriving her son of his title as a Sufi. Could one suggest that the association of Abū ʿAlī with Junayd and his wide success in disseminating the Sufi teachings of the Junaydī-line to Egypt were good reasons for being venerated in his sister's eyes? Meanwhile, such reasons do not explain the negative or at least the cold approach of the mother in reference to her son's spirituality. The phrasing of her statement, it should be noted, implies the existence of two degrees of spiritual life: The first relates to a standard pious life, while the other has more to do with a type of exalted or genius spirituality that turns someone into a real Sufi.

This notion could be a good example of how the dynamics between the personal and the communal domains could take a form that might be essentially different from what we might originally expect. Dignity of the renowned brother, who most probably had acted as one of the Sufi masters of his sister, led the latter to disregard her son when the comparison had to be raised.

Based on the literary and theoretical structure of Sulamī's brief accounts of Sufi mothers, motherhood seems to be a marginal and insignificant concern. It is like describing someone by mentioning his kinship with someone else who was already known to the listener. In Sulamī's case, motherhood was entirely incidental and irrelevant for the pious and Sufi careers of those women. It is, however, still important to ask why the author did not say anything about the roles and support of the mothers. Why was he so eager to describe the support of wives and sisters while mothers seem to have been totally neglected? Would it be possible to suggest, therefore, that Sulamī did not know of any woman who was distinguished, besides her own spirituality, for the unique support of her Sufi son?

THE IMAGE OF MOTHERS FROM THEIR OFFSPRING'S PERSPECTIVE

Sons or daughters (though the sources rarely tell about the latter) who initiated the Sufi path found themselves compelled to reconcile their spiritual careers with their familial obligations and parental commitments. Many of the relevant anecdotes are not exactly autobiographical. Most are narrated through the mediation of the later Sufi biographer. I chose to gather those anecdotes here since the viewpoint of the biographer, the male biographer of course, has a lot in common with those

Sufi figures who had the opportunity to relate their relationships with their pious mothers. The references presented through the later biographers should have reflected the latter's own socio-religious contexts in which the image of mothers in general and of Sufi mothers in particular was an essential element.

When Daylamī, the later biographer of Ibn Khafīf al-Shīrāzī, describes Umm Muḥammad, the pious mother of the renowned Sufi Sheikh, the data presented here should be treated on two levels: The first is related to Daylamī himself and the image of Sufi mothers in his day while the other is related to the early period of Ibn Khafīf and his mother. With the lack of paralleled autobiographical material, our attempt to reconstruct the nature of the relationship between the mother and the son is drawn nearly completely upon the stock of narratives that succeeded in being preserved and circulated until the days of the biographer. Since references of this type are initially few, I would suggest trusting their relevance to the early period of their heroes.

Daylamī reports that this woman occasionally invited Sufi masters to her home when her son was absent.[19] It was also mentioned that Umm Muḥammad used to accompany her son on pilgrimages.[20] Ibn Khafīf took his mother with him on his last visit to Mecca where he met Abū ʿAmr al-Zajjājī who was quick-tempered and peevish. During their meeting, Zajjājī asked Ibn Khafīf: 'Do you possess anything of this world?' The Shirāzian visitor replied: 'Oh master, when we discuss saints' attributes, worldly affairs could not be mentioned.' Zajjājī, probably uncomfortable with the idea that Ibn Khafīf's mother still had a strong influence upon her son, remarked: 'Perhaps you should transfer all you possess on behalf of your mother! (*rubbamā jaʿalta mā tamlik bi-ism ummik*). This remark contains an obvious echo of the early Sufi ideal according to which the 'real Sufi does not possess anything and he is not possessed by anything' (*al-ṣūfī lā yamlik shayʾan wa-lā yamlikuhu shayʾ*).[21] Would it be possible, then, to suggest that Zajjājī's statement implicitly blamed Ibn Khafīf for allowing his 'worldly' connections and family relationships to affect his Sufi career? It was a well-known principle for the early Sufis to avoid emotional and material connections with their native cities during their travels, since physical travelling was considered the equiva-

[19] See Daylamī, *Sīra*, 266. [20] See e.g., ibid., 141.
[21] Qushayrī, *Risāla*, 139, lines 8–9. Cf. Kubrā, *Fawāʾiḥ al-jamāl*, 45.

lent of the inner route of ascent, and both need to be undertaken solely.[22] Travelling for pilgrimage was more appropriate when done without the company of one's family members. If they were to accompany the Sufi, then social and emotional connections could not, logically, be avoided as they should be. Ibn Khafīf's unexpected reply to Zajjājī was: 'Oh master, when the men of God (*rijāl Allāh*) are mentioned, one should not mention women!'[23] Consequently, Zajjājī admired Ibn Khafīf. He invited him to eat and asked him to take some food to his mother.[24] It seems most probable that Ibn Khafīf's reply was the outcome of the debate with Zajjājī's point of view rather than an expression of his real attitude.

The above-mentioned impact of Umm Muḥammad is clearly documented in another story according to which Ibn Khafīf did not allow Abū al-ʿAbbās b. ʿAṭāʾ to remove his, Ibn Khafīf's, *khirqa* in order to dress him with another one because it was his mother who had 'dressed him with this *khirqa* and nobody except her is allowed to take it off'.[25] In one episode of Qushayrī's *Risāla*, Ibn Khafīf asked his mother's permission to travel. He sent someone to ask her for his *muraqqaʿa* (patched robe), and she gave him her permission to go on a journey. Ibn Khafīf, then, commented: '*Fa-lam tuʿāriḍnī al-wālida wa-raḍiyat bi-khurūjī.*'[26] This remark gives the impression that Umm Muḥammad was more than the usual type of mother of a Sufi master. Ibn Khafīf, though very known and highly respected, was attached to his strong-minded mother and did not feel absolutely free to make his own decisions at all times. On the question of travelling, at least, we know that he actually maintained this type of dependence with his mother.

In another anecdote, while Ibn Khafīf was striving to attain divine knowledge on the Night of Power (*laylat al-qadr*) that falls during the last ten nights of Ramaḍān by practising many religious rituals on his roof, his mother was granted the divine revelation effortlessly in her room. She called her son to come and share the divine light with her by saying: 'Oh my son Muḥammad! Here is what you had looked for.' Ibn Khafīf hurried to his mother's place, fell down at her feet and gained some

[22] See e.g., Sarrāj, *Lumaʿ*, 189, line 8 (*ḥaythumā waqaf qalbuhu yakun manziluhu*); Qushayrī, *Risāla*, 143, lines 9–14; ʿIzz-al-Dīn Maḥmūd Kāshānī, *Miṣbāḥ al-hidāya wa-miftāḥ al-kifāya*, ed. by Jalāl-al-Dīn Humāyī (Tehran, 1381 *Shamsī*/2002), 263ff.

[23] See, Daylamī, *Sīra*, 141. [24] Ibid., 142. [25] See ibid., 159.

[26] Qushayrī, *Risāla*, 145, line 21.

of the lights that surrounded her.[27] Moreover, he used to say later: 'Now I recognise the very value of a mother.'[28]

Muḥammad b. al-Munawwar, the grandson of Abū Saʿīd b. Abī al-Khayr (d. 440/1049) mentions Abū Saʿīd's mother at the very beginning of his hagiography *Asrār al-tawḥīd fī maqāmāt al-shaykh Abū Saʿīd*. One night when Bābu Bu'l-Kheyr (Abū Saʿīd's father) was intending to go to a gathering of dervishes, his wife asked him to: 'Take Bū Saʿīd with you so that the gaze of the dervishes and men of spiritual esteem may fall upon him.'[29]

Although Abū Saʿīd's father was intensively involved in Sufi activities, he probably did not believe that his little child was mature enough to take part in Sufi gatherings. His mother, however, seems to have realized the impact of accompanying the pious dervishes upon her child before he acquired his intellectual faculties which, according to the Sufi tradition, only encumber spiritual revelation and stain the purity of the heart. When the father and mother of Abū Saʿīd died, as the author of *Asrār al-tawḥīd* writes: 'The restraints based on consideration for his parents were removed from his path.'[30] Abū Saʿīd was then able to set out for the desert and spent seven years experiencing ascetic austerities.

Frequently in Sufi hagiographies, the term *ḥaqq al-wālida* (lit. mother's duty) appears.[31] In all instances, this term indicates the family restraints that the Sufi has to take into account while considering his need to travel and develop his mystical career. Making the pilgrimage to Mecca contradicted, in some anecdotes, the Sufi's duties towards his own parents. Many sheikhs, therefore, ordered their disciples to keep 'serving' (*khidma*) their parents as long as the latter were alive and not to go on pilgrimages or travel for any other purpose. Kharkūshī tells that Abū 'Uthmān al-Ḥīrī criticized Muḥammad b. 'Abd Allāh al-Farghānī for not asking his mother's permission before travelling. Farghānī, as a result, decided not to travel as long as his mother was alive. When she died,

[27] See e.g., Muʿīn-al-Dīn Junayd Shīrāzī, *Shadd al-izār fī ḥaṭṭ al-awzār 'an zuwwār al-mazār*, ed. by Muḥammad Qazvīnī and 'Abbās Iqbāl (Tehran: Chāpkhānih-yi Majlis 1949), 368; Daylamī, *Sīra*, 250.

[28] Ibid., 369.

[29] Moḥammad Ebn-e Monavvar, *The Secrets of God's Mystical Oneness or the Spiritual Stations of Shaikh Abu Sa'id [Asrār al-towḥid fī maqāmāt al-Šeyḵ Abi Sa'id]*, trans. with notes and introduction by John O'Kane (Costa Mesa, Calif. and New York: Mazda Publishers, 1992), 76.

[30] Ibid., 105.

[31] See e.g., Jullābī Hujwīrī, *Kashf al-maḥjūb*, 111; Jāmī, *Nafaḥāt al-uns*, 191, 322; Tamīmī, *Mustafād*, vol. 2, 106, 129.

Farghānī travelled to Nishapur to visit Abū ʿUthmān and became his close disciple.[32] Uways al-Qaranī (d. 37/657), a Yemenite contemporary of the Prophet, was considered by Hujwīrī as one of the great Sufi masters (*az kibār-i mashāyikh-i ahl-i taṣavvuf*) whose passionate state (*ghalabih-yi ḥāl*) overwhelmed him and whose sincere wish to honour his mother's duty prevented him from meeting the Prophet.[33]

Turning back to Abū Saʿīd's biography, it is told that he was always wandering in the mountains and the desert and would be lost for many days or even for several months until his father eventually found him and brought him home. In order to please his parents, Abū Saʿīd would sometimes give up his wanderings and devotions and agree to come home: 'The sheikh's father was constantly searching for him and would find him every month or so and, out of kindness, bring him back to Meyhana [...] so that he would not suddenly run away again.'[34]

In ʿAṭṭār's biography of Abū Yazīd al-Basṭāmī, the latter's mother was portrayed in a typical spiritual manner. When Basṭāmī heard his master's explanation for the *Qurʾān*ic verse: 'Be thankful to Me and thy parents',[35] he asked his master's permission to go home to tell his mother something. In answer to her surprise he said: '*Man dar dū khānih kadkhudāyī natavānam kard* " (I cannot be manager in two houses at once), explaining that his mother should either ask God to give him entirely to her or apprentice him to God so that he might dwell wholly with Him. By exempting her son from his duties to her, Basṭāmī's mother is quoted by ʿAṭṭār to have told her son to 'go and be God's'.[36] This distinguished image of Basṭāmī's mother seems to have been well established in early Sufi literature.

In Qushayrī's *Risāla*, Basṭāmī tells that his mother used to avoid eating a food that was suspected of impurity when she was pregnant with him.[37] In another source, *al-Nūr min kalimāt Abī Ṭayfūr* of Sahlajī, several related anecdotes appear.[38] According to one anecdote, this woman was

[32] See Kharkūshī, *Tahdhīb al-asrār*, 328.

[33] See Jullābī Hujwīrī, *Kashf al-maḥjūb*, 99–100.

[34] Ebn-e Monavvar, *Asrār al-tawḥīd*, 93. The latter quotation is mentioned in: Ibid., 96.

[35] ʿAṭṭār, *Tadhkirat al-awliyāʾ*, vol. 1, 136. The English translation is based on Arberry's edition of the selected episodes from ʿAṭṭār's work: ʿAṭṭār, *Muslim Saints and Mystics: Episodes from the Tadhkirat al-awliyāʾ (Memorial of the Saints)*, trans. by A. J. Arberry (London: Routledge & Kegan Paul, 1966), 102.

[36] ʿAṭṭār, *Tadhkirat al-awliyāʾ*, 136; idem, *Muslim Saints*, 102.

[37] Qushayrī, *Risāla*, 119, lines 22–23; Ibn Khamīs, *Manāqib al-abrār*, vol. 1, 193; Sahlajī, *Nūr*, 179.

[38] See e.g., Sahlajī, *Nūr*, 92–93.

'unique among her fellow women [. . .]'. Once, when she noticed her son's [spiritual] disturbance she uttered: 'Calm down!' Abū Yazīd tells that this utterance affected him and, as a result, his intensive inner disturbance did indeed calm down.[39] It was also indicated that Abū Yazīd's father waited forty days before he had sexual intercourse with his bride in order to be sure that her stomach was entirely empty of suspected food from her father's home.[40] It is clear that such anecdotes contribute to complement the fictional image of Sufi mothers as supportive figures and were designed especially to add another dimension to the spiritual portrayal of Basṭāmī and other male Sufis.

Even though we are not able to consider the historical dimension of those stories, it seems most probable to assume that Abū Yazīd's mother was really a distinguished woman and that her spiritual support for her son justifies the reference to her character in Sufi literature, even though this reference is brief.

Contrary to the statement that was ascribed to Basṭāmī's mother in 'Aṭṭār's *Tadhkira* ('Go and be God's') in one incident, when Abū Sa'īd sat down before the door of his house, his mother came to the door and said: 'Come inside! You should come inside.' Abū Sa'īd did not come inside but left his home.[41] Here, we come to the serious challenge that mothers of Sufi saints most probably had to face. It should be kept in mind that the very initiation into the Sufi path in the period under investigation subjected a person to extreme devotions and harsh austerities, especially for the early Sufis, whose ideal of actual poverty and physical retreats very often contrasted with the practice of their later successors. For this reason it might be possible to suggest that mothers were not eager to face such a challenge. One saying which was attributed to Basṭāmī's mother: 'Leave the door half open!' might have implied the deep emotional crisis that mothers of some Sufis had to cope with while watching their children giving up their social ties and devoting their entire lives to mystical careers. Abū al-'Abbās b. Masrūq (d. 298/910 or 299/911), for instance, is quoted as saying that his mother was weeping on Saturday nights when seeing her son exhausted of the hard worshipping he would do.[42] The 'half-opened door' in reference to Basṭāmī, might symbolize the mothers' attempt to maintain a strong impact upon their children and the high degree of dependence the latter felt towards them.

[39] Ibid., 62. [40] See ibid. [41] See ibid., 95.
[42] See Anṣārī Haravī, *Ṭabaqāt al-ṣūfiyya*, 72.

In *ḥadīth* literature, the well-known story of the Christian saint Jurayj and his relationship with his mother is interesting in this regard.[43] According to one variation of the story, amidst his ritual prayers, Jurayj's mother called him. When he did not respond to her calling, she screamed for him again and again. As punishment for his disobedience, he was accused later on of adultery.[44] Whether this was a fictional incident that its authors used to accentuate veneration for a mother when compared with religious duties or an authentic event, this story and its parallels might bear correspondence with how mothers might have acted in reality.[45]

Ties of the womb occupy a seminal position in medieval Muslim discourse. Several works had been entitled *birr al-wālidayn* (filial piety), the most famous of which are the works of Ibn al-Jawzī and that of Muḥammad b. al-Walīd al-Ṭarṭūshī (d. 519/1126).[46] Many prophetic traditions were used to emphasize this type of piety. According to one of the most famous traditions, someone asked the Prophet: 'Whom should I respect?' and the Prophet repeated his answer: 'your mother' three times just before he continued: 'Then, [respect!] your father.'[47] Ghazālī indicates that the natural need for the mother explains her precedence over the father, and that is why children are requested to be

43 On this figure see e.g., J. Horovitz, 'D̲jurayd̲j', *Encyclopaedia of Islam*, second edition, ed. by P. Bearman, Th. Bianquis, C. E. Bosworth, E. van Donzel, and W. P. Heinrichs, consulted online on 5 October 2017 http://dx.doi.org/10.1163/1573-3912_islam_SIM_2122.

44 See e.g., Qushayrī, *Risāla*, 176, lines 28–36. This story was told elsewhere to exemplify the idea that filial piety is more important than ritual prayer [see e.g., Ibn al-Athīr al-Jazrī, *Usd al-ghāba fī maʿrifat al-ṣaḥāba*, ed. by Muḥammad al-Bannā and Muḥammad ʿĀshūr (Cairo: Dār al-Shaʿb, 1970), vol. 5, 53 (in the biography of Yūsuf al-Fihrī)]. Cf. Sahlajī, *Nūr*, 92; Makkī, *Qūt*, vol. 2, 579.

45 This was one point that David Herlihy raised concerning the lives of the Christian saints of the later Middle Ages. He writes: 'My point is that evocations of motherhood, childhood, and fatherhood contained in the lives must bear some correspondence with the ways in which mothers, children, and fathers were viewed in the real world. These images were designed to evoke an emotional response on the part of readers or listeners; the sentiments expressed in a devotional context must have had parallels in feelings that prevailed in the natural family, for which we have no records.' (Herlihy, *Medieval Households*, 115.)

46 Abū al-Faraj ʿAbd al-Raḥmān Ibn al-Jawzī, *Birr al-wālidayn*, ed. by Muḥammad ʿAbd al-Qādir ʿAṭā (Beirut: Muʾassasat al-Kutub al-Thaqāfiyya, 1988); Abū Bakr Muḥammad b. al-Walīd al-Ṭarṭūshī, *Birr al-wālidayn: Mā yajib ʿalā l-wālid li-waladihi wa-mā yajib ʿalā al-walad li-wālidihi*, ed. by Muḥammad ʿAbd al-Karīm al-Qāḍī (Beirut: Muʾassasat al-Kutub al-Thaqāfiyya, 1986).

47 Muḥammad b. ʿĪsā al-Tirmidhī, *al-Jāmiʿ al-kabīr*, ed. by Bashshār Maʿrūf (Beirut: Dār al-Gharb al-Islāmī, 1998), vol. 3, 463; Nawawī, *Riyāḍ al-ṣāliḥīn*, 99.

dutiful to their mothers twice as much as to their fathers.[48] Maternal love and filial piety that relate particularly to mothers, by virtue of the difficulties they endure in life, find their expression in different verses of the *Qur'ān*.[49]

In Sufi contexts, dutifulness towards mothers was not only a statement of compliance with the religious law and *sunna* but, rather, one element of a comprehensive system of self-discipline (*mujāhada*) and ascetic austerities. One of the biographical accounts of Iṣfahānī's *Ḥilya* was devoted to a pious man called Abū ʿAbd Allāh Kahmas b. al-Ḥasan who was celebrated for his unique sense of duty towards his mother. On one occasion, a group of his companions came to visit him at his home. His mother, who did not like those people, asked her son not to keep company with them, and he therefore asked them not to come again.[50] Kahmas did not go on a pilgrimage by virtue of his sincere veneration to his mother, and after she died, he went to Mecca and spent the rest of his life there.[51] Muḥammad b. Sīrīn (d. 110/729), the famous renunciant and jurist of Baṣra, is said to have kept silent in his mother's presence so that everyone who looked at him then thought that he was sick.[52] Similar anecdotes are found in the above-mentioned works of Ibn al-Jawzī, Ṭarṭūshī and many others.[53] From another perspective, however, Muslim reality witnessed less ideal cases of filial impiety. Ibn al-Jawzī himself mentions at the beginning of his short treatise that during his lifetime: 'Many young men do not consider filial piety as a religious duty [...] and they cut the ties of the womb (*yaqṭaʿūn al-arḥām*).'[54] Although the anecdotes told by Ibn al-Jawzī gave evidence of the unhappy destiny that awaits those who disobey their parents, many of those who later became renowned Sufis were far from being the ideal examples of filial piety. Even if we consider such anecdotes as not exactly historic, they can reflect a reality in

48 Abū Ḥāmid Muḥammad al-Ghazālī, *Iḥyā' ʿulūm al-dīn*, ed. by Muḥammad ʿAbd al-Malik al-Zughbī (Cairo: Dār al-Manār, n.d.), vol. 2, 323.

49 See Avner Giladi, 'Herlihy's Thesis Revisited: Some Notes on Investment in Children in Medieval Muslim Societies', *Journal of Family History*, vol. 36, no. 3 (2011), 237–238. See also idem, *Muslim Midwives*, 37–56.

50 Iṣfahānī, *Ḥilyat al-awliyā'*, vol. 6, 230.

51 See ibid., 229; Ibn al-Jawzī, *Ṣifat al-ṣafwa*, vol. 3, 235.

52 See Dhahabī, *Siyar*, vol. 4, 620.

53 Such is the case with mothers who ordered their sons to divorce their wives. See e.g., Ibn al-Jawzī, *Akhbār al-nisā'* (incorrectly attributed to Ibn Qayyim al-Jawziyya), ed. by Aḥmad b. ʿAlī (Cairo: Dār al-Manār, 1998), 55–56; Nawawī, *Riyāḍ al-ṣāliḥīn*, 102; Tirmidhī, *al-Jāmiʿ al-kabīr*, vol. 3, 465–466.

54 Ibn al-Jawzī, *Birr al-wālidayn*, the author's *introduction*, 25.

which filial piety was not always observed.[55] Thus, the insistence on the icon of pure religious morality in Muslim and even Sufi works may imply that absolute filial piety was not automatically regarded as the actual reality of Muslim life.

Sometimes, the child–mother relationship is compared with the Sufi–God relationship or, in the later classical period following the fifth/eleventh century, with the disciple–master relationship. The Muslim expression that describes one's purity and chastity in terms of turning back to his day of birth (*rajaʿa ka-yawm waladathu ummuhu*), which was generally related to pilgrimage and its basic conditions of purity and renunciation of sin according to a well-known *ḥadīth*, gained additional significance in Sufi literature.[56] Sufi authors often made use of this expression in their discussions of repentance (*tawba*) and the inner impact of performing the ritual ablution and prayers.[57] In one tradition, exiting from the mother's womb is compared to the idea of 'coming out from the grief into the spirit of the world' (*al-khurūj min al-ghamm ilā rawḥ al-dunyā*).[58] In all these contexts, the very beginning of the child–mother relationship manifests the Sufi concept of *ṭawr al-fiṭra*, the spiritual stage that precedes the actual birth of human beings; it is the stage in which creatures were still corporeally unborn, in contrast with *ṭawr al-khilqa* in which the temporary life of the joy in its corporeal body involves constant commitment of sins and turpitude. While quoting one definition of the *mutawakkil* (the one who has absolute trust in God), Qushayrī writes: 'Just like the new-born baby who knows no shelter except for his mother's breast, *mutawakkil* is not rightly guided to anyone except to God.'[59]

Since Amat al-Raḥīm Karīma al-Qushayrī (d. 486/1093), one of the five daughters of Abū al-Qāsim al-Qushayrī, was the mother of the historian of Nishapur ʿAbd al-Ghāfir b. Ismāʿīl al-Fārisī (d. 529/1135), she gained special attention in her son's *al-Muntakhab min al-siyāq li-taʾrīkh naysābūr*. Fārisī indicates that his mother 'took the path of piety and renunciation from her venerated mother and from her brothers and

55 See e.g., the story of Muḥammad b. Hārūn who killed his mother while he was drunk, in: Ibid., 65.

56 See e.g., Muḥammad b. Ismāʿīl al-Bukhārī, *Ṣaḥīḥ al-Bukhārī* (Beirut: Dār al-Kutub al-ʿIlmiyya, 2001), 282 (no. 1521); Muḥammad b. Aḥmad al-Qurṭubī, *al-Jāmiʿ li-aḥkām al-Qurʾān* (Beirut: Dār al-Fikr, 1993), vol. 1, 378.

57 See e.g., Ghazālī, *Iḥyāʾ*, vol. 1, 237, 284.

58 Iṣfahānī, *Ḥilyat al-awliyāʾ*, vol. 7, 25.

59 Qushayrī, *Risāla*, 85, lines 20–21.

sisters' (*akhadhat ṭarīq al-ʿibāda wa-l-zuhd min wālidatihā al-ḥurra wa-min ikhwānihā wa-akhawātihā*), while she 'took the path of Sufi knowledge from her father and brothers'.[60]

Majd al-Dīn al-Baghdādī (d. 607/1210 or 616/1219) describes the unique spiritual relationship between the Sufi master and his disciple as 'the embryo of servitude' (*janīn al-ʿubūdiyya*), the Sufi's discipleship (*irādā*) being the 'womb' (*raḥim*) in which this 'embryo' is created and the master, who spiritually suckles and educates this disciple being the wet nurse (*ẓiʾr*).[61] The deep influence of the disciple's gaze on his master, as it is known in master–disciple contexts, is also found in parallel contexts of filial piety mainly in reference to the veneration of his mother and the impact of the child's gazing at her.[62]

On other occasions, mothers are portrayed as the heroic visionaries through whom God guides the Sufi and removes some veils of the invisible (*ghayb*) before his eyes.[63] In his autobiographical *Confessions*, Saint Augustine of Hippo portrayed his Christian mother, Monica, as the instrument by which God's words and conduct were manifested before him. Besides the visions of a new spiritual life she foresaw for her son,[64] her personal life manifested an intensive spiritual metamorphosis that paralleled what her son eventually experienced. After a long period of 'a weakness for wine', she was guided towards a deep Christian faith.[65] Telling about her death in his autobiography, Augustine says that Monica not only endowed him with his worldly existence but also caused him to be born 'into the light of eternity'.[66] The symbol of a new or a second rebirth was strongly emphasized by later Sufis who made use of the ancient religious conception of man being spiritually reborn to

60 See Abū al-Ḥasan ʿAbd al-Ghāfir b. Ismāʿīl al-Fārisī, *al-Muntakhab min al-siyāq li-taʾrīkh naysābūr*, selected by Ibrāhīm b. Muḥammad al-Ṣarīfīnī, ed. by Muḥammad ʿAbd al-ʿAzīz (Beirut: Dār al-Kutub al-ʿIlmiyya, 1989), 428–429. Cf. Martin Nguyen, *Sufi Master and Qur'an Scholar: Abū'L-Qāsim al-Qushayrī and the Laṭāʾif al-Ishārāt* (London: The Institute of Ismaili Studies, 2012), 76–77.

61 See Majd-al-Dīn al-Baghdādī, *Tuḥfat al-barara*, in Kubrā, *Fawāʾiḥ*, appendix, 279.

62 See e.g., Ibn al-Jawzī, *birr al-wālidayn*, 41, 47, 49.

63 See e.g., Abū Bakr ʿAbd Allāh b. Muḥammad al-Mālikī, *Riyāḍ al-nufūs fī ṭabaqāt ʿulamāʾ al-qayrawān wa-afrīqiyya wa-zuhhādihim wa-nussākihim wa-siyar min akhbārihim wa-faḍāʾilihim wa-awṣāfihim*, ed. by Bashīr al-Bakkūsh (Beirut: Dār al-Gharb al-Islāmī, 1983), vol. 1, 255.

64 See Saint Augustine, *Confessions*, trans. by Henry Chadwick (Oxford: Oxford University Press, 1998), 49, 88, 108.

65 See ibid., 167. 66 Ibid., 166.

express the idea of a disciple being reborn from his sheikh through the harsh process of training.[67]

Assimilation between the Sufi master and the father as expressed by statement such as: 'The disciple becomes part of his sheikh in the spiritual rebirth as the son is part of his father in the natural birth'[68] may be seen, in my view, as a modification of the deep-rooted maternal ideal of spirituality and sanctification tellingly represented by the idea of the 'mother of God' in very ancient civilizations.[69] Only in few instances in Sufi literature was the sheikh–disciple relationship compared with the mother–child relationship. Certain Sufi theoreticians portrayed the symbols of femininity and motherhood as corresponding to the lower organs in man against which he has to contend, however, they still believed that those organs are capable to attain perfection.[70]

While the positive images of mothers distinguished the general discourse of Muslim piety in early works of *zuhd* and some Sufi writings,[71] the period that followed the fourth/tenth and fifth/eleventh centuries began witnessing different attempts to construct theories about the

[67] See a detailed discussion of the concept of spiritual rebirth (*al-wilāda al-rūḥiyya/al-ma'nawiyya*) in A. Salamah Qudsi, 'Institutionalized *Mashyakha* in the Twelfth Century Sufism of 'Umar al-Suhrawardī', *Jerusalem Studies in Arabic and Islam* 36 (2009), 390–393.

[68] Suhrawardī, *'Awārif*, 104.

[69] See Robert Briffault, *The Mothers: A Study of the Origins of Sentiments and Institutions* (New York: Macmillan, 1927), vol. 3, 48.

[70] See e.g., Abū Ḥafṣ al-Suhrawardī, *untitled treatise*, MS. Jagiellońska (3994), fol. 40a–40b; idem, *'Awārif*, 308–309; Cf. Annemarie Schimmel, 'The Feminine Element in Sufism', in idem, *Mystical Dimensions*, 428–429.

[71] For mothers as the most important companions and counsellors of their sons see e.g., Ibn al-Jawzī, *Ṣifat al-ṣafwa*, vol. 3, 116–117 [on the mother of Sufyān al-Thawrī, who was claimed to urge her son to devote himself to studying while she took upon herself to supply him with his sustenance. On this figure, see also Nelly Amri and Laroussi Amri, *Les Femmes Soufies ou la Passion de Dieu* (St. Jean de Braye: Éd Dangles, 1992), 89]. A similar story was told about Sulamī's mother, who asked her son to take an advance on his inheritance to finance his pilgrimage (see Rkia Cornell in her introduction to Sulamī's *Dhikr*, 36). In a biography of one jurist, the mother is referred to as warning her son against having three types of food at once on his table (see Mālikī, *Riyāḍ al-nufūs*, vol. 2, 363). This ascetic type of mothers, however, is to be compared with another type which seems, in early traditions, to have been used as a literary technique to expose the high degree of piety their sons could attain in their daily life. According to one story, the mother of Wuhayb b. al-Ward of Mecca brought him some milk to drink and told him about the source of this milk. She knew that the goats from which this milk was taken used to graze with the goats of the ruler, but she did not tell her son who, eventually, refused to drink, even when his mother said: 'Drink it my son, and God will forgive you!' (Makkī, *Qūt*, vol. 2, 601).

mother as a symbol of the lower soul and about the father as a symbol of the holy spirit. Such theories partly originated in Plato's philosophy of man's spiritual priority in the world of creation. 'Masculinity is the best nature of human beings' was the Platonic framework that had been introduced to the Muslim world by the translation of *Timaeus* by Ḥunayn b. Isḥāq.[72] As part of this general idea of feminine inferiority, a specific reference to maternal inferiority can be found in philosophical discussions of man's being the microcosm of a universal intercourse of the sun and moon, of the lofty spirit and its corporeal counterpart.[73] The expression '*ābā'unā al-'ulwiyyāt wa-ummahātunā al-sufliyyāt*' (lit. our superior fathers and our inferior mothers), very often, appears in the writings of Muslim philosophers.[74] In reality, however, maternal ties were much more venerated than such abstract debates might suggest.

For Augustine of Hippo, leaving his mother's company in search of a deeper and more independent religious experience was the only gateway to escape what he described as the eternal desire of mothers to keep their children close to them.[75] 'Abd al-Qādir al-Jīlānī (d. 561/1166) is quoted by Jāmī as entreating his mother to release him on God's behalf and allow him to go to Baghdad. Jīlānī's mother, Umm al-Khayr, allowed her son to go while making a pledge that she would not see him till the Day of Judgment.[76] Sha'rānī, in his account of Muḥammad al-Sindāwī, tells us that even though this Sufi was a dutiful son, he used to say to his mother: 'Donate me to God! Our appointed meeting shall be in the day hereafter.' The author adds his explanation: '[...] in order to avoid his mother's expectations from him' (*li-yaqṭa' ṭama'ahā minhu*).[77]

[72] See Ḥunayn b. Isḥāq, *Jawāmi' kitāb ṭīmāwus*, in *Aflāṭūn fi al-Islām*, ed. by 'Abd al-Raḥmān Badawī (Tehran: Mu'assasat-i Muṭāla'āt-i Islāmī-i Dānishgāh-i Mak-Gīl, 1974), 95 and the footnote.

[73] See e.g., Ikhwān al-Ṣafā', *Rasā'il ikhwān al-ṣafā' wa-khullān al-wafā'*, ed. by Khayr-al-Dīn al-Ziriklī (Cairo: al-Maktaba al-Tijāriyya, 1928), vol. 2, 379 (the 25th epistle). This theory of man's being the microcosm of the universe was the basis of *Ikhwān al-ṣafā'*'s system of thought. F. Dieterici, in his German translation of their *Rasā'il*, divided the original text into two parts: macrocosms and microcosms. See F. Dieterici, *Die Philosophie bei den Arabern im IX-ten Jahrhünderten* n. Chr.: *Gesamtdarstellung und Quellenwerke* (Leipzig: J.C. Hinrichs, 1858–1895), vol. VIII, 208.

[74] See e.g., Abū Ḥāmid al-Ghazālī, *al-Ma'ārif al-'aqliyya*, ed. by 'Abd al-Karīm al-'Uthmān (Damascus: Dār al-Fikr, 1963), 21; Muḥyī al-Dīn Ibn 'Arabī, *'Uqlat al-mustawfiz*, in: Ibn 'Arabī, *Kleinere Schriften des Ibn Al-'Arabī*, ed. by H. S. Nyberg (Leiden: Brill, 1919), 82.

[75] See Augustine, *Confessions*, 82.

[76] Jāmī, *Nafaḥāt al-uns*, 507.

[77] Sha'rānī, *Ṭabaqāt*, vol. 2, 165.

Biographies and Sufi hagiographies are full of similar anecdotes.[78] Broadly speaking, the full agreement of mothers to give up their maternal authority by allowing their sons to break away from their family relations is *per se* an attempt to consolidate the utopian literary ethos of a perfect maternal-spiritual support.

In the biography of Majd al-Dīn al-Baghdādī, it was said that his mother, who was a physician, could not bear the way in which the Sufi master treated her son. When she knew that her son was ordered to clean the latrines, she offered to send the master her Turkish slave to replace him. According to the story, the master did not agree because 'as a physician too, if your son is a patient, he will not recover if I provide that Turkish slave with the medication!'[79] Such a story is, in my view, more reliable than the above-mentioned anecdotes about typical and, to use modern terminology 'essentialist' motherhood, which was, for the most part, portrayed in extremely ideal terms to suit those of the Sufi theoretical system, particularly in its early period.

Besides this, it is not clear whether stories about Sufi women who used to stay for long periods in Mecca (*mujāwara*) and others who did not refrain from staying overnight at male Sufis' homes were reliable, and whether those women were celibate or actual mothers and wives.[80] Fāṭima of Nishapur, who was known in Sufi hagiographies due to Dhū al-Nūn al-Miṣrī's confession that this woman was his 'male' teacher (*ustādh*),[81] spent her life in a long *mujāwara*. In none of her biographical accounts was her family status clearly stated.

[78] See e.g., Jāmī, *Nafaḥāt al-uns*, 520. Ibn al-Jazrī, *al-Zahr al-fā'iḥ fī dhikr man tanazzaha 'an al-dhunūb wa-l-makārih* (Cairo: al-Maṭba'a al-Milījiyya, 1906), 37 (the story of Abū al-Ḥasan al-Thawrī and his mother, who, when her son asked her to set him free for the sake of God, she answered him: 'But there is nothing in you that is virtuous to God!' The son, shocked by his mother's answer, left his home for five years spent in self-seclusion. Afterwards, when the 'light of devotion' appeared to him, the son returned home, and his mother eventually agreed to set him free for the sake of God). According to later Sufi sources, the death of mothers, which might be the worst event in the Sufi's private life, would not prevent him from wandering. See e.g., *Tartīb al-sulūk*, attributed to Ibn 'Atā' Allāh al-Sikandarī (d. 917/1511), ed. by Khālid Zuhrī (Beirut: Dār al-Kutub al-'Ilmiyya, 2004), 22.

[79] See, Jāmī, *Nafaḥāt al-uns*, 424.

[80] See e.g., the account of Rayḥāna of Ubulla, whose male companions used to stay overnight at her place (Ibn al-Jawzī, *Ṣifat al-ṣafwa*, vol. 4, 39; Sulamī, *Dhikr*, 307). Jamī mentions an anonymous Persian woman who used to stay overnight at Najīb b. Buzghush's (d. 678/1280) place (see Jāmī, *Nafaḥāt al-uns*, 634).

[81] This word was used by Sulamī in its male variation to indicate the Sufi tradition of elevating exceptional pious women to the status of spiritual men. See Sulamī, *Dhikr*, the editor's *introduction*, 43; note 108. For the first editor of Sulamī's book, the Egyptian Maḥmūd al-Ṭanāḥī, these examples merely display a 'linguistic anomaly' [Sulamī, *Dhikr*, ed. by Maḥmūd al-Ṭanāḥī (Cairo: Maktabat al-Khānjī, 1993), *introduction*, 19].

On many other occasions, pious women were mothers and seem to have enjoyed a certain degree of free mobility and inter-gender relations with male Sufis that other women could not really enjoy. If this was the case, I suggest that children of such women were expected to fall under the direct impact of their mothers' religiosity. However, when children managed to independently assert their own spiritual religiosity and aspire to look for an independent Sufi career of their own, their mothers did not seem to have been exactly entranced with the matter, and their 'maternal authority' might have overpowered the high ideal of absolute maternal support.

Recent scholarship of Sufism in the modern period has shown to what extent mothers, in Sufi environments, are concerned with their children's affiliation to Sufi orders and are, therefore, highly involved in making decisions about their sons during the childbearing years. Fathers, on the other side, have no interest in active ties with Sufi orders until their later years of life when their children are mature enough to make their own decisions.[82]

[82] See Daisy Dwyer, 'Women, Sufism, and Decision-Making in Moroccan Islam', in *Women in the Muslim World*, ed. by Lois Beck and Nikki Keddie (Cambridge, Mass.: Harvard University Press, 1978), 596–597.

4

Sufis as Maternal Uncles

In Sufi hagiographies, maternal uncles frequently play a fundamental role in the Sufi careers of their nephews. In this form of relationship the link between the personal-family and the communal-Sufi spheres becomes clear and very interesting. Early Sufi history includes many cases, the most famous of which are those of Junayd and his maternal uncle, Sarī al-Saqaṭī;[1] ʿAbd al-Wāḥid al-Sayyārī and his uncle Abū al-ʿAbbās al-Sayyārī;[2] Sahl al-Tustarī (d. 283/896) and Muḥammad b. Sawwār[3] and Abū ʿAbd Allāh al-Rūdhbārī and his renowned uncle Abū ʿAlī al-Rūdhbārī.

In ancient matriarchal societies, it was brothers, not fathers or husbands, who were the natural supporters and protectors of their sisters and their sisters' families and children. This basic feature of primitive societies has survived in different forms both in ancient societies and modern civilizations even though the patriarchal constitution has replaced the more primitive matriarchy.[4] Sisters and mothers rather than wives and daughters are viewed in anthropological studies of different cultures, as in our context, as women who could enjoy a high social status and thus play influential and notable roles.[5]

[1] See Qushayrī, *Risāla*, 10, 20; Sulamī, *Ṭabaqāt*, 141. On Junayd's transition of Saqaṭī's Sufi statements and doctrines, see Sulamī, *Ṭabaqāt*, 41–48.

[2] Jāmī, *Nafaḥāt al-uns*, 145–146.

[3] See Qushayrī, *Risāla*, 15–16; Sulamī, *Ṭabaqāt*, 199.

[4] See Briffault, *Mothers*, vol. 1, 498; Margaret Smith, *Muslim Women Mystics: The Life and Work of Rābiʿa and Other Women Mystics in Islam* (Oxford: Oneworld, 2001), 141–142. Cf. Robertson Smith, *Kinship and Marriage*, 194–195. On the importance of matrilineal ties in imperial Rome see e.g., Herlihy, *Medieval Households*, 6–7.

[5] See Susan Sered, 'Mothers and Icons', *Nashim: A Journal of Jewish Women's Studies and Gender Issues*, 3 (2000), 11. One example of the strong influence sisters had in early

In early Sufi hagiographies, we know about sisters who acted as solid support for their renowned Sufi brothers while pursuing their own spiritual careers.[6] Sarī al-Saqaṭī's sister, as previously mentioned, used to supply her brother with sustenance.[7] Jāmī tells that Khawāja Muḥammad b. Abī Aḥmad al-Chishṭī (d. according to Jāmī 411/1020) did not get married until the age of sixty-five and that he had a sister who would serve him and work hard in spinning textiles in order to provide for him. His sister, it is said, remained celibate until the age of forty.[8]

In the light of the high rates of divorce in medieval Muslim societies, an increasing number of women could live as single for long periods of time or even for the rest of their lives after becoming widows or getting divorced. Based on the two prominent *adab* anthologies of Tanūkhī dated from the second part of the third/ninth century and the first part of the fourth/tenth century – *Nishwār al-muḥāḍara* and *al-Faraj ba'd al-shidda* – Nadia Maria el-Cheikh concludes that 'strong relations could exist between an adult male and his mother, and that a son's fondness for his mother did not necessarily diminish after he became completely independent, having reached high positions of power'. The other side of these strong relationships was the general social condemnation of mothers' remarriages, as the sources from early medieval Islam indicate.[9] Scholars of the Muslim family during the Ottoman period, however, rely on *sharī'a* court archives to indicate that remarriage was not necessarily as difficult for women as usually believed. Children of the late Ottoman societies used to live with their mothers in cases of divorce, in light of a general social acceptance of children from previous marriages.[10] Reasonably speaking, when women preferred to remain single after divorce or the death of their husbands, or in cases they remarried and took their

Muslim history can be supported by Ibn 'Asākir in the biography of the sister of 'Abd Allāh b. 'Āmir b. Kurayz, who was mentioned as cursing her brother to the Umayyid *khalīfa* Mu'āwiya. When Mu'āwiya intended to ride his horse, 'Abd Allāh warned him against this woman who was able to stop the *khalīfa* and overwhelm him with an argument at the end of the story. [See Ibn 'Asākir, *Ta'rīkh madīnat dimashq*, ed. by Muḥibb al-Dīn 'Umar al-'Amrawī (Beirut: Dār al-Fikr, 1995–1998), vol. 70, 277–278).]

6 See Sulamī, *Dhikr*, 123, 193, 195, 217.

7 See Kharkūshī, *Tahdhīb al-asrār*, 367.

8 See Jāmī, *Nafaḥāt al-uns*, 325.

9 See Nadia El-Cheikh, 'Women's History: A Study of al-Tanūkhī', in *Writing the Feminine: Women in Arab Sources*, ed. by Manuela Marín and Randi Deguilhem (London and New York: I.B. Tauris Publishers, 2002), 136–137.

10 See Abdal-Rehim, 'The Family and Gender Laws in Egypt during the Ottoman Period', in *Women, the Family, and Divorce Laws in Islamic History*, ed. by Amira El-Azhary Sonbol with a foreword by Elizabeth Warnock Fernea (Syracuse, N.Y.: Syracuse University Press, 1996), 110.

children to live with them, the relationship between children and their mothers' families remained very close.

If these data are relevant in shedding further light on the sister–brother system of relationships in Sufi communities, then might one suggest that the frequency of divorce in early medieval Islam might have acted as an influential factor for the strong ties that Sufi brothers and sisters could have both in social and economic terms? There are few, if any, references in the sources that describe the social background of pious women and their familial attachments. When flashes of references to sister–brother kinship appear in Sufi hagiographies, the text turns out to be hazy and unclear. Shabaka of Baṣra, for example, is introduced by Sulamī as a woman who 'was a companion of her brother, and like him, she was specialized in the way of scrupulousness (*waraʿ*)'.[11] Neither Sulamī nor other authors and biographers provide additional data concerning this woman or her brother.

Recent scholarship on women and Islam points to the existence of 'ancient female-dominated religious cults' in the pre-Islamic society of Arabia. Several social phenomena related to women's lives and positions, particularly inside the institution of marriage, only prove that this society was actually organized on a matriarchal-matrilineal basis. Certain marriage rituals in the pre-Islamic period gave women superiority and guaranteed their authority and control over their own lives. It is shown that sometimes women could remain within their own family circles after marriage and that their husbands used to visit them there. As a result of the ancient pre-Islamic polyandry, mothers kept their absolute authority over recognizing their offspring's kinship and that is why, very frequently, children lived their whole lives in the lap of their mothers' families. Certain traces of the matriarchal-matrilineal system could survive the birth of Islam and the establishment of its social-religious culture. One of those traces is the significant role that maternal uncles could play in the society of Arabia. This role has existed within Arab societies until recent times.[12] W. Robertson Smith points out that 'in historical times, there was more natural affection between children and their maternal uncles and aunts than between them and the brothers and sisters of their father'. He,

[11] Sulamī, *Dhikr*, English translation, 90.

[12] See e.g., Ghada Karmi, 'Women, Islam and Patriarchalism' in *Women and Islam: Critical Concepts in Sociology*, ed. by Haideh Moghissi (London and New York: Routledge, 2005), vol. 1: *Images and Realities*, 173–174. On the matriarchal-matrilineal system in early Islam see Gertrude Stern, *Marriage in Early Islam* (London: Royal Asiatic Society, 1939), especially 66, 70.

further, compares this situation to the Talmudic rule according to which 'children on the whole resemble the brothers of the mother' (*rōv banīm dōmīn li-aḥī ha-em*).[13]

Ancient works of *adab* are full of stories about maternal uncles who embarked upon supporting and protecting their nephews even when the latter had disputes with their parents. Tanūkhī, for instance, points to the story of Ismāʿīl b. Jāmiʿ whose father used to prevent him from singing, which is why he left his family and travelled to Yemen to live with his maternal uncle there.[14] Stories about nephews who used to associate with their maternal uncles in their daily activities are also frequent. Elsewhere in Tanūkhī's work, the author refers to Abū al-Ḥusayn Muḥammad b. ʿUbayd Allāh, known as Ibn Naṣrawayhi, the *qāḍī* of Baṣra, who used to accompany his maternal uncle (whose name was not mentioned) during his visits to Ḥallāj, until one day his uncle became convinced that Ḥallāj was a juggler, and he and his nephew stopped visiting him.[15]

In early Sufi circles, there is scant evidence that could support any research of nephew–maternal uncle relationship or the relevance of this type of relationship to the sister–brother relationship in the Sufi domain. As was the case of studying mothers, authors of Sufi hagiographies were not interested in portraying the family background of their heroes including the latter's ties with their uncles. In only few occasions do we come across autobiographical notions in which Sufi nephews describe their relationship with their maternal uncles. Such notions are primarily preserved in the compendia of later Sufi authors.

The story of Sahl b. ʿAbd Allāh al-Tustarī's initiation into the Sufi way of life is repeatedly mentioned by Sufi and non-Sufi biographies. Sahl's maternal uncle, Muḥammad b. Sawwār, is said to have caused his nephew to follow the Sufi path of life. The story of Sahl's *tawba*, that is the drastic moment when he experienced the shift from a normal life towards a Sufi mode of life, it should be noted, is told in all the sources by Sahl himself.[16] The following is Ṣafadī's version of this story:

The motivation for Sahl's initiation to the Sufi way of life was his maternal uncle Muḥammad b. Sawwār. Sahl reports: 'My maternal uncle once said to me: Don't you remember God Who created you? I answered him: How would I remember Him?. He said: Say in your heart when you move your body beneath your clothes

[13] Robertson Smith, *Kinship and Marriage*, 195 and footnote 1.
[14] See Tanūkhī, *Nishwār al-muḥāḍara*, vol. 6, 170. [15] See ibid., vol. 2, 290.
[16] On *tawba* in early Sufi literature, see Böwering, *Early Sufism between Persecution and Heresy*, 45–54.

three times without moving your tongue: God is with me, God is looking at me, God is witnessing me. I practised that for several nights and later I informed my uncle. He said to me: Say that seven times every night. I practised that and came back to inform him. Then he asked me to repeat the statement eleven times every night. When I practised that I began feeling a certain pleasure in my heart. One year after, my uncle said to me: Remember what I taught you and keep it until the day of your death.' [. . .] This was the beginning of Sahl's spiritual career.[17]

Sufi sources, furthermore, do not devote to Ibn Sawwār himself a separate biographical account. Sulamī, for instance, refers to him in the biography of his nephew: '[Sahl] accompanied (*ṣaḥiba*) his maternal uncle, Muḥammad b. Sawwār.'[18] In Sulamī's biography of Sahl, rather, only few statements of Ibn Sawwār are mentioned. Qushayrī mentions the above-mentioned story; it is interesting, however, to note that, unlike Ṣafadī, he does not refer to the story as the Sufi starting point in Sahl's career. Qushayrī reports another interesting anecdote, which was narrated again by Sahl:

I was three years old, and I used to wake up in the middle of the night watching my uncle praying all night. Sometimes my uncle was saying to me: 'Go to sleep since you have occupied my heart (*nam fa-qad shaghalta qalbī*).'[19]

The latter statement serves Qushayrī to portray the spiritual image of Sahl by placing it within the framework of his early childhood. The structure of Qushayrī's biographical account of Sahl leaves the impression that the use of the character of Ibn Sawwār by itself serves as a strategy to commend the nephew's willingness to initiate Sufism a long time before the definite trigger occurred which other authors (except to Qushayrī) relate to his uncle. The later statements in Sahl's biography in the text of *Risāla* prove that the basic theme that Qushayrī aimed to highlight was Sahl's gradual advancement in his spiritual career, which started from the

17 Ṣalāḥ al-Dīn Khalīl b. Aybak al-Ṣafadī, *al-Wāfī bi-l-wafayāt*, ed. by Aḥmad al-Arnāʾūṭ and Turkī Muṣṭafā (Beirut: Dār Iḥyāʾ al-Turāth al-ʿArabī, 2000), vol. 16, 11–12; Cf. Qushayrī, *Risāla*, 15. As for the biography of Sahl, see e.g., Sulamī, *Ṭabaqāt*, 199–205; Iṣfahānī, *Ḥilyat al-awliyāʾ*, vol. 10, 198–222; Qushayrī, *Risāla*, 15–16; Ibn al-Jawzī, *Ṣifat al-ṣafwa*, vol. 4, 46–48; Muḥammad b. Aḥmad al-Dhahabī, *al-ʿIbar fī khabar man ghabar*, ed. by Ṣalāḥ al-Dīn al-Munajjid and Sayyid Fuʾād (Kuwait: Dāʾirat al-Maṭbūʿāt, 1960–1966), vol. 2, 76.

18 Sulamī, *Ṭabaqāt*, 199.

19 Qushayrī, *Risāla*, 15. This anecdote appears also in Abū Khalaf Muḥammad b. ʿAbd al-Malik al-Ṭabarī's (d. ca. 470/1077) *Salwat al-ʿārifīn wa-uns al-mushtāqīn*. See idem, *Salwat al-ʿārifīn wa-uns al-mushtāqīn*, in Gerhard Böwering and Bilal Orfali, *The Comfort of the Mystics: A Manual and Anthology of Early Sufism* (Leiden and Boston: Brill, 2013), Arabic text, 473, paragraph no. 846.

age of three through the age of six or seven (when he became able to memorize the whole *Qurʾān* and even to perform *ṣawm al-dahr*, that is, daily fasting) and the age of thirteen (when he travelled to *ʿAbbādān* and associated with Abū Ḥabīb Ḥamza b. ʿAbd Allāh al-ʿAbbādānī for Sufi instruction). It is most probable that the wish to consolidate this theme motivated Qushayrī to report Sahl's story with his uncle when he was three years old, and that is why the actual historical content of the story should not be seriously considered. The reader of such a story would be very eager to ask questions such as: What can we infer from this story about the social engagement of maternal uncles in the lives of their nephews? Why did Sahl often stay overnight at his maternal uncle's place?

Besides the above-mentioned intent of Qushayrī, the specific item of data that refers to the three-year-old Sahl with his uncle could be cautiously reconsidered and its social-actual content be re-examined more carefully if similar items of data appear in relation with other Sufi figures. In the biography of Junayd in Ṣafadī's *al-Wāfī bi-l-wafayāt*, Junayd is quoted as having said:

> I used to play in front of (*bayn yadayy*) Sarī al-Saqaṭī when I was seven years old while a group of people used to sit with him and discuss the doctrine of thankfulness. He [that is Sarī al-Saqaṭī!] said to me: 'Oh young boy, what does thankfulness mean?.' I answered: '[thankfulness!] means that you do not disobey God through a grace (*allā taʿṣī Allā bi-niʿma*).' Then he said to me: 'I am afraid that the only grace you got from God is your tongue.'[20]

According to this anecdote, the seven-year-old Junayd used to stay in the company of his renowned maternal uncle from his very early years. Again, it seems that the biographer's intention was to praise Junayd's early preparation and the outstanding spiritual qualities he already possessed at the age of seven. Nevertheless, in this anecdote as well as in that mentioned earlier, the intention of the authors to praise the saintly features of the nephews does not necessarily imply that the components of the stories are literary and that they have nothing to do with their heroes' actual lives. Strong relationships between nephews and maternal uncles were evident in Islamic medieval sources, not only in early Sufi writings. In both cases of Sahl al-Tustarī and Junayd, and even though the very details of the stories may not all be historically authentic, we suggest that the young nephews could enjoy very close relationships with their maternal uncles.

[20] Ṣafadī, *Wāfī bi-l-wafayāt*, vol. 11, 155.

In a later section of Junayd's biography, his uncle appears again. Junayd reports that his maternal uncle asked him to speak before some people. This means that his uncle felt that, he, Junayd, was talented enough to present a speech on Sufi instruction on his own. It was reported that Junayd did not carry out his uncle's request since he felt ashamed before people: '*Kuntu ajid ḥishma ʿan al-nās fa-innī kuntu attahim nafsī fī istiḥqāq dhālika*' ('I felt ashamed before people since I used to accuse myself of not being worthy of doing so').[21] Later on, Junayd saw the Prophet Muḥammad in his dream, and the latter asked him to speak before some people as his uncle had done earlier. When Junayd visited his uncle and told him about the dream, the uncle, in a reproving voice, said to him: 'You did not believe us until you were ordered to do that (*lam tuṣaddiqnā ḥattā qīla lak*).'[22]

It is interesting that the image of Junayd here is completely different from his portrayal in early Sufi writings, where he is usually introduced as a man of self-confidence, sometimes reaching the limits of arrogance, particularly in those references made to his early days as a young Sufi. Junayd, for instance, is reported to have criticized many Sufis of his time, as well as warned his fellows against the closest bad outcome of their shameful behaviours – this is frequently mentioned in the sources. Some of these will be mentioned later in Chapters 5 and 7. References to Junayd's brilliant character as a young man of great knowledge are also frequent. Qushayrī, for instance, relates that 'he [Junayd!] used to deliver legal opinions (*kāna yuftī*) in the teaching session of Abū Thawr in the latter's presence at the age of twenty.'[23] Notably, however, another element of Junayd's character appears in the aforementioned anecdote with his uncle. Junayd, according to the story, could not believe his uncle, who was certain of his nephew's ability to display his knowledge in public. Although authors who quoted this story aimed at highlighting Junayd's modesty, the opposite description of a man who does not trust others, including his own master, his uncle, is also indicated here. The following paragraph, which appears in Sulamī's *Jawāmiʿ ādāb al-ṣūfiyya* strengthens the latter notion:

Junayd said: One day, I saw that Sarī al-Saqaṭī acted as though he was nervous of me (*ka-l-wājid ʿalayya*). Then, he [Sarī!] said to me: 'Who are those who came to my ears that they gather around you?.' Sarī, rather, warned me about that (lit. alienated me from that, *karraha lī dhālika*). I then said: 'Oh Abū al-Ḥasan [that is

[21] Ibid. [22] Ibid. Cf. Ibn Khillikān, *Wafayāt al-aʿyān*, vol. 1, 373.
[23] Qushayrī, *Risāla*, 20. The notable jurist Abū Thawr died in 240/855.

Sarī al-Saqaṭī]! If a hungry man comes to me for the sake of asking food, I feed him, and if a man with blood disease comes to me to ask for cupping (*ḥijāma*), then would it be possible for me to withhold that from him? Or if a naked man comes to me to ask for a dress, then would it be possible to deny his request while I have a dress to offer to him?.' Sarī said to me: 'No, do not withhold that from them,' and he [Sahl!] became delighted (*inbasaṭa*).[24]

It is clear that Sulamī's reference to this story was said to emphasize one component of his ethical system: the necessity to avoid social fame resulting from the master status (*ustādhiyya*) and the great value in serving one's brothers sincerely. Sulamī understood the story in favour of Junayd, even though the latter appears to be the one who sought leadership by means of supporting his disciples and providing their daily needs. According to Sulamī, no avidity of leadership is to be attributed to Junayd, but instead a true and uncompromising commitment to his companions. If we remove the anecdote from Sulamī's context, we come directly across Junayd's independent and very assertive personality, whose respect for his maternal uncle did not limit his aspirations for leadership and influence.

Ibn al-Jawzī provides us with a detailed description of Junayd-Sarī's relationship. The many anecdotes in Ibn al-Jawzī's biographical account of Sarī al-Saqaṭī relate that Junayd was very close to his uncle and that during his youth he used to spend nights at his uncle's place, and, being the senior disciple of his uncle, he was the one who sat close to his uncle's head at the latter's last moments.[25]

Jāmī, in his biographical account of Sarī al-Saqaṭī, makes no reference to Sarī's kinship with Junayd, while introducing the latter as Sarī's senior disciple.[26] In the biography of Junayd, furthermore, Junayd is quoted as having said: 'People think that I am the disciple of Sarī al-Saqaṭī while I am the disciple of Muḥammad b. ʿAlī al-Qaṣṣāb.'[27] Jāmī, on many occasions in his *Nafaḥāt al-uns*, criticizes Junayd and the veneration he gained among the early Sufis. On one occasion, for instance, Jāmī writes about Ruwaym b. Aḥmad that 'he [Ruwaym!] claims that he is one of Junayd's disciples and companions; however, Ruwaym is better than Junayd, and one hair taken from Ruwaym, in my view, is better than one hundred Junayds!'[28] On another occasion, Jāmī places Junayd in the

[24] Sulamī, *Jawāmiʿ*, 15. [25] See Ibn al-Jawzī, *Ṣifat al-ṣafwa*, vol. 2, 209–218.

[26] See Jāmī, *Nafaḥāt al-uns*, 53.

[27] Ibid., 82. Baghdādī mentions this statement in the biography of Abū Jaʿfar Muḥammad b. ʿAlī al-Qaṣṣāb al-Ṣūfī who, according to Baghdādī, died in 275/888 (see Baghdādī, *Taʾrīkh baghdād*, vol. 4, 104).

[28] Jāmī, *Nafaḥāt al-uns*, 95.

third place after Kharrāz and Ruwaym.[29] Returning to Junayd-Sarī relationship according to *Nafaḥāt al-uns*, it might be possible to suggest that Jāmī sought to counter the close relationship between Junayd and his uncle as well as to combine him with other masters such as the above-mentioned Qaṣṣāb as part of his negative attitude towards Junayd. The position of Junayd among his Sufi contemporaries and successors is the focus of a detailed discussion in Chapter 5.

In comparison to Junayd's maternal uncle, a short reference to Junayd's paternal uncle is provided by Kharkūshī in his *Tahdhīb al-asrār*. An interesting anecdote about Junayd and *al-Ḥārith al-Muḥāsibī* was partially mentioned in Chapter 1. Junayd met Muḥāsibī and invited him to eat at his place. When Junayd discovered that there was not enough food, he entered the home of his paternal uncle who was working at the court of the rulers (*wa-kāna ʿammī yaʿmal maʿ hāʾulāʾ al-salāṭīn*) and took a large amount of food back for Muḥāsibī. The latter, with his deep insight, could feel that the source of this food was suspicious and, therefore, refused to eat.[30]

In certain cases, a Sufi's maternal uncle was more famous and honourable than his nephew. Two interesting examples may be mentioned here: that of ʿAbd al-Wāḥid b. ʿAlī al-Sayyārī and his maternal uncle Abū al-ʿAbbās al-Qāsim b. al-Qāsim al-Sayyārī, while the other is that of Abū ʿAbd Allāh al-Rūdhbārī and his renowned maternal uncle, Abū ʿAlī al-Rūdhbārī. I referred to the latter in Chapter 3.

Sufi and non-Sufi biographers refer to ʿAbd al-Wāḥid b. ʿAlī al-Sayyārī only as a *ḥadīth* transmitter of his honourable uncle.[31] There is no separate biography describing him in Sulamī's *Ṭabaqāt*. Sulamī mentions him as a part of his uncle's biography. In his commentary on the *Qurʾān*, on the other hand, Sulamī refers dozens of times to Abū al-ʿAbbās al-Sayyārī without referring to his transmitter.[32] Interestingly, Sulamī, at the very beginning of Abū al-ʿAbbās al-Sayyārī's biography, points to Abū al-

[29] Ibid., 96. Jāmī's criticism was not only directed to earlier Sufi personalities like Junayd, but it could, rather, involve different groups among the people of Herāt in his day. Hamid Algar indicates that Jāmī's numerous criticisms were made while he had not named anyone explicitly in his works so that he criticized the elite and commonality alike. Jāmī criticized in his different works the Muslim scholars (*ʿulamāʾ*), jurisprudents (*fuqahāʾ*) and those who were considered in his eyes as pseudo-Sufis. See Algar, *Jami*, 109–120.

[30] See Kharkūshī, *Tahdhīb al-asrār*, 360.

[31] See e.g., Ṣafadī, *Wāfī bi-l-wafayāt*, vol. 24, 111.

[32] See Gramlich, *Alte Vorbilder*, vol. 2, 416.

ʿAbbās's line of descent through his mother's family: 'His name is al-Qāsim b. al-Qāsim b. Mahdī. He is the grandson of Aḥmad b. Sayyār on the daughter's side (*ibn bint Aḥmad b. Sayyār*).'[33] Like Sulamī himself, Abū al-ʿAbbās al-Sayyārī had also what Ruth Roded called 'semi-matrilineal ascription'.[34] Hujwīrī and Jāmī, on the other hand, point out that Abū al-ʿAbbās al-Sayyārī has 'inherited a large fortune from his father' and that he 'gave the whole of it in return for two of the Prophet's hairs'.[35] Hujwīrī makes no reference to the nephew. Jāmī brings forward the biography of ʿAbd al-Wāḥid immediately after the biography of his uncle and introduces him as the apprentice (Persian. *shāgird*) of his uncle. Jāmī reports that ʿAbd al-Wāḥid endowed his home for the benefit of the Sufis of Merv after a legendary anecdote had taken place. Once he invited the Sufis of Merv to his place, and one of them experienced an intensive state of ecstasy during the *samāʿ* ceremony. He flew up, into the air, and disappeared.[36]

Qushayrī does not mention ʿAbd al-Wāḥid at all in the biographical account of the uncle.[37] The nephew generally acted as a transmitter for his uncle. If we consider the biography of the uncle, we find that few are the statements of Sufi contents in which ʿAbd al-Wāḥid appears as a transmitter. By the end of Abū al-ʿAbbās's biography in Sulamī's *Ṭabaqāt*, for instance, ʿAbd al-Wāḥid reports the following statement of his uncle: 'If it was permitted to pray using a verse of poetry, it could be permitted to use the following verse.'[38] The rest of the statements in which the nephew is mentioned are traditions that are traced to Abū al-ʿAbbās through chains of transmitters that go back to the Prophet himself. In the biography of Abū Bakr al-Wāsiṭī (d. ca 320/932), however, the name of

[33] Abū al-Ḥasan Aḥmad b. Sayyār al-Marwazī (d. 268/881). See Sulamī, *Ṭabaqāt*, 462; Ibn al-Jawzī, *al-Muntaẓam fī tārīkh al-mulūk wa-l-umam*, ed. by Muḥammad ʿAbd al-Qādir ʿAṭā and Muṣṭafā ʿAbd al-Qādir ʿAṭā (Beirut: Dār al-Kutub al-ʿIlmiyya, 1992), vol. 14, 92. Cf. Yūsuf b. ʿAbd al-Raḥmān al-Mizzī, *Tahdhīb al-kamāl fī asmāʾ al-rijāl*, ed. by Bashshār Maʿrūf (Beirut: Muʾassasat al-Risāla, 1983), vol. 1, 323–324. (On Aḥmad b. Sayyār: 'He is the maternal grandfather of Abū al-ʿAbbās b. al-Qāsim al-Sayyārī of Merv.') Dhahabī, in his *Siyar*, does not refer to Aḥmad al-Sayyārī's kinship to Abū al-Qāsim (see Dhahabī, *Siyar*, vol. 12, 609–611); however, Dhahabī mentions that in his *Tārīkh al-islām* [see Dhahabī, *Tārīkh al-islām wa-wafayāt al-mashāhīr wa-l-aʿlām*, ed. by Bashshār Maʿrūf (Beirut: Dār al-Gharb al-Islāmī, 2003), vol. 7, 784]. Cf. also Gramlich, *Alte Vorbilder*, vol. 2, 413.

[34] See Ruth Roded, *Women in Islamic Biographical Collections from Ibn Saʿd to Who's Who* (Boulder: Colorado and London, 1994), 12, 56–57, 140–141. Cf. Sulamī, *Dhikr*, Cornell's *introduction*, 32.

[35] Jāmī, *Nafaḥāt al-uns*, 145.

[36] See ibid., 146.

[37] See Sulamī, *Ṭabaqāt*, 462–464; Qushayrī, *Risāla*, 30.

[38] Sulamī, *Ṭabaqāt*, 468.

ʿAbd al-Wāḥid as a transmitter of Wāsiṭī's sayings through his uncle appears frequently.[39] ʿAbd al-Wāḥid al-Sayyārī was, most likely, the connecting link through which the bulk of Abū Bakr al-Wāsiṭī's work passed on to Abū ʿAbd al-Raḥmān al-Sulamī, who relied heavily on Wāsiṭī's interpretation of the *Qurʾān* in his two Sufi exegeses of the holy text: the *Ḥaqāʾiq al-tafsīr* and *Zubdat al-ḥaqāʾiq*.[40]

The biographical material available does not allow us to reach any definite conclusions concerning the nature of the relationship between the two Sayyārīs. Gramlich points out the problematic fact that the early sources rarely refer to the followers of Abū al-ʿAbbās al-Sayyārī and that in most textual evidence Abū al-ʿAbbās is the only figure to be mentioned while discussing *Sayyāriyya*.[41] From the collection of sayings that the nephew transmitted from his uncle, we come across no references that can shed light on the personal level of the relationship between the two, as in the case of other Sufi figures. On some occasions in early Sufi writings, we come across such autobiographical notions made by Sufi authors to describe the personal experiences they had with their masters. Abū Ḥafṣ al-Suhrawardī, whose paternal uncle was his most influential master, provides few references of this kind in his *ʿAwārif*.[42]

The suggestion is that the nephew who succeeded in transmitting the esoteric statements of Wāsiṭī could not do so without having a strict Sufi training under his uncle in addition to other masters of his day. In the biography of Sulamī's maternal grandfather Abū ʿAmr b. Nujayd in his *Ṭabaqāt*, Sulamī refers to ʿAbd al-Wāḥid as one of Ibn Nujayd's close disciples in Merv.[43] This notion might provide an explanation for two issues: The first is the contact between Sulamī and ʿAbd al-Wāḥid through which the teachings of Wāsiṭī passed to Sulamī, and the other is the evidence that ʿAbd al-Wāḥid had more than one sheikh under whom he acquired his Sufi training. In addition to his uncle and Ibn Nujayd, ʿAbd al-Wāḥid seems to have been interested in the teachings of Ḥallāj. He contacted Aḥmad b. Fāris and transmitted some of Ḥallāj's sayings from him.[44] ʿAbd al-Wāḥid's major contribution in maintaining the teachings of his uncle is shown by the fact that Jullābī Hujwīrī, who

[39] See ibid., 304–305; Jullābī Hujwīrī, *Kashf al-maḥjūb*, 323.

[40] See Gramlich, *Alte Vorbilder*, vol. 2, 413–417; See also Laury Silvers, *A Soaring Minaret: Abū Bakr al-Wāsiṭī and the Rise of Baghdadi Sufism* (Albany: State University of New York Press, 2010) *introduction*, 4.

[41] See Gramlich, *Alte Vorbilder*, vol. 2, 416.

[42] See e.g., Suhrawardī, *ʿAwārif*, 284.

[43] See Sulamī, *Ṭabaqāt*, 479.

[44] See ibid., 30. See also Gramlich, *Alte Vorbilder*, vol. 2, 416.

lived about one hundred years after the foundation of Sayyārī's Sufi circle in Merv, reports the existence of numerous followers of Sayyārī in Merv and Nasā in his day. Hujwīrī states that the followers of Abū al-ʿAbbās were concerned with keeping his legacy unchanged for a long time after his death.[45] This latter notion makes it possible to assume that ʿAbd al-Wāḥid, besides his above-mentioned significant contribution, was able to operate but only in the shadow of his celebrated maternal uncle. This is to say that, in both the cases of ʿAbd al-Wāḥid al-Sayyārī and Abū ʿAbd Allāh al-Rūdhbārī, the nephews were not able to compete with the high spiritual positions of their maternal uncles.

The specific form of kinship between Bishr b. al-Ḥārith and ʿAlī b. Khashram (d. 257/870), a famous *ḥadīth* transmitter, was a matter of dispute in both Sufi and non-Sufi biographies. Some biographers state that Bishr was the maternal nephew of ʿAlī b. Khashram,[46] while others, like Baghdādī and Ibn al-ʿImād, claim Bishr was ʿAlī's cousin.[47] Ṣafadī, on one occasion in his work, indicates that Bishr al-Ḥāfī was ʿAlī b. Kashram's cousin, while on another occasion he reports that Bishr was ʿAlī b. Khashram's uncle.[48]

Notably, Abū Nuʿam al-Iṣfahānī does not refer to ʿAlī b. Khashram as one of Bishr's relatives at all. He indicates one statement of Bishr that ʿAlī transmitted from him,[49] while on another occasion of *Ḥilya*, Iṣfahānī reports a long letter that Bishr sent to ʿAlī. Bishr addressed his letter to 'Abū al-Ḥasan ʿAlī b. Khashram' and advised him to follow his ancestors' footsteps, to be satisfied with their example of sincere piety and to abandon the association of his contemporaries because this would distance him from the path of the Prophet's companions. Frequently in his letter, Bishr warns ʿAlī b. Khashram of the people of his time (*iḥdhar ahl zamānika*) since those might lead him to affliction (*fitna*) and urges him to commit himself to a life of seclusion.[50] The general structure and

[45] See Jullābī Hujwīrī, *Kashf al-maḥjūb*, 323.

[46] See Anṣārī Haravī, *Ṭabaqāt al-ṣūfiyya*, 71. Qushayrī, *Risāla*, 11; Sulamī, *Ṭabaqāt*, 33; Ibn Manẓūr, *Mukhtaṣar taʾrīkh dimashq*, vol. 5, 191. References to ʿAlī b. Khashram are frequent in works of historiography and biographies. See e.g., Kamāl al-Dīn ʿUmar b. Aḥmad b. al-ʿAdīm, *Bughyat al-ṭalab fī tārīkh ḥalab*, ed. by Suhayl Zakkār (Beirut: Dār al-Fikr, 1988), vol. 3, 2388; Ṣafadī, *Wāfī bi-l-wafayāt*, vol. 21, 55 (here the date of death is 257).

[47] See Baghdādī, *Taʾrīkh baghdd*, vol. 7, 545; ʿAbd al-Ḥayy b. Aḥmad b. al-ʿImād, *Shadharāt al-dhahab fī akhbār man dhahab*, ed. by ʿAbd al-Qādir al-Arnāʾūṭ and Maḥmūd al-Arnāʾūṭ (Damascus: Dār Ibn Kathīr, 1988), vol. 3, 123.

[48] See Ṣafadī, *Wāfī bi-l-wafayāt*, vol. 21, 55.

[49] See Iṣfahānī, *Ḥilyat al-awliyāʾ*, vol. 9, 182

[50] See ibid., vol. 8, 383–385.

discourse of this letter might give preference to the second possible form of kinship according to which they were cousins.

In some biographical accounts of Bishr, we come across the idea that, in spite of the fact that he had an excellent knowledge of *ḥadīth* science, 'he did not nominate himself to the position of *ḥadīth* transmitter', and that Bishr 'disliked *riwāya*' (oral transmission of prophetic traditions). The latter notion might explain why Bishr buried his books according to certain non-Sufi sources.[51] It appears as though Sufi biographies found no interest in this piece of data. The work of Baghdādī, for instance, brings to the fore numerous statements of Bishr in which he considers *ḥadīth* transmission as a major cause of self-conceit, a negative impact of the lower soul according to early Sufi doctrines. It is reported that someone asked Bishr: 'Why do you not transmit *ḥadīth*?' and that he answered: 'I like to do that, and that is exactly the reason why I abandon everything that I yearn to do.'[52] Bishr's negative attitude towards men of *ḥadīth*, most probably, serves as the background of his above-mentioned letter to ʿAlī b. Khashram. He might have sought to criticize his uncle/cousin's strong engagement in *riwāya* instead of practising a pious Sufi pattern of life. From another perspective, it is still appropriate to ask here why the majority of Sufi biographies mention the nephew–maternal uncle kinship, while non-Sufi biographies tend to emphasize the cousin–cousin kinship in particular. Had the letter in Iṣfahānī's *Ḥilya* any influence on those authors who gave preference to the second form of kinship between the two figures?

In his biography of Bishr in *Ṣifat al-ṣafwa*, Ibn al-Jawzī mentions several quotations of Bishr that were reported by his nephews, Abū Ḥafṣ and ʿUmar.[53] Bishr had strong relationships with his sisters; three were

[51] See Baghdādī, *Taʾrīkh baghdād*, vol. 7, 545; Ibn Manẓūr, *Mukhtaṣar taʾrīkh dimashq*, vol. 5, 191; Ibn al-ʿImād, *Shadharāt al-dhahab*, vol. 3, 122.

[52] Baghdādī, *Taʾrīkh baghdād*, vol. 7, 545. Bishr's negative attitude towards politics is beautifully asserted in the following anecdote at the end of Ibn Khafīf's *Kitāb al-iqtiṣād*: It was stated that the Abbasid ruler al-Muʿtaḍid invited Bishr b. al-Ḥārith to his court. When the messenger told Bishr of al-Muʿtaḍid's wish, Bishr said: 'Tell him that I sware of God that if I know that he addresses me again I will abandon his proximity in Baghdad.' When the Abbasid ruler heard Bishr's reply, he said: 'Tell him that I will not address him again.' [Ibn Khafīf, *Kitāb al-iqtiṣād*, in Florian Sobieroj, *Ibn Ḫafīf aš-Šīrāzī und seine Schrift zur Novizenerziehung (Kitāb al-Iqtiṣād): Biographische Studien, Edition und Übersetzung*, Inaugural-Dissertation zur Erlangung der Doktorwürde der Philosophischen Fakultäten der Albert-Ludwigs-Universität zur Freiburg, 1992, Arabic text, 42.]

[53] See Ibn al-Jawzī, *Ṣifat al-ṣafwa*, vol. 2, 185–186. See an additional quotation of Bishr made by his nephew Abū Ḥafṣ in Sulamī, *Jawāmiʿ*, 5–6.

mentioned by name in the works of Sulamī and Ibn al-Jawzī. In their biographical accounts, it was noted that Bishr's sisters used to spin textiles on the roof of their house at nights.[54] The latter notion might indicate that those women would have had to make their own living. No additional data can provide us with the familial background of Bishr's sisters or to tell whether they worked in the production of textiles as a result of becoming single or not.[55]

Other pious sisters had the opportunity to share their Sufi brothers' lives of devoutness and renunciation. In addition to Bishr's sisters, the cases of Maymūna, the sister of Ibrāhīm al-Khawwāṣ,[56] and ʿAbda bint Aḥmad bint ʿAṭiyya, the sister of Abū Sulaymān al-Dārānī, could be mentioned here. Ibn ʿAsākir refers to the following statement made by Sulaymān al-Dārānī, that is, the son of the great Syrian mystic: 'My paternal aunt is more renunciant than my father (*ʿammatī azhad min abī*).'[57]

ʿAbd Allāh b. Ḥāḍir of Rayy was the maternal uncle of Yūsuf b. al-Ḥusayn, a personality that will receive a detailed consideration in Chapter 8. Ibn Ḥāḍir, Ibn Abī Yaʿlā (d. 526/1132) states, was a *ḥadīth* transmitter who came from Rayy and settled for many years of his life in Baghdad, where he associated with Dhū al-Nūn al-Miṣrī. The basic element in his biography is that he transmitted *ḥadīth* from Aḥmad b. Ḥanbal, although Baghdādī refers to him as a weak transmitter.[58] None of the early Sufi biographers devotes a biographical account to him. Sulamī mentions him once in the biography of Yūsuf b. al-Ḥusayn as a narrator of *ḥadīth* and does not refer to his kinship with Ibn al-Ḥusayn.[59] Jāmī, who chose to write a separate biography of Ibn Ḥāḍir, refers in much detail to his relationship with Yūsuf b. al-Ḥusayn. According to Jāmī, Ibn Ḥāḍir was one of Dhū al-Nūn's companions and, even, preferable to him. The 'pseudo-nephew' was a disciple of

[54] See Ibn al-Jawzī, *Ṣifat al-ṣafwa*, vol. 2, 294–296; Sulamī, *Dhikr*, 322–325.

[55] On the relationship between high rates of divorce and women's involvement in gender-specific professions in medieval Muslim societies, see Rapoport, *Marriage*, 31–50.

[56] See her biography in Sulamī, *Dhikr*, 217; Ibn al-Jawzī, *Ṣifat al-ṣafwa*, vol. 2, 296.

[57] Ibn 'Asākir, *Taʾrīkh madīnat dimashq*, vol. 69, 262–263. See the biography of ʿAbda in Ibn al-Jawzī, *Ṣifat al-safwa*, vol. 4, 272–273. Sulamī mentions another sister of Abū Sulaymān, Āmina. See Sulamī, *Dhikr*, 195.

[58] See Abū al-Ḥusayn Muḥammad b. Abī Yaʿlā, *Ṭabaqāt al-ḥanābila*, ed. by ʿAbd al-Raḥmān al-ʿUthaymīn (Makka: al-Amāna al-ʿĀmma li-l-Iḥtifāl bi-Murūr Miʾat ʿĀm ʿalā Taʾsīs al-Mamlaka, 1999), vol. 2, 25; Cf. Baghdādī, *Taʾrīkh baghdād*, vol. 11, 112–113, 292–293.

[59] See Sulamī, *Ṭabaqāt*, 176.

Dhū al-Nūn, as many sources indicate. When he returned from a visit to Dhū al-Nūn, his uncle met him in Baghdad and asked him to gather all his collections of the sayings and teachings of the Egyptian Sufi master and to throw them into the Tigris. It was reported that Ibn al-Ḥusayn was not able to carry out his uncle's first request, and when turning back to his uncle, the second request came: 'When you arrive at Rayy, do not tell anyone that you had associated with Dhū al-Nūn.'[60] If this anecdote was authentic, and the kinship between the two figures was true, then one can suggest that the uncle whose fame could not go along with that of the great Egyptian master, probably attempted to undercut the firm disciple–master relationship of his nephew and Dhū al-Nūn. I would call attention here to Jāmī's tendency to disregard certain Sufi personalities of the early period. In addition to the above-mentioned case of Junayd, Dhū al-Nūn appears here as the subject of Jāmī's sarcastic and offensive remarks.

Both al-Khaṭīb al-Baghdādī and Samʿānī refer to Shiblī's maternal uncle, who had won a senior administrative position in Egypt. Neither Baghdādī nor Samʿānī provide us with the uncle's name, yet both of them mention Sulamī as the source for this piece of information.[61] Unfortunately, there is no reference to Shiblī's relationships with his uncle. Kāmil al-Shaybī, in his introduction to Shiblī's *Dīwān* considers it most probable that Shiblī spent a certain period of time during his youth in Alexandria, where his maternal uncle lived and worked, and that Shiblī adopted the Mālikī school of jurisprudence, which was the most widespread school in Egypt and North Africa of the time, as a result of his stay there.[62] Among early Sufi biographers, it was ʿAbd Allāh Anṣārī of Herāt who indicated that Shiblī was in fact an Egyptian Sufi.[63] This notion, among others, brought Shaybī to his conclusion. Regardless of the important position that his maternal uncle occupied in Egypt, the references to this uncle in the aforementioned sources came to emphasize Shiblī's sincere choice of the renunciatory life, in spite of a wealthy familial environment of which he could easily take advantage.

Despite the problematic nature of the available material, tackling the issue of nephew–maternal uncle relationships in early Sufi spheres helps one to understand the points of conjunction between the personal and the

60 Jāmī, *Nafaḥāt al-uns*, 98–99.

61 See Baghdādī, *Taʾrīkh baghdād*, vol. 16, 564; Samʿānī, *Ansāb*, vol. 8, 53. In Sulamī's *Ṭabaqāt*, there is no reference to Shiblī's maternal uncle at all.

62 See Abū Bakr al-Shiblī, *Dīwān Abī Bakr al-Shiblī Jaʿfar b. Yūnus*, ed. by Kāmil Muṣṭafā al-Shaybī (Baghdad: Dār al-Taḍāmun, 1967), 37–40.

63 See Anṣārī Haravī, *Ṭabaqāt al-ṣūfiyya*, 120.

communal aspects of life on both sides. When the Sufi master is none other than the maternal uncle, one should suggest the existence of a firm disciple–master relationship. This situation necessarily involves a strong connection between the two sides since the family space turns into one of continuous discipleship. It is here that the boundaries between the family space and the Sufi space where the devotee gets his spiritual guidance through intensive meetings with his sheikh dissolve to become one integrative unit. The devotee obtains his Sufi education within the limits of the family bonds. In many cases, sources report that young nephews could grow up within the spiritual environment that their influential uncles-masters had established. The physical closeness with the odour of spirituality revealed the world of Sufism to the young nephews from a very young age. They were able to spend their early years in their uncles' company to attend with them gatherings of great masters, travel with them, accompany them on pilgrimages, present their doctrines and help pass on the teachings that their uncles had received from their ancestors. Jāmī tells that Yūsuf b. Muḥammad b. Simʿān (d. according to Jāmī 459) was the disciple of his maternal uncle Muḥammad b. Abī Aḥmad. Since the maternal uncle remained unmarried for a very long time and, thereby, his own sons were not mature at the time he was able to guide disciples, he decided to adopt his nephew and raise him as his son. After the uncle's death, his nephew replaced him in guiding the disciples.[64]

Even when Sufism came to be an organized institution of the spiritual family of 'brothers' (*ikhwān*) throughout the late sixth/twelfth century, the disciplined form of affiliation to the Sufi-organized *ṭarīqa* was founded, particularly, on family bonds and family networks. In many *ṭarīqa*s like *rifāʿiyya*, for instance, the very heart of the *ṭarīqa* was founded on the activities of the offspring of the *ṭarīqa*'s eponym, that is the great Sufi master to whom the *ṭarīqa* is attributed, Aḥmad al-Rifāʿī (d. 578/1182) in this case. Later on, this family-based structure of the *ṭarīqa* could break out of the close blood relationship of the founder's offspring and turn into a wider and non-familial framework of affiliation to the *ṭarīqa*.[65]

[64] See Jāmī, *Nafaḥāt al-uns*, 325.

[65] See e.g., C. E. Bosworth, 'Rifāʿiyya', *Encyclopaedia of Islam*, second edition, ed. by P. Bearman, Th. Bianquis, C. E. Bosworth, E. van Donzel, and W. P. Heinrichs, consulted online on 9 October 2017 http://dx.doi.org/10.1163/1573-3912_islam_SIM_6296.

In certain cases, paternal uncles were the influential masters of renowned Sufi personalities. The case of ʿUmar al-Suhrawardī and his paternal uncle Abū al-Najīb al-Suhrawardī (d. 564/1168) is a good example. Though the master, Abū al-Najīb, left his mark on Baghdadi Sufism by the composition of his *Ādāb al-murīdīn* (*Sufi Rules for Novices*) and his preaching talents, the nephew, Abū Ḥafṣ al-Suhrawardī, came to be the influential Sufi master whose influential *magnum opus ʿAwārif al-maʿārif* remained the basic textbook of many later *ṭarīqa*s in the world of Islam.[66]

Broadly speaking, if we compare the textual data noted in the previous subchapter on mothers and the data presented here, we might conclude that the influence of maternal uncles on the Sufi careers of their nephews was, most probably, more effective and supportive than that of their mothers. If, to speak about the ideal of the 'maternal lightning trigger' in early Sufi spheres, then maternal uncles, not mothers, appear more often as its characteristic representatives.

[66] See ʿUmar b. Muḥammad al-Suhrawardī, *Die Gaben der Erkenntnisse des ʿUmar as-Suhrawardī (ʿAwārif al-Maʿārif)*, ubersetzt und eingeleitet von Richard Gramlich (Wiesbaden: Steiner, *1978*), Vortwort, V; Einleitung, 3. On Abū al-Najīb al-Suhrawardī and his work, see ʿAbd al-Qāhir b. ʿAbd Allāh Abū al-Najīb al-Suhrawardī, *A Sufi Rule for Novices*, an abridged translation and introduction by Menahem Milson (Cambridge, Mass.: Harvard University Press, 1975); and on the work of his nephew, Abū Ḥafṣ al-Suhrawardī, see Erik Ohlander, *Sufism in an Age of Transition: ʿUmar al-Suhrawardī and the Rise of the Islamic Mystical Brotherhoods* (Leiden and Boston: Brill, 2008); A. Salamah-Qudsi, *Bayn sayr wa-ṭayr: al-Tanẓīr, ḥayāt al-jamāʿa, wa-bunā al-muʾassasa fī taṣawwuf Abī Ḥafṣ al-Suhrawardī* (Beirut: Dār al-Kutub al-ʿIlmiyya, 2012).

PART II

COMMUNAL NARRATIVES

Early Sufis' Modes of Operating in the Framework of Sufi Communal Lives

5

Consensually Acclaimed Sufis and Lenient Approaches

In the following four chapters, I am going to discuss in detail the emergence and evolution of different communal aspects of Sufi piety. The latter will be approached from four different perspectives: The first perspective is that of early Sufi personalities who successfully portrayed the accepted boundaries of Sufi codes of behaviour in the framework of their communal lives and activities or 'the consensually acclaimed Sufis'. The second is the perspective of marginal personalities such as Niffarī. The third is the perspective of Sufi personalities who had their own ways of negotiating the monopoly of mainstream Sufism and disputing its representatives and, finally, the perspective of certain controversial Sufis, whose names were linked with the custom of association with youth (*ṣuḥbat al-aḥdāth*), as well as Sufi authors who referred in their writings to that custom. This chapter, thereby, will put the focus on Sufi personalities who played key roles in establishing the high Sufi ethos, a process in which all accepted codes of behaviour and rules of ethics were integrated into one solid system. David Martin summarizes the basic achievement of these Sufi personalities as follows: 'This is to say they established a consensus, an *ijmā'*, among themselves as to what was within the pale of Sufism and what heresy.'[1] I agree with this reference to a sort of internal consensus within the boundaries of the group of *ṣūfiyya*; however, I would add to the last part of the notion my own notion: Consensus in the case of Iraqi *ṣūfiyya* was not designated to exclude controversial Sufi figures. Except for a small number of cases, the *ṣūfiyya*'s main target was to blur

[1] Martin, *Account of Ruwaym*, 28.

individual tendencies among the Sufis and hide probable differences and unique modes of piety. The representatives of this line were most likely not interested in highlighting any individuality, any personal tone or any abnormal behaviour or thought. Accordingly, controversial cases should have been included under the ultimate umbrella of the *ṣūfiyya*, and interpersonal tensions should have been left aside. This was actually an internal consensus, which was grounded in the criteria that the *ṣūfiyya* and their successors dictated in the early phase of Sufism. The *ṣūfiyya* aimed at creating a homogenous group that would include all Sufi trends and streams, at least in theoretical terms. It appears that, to a remarkable extent, they were successful. Anyone who reads the classical Sufi compendia can outline a general system of thought that would easily fall under the broad title of *taṣawwuf*. Though this consensus was effective, differences between some of its founders were unavoidable. The case of Ruwaym b. Aḥmad with Junayd and other representatives of the *ṣūfiyya* might be the most blatant example. Scholars have pointed to Ruwaym's differences with the general line of mainstream Sufism of his day. He was portrayed in Sufi hagiographies as the one who did not practise the same austerities that his contemporaries practised and urged their disciples to practise. In Chapter 7, I will draw on these notions on Ruwaym and other early personalities as starting points for tackling some aspects of the interpersonal networks that defined Sufis' communal lives.[2] As we will see later in this chapter, attempts to doubt the authoritative characteristic of this consensus as well as that of its founders are also found in the early sources.

The process of establishing the high Sufi ethos, as evident in the sources, could have been undertaken by means of different procedures and strategies. Key personalities like Junayd chose, for instance, to bind themselves to what I call the 'lenient approaches'. I argue that this was indeed one of the most influential procedures in early Sufism to exempt new initiates from strict codes of behaviour and spiritual practice, as a measure of facilitating broader and more solid recruitment.

While this approach was not common in the early part of the considered period here, over the course of the sixth/twelfth century, it became one of the major traits of the Sufi practical system and actual communal life of the Sufis. Mustamlī Bukhārī makes use of one tradition narrated by

[2] See Schimmel, *Mystical Dimensions*, 59. Cf. Martin, *Account of Ruwaym*, 29.

Anas b. Mālik (d. between 91/709 and 93/711) on the leniency of the Prophet Muḥammad in order to highlight the idea of mutual compassion (*shafaqat*) among the Sufis.[3] This chapter discusses Sufi personalities who managed to gain renown within their communities due to their commitment to establishing a solid Sufi ethos through facilitating the very concept of joining the Sufi community. The names of these personalities became one with famous Sufi schools and doctrines, and their sayings and deeds were the building blocks of the main body of early Sufi doctrinal system. This was the case of Junayd and other figures of the group of *ṣūfiyya*, who, according to Karamustafa, were the authoritative elite of the Sufis of Baghdad and who managed to firmly plant themselves into the social fabric of the Abbasid capital.

Interestingly, Junayd advises his followers to avoid strictness with Sufi novices.[4] This technique is recommended by Junayd in order to avoid scenarios in which those novices find themselves unable to commit to all the responsibilities required from the advanced Sufis and who would eventually give up their interest in the path entirely.

This lenient approach, as one form of communication between certain masters and their counterparts in the framework of Sufi communal lives, deserves to be treated here. According to this approach, an initiate should not be required to commit to the strict codes of behaviour and spiritual practices of their veteran fellows. This was not the common approach in the early part of the considered period; however, it progressively succeeded in gaining the support of certain masters, such as Junayd and, later on, Aḥmad al-Ghazālī (d. 517/1123 or 520/1126) and both Abū al-Najīb al-Suhrawardī and his nephew ʿUmar al-Suhrawardī. In the course of the sixth/twelfth century, the position of those individuals who imitate the Sufis without becoming disciplined fellows of theirs (*mutashabbihūn bi-l-ṣūfiyya*) grew into a major feature of the Sufi institution of that time, with the strong theoretical support in the teachings of the latter two Suhrawardīs.[5]

Besides Junayd, this chapter seeks to discuss the cases of Abū Saʿīd al-Kharrāz and Abū Ḥafṣ al-Ḥaddād (d. c. 265/878-879).

[3] See Mustamlī Bukhārī, *Sharḥ kitāb al-taʿarruf*, vol. 1, 195–196.

[4] See e.g., Sulamī, *Ṭabaqāt*, 146. This reference as it appears in Sulamī's work as well as in other sources will be examined later in this chapter.

[5] On the position of *mutashabbih* see Salamah-Qudsi, *Idea of Tashabbuh*, 175–197.

ABŪ AL-QĀSIM AL-JUNAYD (D. 298/910–911): A MAN OF CHARISMA AND LENIENCY

The character of Junayd launched many scholarly endeavours in recent decades.[6] The main focus has been put on Junayd's doctrine of 'unification' (*tawḥīd*), as well as the origins of his position as the typical representative and leader of what is traditionally known as the School of Baghdad, or the School of Sobriety. In spite of the differences between the teachings of the major representatives of this school, which were not negligible, the overall image of the School of Baghdad is by all means a direct outcome of the teachings of Junayd and of his close circle of disciples. The works of Josef van Ess, Ali Hassan Abdel-Kader, David Ludwig Martin, Elsayed M. H. Omran and Shams C. Inati are among the most outspoken scholarly attempts to thoroughly examine this unique figure who stood at the helm of the Sufi movement in Islam and who successfully left his mark on its development from the third/ninth century until today.

I do not seek here to refer again to Junayd's doctrines, as these are displayed in the body of statements and fragments ascribed to him in the Sufi compendia. Instead, I seek to look into Junayd's dynamic relationships with his Sufi contemporaries, the nature of his position as a consensually acclaimed Sufi leader and the ways in which this position fits together with Junayd's practical agenda in treating novices leniently.

It is interesting to note, further, that the consensual veneration of Junayd in early Sufi and non-Sufi sources was challenged in Persian Sufi

[6] See Abū al-Ḥasan ʿAlī b. Muḥammad al-Daylamī, *A Treatise on Mystical Love*, trans. by Joseph Norment Bell and Hassan Maḥmūd al-Shāfiʿī (Edinburgh: Edinburgh University Press, 2005), the editors' *introduction*, lix. Cf. A. J. Arberry, 'al-Djunayd', *Encyclopaedia of Islam*, second edition, ed. by P. Bearman, Th. Bianquis, C. E. Bosworth, E. van Donzel, and W. P. Heinrichs, consulted online on 9 October 2017 http://dx.doi.org/10.1163/1573-3912_islam_SIM_2117. Most recently, Ahmet Karamustafa, '*Walāya* According to al-Junayd (d. 298/910)', in *Reason and Inspiration in Islam: Theology, Philosophy and Mysticism in Muslim Thought: Essays in Honour of Hermann Landolt*, ed. by Todd Lawson (London: Tauris, 2005), 64–70; idem, *Sufism*, 15–18; Josef Dreher, 'Comment un Homme Peut-il Perdre plus qu'il ne Possède? Essais d'Explication d'une Sentence Énigmatique d'al-Junayd (m. 298/910) Concernant les Progrès et les Dangers sur le Chemin vers Dieu', *Institut Dominicain d'Études Orientales du Caire: Mélanges (MIDEO)*, vol. 27 (2008), 413–422; Jawid Mojaddedi, 'Getting Drunk with Abū Yazīd or Staying Sober with Junayd: The Creation of a Popular Typology of Sufism', in *Sufism, Volume I: Origins and Development*, ed. by Lloyd Ridgeon (London: Routledge, 2008), 171–187; idem, 'Junayd in the *Ḥilyat al-awliyā*ʾ and the *Nafaḥāt al-uns*', in *Tales of God's Friends: Islamic Hagiography in Translation*, ed. by John Renard (Berkeley: University of California Press, 2009), 79–91.

hagiographical works. Attempts to defame Junayd's image began with the early fourth/tenth century biographer ʿAbd Allāh Anṣārī of Herāt and continued with his successor ʿAbd al-Raḥmān Jāmī in the later ninth/fifteenth century. Some of the negative references to Junayd in Jāmī's *Nafaḥāt al-uns* will be raised in Chapters 7 and 8. Both Anṣārī and Jāmī tell that 'one hair of Ruwaym [b. Aḥmad, al-Junayd's contemporary!] is better than a hundred Junayds.' Besides, Junayd was portrayed in the biography of Ruwaym in the works of these two authors as the one who tried to harm his companion by forbidding novices to visit him. In Chapter 8, I will show how the character of Junayd appears in early anecdotes about Sufis who fall into the fault of the illegal gaze. In the majority of these anecdotes, Junayd is mentioned to have warned his fellow of the negative consequence of the fault he committed. He is usually portrayed there as the perfect Sufi sheikh that knows everything and can predict the consequences of certain forms of behaviour that do not fit with the 'ideal' and 'high' Sufi ethos, of which he himself was a main founder. The reasonable nature of Junayd was not approached positively by all Sufi authors. A critical approach towards his reasonability and 'scientism' is documented in both Anṣārī's and Jāmī's works.[7] However, this critique did not manage to affect Junayd's image as a consensual figure, or even as the most consensually acclaimed figure in the history of early Sufism.

The study of Junayd's personality should be shifted to new arenas, where his image is portrayed in different, less sympathetic, tones. His tense relationships with certain figures of his time are difficult for the modern scholar to approach. In order to reveal more of such tensions, I suggest treating his *Rasāʾil* not only as a document of his secret teachings but also as a source of many implied nuances of the nature of his relationships with his contemporary Sufis. At the very basis of writing his *Rasāʾil* lies Junayd's doctrine, according to which the secret Sufi theories should be kept as the elect's estate. The discourse of this work leaves no doubt that Junayd addressed it to those who he was sure would understand it. His *Rasāʾil* are by all means 'the personal documents of a great mystic of the third century A.H.', as Abdel-Kader phrases it.[8]

[7] See Anṣārī Haravī, *Ṭabaqāt al-ṣūfiyya*, 49; Jāmī, *Nafaḥāt al-uns*, 74.

[8] Ali Hassan Abdel-Kader, *The Life, Personality and Writings of al-Junayd: A Study of a Third/Ninth Century Mystic with an Edition and Translation of His Writings* (London: Luzac & Company, 1962), *introduction*, xvii.

Throughout his *Rasā'il* as well as in the fragments of his sayings that are scattered in different sources, Junayd presents his life project: to formulate the pragmatic boundaries of *taṣawwuf* that guarantee the Sufis become consensually acclaimed when they take upon themselves to act within these boundaries in their communal lives. In one of his *Rasā'il*, he appears to urge the Sufis to exercise caution in association with others, to keep their distance and to conceal their own inner states from others' eyes (*al-ḥadhar wa l-taqiyya*).[9] On another occasion, Junayd calls on his fellows to keep themselves in the celebrated situation of 'strength (*quwwa*), stability (*tamkīn*), and tranquillity (*hudū'*)'.[10]

It seems most likely that Junayd looked forward to establishing contacts with Sufis of the eastern parts of the Muslim world of his time in the same way he used to do with his contemporary Sufis of Syria and Iraq. It is probable that, after the great preacher and mystic of Rayy, Yaḥyā b. Mu'ādh al-Rāzī (d. 258/872) left Baghdad after a short visit, the young Junayd decided to send him a very gloomy letter. Fragments of this letter are preserved in Junayd's *Rasā'il* while others appear in Sarrāj's *Luma'*.[11]

The reader of the two texts notices Junayd's clear attempt to boast before the elder sheikh of Rayy of his generous knowledge of Sufi terminology and his genius writing talents. Yaḥyā, as Christopher Melchert points out, might be seen as either an ascetic or a mystic, based on his sayings, advice and teachings.[12] He was a truly honourable preacher and *zāhid* according to Sulamī. Meanwhile, some of the sayings ascribed to him in the latter's *Ṭabaqāt* refer to the knower of God (*'ārif*) parallel to the ascetic (*zāhid*), while in one saying he refers clearly to the category of *mutaṣawwifa*.[13] My suggestion to deduce Junayd's boasting tone from the traces of his original letter to Yaḥyā b. Mu'ādh becomes more interesting if the references to this letter are cross-checked with one anecdote that appears in the works of the non-Sufi historians al-Khaṭīb al-Baghdādī and Ibn Khillikān. Both authors tell that, during one of the sessions that Yaḥyā b. Mu'ādh held in Baghdad, Junayd rose to speak, and Yaḥyā said to him: 'Keep silent, O sheep! Who are you to speak when

9 See Junayd, *Rasā'il*, in Abdel-Kader, *Junayd*, Arabic text, 19.

10 Ibid., 1.

11 See ibid., 2; Cf. Sarrāj, *Luma'*, 358.

12 See Christopher Melchert, 'The Transition from Asceticism to Mysticism at the Middle of the Ninth Century C.E.', *Studia Islamica*, 83 (1996), 57–58.

13 See Sulamī, *Ṭabaqāt*, 102, 104.

true men speak?' *(uskut yā kharūf! mā laka wa-l-kalām idhā takallam al-nās?)*.[14] The biography of Yaḥyā b. Muʿādh in Sulamī's *Ṭabaqāt* does not include any references to his visit to Baghdad. At one point in *Lumaʿ*, Sarrāj refers to Yaḥyā b. Muʿādh as the one who used to wear woollen and worn-out clothes in his early years; however, later in life, he was said to have turned to wearing silk. Sarrāj went on to tell that, when Abū Yazīd al-Basṭāmī was told that Yaḥyā used to wear silk, he made the following comment: 'O poor Yaḥyā! He was not able to bear patiently (*lam yaṣbir*) what is inferior, thereby how will he be able to bear patiently what is superior?'[15] This story is narrated in a context where contentment with one garment only in one's daily life was highly praised in the eyes of the *ṣūfiyya*. The names of both Junayd and his celebrated disciple Jaʿfar al-Khuldī appear as the main representatives of this line, while the name of Abū Ḥafṣ al-Ḥaddād al-Naysābūrī appears in the same place as the representative of the group of Sufis who acted outside the boundaries of *ṣūfiyya*. Yaḥyā b. Muʿādh is cited to have worn silk and wool since the true Sufi in his eyes does not pay any attention to what he wears. This notion fits well with the idea that Yaḥyā b. Muʿādh appears in the sources to have emphasized hope over fear and, therefore, provoked the rebuke of his Sufi contemporaries.[16] Is it possible, then, that Basṭāmī's criticism of Yaḥyā b. Muʿādh was an outcome of Sarrāj's attempt to demonstrate the negative approach of Junayd and his close circle of disciples to Yaḥyā and his spiritual world view? In other words, would it be possible to suggest that, by narrating Basṭāmī's critical statement, Sarrāj sought to demonstrate Junayd's approach towards Yaḥyā and his renunciatory life? It is probable that Yaḥyā, who was known for undertaking a strict life of renunciation in the history of early Sufism, became here a voluptuary man in the way Junayd and his milieu chose to conceive his personality and religiosity.

In addition to Yaḥyā, Junayd sent a letter to another mystic of Rayy, Yūsuf b. al-Ḥusayn. It is evident that this letter was one among a series of correspondence between Junayd and this figure, as different sources state. While Abdel-Kader refers in some detail to the relationship between Junayd and Yūsuf b. al-Ḥusayn, who was at that period a distinguished

[14] The English translation is provided by Abdel-Kader in: Abdel-Kader, *Junayd*, English part, 31. See also Baghdādī, *Taʾrīkh baghdād*, vol. 16, 306; Ibn Khillikān, *Wafayāt al-aʿyān*, vol. 6, 166.

[15] Sarrāj, *Lumaʿ*, 188.

[16] See most recently: Christian Lange, *Paradise and Hell in Islamic Traditions* (New York: Cambridge University Press, 2016), 223 and footnote 27.

mystic of Rayy and the region of *Jibāl*.[17] However, Abdel-Kader does not refer to the content of these correspondence or the way in which they imply interpersonal conflicts and tensions. It is most probable that the one who initiated this controversial correspondence was Junayd and that Yūsuf b. al-Ḥusayn's letter, or even numerous letters to Junayd, came in response. By the end of Junayd's letter, he clearly indicates that he initiated the correspondence: '*Bada'tuka bi-kitābī.*'[18] I consider it more probable that Junayd, by initiating such correspondence, aspired to consolidate his contacts with contemporary Sufis in the eastern territories of the Islamic world and to integrate them under the umbrella of the high Sufi ethos that he wanted to establish and transmit. Abū Nuʿaym al-Iṣfahānī preserves a very short passage from one of Ibn al-Ḥusayn's letters to Junayd. Though there is no evidence to any theoretical controversy, it is likely that this passage was taken from a long-missing letter in which Yūsuf b. al-Ḥusayn defended himself against the accusations of heresy (*zandaqa*) addressed to him by the people of Rayy, alongside a possible controversial approach of the Baghdadi Sufis whom Junayd represented. A detailed discussion of what appears to be this missing letter from Yūsuf b. al-Ḥusayn will be presented below. Qushayrī indicates that Ibn al-Ḥusayn wrote to Junayd and recommended that he keeps himself away from 'tasting his lower soul's flavour' because 'by doing so he will not obtain any goodness forever'.[19] This statement could have been a rebuke of the covert letter of the great master of Baghdad and its arrogant tone, and it is also found in the same letter that I will discuss hereinafter.

Muḥammad Muṣṭafā in his *Tāj al-ʿārifīn* from 1987 undertook the endeavour of republishing Junayd's previously known works, along with bringing to light other unknown works of the great master of Baghdad as well as relevant letters that were addressed to him. Among those letters, two were allegedly composed by Yūsuf b. al-Ḥusayn in response to Junayd's aforementioned letter to him.[20]

The first among these two letters begins with a tone that is fraught with admonition. Immediately after praising his addressee, Ibn al-Ḥusayn writes:

[17] See Abdel-Kader, *Junayd*, 33.

[18] Junayd, *Rasāʾil*, Arabic text, 30. Cf. Sarrāj, *Lumaʿ*, 239.

[19] Qushayrī, *Risāla*, 24.

[20] See Junayd, *Rasāʾil wa-rudūd*, in *Tāj al-ʿārifīn: Dirāsāt wa-nuṣūṣ manshūra wa-ghayr manshūra*, ed. by Muḥammad Muṣṭafā (Cairo: Dār al-Ṭibāʿa al-Muḥammadiyya, 1987), 338–351.

You preached to me and fulfilled your duty of advice perfectly (*wa'azta fa-bālaghta*) [. . .] and you beat me and caused me pain (*ḍarabta fa-awja'ta*). You followed the example of the great prophets by committing yourself to leniency while talking to people and advising them, so that during reading your letter I was able to imagine Moses and Aaron, both of whom God asked to be lenient [with Pharaoh!]. It was difficult for me to imagine myself in Pharaoh's position, being the one who you were diligent to treat him leniently, since the one who needs to be treated leniently is either the insolent (*al-'ātī*) or the ignorant (*al-jāhil*) or even the boy (*al-ṣabī*)![21]

It is clear from this passage that Yūsuf b. al-Ḥusayn wanted to lash out at his addressee and defend himself against the arrogant and patronizing tone of the original letter that had been sent to him. While Ibn al-Ḥusayn compares his addressee to the prophets, those who chose leniency while guiding their people down the path of truth and belief, he insists that, like all prophets, his addressee is not able to guide anyone alone since no one other than God is capable of guiding people: 'All prophets had the divine mission; however, they did not have the authority for divine guidance' (*malakū al-risāla, wa-lam yamlukū al-hidāya*).[22]

Immediately, after this implied injury, Ibn al-Ḥusayn makes use of different rhetoric strategies to preserve a certain degree of restraint and to refrain from sliding into plainly personal dispute. The use of phrases like 'O my brother and delight of the eye' (*akhī wa-qurrat 'aynī*), 'my dear' (*'azīzī*) and 'my beloved' (*ḥabībī*) is one such strategy. Another strategy is the emphasis on the idea that this addressee sought to support him through his sincere advice and that he recruited leniency and mildness in order to do so. Ibn al-Ḥusayn refers in his letter to some of the requirements that his addressee asked him to follow. The text reads as follows:

Oh my dear. You mentioned [in your letter!] that what motivated you to write to me was the need you felt to urge me to avoid associating with people who are not of my own kind (*an ajtanib mujālasat ghayr abnā' jinsī*). You sought to express this idea and, thereby, you chose to do that gently and leniently (*rafaqta wa-talaṭṭafta*).[23]

In spite of the tone of admonition in the first part of the letter, the latter part of the text relies heavenly on apologies, self-blame and acknowledg-ment of the author's inferiority in comparison with the elevated position of his addressee. He blames himself for acting in a way that did not conform with the general codes of behaviour imposed by his addressee;

21 Ibid., 339–340. 22 Ibid., 341. 23 Ibid., 342.

however, he still does not seek to receive any public praise by showing people his self-blame: 'I seek refuge with God of being adorned with self-blame' (*a'ūdhu bi-llāh min al-tazayyun bi-lawm al-nafs*).[24] He insists that his addressee's requirements were completely sincere and that he himself does not deserve the title 'one of the most pious at his age', which was originally mentioned by his addressee in his former letter. Ibn al-Ḥusayn presents here very sophisticated *malāmatī* teachings. As I will show in the course of Chapter 8, he himself had strong ties with Abū Turāb al-Nakhshabī (d. 245/859), whose impact on the Khurāsānian founders of *malāmatiyya* school is commonly known. According to *malāmatī* teachings, good deeds should be concealed as a means to avoid self-conceit. Self-blame is considered one good deed, and thereby it should be completely concealed from people's eyes. When it is concealed, the mystic, according to Ibn al-Ḥusayn's doctrinal system, should not feel any satisfaction with the very act of concealing. A satisfaction of this type might be another trigger for self-conceit.

Interestingly, immediately after criticizing self-conceit and the act of 'being adorned (*tazayyun*) with self-blame', Ibn al-Ḥusayn refers to his addressee using the phrase '*zayyantanī bi-kitābika*' (you adorned me with your letter).[25] It might be possible to understand this usage as an implied criticism by the author of his addressee's tendency of showing off by initiating the correspondence with him as well as with many other figures of his time. Ibn al-Ḥusayn, rather, writes that if he could enjoy a situation of sobriety (*law ṣādafta himma mutayaqqiẓa*) like his addressee, he would then completely benefit from the instructions and advice provided in his former letter to him; however, sobriety is not for him. He goes on to indicate that he chose to use his addressee's style of writing: 'Oh my beloved! I addressed you by using the same language that you had already used' (*ḥabībī; bi-lisānika khāṭaabtuka*). This style combines tongue lashing, haughtiness and lenient discourse at once. These are the components of Ibn al-Ḥusayn's letter as well. Ibn al-Ḥusayn tells his addressee that he benefitted from his strategies of writing since Ibn al-Husayn and his addressee had corresponded frequently in the past: 'I benefitted from your letters in the past and present.'[26]

Towards the end of the letter, Ibn al-Ḥusayn praises his addressee, using expressions like 'you are one of the last remains of the recluses (*nussāk*)', and 'you are the undisputed leader of the wise men and the

[24] Ibid., 345. [25] Ibid. [26] Ibid.

knowers of God' (*sayyid al-ḥukamāʾ wa-l-ʿārifīn*).[27] After this praise, the author makes the following unclear statement:

I had no doubt that some of the recluses (*nussāk*) and those who tend to renunciation (*al-māʾilīn ilā al-taqallul*) who visited you from my region asked me to scale up (*istazādūnā*). By my life (*la-ʿamrī*)! Am I able to be in the position of the one who is urged to scale up (*mawḍiʿ al-mustazād*)?.[28]

For the editor of *Tāj al-ʿārifīn*, this passage leaves the impression that a group of people insulted Junayd in Ibn al-Ḥusayn's presence, and that is why the latter responds to their behaviour here.[29] This interpretation is not convincing in fact. The verb *istazādūnā* in the text carries the meaning of 'asked us to augment or to scale up something'. I think Ibn al-Ḥusayn probably refers here to the controversy that he had been involved in with the group of renunciants in his homeland *Rayy*. It appears that those could not bear Ibn al-Ḥusayn's *malāmatī* behaviour, according to which he used not to show any of his renunciatory exercises and austerities in public.[30] It seems most likely that they asked him to show his commitment to Muslim supererogatory performances and that he refused to do so. He goes on to write that it is impossible to satisfy everyone and that the best thing to do is to purify one's inner truth so that God, in response, will purify his ties with all people.

The style of the second letter published by Muṣṭafā is similar to the aforementioned response of Yāsuf b. al-Ḥusayn. Some of its passages appear in Sulamī's *Ṭabaqāt* and Iṣfahānī's *Ḥilyat al-awliyāʾ*. This letter is shorter than the first, and its language is vaguer. In one interesting passage, the author writes:

Oh my dear. You asked me to avoid writing to you in an irrational language (*hadhayān*) as well as to avoid the talk of the insane (*kalām al-maʿtūh*) or the talk of the one who suffers from pleurisy (*mubarsam*). [...] I am certain that you believe that man is completely controlled by God's predestination (*qaḍāʾ*) and not by his own will (*ʿazmihi*).[31]

It appears that Ibn al-Ḥusayn felt a crucial need to justify his passionate language that might be conceived in the eyes of the addressee as a clear expression of intoxication and spiritual insanity. The latter, as the text reads, had already tried to convince Ibn al-Ḥusayn to avoid this form of

[27] Ibid., 346. [28] Ibid. [29] See ibid., footnote 5.

[30] See a detailed reference to Ibn al-Ḥusayn's relationships with the *zuhhād* of Rayy is in Chapter 8.

[31] Junayd, *Rasāʾil wa-rudūd*, 349–350.

writing or even to avoid the particular mode of piety which is implied in this form of writing.

Junayd's haughty tone is deduced from his letter to an unknown personality who, as the text reads, sent Junayd a letter first in which he described the secret Sufi science. As a response, Junayd explains to him in a letter that what he already described was nothing but an outcome of illusion or misunderstanding (*tawahhum*).[32] It is not a high state of grace as the person who described it thought but, rather, an expression of an intermediate state between two other states (*wāsiṭa bayn ḥālayn*). What Junayd wants to say here is that the spiritual state that this man was proud to share with Junayd is to be seen as the second state that follows the starting point and precedes the highest and ultimate state. At the very end of this letter, Junayd shows a distinguished degree of pragmatism and indulgence while referring to the person to whom he wrote his letter by saying: 'You are indeed one of my close companions; you share in my longings and are one of the leaders of my fellowship. You are of the friends of the heart for whom my devotion is sincere.'[33] Junayd, on the one hand, disparages the spiritual achievement on this man, while, on the other hand, celebrates this man's position as one of the persons granted the prestige of being one of Junayd's close companions.

Junayd's letter to ʿAmr b. ʿUthmān al-Makkī is very interesting. It is the longest letter among Junayd's *Rasāʾil*. Junayd indicates in the body of the letter that he wrote it as a response to someone who had asked him to define the states of those who achieved the ultimate destination of the path of truth (*naʿt al-muḥaqqaqīn*).[34] It might be possible that Junayd had in mind the idea of addressing the letter with all the issues it contains to ʿAmr b. ʿUthmān without being asked to do so by anyone. He, most likely, intended to send a particular message to this particular personality. Dhahabī in his *Siyar* indicates that:

> ʿAmr b. ʿUthmān al-Makkī was one of the honourable masters of jurisprudence, and when he was appointed to the position of *qāḍī* of the city of Jeddah, Junayd abandoned his association (*hajarahu al-Junayd*). He [ʿAmr b. ʿUthmān!] used to dispraise Ḥallāj.[35]

Unfortunately, we are unable to determine when Junayd decided to send this letter to Makkī and what exactly the surrounding circumstances

32 Junayd, *Rasāʾil*, 5.

33 Ibid., 6. The English translation here is of Abdel-Kader in Abdel-Kader, *Junayd*, 127.

34 See Junayd, *Rasāʾil*, 23–24.

35 Dhahabī, *Siyar*, vol. 14, 58.

were. We only have the main body of the long letter in which Junayd indicates aspects of his personal approach towards Makkī and his Sufi fellows in general alongside other fragments in Sarrāj's *Luma'* that might contribute to our attempt to reconstruct the historical and interpersonal context of this letter.

Junayd chooses to adopt a narrative style in this letter. He imagines a dialogue between two characters: the character of a scholar (*'ālim*) and the character of a wise man (*ḥakīm*). The scholar, according to Junayd, 'donned the outward decoration of learning' (*labisa min al-'ilm ẓāhir ḥilyatihi*).[36] The wise man tries to instruct the scholar how to move on from the stage of the outward science to the exalted stage of the inward science and how to abandon the earthy and material motivations for religious attainments for another type of motivation that is completely free of the greed for social fame and earthy benefits. It is here that Junayd accuses Muslim religious scholars, jurisprudents, judges and theologians of their greed for money, leadership and fame by their engagements in religious science. It seems that the latter notion, that is his critique against scholars' greed for wealth, was very important for him since it was at this point that he chose to quote several *Qur'ān*ic verses in order to justify his view.[37] Junayd also assails the tendency of religious scholars to flatter statesmen as a means to obtain authority and influence.[38] The question that should be raised here is as follows: Why does Junayd refer to such issues in the framework of this letter in particular? Is it possible that he adopts a strategy of presenting his teachings and critical views in the framework of his correspondence in general and regardless of who the addressee is? Could his notions here, in the letter he addresses to 'Amr b. 'Uthmān al-Makkī, be one example of this strategy? I argue that this is not necessarily true and that Junayd, through his letter to Makkī, intended to attack mainly those religious scholars who occupied the position of *qāḍī* and earned a livelihood from the state. Makkī, in fact, was one of those. Junayd urges his addressee to leave his engagement in jurisprudence and *ta'wīl* (literally means 'going back to the origins' and technically means the interpretation of sacred sources).[39] The latter might have implied, according to Junayd, the commitment to academic and intellectual conduct in attaining a religious mode of life. Working in

[36] Junayd, *Rasā'il*, 8. [37] See ibid., 14. [38] See ibid., 16.

[39] See e.g., John Renard, *Historical Dictionary of Sufism* (Historical Dictionaries of Religions, Philosophies, and Movements, No. 58) (Lanham, Md., Toronto and Oxford: The Scarecrow Press, 2005), 83.

jurisprudence, accordingly, cannot lead man to the inner life with God. The shift from the form of commitment to religious scholarship towards an essentially different form of commitment to Sufi discipleship and training is compared to the quest of the sick for medication.[40]

Towards the end of the letter, Junayd presents in great detail his practical teachings of initiating the Sufi path, which begins with 'fixing the intention' (*iṣlāḥ al-niyya*), progressing to caution and concealing one's inner life from public (*ḥadhar wa-taqiyya*), keeping silence, abstaining from associating with others and remaining committed to the principle of ordering good and prohibiting evil (*al-amr bi-l-maʿrūf wa-l-nahī ʿan al-munkar*).[41] Based on these teachings, a complete situation of seclusion is not necessarily needed. A certain group of Sufis, Junayd asserts, are still allowed to associate in public spheres by spreading morality (*faḍīla*) and religious science on the condition that this act is carried out with sincerity and purity. Junayd insists on the crucial need for each Muslim to keep loyalty to the high ideal of *jamāʿa,* that is, living and acting within the boundaries of one's community, both his close Sufi community and his wider Muslim community. This is, according to him, a matter of necessity. A true Sufi 'should not pull out one hand from his *jamāʿa*' (*lā yanziʿ yadan min jamāʿa*). He, furthermore, needs to be committed to the *sunna*, to abstain from both religious innovation (*bidʿa*) and theological debate and to avoid slandering the rulers and revolting against them. Conciliation and moderation are key concepts: '*mutawassiṭ bi-jamīʿ al-madhāhib*.' By means of these techniques, each Sufi could protect himself and gain an honourable place within the boundaries of Muslim consensus (*ijmāʿ*) in a way similar to that of Junayd himself.

Sarrāj at one point in his *Lumaʿ* writes:

> ʿAmr b. ʿUthmān al-Makkī sent a letter to the Sufi community (*jamāʿat al-ṣūfiyya*) of Baghdad. This letter reads: 'You will not reach to the truth of the absolute Truth, until you pass that hidden track and travel along those dangerous deserts.' Junayd, who attended the Sufi session where Makkī's letter was read together with Shiblī and Jurayrī [d. 311/923–92!], said: 'I wish I knew who will be able to enter that tracks and deserts.'[42]

This passage leaves the impression that correspondence was a well-known fashion among early Sufis and that through this type of contact they used to respond to their counterparts who lived and acted in different and faraway regions of the Muslim world. It is a pity that the sources

[40] See Junayd, *Rasāʾil*, 18. [41] See ibid., 19–20. [42] Sarrāj, *Lumaʿ*, 233.

provide us only with fragments taken from the original complete letters. As for the previously quoted passage from *Luma'*, we do not have enough information to determine when Makkī wrote this letter and sent it to the Sufis of Baghdad, after his appointment to the formal position of *qāḍī* or prior to it. We do not know, further, whether Junayd's letter to Makkī, the long one that we are discussing here, followed that of Makkī's to the Sufis of Baghdad or preceded it. What we might see here is that the nuances and tone that could be derived from the available fragments of the two original letters indicate a tense interrelationship between the two figures, Junayd and Makkī. Elsewhere in *Luma'*, interestingly, Junayd is quoted to have described the Sufis of Khurāsān as 'men of hearts' (*aṣḥāb qulūb*).[43] This statement should be understood as Junayd's way to underestimate the Sufis of Khurāsan. On the same occasion, Junayd is quoted as saying that the one who reaches to the truth of knowledge passes all states and situations (*ya'bur al-aḥwāl wa-l-maqāmāt*).[44] The Sufi whose heart controls him, like in the case of the Khurāsānian Sufis according to Junayd, is not capable of behaving and speaking as a reasonable man or guiding others along the path. This statement suits the general frame of Junayd's teachings, and, thereby, it is possible to consider it authentic.

In other letters, Junayd frequently urges his fellow Sufis to abandon their utilitarian relationships with rulers and men of authority. In his letter to Abū Isḥāq al-Māristānī (d. 309/921–922)[45] which does not appear in Abdel-Kader's edition of *Rasā'il*, he uses a very severe tone of blame, admonition and condemnation. Māristānī himself was a member of the Baghdadi *ṣūfiyya*, and early hagiographers indicate that Junayd adopted him as his close spiritual brother.[46] Junayd explicitly accuses his addressee of 'being a slave for other slaves of this world'[47] and embarrasses him for being a religious man with a tendency towards vain pleasures of this world: 'O my dear brother! Cast down your heart's eyes away from them [the people of this world!], and protect your conscience from being their associate and friend.' By the end of the letter, Junayd asks his addressee to excuse him for his severe criticism.[48] Junayd's criticism

[43] Sarrāj, *Luma'*, 359. [44] Ibid.

[45] Abū Isḥāq Ibrāhīm b. Aḥmad al-Māristānī, a contemporary of Junayd. See references to him in Abū Khalaf al-Ṭabarī, *Salwat al-'ārifīn*, 97, 509.

[46] See Baghdādī, *Ta'rīkh Baghdād* (the biography of Ibrāhīm b. Aḥmad); Iṣfahānī, *Ḥilyat al-awliyā'*, vol. 10, 353 (*'kāna al-Junayd lahu mu'ākhiyan'*).

[47] See this letter in Su'ād al-Ḥakīm's edition of *Tāj al-'ārifīn al-Junayd al-Baghdādī: al-a'māl al-kāmila* (Cairo: Dār al-Shurūq, 2004), 290.

[48] Ibid., 292.

against some of his contemporaries' flattery of men of authority is also documented through other fragments that Abū Nuʿaym al-Iṣfahānī preserves in his *Ḥilya*.[49]

Junayd's custom of criticizing his contemporaries appears very frequently throughout his *Rasāʾil* as well as in the statements and fragments of other letters ascribed to him and preserved by Sarrāj. He criticizes Shiblī and Basṭāmī. While Shiblī was considered in Junayd's eyes as a Sufi who 'was stopped in his place' (*ūqifa fī makānihi*),[50] Basṭāmī was described as the one who 'did not manage to leave the starting point' (*lam yakhruj min ḥāl al-bidāya*).[51] On another occasion, Junayd appears to blame Shiblī and even invoke God against him for disseminating the Sufi science in public.[52] Meanwhile, we should keep in mind that, in spite of this critical tone, Junayd was the major representative of the Baghdadi group of *ṣūfiyya* who endeavoured to explain the ecstatic utterances (*shaṭaḥāt*) of both Shiblī and Basṭāmī. His detailed commentaries of the most 'problematic' and esoteric utterances of the latter leave no doubt that besides, or in spite of, his personal critique against the Sufis of ecstasy, Junayd's pragmatism moved him to grant them a moderate portrayal by supporting their statements with his own reservations and explanations. By doing so, Junayd indeed did a remarkable favour to these figures: He contributed to saving their images, which had been seriously threatened by their own controversial statements and strange codes of behaviour. Due to Junayd's lenient approach towards Shiblī, among other reasons and motivations, Sarrāj chose to make serious efforts to portray Shiblī as a moderate Sufi completely committed to Islamic duties and mores. At one point in *Lumaʿ*, for instance, Jaʿfar al-Khuldī tells that he met Shiblī's close disciple who had remained with his master during the latter's dying moments. Shiblī's disciple told Jaʿfar that when his master lost his ability to speak as he was drawing his last breath, he called for his assistance in performing ablution. When this disciple forgot to wash his master's beard in those moments, Shiblī grasped his disciple's hands and brought them into his own beard to wash it. It was

[49] See Iṣfahānī, *Ḥilyat al-awliyāʾ*, vol. 10, 279, 286.
[50] Sarrāj, *Lumaʿ*, 404.
[51] Ibid., 397.
[52] See Mustamlī Bukhārī, *Sharḥ kitāb al-taʿarruf*, vol. 1, 216. What is narrated here is that Shiblī replied in a very rude manner to Junayd, and that is why Mustamī Bukhārī chose to provide his own interpretation for Shiblī's statement (see ibid., 216–217). On a later occasion in the same work, Shiblī himself asks God to explain to him why Ḥallāj was executed, and God told him that this occurred since 'We granted him [Ḥallāj!] one of Our secrets and he disseminated it in public!' (ibid., 218–219).

told that Ja'far was extremely astonished to hear that there was a Sufi who was not ready to abandon even one small detail in the Muslim ritual of ablution, not even on his last breath.[53]

Junayd's pragmatism motivated him to pass over his personal criticism for the sake of achieving unity with his contemporary Sufis under the high Sufi ethos that he and his circle of Baghdadi *ṣūfiyya* founded. This type of defence that Basṭāmī and Shiblī was granted by a charismatic personality like Junayd, as well as the similar defence that other figures like Abū Bakr al-Wāsiṭī were granted by Sarrāj the author of *Luma'*,[54] was crucial in the process of establishing the boundaries of the Sufi ethos, under which all these figures, regardless of their different doctrines and controversial statements, came to be united. This unity was the ultimate destination for Junayd. As I will show in Chapter 6, Niffarī differs from other controversial figures of early Sufism in the fact that he most likely intended to detach himself from the *ṣūfiyya*, and that is why none of the charismatic Sufi personalities of his time defended his statements or attempted to moderate the way his image was conceived in public.

Sarrāj devotes a separate section in his work to what he calls '*ṣudūr al-kutub wa-l-rasā'il*'. He refers here to the opening sections of Sufi correspondence and letters. A remarkable portion in this section is given to Junayd and his opening sections. The rationale behind preserving these texts in Sarrāj's view is to lead readers to contemplate the words that Sufi masters chose to put at the very beginning of their letters and to recognize the implied significance behind them.[55] The data brought about here make a strong impression that Junayd had a wide network of contacts made up of his contemporaries and that he was very active in addressing them through letters as well as in trying to unite them under the umbrella of one homogenous and pragmatic Sufi ethos that matches the general frame of his own doctrinal system. In many instances, the structural and thematic makeup of what is available today from the original correspondence leads us to think that it was Junayd who initiated contact and that the letters that he received from certain personalities came in response. In some cases, furthermore, the initiation undertaken by Junayd in a form of a letter to one of his colleagues could provoke a series of letters between the two. This was the case of Junayd's correspondence with Yūsuf b. al-Ḥusayn.

[53] See Sarrāj, *Luma'*, 104.
[54] See Sarrāj's defence on Wāsiṭī in: Sarrāj, *Ṣuḥuf min kitāb al-luma'*, 12–16.
[55] See Sarrāj, *Luma'*, 243.

Fragments of an original longer letter that Abū al-Ḥusayn al-Nūrī sent to Junayd in *Luma*ʿ might imply that Junayd was the one who first wrote to his controversial counterpart Nūrī.[56] The latter is one of the early Sufi personalities Sarrāj refers to in much detail in his treatment of Sufis who were targets of persecution and accusations of heresy during the early phase. It is here that the author of *Luma*ʿ gathers many of the problematic sayings of Nūrī. He, for instance, does not hesitate to mention that Nūrī, once he heard the call for prayer, said, 'It is the thrust of the mark of death' or that when he once heard the barking of dogs, he said: 'Here I am at Your service!' (*labbayka*!).[57] Meanwhile, Sarrāj was very eager to describe Nūrī's attempts to moderate the shocking nature of his words as well as to indicate his own attempts to do so. In Sarrāj's words, Abū al-Ḥusayn al-Nūrī is 'one of the men of ecstasy' (*min al-wājidīn*) and 'he used to ladle from a giant sea' (*kāna yaghrif min baḥr kabīr*).[58] Though Junayd does not appear in the text of *Luma*ʿ to have written any commentary to Nūrī's ecstatic utterances, as he did in the cases of Basṭāmī and Shiblī, it might be possible that he tried to monitor Nūrī's strange behaviour through correspondence, and this is why I suggested that the abovementioned reference to Nūrī's letter to Junayd followed a previous letter from Junayd to Nūrī. Interestingly, somewhere else in *Luma*ʿ, the following anecdote appears:

> Ibn ʿAṭāʾ told that he heard Abū al-Ḥusayn al-Nūrī saying: 'I yearned to be granted with the ability to perform *karāmāt* [supernatural wonders!]. I took a cane from a group of boys, and I seated myself between two watercrafts and applied to God by saying: "By Your Majesty! (*wa-ʿizzatika!*) If You do not take out to me a fish that weighs three rotls, then I will sink myself." Nūrī went on to say: "A fish that weighs three rotls came out to me from the water."'[59]

Hellmut Ritter combines Nūrī's behaviour here with similar anecdotes about early Sufis who were affected by their deep state of intimacy with God to a degree that motivated them to strife with Him or to challenge Him through their demands.[60] Turning back again to Nūrī and Junayd, Sarrāj states that, when the anecdote reached Junayd, he commented: 'Nūrī was worthy of getting a snake that stings him' (*kāna ḥukmuhu an*

[56] On Abū al-Ḥasan al-Nūrī and the nature of his piety, see: P. Nwyia, 'Textes Mystiques Inédits d'Abū al-Ḥasan al-Nūrī', *Mélanges de L'Universitat St-Joseph*, vol. 44 (1968), 117–120.

[57] Sarrāj, *Ṣuḥuf min kitāb al-luma*ʿ, 5.

[58] Ibid., 6.

[59] Sarrāj, *Luma*ʿ, 327. Cf. ibid., 325.

[60] See Hellmut Ritter, 'Muslim Mystic's Strife with God', *Oriens*, 5 (1952), 1–16.

yakhruj lahu afʿā taldaghuhu). While Junayd's statement here is without a doubt a severe criticism of Nūrī's audacity and impudence, Sarrāj, in his turn, interferes and imposes his own way of understanding Junayd's comment: 'He [that is Junayd!] means that if a snake stung Nūrī this would be more beneficial for him, since the appearance of a fish implies a temptation, while the snake's sting implies purification (*taṭhīr*) and atonement (*kaffāra*).'[61] In spite of Sarrāj's note, the criticism of Junayd, in fact, could not be ignored.

Junayd was pragmatic. In spite of the fact that he had a lot of personal criticism for some of his companions and contemporaries, he tried to put aside this criticism and rise above the interpersonal disputes he most probably had with many Sufi personalities. He spared no effort to indulge those who showed problematic behaviour in public or made controversial statements. Junayd, furthermore, suggested a strategy of facilitation and leniency with new initiates to the Sufi path, an interesting topic by itself which will be discussed in detail. Junayd's pragmatism is best manifested in his attempts to moderate the ecstatic utterances, which implies, at the very essence, his disdain of all interpersonal differences and his commitment to the general interests of the Sufi community. Junayd's greatness lies for the most part in his ability to separate his personal approaches from the common interests of all Sufis under the united umbrella of the Sufi community (*jamāʿat al-ṣūfiyya*). He urged the Sufis of his time to keep their hands within the boundaries of *jamāʿa*, to comply with all religious duties, to show a great extent of respect for Muslim law and to keep their Sufi knowledge away from people's eyes. His letters were, in my view, a very effective instrument to bridge the gaps and overcome the controversies between the Sufis themselves, as well as to achieve a sort of a unity, on general terms at least, among the *ṣūfiyya*.

The body of ecstatic utterances and unusual behaviour of certain Sufis would have led to the expulsion of Sufis from within the boundaries of the legal forms of Islam had Junayd and other moderate Sufi thinkers not written their own commentaries of the most problematic components of that body.[62] Meanwhile, this defence provided by Junayd and later on by Sarrāj and others, to ecstatic Sufis like Nūrī, did not lack advantages that these defenders themselves could enjoy: It helped them establish a type of

[61] Sarrāj, *Lumaʿ*, 327.

[62] Melchert wrote that Junayd converted Basṭāmī's mysticism into 'something unthreatening to ascetics'. See Melchert, *Transition from Asceticism to Mysticism*, 66. See also Avery, *Shiblī*, 99.

a monopoly in the hands of the Baghdadi *ṣūfiyya,* the representatives of the high Sufi ethos, upon the whole matrix of Sufis around the world of Islam. This monopoly implies an ultimate authority to approve or reject certain codes of behaviour or statements made by their contemporary Sufis, wherever they live and act. By creating the boundaries of the Sufi ethos and the main body of accepted Sufi teachings and practices, the Baghdadi *ṣūfiyya*, and later Sufi authors who complied with their general line of Sufi piety, managed to concentrate a kind of monopoly in the hands of Junayd, his circle and successors. It is interesting, for instance, to rely on the following fragment in *Luma*ʿ to understand what a Sufi monopoly could look like: Sarrāj notes that 'Baghdadi Sufis used to supervise the inner states of their beginner companions due to their high spiritual knowledge. Those masters were not allowed to forgive those companions in case that the latter overstepped all bounds and pretended the states of others' (*wa-lā yajūz lahum an yusāmiḥūhum idhā jāwazū ḥudūdahum wa-iddāʿū ḥāl ghayrihim*).[63] These masters (*mashāyikh* in Sarrāj's words) enjoyed a great deal of authority over their companions. They could rebuke their companions in the event the latter showed certain codes of behaviour that did not correspond with the codes that the masters themselves had introduced and, in certain cases, tried to impose. At another part in *Luma*ʿ, it was Jaʿfar al-Khuldī again who told that a Khurāsānian man entered a session of Junayd in Baghdad. This man asked Junayd: 'When do the one who praises a person and that one who dispraises him come to be equal in the eyes of that person?' One of the attendees of Junayd's session replied: 'When that person is introduced to the hospital and becomes enchained with two handcuffs' (*idhā udkhila al-māristān wa-quyyida bi-qaydayn*). Junayd, in response, did not hesitate to ask this anonymous companion not to interfere since the matter was none of his business. Afterwards, Junayd turned to the man of Khurāsān and told him his level-headed definition of the spiritual state in which that man was interested: 'O my beloved (*yā ḥabībī*)! When a person knows and becomes certain of the fact that he himself is created.'[64] It seems probable that the anonymous companion who tried to reply to the Khurāsānian man's question before the great master of Baghdad was none other than Shiblī. At one previous point of *Luma*ʿ, the famous episode of Shiblī's friends visiting him in the hospital (*māristān*) is introduced. While narrating the episode, Sarrāj made use of the same

[63] Sarrāj, *Luma*ʿ, 289–290. [64] Ibid., 295.

statement that appeared in the aforementioned reply of Junayd's companion to the Khurāsānian man: 'When Shiblī was introduced to the hospital and became enchained, his friends came to visit him.'[65] Thereby, in spite of the fact that Junayd's mode of piety was different from that of Shiblī, Junayd allowed the young Sufi with an apparent insanity to associate with him. However, Junayd was absolutely unable, as *Luma*''s fragments tell, to allow Shiblī to leave his prints on the Sufi ethos he sought to consolidate and distribute. In several places in *Luma*', Junayd expresses his concern towards Shiblī's rashness and passionate statements.[66]

By using the term *leniency*, we refer to several characteristics of Junayd's approach towards his Sufi contemporaries, including his overall acceptance of Sufis whose teachings demonstrate disparate modes of piety, even those who were known as ecstatic and passionate, as the previous discussion showed. Leniency also has to do with Junayd's frequent calls, in both his *Rasā'il* and other preserved fragments, to show more sympathy towards one's novices since sympathy is the most important thing to those at the beginning of their spiritual careers. In Junayd's letter to Yūsuf b. al-Ḥusayn, for instance, he urges him to put more effort into guiding his novices and sympathizing with them.[67]

Junayd's leniency also manifests in the frequent references in the text of *Luma*' to his gentle treatment of companions. He tended to show a remarkable degree of mildness towards them during fasting, for example, by breaking his fast when his companions visited him. 'The religious value in sharing meals with one's brothers is not inferior to the religious value of fast itself for the one who performs it', Junayd used to say on such occasions.[68] Junayd attempted to portray, and for a large degree to establish, a communal life in which all Sufis enjoy mutual support and stand together in every aspect of their religious and social lives. In several quotations from him preserved by Sarrāj through Junayd's renowned disciple Ja'far al-Khuldī, Junayd indicates the importance of performing Sufi rituals, such as *samā*', in a group on the condition that the members of this group are true brothers: 'Sufi *samā*' could not be held unless three basic constituents are existed: [sincere!] brothers (*ikhwān*), time, and place.'[69] Having meals together, breaking fast together and being committed to mutual aid and financial backing are examples of the idea of social-communal collaboration to which Junayd looked forward. It was Sarrāj again who devoted a separate section to mutual financial backing

[65] Ibid., 50. [66] These are presented in detail in Avery, *Shiblī*, 99–104.
[67] See Junayd, *Rasā'il*, Arabic text, 29–30. [68] See Sarrāj, *Luma*', 165. [69] Ibid., 186.

between the members of the Sufi community. Junayd was quoted three times in this short section. He appears to call on the Sufis to give charity to their fellow men. Two anecdotes cover Junayd's own activities in this area: The first tells that one day he visited Abū Jaʿfar Ibn al-Karanbī,[70] the Sufi who later became his master, in order to give him money. Ibn al-Karanbī, who did not know Junayd at that time, refused to take the money. However, when Junayd told him that, if he accepted, it would give him, that is, Junayd himself, great joy, Ibn al-Karanbī became convinced and took the money. The other episode describes how Junayd intended to give charity to Ḥusayn b. al-Miṣrī whose wife had given birth in the desert while no neighbour could provide them with any support. It was told that the man refused to take his charity, and that is why Junayd decided to throw the money in the wife's place while calling on her to pick it up. Thus, the man had nothing to do.[71] On another occasion, Junayd appears to have ordered one of his novices not to give all his money as charity in order to prevent a situation in which his lower soul would push him later to get back the money that he gave.[72] The need to consolidate the practical boundaries of mutual financial support among the members of the Sufi community stood behind such episodes. It seems like successfully establishing a religious community whose members are capable of supporting one another, a community that is united in solidarity was one of Junayd's targets. By establishing this pillar of support in the actual daily life of the Sufi *jamāʿa*, Junayd and his colleagues in the *ṣūfiyya* of Baghdad intended to maintain their control on the development of the movement and keep it as homogenous as possible under their ultimate umbrella. Such financial solidarity became one of the common features of Sufi ethics, according to later Sufi biographies. Jāmī tells that Abū Jaʿfar Muḥammad b. Fādhih, the disciple of Muḥammad b. Yūsuf b. Maʿdān al-Bannāʾ (d. 286/899), used to provide for the family of his master since he had inherited a sizeable legacy from his father.[73]

It seems highly likely that Junayd did not urge his disciples to undertake a renunciatory life of constant roving. While *safar* was a general term that referred to a wide spectrum of traditions and customs included in the medieval Islamic culture of travel, the term *siyāḥa,* as it emerged from

[70] In Nicholson's edition of *Kitāb al-lumaʿ*, the name appears as 'Ibn al-Kurrīnī' (see ibid., 198). See Ibn al-Karanbī's biography in: Baghdādī, *Taʾrīkh baghdād*, vol. 16, 594–596; Iṣfahānī, *Ḥilyat al-awliyāʾ*, vol. 10, 238; Jāmī, *Nafaḥāt al-uns*, 83; Dhahabī, *Tārīkh al-islām*, vol. 6, 859 (among those who died between the years 281–290).

[71] Both episodes are provided in Sarrāj, *Lumaʿ*, 198. [72] See ibid., 205.

[73] See Jāmī, *Nafaḥāt al-uns*, 105–106.

early Sufi and non-Sufi sources, has indicated the custom of roving in solitude without provisions undertaken by some early renunciants and Sufis.[74] Sarrāj indicates that, except for the sake of performing pilgrimage, Junayd did not bind himself to roving.[75] Qushayrī in his turn names Junayd among the Sufi masters who preferred residing (*iqāma*) over travelling. Qushayrī chooses to place this chapter among the chapters devoted to *aḥwāl*, and particularly after the chapter on *adab* (rules of ethics), and before the chapter on *ṣuḥba* (companionship) and the chapter on *tawḥīd* (unity). He probably intended to show that Sufi principles of travel combine ethics with companionship as part of his interest to establish a reconciliatory discourse in which Sufi roving keeps the communal medium. Like Sarrāj, Qushayrī prefers the term *safar*. He does not, in fact, use either the word *siyāḥa* or its plural form *siyāḥāt* throughout his *Risāla*, except for in one place: the biographical account of Abū Bakr al-Warrāq al-Tirmidhī (d. 240/854). Here, Qushayrī begins the biographical account with the verb *aqāma* (resided), and then he indicates that Warrāq used to prevent his fellowmen from both *safar* and *siyāḥa* (*yamnaʿ aṣḥābahu ʿan al-asfār wa-l-siyāḥa*).[76] In order to justify his approach, Warrāq himself says that enduring the hardships of life in the place of settlement would be a sufficient reason for attaining the divine grace. In his own definition of *safar*, Qushayrī divides the Sufis into three major categories, while not giving preponderance to any of them: The first category rejected *safar* and restricted it to pilgrimage and mandatory reasons; the second was committed to *safar* as a mode of life and the third category used to perform *safar* in the beginning of their Sufi lives but preferred to settle down when achieving the high spiritual ranks.[77] It appears that certain Sufis of Qushayrī's time and prior to it were accused of neglecting religious duties while travelling frequently. In Qushayrī's view, true Sufis are committed to worship during their roving, as 'dispensations (*rukhaṣ*) are allowed only to those whose travel is mandatory,

[74] Sufi and non-Sufi sources refer frequently to anonymous *ʿubbād* who used to rove in the deserts of *Tabūk* and Sinai (*tīh Banī Isrāʾīl*) and in the mountains of Lebanon and Lukkām (see e.g., Tanūkhī, *Nishwār al-muḥāḍara*, vol. 2, 349: the story of Abū ʿAbd Allāh al-Mazābilī in the mountain of Lukkām). For stories about renunciants' wanderings in the desert of the Sinai, see e.g., Qushayrī, *Risāla*, 12 (in the biography of Bishr al-Ḥāfī); ibid., 23 (in the biography of Abū Bakr al-Zaqqāq). And for stories related to the desert of Tabūk, see e.g., Iṣfahānī, *Ḥilyat al-awliyāʾ*, vol. 10, 324 (the biography of Bunān al-Baghdādī). The literature of *adab* going back to the fourth/tenth century provides us with sarcastic anecdotes concerning groups of Sufis who used to make *siyāḥa* for the sake of alms.

[75] See Sarrāj, *Lumaʿ*, 167. [76] Qushayrī, *Risāla*, 24, lines 23–24. [77] See ibid., 143.

while Sufis' travel is optional'.[78] Junayd, it is argued, did not urge the Sufis of his days to undertake the custom of *siyāḥa* due to its problematic image as an extreme renunciatory practice that would have required abandoning one's family and social networks for the sake of practising a renunciatory mode of roving in solitude or, sometimes, in small groups. This custom, at least in its earliest manifestations, was undertaken without provisions as means to prove one's absolute trust in God.[79]

By the end of the section that Sarrāj devoted to the Sufis' ethics in their associations, the following statement of Junayd is quoted: 'If you encounter a poor man, then use mildness instead of discussing science with him, since mildness contributes to creating a friendly atmosphere with him, while the act of discussing science alienates him' (*idhā laqīta al-faqīr fa-ilqahu bi-l-rifq wa-lā talqahu bi-l-ʿilm fa-inna al-rifq yuʾnisuhu wa-l-ʿilm yūḥishuhu*).[80] This statement might be understood in two ways: According to the first, the great master of Baghdad calls for mutual sympathy and solidarity between the Sufis in general terms, and this is in great harmony with the general framework of Sarrāj's particular section. The other way to understand the statement, which is more likely in my view, is to refer to Junayd's pragmatism in treating new initiates to the Sufi path. He urges his contemporary Sufis to approach potential Sufis leniently by means of hiding real Sufi theories from their eyes. The latter implies, in fact, two significant benefits: one for the Sufi community itself and one for the potential novice who is not ready yet to hear sophisticated spiritual theories. This strategy was not designed by itself for the benefit of the beginner Sufis or potential initiates only. The statement was mainly designed for the benefit of the existing Sufi community whose members needed to protect their mystical heritage in that historical context by concealing it from everyone's eyes, including new initiates. This idea grows stronger and clearer the more we get into Junayd's preserved fragments. In his letter to Abū Bakr al-Kisāʾī al-Dīnawarī,[81] to which

[78] Ibid., 144. The term *rukhaṣ* in Qushayrī's statement refers to the Sufi definition of what was originally a well-known term in Islamic law.

[79] See Houari Touati, *Islam and Travel in the Middle Ages*, translated from the original French edition (*Islam et Voyage au Moyen Âge: Histoire et Anthropologie d'une Pratique Lettrée* (Paris: Le Seuil, L'univers historique, 2000) by Lydia Cochrane (Chicago and London: The University of Chicago Press, 2010), 164–165.

[80] Sarrāj, *Lumaʿ*, 176.

[81] Apparently, this person was not Abū Bakr Muḥammad b. Dāwūd al-Dīnawarī known in Sufi biographies as al-Duqqī, the Syrian Sufi master who died around 260/874. See the latter's biography in Sulamī, *Ṭabaqāt*, 469–471. As for Kisāʾī in the above-mentioned reference, I did not succeed in finding any further data.

Sarrāj refers twice in the text of *Luma*ʿ,[82] Junayd declares that he decided to address this letter out of compassion and deep pity towards Kisāʾī, particularly after the latter had addressed several letters to Junayd. At one point in the letter, Junayd writes: 'Your situation [that you described to me previously!] is not to be blamed, but it is rather to be sympathized with (*ḥāl maʿṭūf ʿalayhi*) [. . .] I feel compassion for you.' It appears that Junayd waited a certain amount of time after receiving Kisāʾī's first letter. Junayd goes on to explain to his addressee that what had prevented him from immediately replying was not 'what came to your imagination' (*mā waqaʿa fī wahmika*), but the hesitation and delay were fed by the fear that his letter might fall in the hands of those who would be incapable of understanding it. Junayd attempts to convince his addressee that this fear is serious by informing him that it had actually happened in the past that one of his letters fell into the hands of a group of people from Iṣfahān and that he did experience the difficulty of escaping from that situation. Thereby, Junayd gets to the following conclusion:

> Human beings need mildness and leniency. Addressing them with discussions that they are incapable to conceive has nothing to do with leniency. Sometimes this [addressing these people with sophisticated discussions!] might take place unintentionally.[83]

Leniency in Junayd's worldview was not meant to disseminate Sufi theories and practices among Muslims as it came to be in later stages in the development of Sufism. It was, rather, Junayd's pragmatic strategy to establish and maintain the elite nucleus of Sufism, which derives its legitimacy and support from the Sufi ethos as it was formulated by the Baghdadi group of *ṣūfiyya*. This pragmatic theorization which succeeded to manifest itself in terms of leniency, mildness and communal solidarity was, in fact, elitist and selective. It was Junayd who, by the end of his letter to the abovementioned Kisāʾī, quoted the following prophetic tradition: 'People are like a hundred camels that have no single riding camel among them', and goes on to say that 'God created the men of knowledge and wisdom due to His mercy, and He granted them to people.'[84] It is interesting to note that the prophetic tradition that Junayd uses here in his letter could originally carry

[82] The main body of the letter appears in Sarrāj, *Luma*ʿ, 239–240; however, Sarrāj refers to it very briefly again in ibid., 358.

[83] See Sarrāj, *Luma*ʿ, 240.

[84] Ibid., 241. The prophetic tradition on the hundred camels is found in: Bukhārī, *Ṣaḥīḥ al-Bukhārī*, Muḥammad b. Ismāʿīl (Beirut: Dār al-Kutub al-ʿIlmiyya, 2001), 1185, *ḥadīth* no. 6498; Muslim b. al-Ḥajjāj, *Ṣaḥīḥ Muslim*, vol. 4, 1973, *ḥadīth* no. 2547.

several meanings as Muslim traditionalists point out: It could refer to the principle of equality between all Muslims. All people are equal in committing to the same religious duties and enjoying the same equal rights. Nonetheless, this tradition could be also understood as referring to the majority of people who are not to be trusted like the hundred camels that are not suitable for riding. Noble riding camels are very rare. Junayd's use of the tradition confirms the second interpretation. Solidarity and leniency were kept, according to him, within the group of close spiritual elite whose chosen members exercised caution while interacting with potential new candidates. The latter should not be exposed to the Sufi doctrinal system until they successfully develop a great degree of openness and a sort of religious flexibility.

Later on, in the course of the fifth/eleventh and sixth/twelfth centuries, leniency and mildness with potential new initiates to the Sufi path became one of the major pillars of the Sufi system of thought, as this was consolidated by the authors of the great and most influential Sufi manuals. Leniency, according to the works of both Abū al-Najīb al-Suhrawardī and his nephew ʿUmar al-Suhrawardī became a key instrument to attracting more and more people to the Sufi community. Leniency (*rifq*) here was given its original meaning as a way to practise open-mindedness with potential initiates, or even with normative Muslims who had a certain degree of sympathy towards the Sufis and their way of life. A significant shift that accrued in the Sufi system of thought concerning the position of those who accompany the Sufi community and try to imitate some of its customs without being able to fully undertake the Sufi mode of life could support a parallel shift in Sufi realities. It is interesting to note that Junayd, who was the key personality that early Sufi authors like Sarrāj engaged to criticize the exposure of new initiates to Sufi theories, became an important authority in the writings of the two Suhrawardīs whose teachings on leniency support the doctrinal system behind the increasingly legitimate position of those who 'imitate the Sufis' (*al-mutashabbihūn bi-l-ṣūfiyya*) without being able to act as full disciplinary Sufis.

In the text of *Lumaʿ* Junayd indicates that what he has said about being lenient is not to be understood as revealing the deep secrets of the path because telling someone about matters he cannot understand is not considered as lenience.[85] Elsewhere in the section devoted to Sufi terminology, the term *taḥallī* (lit. beautifying oneself) appears. Sarrāj succinctly

[85] See Sarrāj, *Lumaʿ*, 240.

defines it by stating that '*taḥallī* is to imitate pious men in word and deed.'[86] Hujwīrī quotes this definition; however, he mentions the critical views of some Sufis regarding the pretence of pious behaviour: '*Taḥallī*, then, is to imitate people without really acting as they do. Those who seem to be what they are not will soon be put to shame, and their secret character revealed.'[87] This early negative approach towards imitators gradually changed after the fourth/tenth century. The author of *Bawāriq al-ilmā' fī al-radd 'alā man ḥarram al-samā'*, whether being Aḥmad al-Ghazālī or someone else,[88] referred to the meaning of *muḥibbūn* (lovers) in discussing the Sufi *samā'* (listening to music). He welcomes those able to offer the Sufis support in the form of money and help in their daily needs as persons to be accepted and warmly received in the Sufi community. Such followers, though without the qualifications of true disciples, may accompany the Sufis and through their sincerity and loyalty acquire a degree of Sufi light and purity, just as smooth wax holds the heat of the sun.[89] This idea obtained its consolidation in Abū al-Najīb al-Suhrawardī's *Ādāb al-murīdīn*. In the last chapter of this work, the author surveys forty dispensations (*rukhṣa*, pl. *rukhaṣ*) that in his view may be granted to those whom he calls the imitators of the Sufis.[90] The main purpose of this chapter is to support the idea that those who imitate disciplined Sufis,

[86] Ibid., 362.

[87] Jullābī Hujwīrī, *Kashf al-maḥjūb*, 504. The English translation is of Nicholson. For Sulamī, every reasonable man should know Sufi principles to some extent so as to differentiate between true Sufis and their imitators (*al-mutashabbihūn bihim*) who dress like them and carry their outward qualities (*al-mutalabbisūn libāsahum wa-l-muttasimūn bi-simātihim*) so that he can distance himself from the latter [see Abū 'Abd al-Raḥmān al-Sulamī, *al-Muqaddima fī al-taṣawwuf wa-ḥaqīqatihi*, ed. by Yūsuf Zaydān (Cairo: Maktabat al-Kulliyāt al-Azhariyya, 1987), 84. See also the English translation of the whole paragraph in: Ohlander, *Sufism in an Age of Transition*, 192]. Besides, Sulamī disapproves the affectation of ecstasy in Sufi devotional rituals. According to a statement of his, one who simulates an act that he has not been entrusted with shall waste what he has actually been entrusted to him (*man takallaf mā lam yukallaf ḍayya'a mā qad kullif*). (See Sulamī, *Jawāmi'*, 30.)

[88] This work, which was introduced to Western scholarship of Sufism by James Robson in 1938 as *Tracts on Listening to Music*, has been proven to be not a work of Aḥmad al-Ghazāli. See the dissertation of Joseph Lumbard on Aḥmad al-Ghazālī, *Aḥmad al-Ghazālī (d. 517/1123 or 520/1126) and the Metaphysics of Love* (Yale University, 2003) in which Lumbard builds on the previous work of the Iranian scholar Aḥmad Mujāhid.

[89] Majd al-Dīn Aḥmad al-Ṭūsī al-Ghazālī, *Tracts on Listening to Music Being Dhamm al-Malāhī and Bawāriq al-Ilmā'*, ed. by James Robson (London: Printed and published under the patronage of the Royal Asiatic Society, 1938), 126. (The author of this work most probably was not Ghazālī. However, this is the author's name that appears on this publication.)

[90] Abū al-Najīb al-Suhrawardī, *Ādāb al-murīdīn*, 80–99.

mainly in their morals and patterns of behaviour, are warmly welcome to accompany them. *Ādāb al-murīdīn* could be considered by all means as the earliest Sufi manual in which this special type of affiliation is clearly presented.[91] The teachings of Abū Ḥafṣ al-Suhrawardī more than those of his uncle, however, provide the theoretical background for a view of the dynamic functions of *mutashabbihūn* in Sufi communities. On the very basis of *tashabbuh* theory, the technique of lenience with prospective beginners finds its legitimacy in statements attributed to Junayd, and that is why Junayd was often quoted in this context by Suhrawardī. His famous statement on treating the beginner initiate leniently was previously mentioned.[92] Sulamī quotes another statement by Junayd in which he advises Shiblī to accept whoever agrees with him, even if this person agrees with only a single word of his.[93] Junayd's leniency, which had earlier been a strategy to protect the close particularity of the Sufi community, turned into an indication of a liberal system of initiation that opened its gates before anyone who was interested, regardless of the real nature of his interest whether strong or weak, in Sufi communal life. According to this system, the *mutashabbih* is allowed to associate with the Sufis as well as become exposed to their inner science. This development should be combined with the wider shift in Sufism in the course of its late classical phase: the shift from a closed elitist movement towards a popular movement with a strong missionary nature.

Before leaving Junayd, I would like to draw attention to an additional fact: Junayd was not a completely consensual acclaimed personality. Negative approaches towards him could be found in some early sources. The early biographical work of ʿAbd Allāh Anṣārī of Herāt presents a different portrait of the renowned Sufi master of Baghdad. Anṣārī Haravī did not hesitate to defame Junayd and celebrate Ruwaym whose case was unique on the scene of early Sufism. As I will show in Chapter 7, it seems that Anṣārī Haravī was not satisfied with portraying Ruwaym as equal to Junayd, and that is why he went on to emphasize the higher spiritual rank of Ruwaym over that of Junayd. This coldness towards Junayd in the work of Anṣārī Haravī turned into a systematic tone of defaming Junayd

91 See ibid., Milson's *introduction*, [8]-[9]. More recently, Eric Ohlander devoted three pages in his *Sufism in an Age of Transition* to what he called 'lay affiliates' in both Abū al-Najīb and Abū Ḥafṣ al-Suhrawardī's teachings. Ohlander attributes the authenticity of this matter for the most part to Abū al-Najīb. See Ohlander, *Sufism in an Age of Transition*, 243–246.

92 See Suhrawardī, *ʿAwārif*, 97; Sulamī, *Ṭabaqāt*, 146; Sarrāj, *Lumaʿ*, 176.

93 See Sulamī, *Ṭabaqāt*, 146.

and attacking his consensually acclaimed persona later on in Jāmī's *Nafaḥāt al-uns*. In the biography of Abū Saʿīd al-Kharrāz, for instance, Jāmī writes: 'Abū Saʿīd used to visit Junayd and pretend to be his disciple despite the fact that he was not indeed his disciple. Abū Saʿīd used to associate with Junayd as one of his companions; however, he was superior to him.'[94] Elsewhere, Jāmī insists that Junayd should have advanced from his position as a man of dry science.[95]

Ibn al-Sāʿī's (d. 674/1276) *Akhbār al-Ḥallāj* from the mid-seventh/thirteenth century refers to tense encounters between Junayd and certain Sufi figures who supported Ḥallāj around the period of his trial, the most famous of which was Ibn Khafīf of Shīrāz. According to one anecdote, Junayd defamed Ḥallāj and accused him of magic and jugglery in a Sufi gathering in Baghdad. In the story, all the attendees kept silent due to their deep veneration for Junayd except for Ibn Khafīf who said to Junayd: 'Oh master, please be patient! The ability to answer prayers and foresee inward thoughts has nothing to do with magic and jugglery.' It was said, then, that the majority of the Sufis in the gathering appeared to believe Ibn Khafīf' defensive words and were suspicious of Junayd's accusations. The narrator, Aḥmad b. Yūnus, went on to say that afterwards he went to Ḥallāj's place and told him what had happened. Ḥallāj laughed and said: 'As to Muḥammad b. Khafīf, he took sides fanatically (*taʿaṣṣaba*) with God, and he will be rewarded accordingly, on the other hand, Abū al-Qāsim al-Junayd said that he [that is Ḥallāj!] lied, and you should say to him [to Junayd!] in response: 'And those who do wrong shall surely know by what overturning they will be overturned.'[96]

ABŪ SAʿĪD AL-KHARRĀZ (D. 286/899 OR A FEW YEARS EARLIER):[97] A MAN OF PRIVATE AUSTERITIES

Another Sufi personality who successfully established a position of fame and gained a certain degree of consensus within the boundaries of his particular network of Baghdadi *ṣūfiyya* was Abū Saʿīd al-Kharrāz. Abū Saʿīd was older than Junayd. He died at least twelve years before Junayd

[94] Jāmī, *Nafaḥāt al-uns* 73. [95] See ibid., 74.

[96] *Sūra* 26, verse 227. See the anecdote in ʿAlī b. Anjab Ibn al-Sāʿī, *Akhbār al-Ḥallāj aw munājayāt al-Ḥallāj*, ed. by L. Massignon and B. Kraus (Paris: Maktabat Laroze, 1936), 90.

[97] According to Sulamī, Kharrāz died in 277/890–891 (see Sulamī, *Ṭabaqāt*, 223). Others suggest that he died 286/899 or a few years earlier (see e.g., Dhahabī, *Siyar*, vol. 13, 419).

(if this was the case he died in 286 and not before). When Jāmī sought to humiliate Junayd and cast doubt on his ultimate position, he used the figure of Kharrāz as the above-mentioned quotation from *Nafaḥāt al-uns* indicates.[98] Jāmī furthermore declares that 'Kharrāz was on the brink of being a prophet due to his honourable position.'[99] Jāmī's ancestor Anṣārī Haravī indicates that Kharrāz was indeed 'superior to all Sufi sheikhs in the science of *tawḥīd*'.[100]

The references to Kharrāz's statements on *fanāʾ* (annihilation) and *baqāʾ* (subsistence) often gained the interest of early biographers as well as of modern scholars and kept their treatments of this figure within the bounds of his esoteric teachings deduced from his remaining works and *Rasāʾil*. Sarrāj refers very frequently to Abū Saʿīd al-Kharrāz in his *Lumaʿ*. Kharrāz's definitions of *tawḥīd* and its relation to the state of annihilation were given prominent attention.[101] Focusing on the state of passionate love and burning thirst to gain intimacy with the Beloved appears as one of the key aspects of Kharrāz's teachings.[102] Sarrāj's *Lumaʿ* draws heavily on sayings and anecdotes on Kharrāz. Nada Saʿb notes that the text of *Lumaʿ* is a major source on Kharrāz's life and teachings due to Sarrāj's proximity to the time of Kharrāz as well as his association with Sufi personalities who learned under Kharrāz or at least were his companions during his lifetime.[103]

Following up on Kharrāz's fragments in Sarrāj's work reveals an additional interesting facet of his unique mode of piety: In several places in the text of *Lumaʿ* Kharrāz points out a distinctive technique of summoning spiritual revelations through listening to the *Qurʾān* and contemplating the secret meanings of its verses. It seems very likely that, over his Sufi career, Kharrāz developed a practical technique that enables the Sufi to make use of the *Qurʾān* as an effective trigger for spiritual states. He explains this technique by saying:

> The first degree in listening to the *Qurʾān* is to listen to it as it is recited to you by the Prophet. Then you progress to a situation in which you listen to the *Qurʾān* as it is recited to you by the angel Gabriel. [. . .] Later on, you progress to a situation in which you listen to the *Qurʾān* as it is recited by God Himself.[104]

[98] See Jāmī, *Nafaḥāt al-uns*, 73. [99] Ibid., 74.

[100] Anṣārī Haravī, *Ṭabaqāt al-ṣūfiyya*, 50. [101] See e.g., Sarrāj, *Lumaʿ*, 33.

[102] See ibid., 64, 214.

[103] See Nada Saʿb, *Ṣūfī Theory and Language in the Writings of Abū Saʿīd Aḥmad ibn ʿĪsā al-Kharrāz (d. 286/899)*, a dissertation presented to the faculty of the Graduate School of Yale University, dissertation director: Gerhard Böwering (December 2003), 80.

[104] Sarrāj, *Lumaʿ*, 80.

This technique is related to the concept of *fahm* in Kharrāz's doctrinal system. Going further with him in the above quotation, we see that after the advancement through the three stages of listening to the *Qur'ān* the mystic becomes able to experience *fahm*, that is, a deep observation (*mushāhada*) of God's hidden worlds.[105] If we add this interesting doctrine to another piece of information according to which Kharrāz composed a separate work on the Sufi rules of conduct in prayer (*adab al-ṣ alāt*) as Sarrāj indicates, then we realize why Kharrāz is quoted heavily in Sarrāj's chapter on prayer.[106] Based on the information presented by Sarrāj, Kharrāz developed a sophisticated system of practising an extended type of prayer in which the mystic goes on contemplating each movement that he performs during his prayer and treats each word that he recites as an instrument to obtain *fahm*. At the end of the discussion on the Sufi mode of prayer, Sarrāj makes the following comment: 'This is what I found in Abū Sa'īd al-Kharrāz's book, may he rest in peace. I saw a group of people who disregarded the extension of prayer and preferred to minimize it as means to close the door before *waswās* [that is, any evil idea that might tempt the mystic and, thereby, distract him from his pure state with God amidst prayer!] (*yakrahūn taṭwīl al-ṣalāt wa-yuḥibbūn al-takhfīf li-mubādarat al-waswās*).'[107] It is to say that a certain group of Sufis believed that extending the time of prayer is expected to open the door for the lower soul in order to tempt the mystic and expel him from the same state of concentration and intimacy with which he started the prayer.

Kharrāz's unique practicum of *ṣalāt* was not restricted to the element of extension. Aspects of a broader system of thought that involves prayer as well as reciting the *Qur'ān* in general could be deduced from Sarrāj's work. Kharrāz is quoted in another place as having presented his doctrine on conducting God's words and even the very letters of His holy words: 'If you hear the verse "*Alif. Lām. Mīm* " [verse 1 in *Sūra* 2!], then you should perceive by *fahm* the inner science behind the letter *Alif* which differs essentially from that inner science that is to be sought behind the letter *Lām*.' Abū Sa'īd tells us here how he used to conduct a single verse for five whole nights, trying to contemplate each letter that it included, and how sometimes he lost his mind while reciting one single verse.[108] Qāsim al-Sāmirrā'ī refers to this part in *Luma'* to indicate that Kharrāz

[105] Ibid., 79–80. [106] See ibid., 152–154. [107] Ibid., 154. [108] See ibid., 89.

was influenced in certain aspects of his teachings by gnostic trends in Shīʿism that found their most outspoken manifestation in the group of *ḥurūfiyya*.[109]

Kharrāz had a renunciatory mode of life that might have differed from the general renunciatory piety of the Baghdadi Sufis of his time. Looking at the fragments that the sources ascribe to him along with the references to him made by his contemporaries and near successors supports our assumption that Kharrāz committed himself to a very rigid system of renunciatory exercises. He performed Sufi roving for long sections of his lifetime. Sulamī indicates that Kharrāz used to rove with Abū Turāb al-Nakhshabī and Abū Ḥamza al-Khurāsānī.[110] Interestingly, both of these figures were well known in the history of early Sufism due to their engagements in controversial behaviour and ecstatic sayings. Abū Turāb al-Nakhshabī had unique teachings on *tawakkul*, and he committed himself thereby to a rigid roving life that led to his tragic death in the desert.[111] On the other hand, Sufi hagiographers describe Abū Ḥamza as a passionate Sufi who despite his ecstatic utterances succeeded in affiliating himself with the Baghdadi *ṣūfiyya*. Sarrāj surveys the accusations of heresy surrounding Abū Ḥamza coming from his contemporaries, and he defends him in a separate section of his *Lumaʿ*.[112]

Kharrāz performed both forms of Sufi roving, *siyāḥa*, individual and collective, as documented in the sources. He appeared to have frequently roved alone and sometimes even without provisions.[113] Ibn Khamīs al-Mawṣilī, for instance, mentions a story that was narrated by Kharrāz himself as follows: 'I entered the desert [alone!] without provisions and food' (*dakhaltu al-bādiya bi-ghayr zād*) until an extreme neediness harmed me (*aṣābatnī fāqa shadīda*). Kharrāz goes to tell that when he saw an animal, he could finally calm down. However, afterwards he knew that this tranquillity was a result of his trust in something other than God, and therefore he decided to bury his body under the soil as punishment

[109] See Aḥmad b. ʿĪsā Abū Saʿīd al-Kharrāz, *Rasāʾil al-Kharrāz*, ed. by Qāsim al-Sāmirrāʾī (Baghdad: Maṭbaʿat al-Majmaʿ al-ʿIlmī al-ʿIrāqī, 1967), *introduction*, 4.

[110] See Sulamī, *Ṭabaqāt*, 328 (in the biography of Abū Ḥamza).

[111] See his biography in: Sulamī, *Ṭabaqāt*, 136–140; Qushayrī, *Risāla*, 18; Jullābī Hujwīrī, *Kashf al-maḥjūb*, 151–152; Iṣfahānī, *Ḥilyat al-awliyāʾ*, vol. 10, 46–52; Gramlich, *Alte Vorbilder*, vol. 1, 325–344.

[112] See Sarrāj, *Ṣuḥuf min kitāb al-lumaʿ*, 6–7.

[113] See e.g., Sarrāj, *Lumaʿ*, 329 (Kharrāz tells a story that happened to him when he entered the desert solely). For Kharrāz's collective *siyāḥa* see e.g., Ibn Khamīs al-Mawṣilī, *Manāqib al-abrār*, vol. 1, 424 (with Abū al-Qāsim al-Nahawandī and Abū Bakr al-Warrāq).

for his lower soul, which momentarily lost its absolute trust in God.[114] Practising *ṣiyāḥa* was one of the rigid and harrowing austerities that Kharrāz performed. Ibn ʿAsākir and other medieval biographers like Abū al-Fidāʾ Ibn Kathīr (d. 774/1373) preserved several anecdotes on Kharrāz's hardships during *siyāḥa* as well as while practising constant fast (*ṭayy*).[115] Junayd is frequently quoted in the sources as having compared Kharrāz's mode of piety with that of his close Sufi circle: 'If we demand from God to grant us the essential nature of Abū Saʿīd al-Kharrāz's spiritual state, then we will be wiped out' (*law ṭālabnā Allāh bi-ḥaqīqat mā ʿalayhi Abū Saʿīd al-Kharrāz la-halaknā*).[116]

In the comparison between Junayd and Kharrāz in early medieval sources, as expected, the first is preferred: 'He [that is Kharrāz!] was preferred over all Sufis for his rhetorical talents, except for Junayd, who was by all means the greatest *imām* ', asserts Ibn ʿAsākir, among many other authors.[117] The case of Jāmī, however, stands out. In his article on the mystics of the late third/ninth century (1968), W. Montgomery Watt points out to Kharrāz's distinction from the general line of the *ṣūfiyya* of his time. Watt shows that Kharrāz differed from the Baghdadi Sufis despite the fact that he maintained contacts with them.[118] Towards the end of this paper, Watt further indicates that Kharrāz's main contribution to early Sufism lies in his attempts to establish a distinguished Sufi line under the general umbrella of the school of Baghdad as his fragments in Sarrāj's *Lumaʿ* imply. No further discussion of the actual contents of that line is provided by Watt.[119] Karamustafa refers to Kharrāz as a prominent member of the Sufi circle in Baghdad and goes on outlining the major constituents of his doctrinal system as those could be deduced from his surviving short works.[120]

Kharrāz's personality differs from other figures in the Baghdadi line. He differs completely from Junayd. Kharrāz, most likely, paid only little attention to the mechanism of Sufi interpersonal relationships and issues of discipleship. In one long reference made to him by Ibn ʿAsākir, Kharrāz

114 See Ibn Khamīs al-Mawṣilī, *Manāqib al-abrār*, vol. 1, 421–422.

115 See Ibn ʿAsākir, *Taʾrīkh madīnat dimashq*, vol. 5, 135–156; Ismāʿīl b. ʿUmar Abu al-Fidāʾ Ibn Kathīr, *al-Bidāya wa-l-nihāya* (Beirut: Maktabat al-Maʿārif, 1991), vol. 11, 58.

116 Baghdādī, *Taʾrīkh baghdād*, vol. 5, 455; Ibn ʿAsākir, *Taʾrīkh madīnat dimashq*, vol. 5, 131.

117 See Ibn ʿAsākir, *Taʾrīkh madīnat dimashq*, vol. 5, 130.

118 See W. Montgomery Watt, 'Some Mystics of the Later Third/Ninth Century', *Islamic Studies*, vol. 7, no. 4 (1968), 314–315.

119 See ibid., 315.

120 See Karamustafa, *Sufism*, 7–10.

is quoted as saying: 'If the novice, *murīd*, is truthful at the beginning of his path, God will grant him success and will give him a guide from within himself.'[121] This notion does not necessarily mean that Kharrāz did not believe in the essential need for a Sufi master or that he completely believed in one's ability to guide himself along the Sufi path through independently cultivating Sufi learning and training. What he says here is that one's truthfulness at the very beginning of his initiation to the path is expected to bestow purity upon his lower soul (*nafs*) and to turn it, that is, his lower soul, into a real motivation for spiritual progress instead of being an obstacle to it.[122] Kharrāz had a close circle of disciples. Sulamī indicates that one of them, Abū al-Ḥusayn b. Bunān, used to display intensive signs of passion during *samāʿ* and that Kharrāz himself used to clap his hands for him at that time. The biography of Ibn Bunān does not leave any doubt that he was a passionate Sufi whose life was based around ecstatic situations and deep passion that motivated him to perform hard *siyāḥa* that brought about his tragic death in the desert.[123] One of the disciples or close companions of Kharrāz was Yūsuf b. al-Ḥusayn, the aforementioned mystic whose correspondence with Junayd were mentioned in the first part of this chapter. It is interesting to note that many of the key figures in Kharrāz's circle of companions were the same addressees of Junayd's *Rasāʾil*. Beside Ibn al-Ḥusayn, ʿAmr b. ʿUthmān al-Makkī was another close disciple of Kharrāz who himself received a critical letter from the renowned master of Baghdad. It appears that Makkī initiated to *taṣawwuf* through the teachings of Kharrāz, while Yūsuf b. al-Ḥusayn was not exactly a disciple but rather a close companion basically during performing a collective *siyāḥa*.[124]

Kharrāz was likely an introvert, an unsociable Sufi who detached himself from the general communal activities of his contemporaries. He preserved limited interpersonal ties with the broad scene of the *ṣūfiyya*'s activities. His mode of engagement in the religious life of *ṣūfiyya* was

[121] Ibn ʿAsākir, *Taʾrīkh madīnat dimashq*, vol. 5, 135. The English translation is of Nada Saʿb in: Saʿb, *Ṣūfī Theory*, 13.

[122] Nada Saʿb draws on the same statement of Kharrāz brought about in Ibn ʿAsākir's work to argue that 'to al-Kharrāz, the best guide for a Sufi is his own self as he controls his ego, *nafs*, and cultivates his religious learning independently' (ibid.). I consider most probable to understand Kharrāz's reference to the novice's beginning of the path in more general and neutral terms without combining it with any broader sense of the necessity or the absence of necessity of a Sufi master.

[123] See Sulamī, *Ṭabaqāt*, 404; Qushayrī, *Risāla*, 29. No date of death is provided in his biography.

[124] See e.g., Qushayrī, *Risāla*, 24.

probably looser than that of other key figures operating within the boundaries of this group. No historical evidence supports the occurrence of a meeting between Kharrāz and Junayd. Meanwhile, indirect contact between the two could have taken place through their circles of companions, although, unlike Junayd, Kharrāz had no interest in a broad circle of companions. It is said, for instance, that Kharrāz asked his disciple ʿAmr al-Makkī to ask for Junayd's guidance.[125] Junayd's superciliousness and arrogant tone in criticizing many of his contemporaries affected active disciples of Kharrāz. Junayd could not criticize Kharrāz in any of his fragments. On the contrary, in all available statements where Junayd refers to Kharrāz, he praises Kharrāz and pays tribute to his outstanding position. Kharrāz himself was not a domineering master. References to his behaviour with his companions during *samāʿ* ceremonies and travels leave a strong impression that he had a modest and lenient character. His leniency, meanwhile, had nothing to do with pragmatism as in the case of Junayd. According to a long quotation from Kharrāz, one piece of evidence for the truthfulness of the novice is related to his leniency, compassion and patience towards all people. This rule of conduct draws the Sufis closer to the high position of God's prophets. Each novice, according to Kharrāz, should behave as a dutiful son with his master, as a compassionate father with a young man, and to exercise leniency with all kinds of people.[126] As for Sufi 'brothers' and behaviour in their association, Ibn ʿAsākir quotes the following statement of Kharrāz: 'I associated with the *ṣūfiyya* for a very long time, and it had never happened to me that I quarrelled with them.' When Kharrāz was asked to explain why, he replied: 'Because, in their company, I used to act against my lower soul' (*li-annī kuntu maʿahum ʿalā nafsī*).[127] Associating with the Baghdadi *ṣūfiyya* in his time imposed upon him, as this statement reads, to practise patience and compassion by subordinating and oppressing his *nafs*, with all its pride, egotism and passion for leadership, for the sake of maintaining his relationship with those whose lives and outward behaviour and appearance totally differed from his.

If Junayd and his close circle of companions looked forward to unifying the different edges of Sufism while establishing the Baghdadi monopoly upon that desired unified movement, Kharrāz had nothing to do with this comprehensive project. His major interest was directed towards his inner life with God, and he guided his few disciples accordingly. Junayd, who did

[125] Jullābī Hujwīrī, *Kashf al-maḥjūb*, 176. Cf. Saʿb, *Ṣūfī Theory*, 36.
[126] See Sarrāj, *Lumaʿ*, 206. [127] Ibn ʿAsākir, *Taʾrīkh madīnat dimashq*, vol. 5, 130.

not refrain from criticizing many Sufis, praised Kharrāz in his references to him. It is very likely that Junayd sought to bring Kharrāz's Sufism together under the comprehensive and united framework of *taṣawwuf* that he wanted to establish and strengthen. Therefore, it is possible that Junayd was in need of Sufi leaders who could join him on the difficult path towards achieving that goal. Kharrāz, whose teachings on *fanā'* and practical life of hardships and rigid austerities did not exactly complement Junayd's pragmatism and ideal image of *taṣawwuf*, was in Junayd's eyes a necessary support for establishing his own agenda. Kharrāz was not satisfied with practising this type of life. He rather was a great theoretician and a man of letters. Kharrāz's case is completely different from that of Shiblī or Nūrī even though the passionate aspects of his *taṣawwuf* seem to be similar. Kharrāz was older than Junayd, and his character had nothing in common with the disordered character of Shiblī, for instance. His renunciatory mode of life was completely different from that of many other members of the *ṣūfiyya* who simply chose to maintain their engagement in social, political and economic positions of fame like Ruwaym and ʿAmr al-Makkī. Imagining the general scene of *taṣawwuf* during those days helps us to understand Junayd's agenda and better contemplate his distinctive approaches towards his contemporaries: the teachings and activities of Ḥallāj, Nūrī, Shiblī, Abū Ḥamza al-Baghdādī and others in one group; social-oriented Sufi personalities like Ruwaym and Makkī in another and personalities that came from the Sufi circles while choosing to attack the Sufis, like Ghulām Khalīl (d. 275/888) and Ibn Yazdānyār,[128] in the third group. Among all these, Kharrāz stood out as the one whose character could provide Junayd's agenda with a great deal of support.

ABŪ ḤAFṢ AL-ḤADDĀD (D. C. 265/878–879)[129] OF NISHAPUR

The teachings of the early founders of the *malāmatiyya* in the eastern parts of the world of Islam show us interesting strategies of approaching

[128] No date of death is provided in his biography. See e.g., Sulamī, *Ṭabaqāt*, 423–426; Qushayrī, *Risāla*, 30. See also the detailed reference to him in Chapter 7.

[129] Sulamī indicates three options for his date of death: 264 or 267 or 270. See Sulamī, *Ṭabaqāt*, 105–106. For the biography of Abū Ḥafṣ, see, in addition to Sulamī's *Ṭabaqāt*: Qushayrī, *Risāla*, 18; Baghdādī, *Ta'rīkh baghdād*, vol. 14, 133–136; Iṣfahānī, *Ḥilyat al-awliyā'*, vol. 10, 244–245; Anṣārī Haravī, *Ṭabaqāt al-ṣūfiyya*, 38–40; Jullābī Hujwīrī, *Kashf al-maḥjūb*, 154–156.

new affiliates. The character of Abū Ḥafṣ al-Ḥaddād al-Naysābūrī is of great significance here. One of the earliest sources for his image and his role in guiding novices in the Sufi path is Sulamī's *Risālat al-malāmatiyya*. Throughout this short work, the founders of *malāmatiyya* and their successors are described as having guided their novices to practising a normative mode of social life and 'attending the markets' (*luzūm al-aswāq*) as means to conceal their inner truth and to avoid people's praise.[130] At the very beginning of the work, Sulamī differentiates between three ranks of 'the people of religious sciences and spiritual states' (*arbāb al-ʿulūm wa-l-aḥwāl*): Muslim traditionalists in the first, the 'people of divine knowledge' in the second rank and finally the group of *malāmatiyya* in the third rank. Sulamī indicates that the description of the second group is 'analogous to the state of *ṣūfiyya*' (*shabīh bi-ḥāl al-ṣūfiyya*).[131] This, most likely, refers to the Sufis of Baghdad. Sulamī goes on to provide us with comparisons between *ṣūfiyya* and *malāmatiyya*, while praising and favouring the latter. In order to celebrate *malāmatiyya*'s preference over the other famed Baghdadi group, Sulamī quotes the following statement of Abū Ḥafṣ al-Ḥaddād, who presents an interesting comparison between the novices of *ṣūfiyya* and the novices of *malāmatiyya*:

> The novices of *malāmatiyya* are unstable in the position of manhood (*mutaqallibūn fī al-rujūliyya*); their lower souls have no impact on them [...] since their outwards are unveiled while their inwards are hidden. The novices of *ṣūfiyya* bring into view the imprudence of their *karāmāt* in a way that motivates the men of truth to laugh at them due to their plentiful impure claims and the rarity of their true states.[132]

Abū Ḥafṣ al-Ḥaddād criticizes the *ṣūfiyya* for not warning their novices against showing off their spiritual capacities. Meanwhile, the novices of *malāmatiyya* keep wavering and do not feel that they arrive at the ultimate spiritual rank that allows them to celebrate this achievement. The word *rujūliyya* in the above quotation indicates the *malāmatiyya*'s way to obtaining inner states of closeness and purity and ignoring every external indication for them. The behaviour of the *ṣūfiyya*'s novices, on the other hand, causes contempt and sarcasm since it focuses specifically on external indications for spiritual states. *Karāmāt* are nothing but the typical example for such indications. Controversies regarding different Sufi doctrines and practices between the line of Abū Ḥafṣ and his

[130] See Sulamī, *Risālat al-malāmatiyya*, 91, 101. [131] Ibid., 87. [132] Ibid., 88–89.

companions on the one hand and Junayd and his circle on the other are frequently referred to by the authors of early sources.[133] At one point in *Luma'*, for instance, Sarrāj finds Abū Ḥafṣ's custom of wearing silk and magnificent clothes contrary to the representatives of Baghdadi *ṣūfiyya* such as Ibn al-Karanbī, one of Junayd's masters, who committed themselves to austere codes of dress. The tone of Sarrāj's comment that follows this comparison shows preference to *ṣūfiyya*'s customs over that of the Nishapurian leader, even though Sarrāj concludes that the true Sufi is allowed to wear whatever God wishes him to wear.[134]

Based on *Risālat al-malāmatiyya*, Abū Ḥafṣ al-Ḥaddād did not allow his novices to perform *siyāḥa* that was not specified as *ḥajj*, religious war (*jihād*) or the search for religious science. Sufi roving that was not included under one of these legal reasons for travelling (*al-asfār 'alā al-murād*, which literally means travelling in accordance with God's will) as Sulamī calls it, was not acceptable to him.[135] This doctrine might be seen as one aspect of Abū Ḥafṣ's lenient approach towards novices, and it should be added to his unique method of attracting these novices to the path of blame, as Sulamī presents it. In one occasion of *Sharḥ kitāb al-ta'arruf*, for instance, Mustamlī Bukhārī tells that when Abū Ḥafṣ came to Baghdad to visit Shiblī, the latter said to him: 'You educated your companions using the etiquette of the sultans' (*addabta aṣḥābaka ādāb al-salāṭīn*). In response, Abu Ḥafṣ said to shiblī: 'No, O Abū Bakr [that is, Shiblī!]. The veracity of the title is an indication of the veracity of the very content of the book [...] one's outwards is an indication of his inwards (*zāhir-i khalq 'unvān-i bāṭin ast*).'[136]

Abū Ḥafṣ differed from other leaders of *malāmatiyya* in his interesting technique to awaken his novices' desire for ascetic exercises, to which they needed to commit themselves after initiation to the Sufi life. By praising these exercises, and putting the focus on their spiritual traits, Abū Ḥafṣ and his successors sought to arouse the interest of novices in renunciatory customs, and to urge them to systematically adhere to these.[137] Unlike the act of observing one's companions for the sake of protecting them against unaccepted behaviour in the doctrinal system of Baghdadi *ṣūfiyya*, as Chapter 7 will show, Abū Ḥafṣ called on his companions to commit themselves to a merciful and compassionate approach towards new

133 See e.g., Dhahabī, *Siyar*, vol. 12, 510–512 (the biography of Abū Ḥafṣ al-Naysābūrī).
134 See Sarrāj, *Luma'*, 188. 135 See Sulamī, *Risālat al-malāmatiyya*, 94.
136 Mustamlī Bukhārī, *Sharḥ kitāb al-ta'arruf*, vol. 1, 192–193.
137 See Sulamī, *Risālat al-malāmatiyya*, 103.

affiliates. He urged Sufis to stay patient towards any unaccepted behaviour by their brothers since, according to him, one of the major pillars of *malāmatiyya* is 'the exaltation of people and keeping favourable judgment of them, and considering the well-meaning of their shameful deeds'.[138]

Abū Ḥafṣ's contemporary, Ḥamdūn al-Qaṣṣār (d. 271/884–885) was another great master of the *malāmatī* line in Nishapur. His biography in early sources leaves the impression that he was highly profound of renunciatory exercises that, according to him, should be undertaken and whose spiritual values should nevertheless not be exaggerated.[139] Unlike Abū Ḥafṣ al-Ḥaddād, it appears that Ḥamdūn imposed upon his novices the custom of roving.[140] His strategy in treating novices was different from that of Abū Ḥafṣ. He used to disparage renunciatory exercises in the eyes of novices as well as to show them their deficiencies for the sake of protecting them from conceit.[141] While Abū Ḥafṣ's technique suited normative Sufi novices and it paved the way for them to join Sufism, Qaṣṣār's technique could only work for novices with genuine intentions whose inclination to the Sufi path was not subordinated to terms of compensation and material benefit. This difference between the two figures, beyond other reasons, motivated A. Karamustafa to argue that it was this group of Khurāsānian disciples of Abū Ḥafṣ al-Ḥaddād and Abū ʿUthmān al-Ḥīrī, not of Ḥamdūn al-Qaṣṣār, whose members studied with the Sufis of Baghdad and managed, in the course of time, to represent 'a fusion between Sufis of Iraq and *malāmatiyya* of Khurāsān'.[142]

138 Ibid., 90.
139 See his biography in Sulamī, *Ṭabaqāt*, 114–119; Anṣārī Haravī, *Ṭabaqāt al-ṣūfiyya*, 40–41; Jullābī Hujwīrī, *Kashf al-maḥjūb*, 156–157. Cf. Watt, *Some Mystics*, 309–310.
140 See Sulamī, *Risālat al-malāmatiyya*, 94.
141 See ibid., 103; Cf. Karamustafa, *Sufism*, 49.
142 Karamustafa, *Sufism*, 61.

6

Marginal Piety

The Case of Niffarī (d. c. 354/965)

The case of Muḥammad b. ʿAbd al-Jabbār al-Niffarī[1] demonstrates a unique instance of a pious figure who was completely ignored by his contemporaries, as well as by the majority of later Sufi authors and theoreticians. It was not until the days of Ibn ʿArabī that Niffarī was introduced into the world of medieval Islamic religiosity after nearly three centuries of neglect. This chapter will attempt to place the unique case of Niffarī within the general scene of Muslim spirituality during the fourth/tenth century and to bring to the fore the discussion of his complete neglect both in Sufi and non-Sufi writings of his time. This neglect was complete in a way that no imprint of his life and writings was seen in the Sufi works of the fourth/tenth century and the following two centuries. Neglect as such raises the question: Was Niffarī a real Sufi of the fourth/

This chapter benefits from an earlier work of mine, particularly in dealing with the question of Niffarī's neglect by his contemporaries. See A. Salamah-Qudsi, 'Remarks on al-Niffarī's Neglect in Early Sufi Literature', *British Journal of Middle Eastern Studies*, vol. 41, no. 4 (2014), 406–418.

1 A. J. Arberry suggests that 'all the authorities agree' on Niffarī's name that is Muḥammad b. ʿAbd al-Jabbār b. al-Ḥasan al-Niffarī [See the *Mawāqif and Mukhāṭabāt*, ed. and trans. by A. J. Arberry (London: J. W. Gibb Memorial Series, 1935), 2. Afterwards: Arberry (ed. and trans.), *Mawāqif and Mukhāṭabāt*]. However, recent scholars have concluded that this name was in fact the name of Niffarī's grandson who collected his grandfather's work, as Arberry himself also indicated [see Arberry (ed. and trans.), *Mawāqif and Mukhāṭabāt*, 6]. Cf. ʿAfīf al-Dīn al-Tilimsānī, *Sharḥ mawāqif al-Niffarī*, ed. by Jamāl al-Marzūqī (Cairo: al-Hayʾa al-Miṣriyya al-ʿĀmma li-l-Kitāb, 2000), 20; ʿAfīf al-Dīn al-Tilimsānī, *Sharḥ mawāqif al-Niffarī: Muḥammad b. ʿAbd al-Jabbār b. al-Ḥasan*, ed. by ʾĀṣim Ibrāhīm al-Kayyālī (Beirut: Dār al-Kutub al-ʿIlmiyya, 2007), 19. Concerning the date of Niffarī's death see the different suggestions in: Jamāl al-Marzūqī, *Falsafat al-taṣawwuf: Muḥammad b. ʿAbd al-Jabbār al-Niffarī* (Beirut: Dār al-Tanwīr, 2007), 21–25.

tenth century? To some extent, L. Massignon was convinced that Niffarī was not a tenth-century mystic, and that is why he did not mention him in any of his scholarly works about the Sufis who lived in the fourth/tenth century.[2]

In his own writings, Niffarī did not define himself as a *ṣūfi*, nor did he define his teachings as components of *taṣawwuf*. For this reason, an examination of Niffarī's individual case would enable us to understand the boundaries between the mystic's awareness of his religious life, that is, how he defines his own piety and the way in which later authors and theoreticians defined that piety. In other words, studying Niffarī can be a gateway to resolving why such a unique figure is usually associated with early Sufism while he himself, apparently, was not eager to do so.

The questions that should be asked are: How did Niffarī himself consider his own spirituality in connection with the Sufi institutions of his time, as well as in connection with Islamic piety in general? How did he set his spiritual system apart both from the exoteric stream of the traditionalists as well as from the esoteric streams known in early medieval Islamic society? Would it be legitimate to consider as a Sufi someone who made every effort to detach himself from Sufi institutions? What are, then, the boundaries between the awareness of one's own individual piety and the way in which later figures choose to define it?

The statement made by Jaʿfar al-Khuldī to exclude al-Ḥakīm al-Tirmidhī from the group of *ṣūfiyya*: '*Mā ʿadadtuhu fī al-ṣūfiyya* ',[3] reflects the process in which Baghdadi Sufis around that time became increasingly conscious of their collective spiritual identity. Ahmet Karamustafa, in his pioneering work on the formative period of Sufism, provides us with a detailed discussion of the foundation of a distinct Baghdad-centred movement whose members became known as *ṣūfiyya* in the course of the third/ninth century. The group of *ṣūfiyya*, according to Karamustafa, came, from the mid-third/ninth century, 'into full view as members of a distinct mode of mystical piety', that applied to itself exclusively the title and could differentiate itself with particular characteristics that had not, any longer, to do with mere renunciation.[4] Those first Sufis, as Karamustafa indicates, formed an intellectual elite who were highly literate and learned in the *Qurʾān* and the *ḥadīth*, and they constituted a distinctly urban

[2] Louis Massignon, *Essay on the Origins of the Technical Language of Islamic Mysticism* (Notre Dame, Ind.: University of Notre Dame Press, 1997), 90 ff.

[3] See the detailed discussion of Tirmidhī's case later in this chapter.

[4] See Karamustafa, *Sufism*, 1–19.

phenomenon of middle-class urbanites of artisanal and merchant origins, in addition to certain cases of the upper classes. They succeeded in planting themselves strongly into the social fabric of Baghdad and came to be central players in the urban scenes of early medieval Muslim communities.[5]

Certain members of this movement, most probably, did not hesitate to exclude those whose piety did not fit in with theirs. From another viewpoint, Khuldī's statement helps us to realize that the growing and more established group of *ṣūfiyya* could hardly embrace persons with modes of spirituality that differed from the structured and systematic Sufism which became increasingly linked to the master–disciple relationship besides other elements of religiosity.

Niffarī's actual ties with the Sufi circles of his days were, apparently, weak or even missing. The structure of his spiritual system does not correspond with the Sufi writing tradition of his days even though the very components of his discourse cannot be totally separated from those in 'normative' Sufi works.

To understand Niffarī's case, I suggest taking the following steps:

I. The first step is to outline the foundations of Niffarī's teachings as presented in his *Mawāqif* and *Mukhāṭabāt* in an attempt to find out the most probable attitude of Niffarī towards both institutionalized Sufism and the general body of traditional Islam. This brings us to the question: Are his utterances daring enough to justify the neglect by his contemporaries?

It is not the aim of this chapter to present a thorough reading of Niffarī's writings, even though this, as far as I know, has not yet been undertaken. Most of the references to him in recent scholarship are terse and mundane and are usually presented with a focus on specific elements in his doctrinal system.[6]

[5] Ibid., 21–24.

[6] See the works of Alexander Knysh, *Islamic Mysticism: A Short History* (Leiden, Boston, Koln: Brill, 2000), 102–105; John Renard, *Knowledge of God in Classical Sufism: Foundations of Islamic Mystical Theology* (Mahwah, N.J.: Paulist Press, 2004), 27–28 (here, Niffarī's case is discussed in the section that also includes the three influential authors of the tenth century: Sarrāj, Kalābādhī, and Abū Ṭālib al-Makkī); and Khālid Belqāsim, *al-Ṣūfiyya wa-l-farāgh: al-Kitāba 'ind al-Niffarī* (Beirut: al-Markaz al-Thaqāfī al-'Arabī, 2012). Though the last is a significant and thorough contribution to the study of Niffarī, it does not place Niffarī apart from the sophisticated portrait of Islamic medieval spirituality. Many sections are even presented in a metaphorical and barely comprehensible Arabic.

II. In discussing the dynamics between Niffarī's individual case and the general religious scene of his time, it would be very useful to compare him with other controversial Sufi figures such as Abū Bakr al-Wāsiṭī, al-Ḥakīm al-Tirmidhī and Abū Yazīd al-Basṭāmī. This comparison might enable us to place Niffarī within the general context of the accepted Islamic piety of his period.

To begin with, it would be most important for us to set aside the common tendency to combine Niffarī with normative Sufism that came to be designated by the term *ṣūfiyya*. Niffarī's religiosity, although it shared a few features and terminology with normative Sufism, is a distinctive mode of piety. If the word *ṣūfī* in Niffarī's time referred to 'a clearly identifiable social movement in Baghdad that was based on a distinct type of piety',[7] then Niffarī could not be considered a *ṣūfī*. In addition to the figures of Dhū al-Nūn al-Miṣrī and al-Ḥārith al-Muḥāsibī, who are both mentioned by Christopher Melchert as those to whom one should be careful not to apply the term *ṣūfī* since they were not known as such in their own lifetimes, I would also add the figure of Niffarī while keeping in mind the essential differences between him and these two figures.[8] The problem of applying the term to Niffarī is precluded by the very fact that he was not known by this term during his life. Niffarī, very simply, was not known at all. The statements that are attributed to Dhū al-Nūn in the Sufi compendia of the fourth/tenth century, if they are presumed to be original, harmonize more or less with a common Sufi ethos that emerged in the course of the third/ninth century. This is not the case with Niffarī's statements in which both their structure and contents seem to challenge the fundamentals of the Sufi ethos of his day.

In modern scholarship, various possible explanations for Niffarī's neglect have been provided. A. J. Arberry, in the introduction to his edited *Mawāqif and Mukhāṭabāt*, asserts that 'Niffarī himself did not trouble to make a collection of his own writings.'[9] This historical notion serves Arberry and other scholars to explain the neglect of Niffarī.

In addition to the previous assertion, the common explanation in recent scholarship emphasizes the strange and obscure character of

[7] See the discussion of the various stages of development that witnessed changes in the semantic contents of this term in Karamustafa, *Sufism*, 6–7.

[8] See Melchert, *Origins and Early Sufism*, 14.

[9] Arberry draws our attention to numerous places in the commentary of ʿAfīf al-Dīn al-Tilimsānī (d. 690/1291), where passages out of context were noted. See Arberry (ed. and trans.), *Mawāqif and Mukhāṭabāt, introduction*, 7.

Niffarī. William Chittick, for instance, phrases this explanation as follows: 'He has not received nearly as much attention as he deserves mainly because of the extreme density and obscurity of what he is saying.'[10] Alexander Knysh suggests that the neglect of Niffarī in Sufi literature is partly originated in the fact that he was not affiliated with any mystical school or Sufi sheikh and, on the other hand, in his shocking views.[11] In her short MA thesis, Elizabeth Kendig summarizes the references to Niffarī and the scholarly attempts to explain his neglect in modern scholarship while offering her own suggestions. She figures that 'density and obscurity are not in themselves enough reasons to explain why Niffarī or any other mystical writer has not found a large audience.'[12] Kendig refers to what she calls Niffarī's 'extended *shaṭḥ*', that is, his intensive use of ecstatic utterances in a way that captured his literary attempts to describe the deep and intimate relation between man and God. Such descriptions could shock many people;[13] however, it is still not enough to identify the reasonable motivations for the complete silence about Niffarī's life and writings in the course of the three centuries that followed his death. Being isolated from society and out of touch with his contemporaries while absorbed in the company of the divine should be added, in Kendig's view, to explain the neglect of Niffarī in the fourth/tenth, fifth/eleventh and sixth/twelfth centuries.[14]

If the writings of Niffarī were really shocking for his contemporaries, why do we not come across any evidence of attempts to confront him or accuse him of heresy for instance? Why did Basṭāmī and Ḥallāj succeed in occupying a remarkable position in the collective consciousness of their times, while Niffarī's only share was a consensual neglect and a mysterious lack of recognition?[15]

[10] William Chittick, *Sufism: A Short Introduction* (Oxford: One World, 2000), 144.

[11] Knysh, *Islamic Mysticism*, 102–105.

[12] Elizabeth Kendig, 'Niffarī and His Audiences: The *Mawāqif* of Muḥammad Ibn 'Abdi 'l-Jabbār al-Niffarī (d. ca. 359/970),' (MA thesis), (University of Toronto, 2006), 5.

[13] See ibid., 8. [14] See ibid., 89.

[15] As for Ḥallāj, he was granted a separate biographical account in Sulamī's work (see Sulamī, *Ṭabaqāt*, 308–313) and, later, by Hujwīrī (see Jullābī Hujwīrī, *Kashf al-maḥjūb*, 189–193). Qushayrī does not mention him among the Sufi masters whose biographies he chose to collect in his *Risāla*. However, Qushayrī preserves several statements of Ḥallāj in different chapters of his work (see e.g., Qushayrī, *Risāla*, 4, 66, 83–84). In one occurrence in *Risāla*, Qushayrī tells an interesting anecdote according to which his master, Daqqāq, asked him to go to Sulamī's house and bring him one of Ḥallāj's works of poetry that Sulamī held at his place. See an earlier reference to this anecdote in Chapter 2.

Jamāl al-Marzūqī suggests that Niffarī's neglect in the early sources originated in the very fact that he himself did not describe his private life in his writings as did most of the Sufis. This fact, continues Marzūqī, might be added to Niffarī's errant life, which he spent in travel and solitude while having no colleagues and disciples.[16] Yūsuf al-Yūsuf suggests that Niffarī committed himself to the principles of *taqiyya* (dissimulation) and secrecy (*takattum*), and that this is the reason he was denied recognition by his contemporaries and successors.[17] The latter is, indeed, an interesting explanation, especially when we use it to compare Niffarī's case with those of other controversial figures in the history of Sufism, such as Tirmidhī, Basṭāmī, Ḥallāj, Rūzbihān Baqlī, and Ibn ʿArabī.

NIFFARĪ'S DOCTRINES IN HIS *MAWĀQIF* AND *MUKHĀṬABĀT*

In the following discussion, I intend to reappraise the system of thought implied in the two works of Niffarī in order to resolve the following questions: Were Niffarī's ideas considered daring and shocking enough to justify his neglect? If those ideas are compared with shocking statements of certain contemporary mystics, such as Wāsiṭī for instance, then what distinguishes Niffarī's thought, and why do I suggest treating his case as a manifestation of a separate mode of early medieval spirituality and not as a part of the Sufi institution as in the case of Wāsiṭī? In addition to Niffarī's actual solitary life, how does a unique system of thought which is founded on a considerable number of extreme statements and critical references both to the traditional Islamic system of worship and Sufi practices contribute to setting apart Niffarī's individual world?

According to Niffarī's famous commentator, ʿAfīf al-Dīn al-Tilimsānī, Niffarī himself was not responsible for the literary form and setting in order the text of *Mawāqif*.[18] The text of *Mawāqif* contains seventy-seven sections each called *mawqif*. In Arabic, this word could originally signify different meanings. It might indicate the staying or stopping place or the situation of staying itself.[19] The term lies at the very basis of Niffarī's theoretical framework. Without going too deeply into the various

[16] See Marzūqī, *Falsafat al-taṣawwuf*, 28–29.
[17] See Yūsuf Sāmī al-Yūsuf, *Muqaddima li-l-Niffarī* (Damascus: Muʾassasat ʿAlāʾ al-Dīn, 2004), 19–20.
[18] See Arberry (ed. and trans.), *Mawāqif and Mukhāṭabāt, introduction*, 6.
[19] See Ibn Manẓūr, *Lisān al-ʿarab*, vol. 9, 359.

interpretations of the term offered by later Sufi authors,[20] we might want to draw attention to the meaning provided in Ibn ʿArabī's *al-Futūḥāt al-makkiyya*. There, the term *mawqif* is said to refer to the state in which the Sufi, who advances through the various stages of the Sufi path, pauses between two stages in order to obtain the divine commands and provisions concerning the higher degree to which God desires to transfer him.[21]

Niffarī himself devotes *mawqif* 8 (*mawqif al-waqfa*) to explain in his own language the meaning of *waqfa*. In spite of the ambiguous language, a careful reading of this section could draw attention to the following components of *waqfa* theory:

a. *Waqfa* involves a complete seclusion from the *siwā* (everyone and everything other than God).
b. *Waqfa* is the source of knowledge (*al-waqfa yunbūʿ al-ʿilm*). This *ʿilm* is derived from the *wāqif* (the one who experiences *waqfa*) himself and not from any external source.
c. *Waqfa* implies the complete absence of the mystic's will and its annihilation in the absolute existence of the divine.[22] In the state of *waqfa*, there is no conciseness and the power of the intellect is absent. It is the point where contradictions meet in the utmost state of closeness to God.
d. *Waqfa* involves vision (*ruʾya*) of the divine.
e. The various descriptions presented by Niffarī to *waqfa* in the following lines of the section give the impression that the *wāqif* is granted a spiritual rank which is higher than the state of *maʿrifa*. He is, therefore, blessed by the divine majesty and power so that he becomes partly divine. Nothing except to God could affect him:

[20] In this regard, see the references to Niffarī in the works of Ibn ʿArabī, ʿAbd al-Wahhāb al-Shʿrānī and others in Arberry (ed. and trans.), *Mawāqif and Mukhāṭabāt, introduction*, 8–14.

[21] See Muḥyī al-Dīn Ibn ʿArabī, *al-Futūḥāt al-makkiyya* (Cairo: *al-Bābī al-Ḥalabī*, 1293/1876), vol. 2, 805.

[22] Niffarī writes: '*Kāda al-wāqif yufāriq ḥukm al-bashariyya*' (the *wāqif* almost exceeded the condition of humanity). Niffarī, *Kitāb al-mawāqif wa-yalīhi kitāb al-mukhāṭabāt*, ed. by Arthur J. Arberry (Cologne: Manshūrāt al-Jamal, 1996), 11 [Afterwards: Arberry (ed.), *Mawāqif*]; Arberry (ed. and trans.), *Mawāqif and Mukhāṭabāt*, 34. Cf. the first definition of *waqfa* provided by Tilimsānī: '*Al-waqfa hiya maqām fanāʾ dhāt al-ṭālib fī dhāt al-maṭlūb*' [*waqfa* is the station of the annihilation of the seeker's essence in the essence of the divine *maṭlūb* (lit. the one who is sought or desired). (Tilimsānī, *Sharḥ mawāqif al-Niffarī*, 115)].

> *'al-wāqif ḥurr'* (the *wāqif* is free).[23] The section ends with the divine saying: *'Ikhbārī/akhbārī*[24] *li-l-'ārifīn wa-wajhī li-l-wāqifīn.'*[25] Apparently, Niffarī chose to close this key section by emphasizing the supreme degree of *waqfa* and *wāqif* when compared with *ma'rifa* (divine knowledge) and *'ārif* (the one who obtains divine knowledge). The *'ārif* obtains the divine revelations with the help of God Himself who reveals to him His secrets. This process could be described as *ta'arruf*, an early term invented by the authors of the famous Sufi textbooks in the fourth/tenth century to indicate the way in which God reveals His secrets to His knowers. *Ta'rīf* differs from *ta'arruf* since it indicates a spiritual technique by which the Sufi, usually the beginner Sufi, seeks to realize the divine signs through his own human efforts.[26] The final utterance in *mawqif al-waqfa*, therefore, should be understood as follows: Those who know God obtain the divine revelations via God's *ta'arruf*. They listen to the secrets He chooses to tell them. In a more sublime position stand the *wāqifūn*, whom God chooses to grant not with His speech but rather with the vision of His own eternal face.

Another interesting section in *Kitāb al-mawāqif* is the *Mawqif of the Sea*. Niffarī's contemporary Sufis made use of the symbol of the sea in addition to other symbols that are related to water. Water and rain are common symbols of mercy in the *Qur'ān*.[27] As for the early Sufis, references to the sea are known to us in different sayings of Ḥallāj, Shiblī and Wāsiṭī.[28] The sea, in Niffarī's text, might be understood as the path towards the

[23] Arberry (ed.), *Mawāqif*, 14.

[24] In Arberry's edition the statements read *akhbārī*, and the English translation given to the whole statement is 'The gnostics have my communications, the stayers have my face' [Arberry (ed. and trans.), *Mawāqif and Mukhāṭabāt*, 37]. In the commentary of Tilimsānī, however, the statement reads *ikhbārī li-l-'ārifīn* (see Tilimsānī, *Sharḥ mawāqif al-Niffarī*, 152). Both variations convey the same meaning.

[25] Arberry (ed.), *Mawāqif*, 16.

[26] See e.g., Abū Bakr al-Kalābādhī, *Kitāb al-ta'arruf li-madhhab ahl al-taṣawwuf*, ed. by 'Abd al-Ḥalīm Maḥmūd and Ṭāha Srūr (Cairo: 'Īsā al-Bābī al-Ḥalabī, 1960), 64.

[27] See e.g., Martin Lings, 'The *Qur'an*ic Symbolism of Water', *Studies in Comparative Religion*, vol. 2, no. 3 (1968), 6 pp. This article is found on the following website www.studiesincomparativereligion.com/uploads/articlepdfs/62.pdf (accessed on 24 March 2015).

[28] In the *Kitāb al-Ṭawāsīn*, the following statement appears: 'All sciences are one drop of His sea' [al-Ḥusayn b. Manṣūr al-Ḥallāj, *Kitāb al-ṭawāsīn*, ed. by Louis Massignon (Paris: Geuthner, 1913), 13]. Sarrāj quotes Shiblī to have said: 'My sea is without any coast' (*baḥrī bi-lā shāṭi'*) (Sarrāj, *Luma'*, 365). As for Wāsiṭī, he is quoted by Abū Ḥafṣ al-Suhrawardī in his discussion of *sukr* and *ṣaḥw* (intoxication and wakefulness) to have

ultimate experience of *waqfa*. 'I saw the ships sinking and the planks floating; then the planks sank also.'[29] Ships and planks are both symbols of the instrumental religious patterns to obtain God's closeness. Those could refer to Islamic rituals as well as to different austerities and ascetic practices known among the Sufis. Both, according to Niffarī, could not help in reaching the *waqfa*. Only a complete sinking in the sea could bring about deliverance and salvation. While the first *Mawqif of Glory* (*'izz*) emphasizes the idea of God's immanence and leaves the impression that obtaining His closeness is barely possible, the *Mawqif of the Sea* provides a glimpse of hope of achieving this closeness under strict and even very rare conditions. Since the *siwā* involves, by its very essence, everything that exists, the ambitious will to reach the closeness of *waqfa* is broken all the time by the impossibility of becoming totally free of that *siwā*. The latter includes human will, desires, actions, religious rituals and speech. Formal religious codes and mechanisms including ritual prayer, reciting the *Qur'ān* and remembering God's name (*dhikr*) are nothing but different aspects of the *siwā*. It is Wāsiṭī who comes to mind again here. According to Wāsiṭī, God makes Himself known through the world of creation; however, the latter veils God from being known because what becomes known are the objects, which are the veils themselves, not God. According to Wāsiṭī, God alone is the true reality, and everything else is nothing.[30] In another saying of Wāsiṭī, he even makes use of the word *siwā* itself (see below).

The text of *Mukhāṭabāt* is drawn from a series of divine addresses, and each begins with the expression 'O servant' (*yā 'abd!*). It has been noted that, unlike the *Mawāqif*, the text of *Mukhāṭabāt* lacks any attempt to put its parts in order.[31] The very idea that God Himself chooses to address the mystic and to confide His secrets to him was not unusual in early Sufi tradition. Sarrāj in his *Luma'* refers to what can be seen as a problematic feature of some of Basṭāmī's statements in which God is said to have

described wakefulness that follows intoxication as a state in which one enters the sea, and later the waves take him back to the coast. (See Suhrawardī, *'Awārif*, 355–356.)

29 Arberry (ed.), *Mawāqif*, 7; Arberry (ed. and trans.), *Mawāqif and Mukhāṭabāt*, 31.

30 See e.g., Sulamī, *Ḥaqā'iq al-tafsīr: Tafsīr al-Qur'ān al-'azīz*, ed. by Sayyid b. 'Imrān (Beirut: Dār al-Kutub al-'Ilmiyya, 2001), vol. 2, 221–222 (his exegesis of verse 53 of *Sūra* 41); 224 (his reference to verse 11 of *Sūra* 42). See the detailed discussion of Wāsiṭī's teachings in Laury Silvers, 'Theoretical Sufism in the Early Period: With an Introduction to the Thought of Abū Bakr al-Wāsiṭī (d. ca. 320/928) on the Interrelationship between Theoretical and the Practical Sufism', *Studia Islamica*, vol. 98/99 (2004), 71–94, and particularly 81.

31 See Arberry (ed. and trans.), *Mawāqif and Mukhāṭabāt*, *introduction*, 7.

initiated the deep experience of closeness with the mystic and to have addressed him. Sarrāj indicates that the verb *qāla lī* (He said to me) in Basṭāmī's utterances should be understood as the words of the inner voice of the mystic himself. When the latter feels entirely obliterated in the divine presence, he ascribes every notion he hears to God since 'all notions and heart secrets begin from God and go to God'.[32] Niffarī's *Mukhāṭabāt* as well as his *Mawāqif* rely entirely upon the idea of God addressing man and not on man's addresses to or invocations of God. This affirmation could serve those who might accuse Niffarī of the desire to provide a sacred text that would contradict the holy speech of God, mainly the *Qur'ān* itself. I do not believe that Niffarī sought to challenge the holy text of Islam. In the few passages where Niffarī refers to *Qur'ān*ic verses, he does so in order to establish his doctrine concerning the superiority of the state of *waqfa* over all forms of institutionalized religiosity. Both Sufism and traditional Islam during the fourth/tenth century seem very far from accepting Niffarī's individual-personal experience of *waqfa*. Both are full of ritual practices that hinder man from attaining the goal of becoming a *wāqif* by using obstacles or veils. The act of reciting the *Qur'ān* is not rejected in itself but is rejected only during the temporary state of *waqfa*

Niffarī uses the word *dhikr* while announcing that 'My recollection is a veil' (*dhirkī ḥijāb*).[33] In addition to its different meanings, the word *dhikr* could indicate the *Qur'ān* itself as well as the practice of recollecting God's name in Sufism.[34] During the very delicate state of *waqfa*, when man's ties with the world of creatures are totally cut off and his spiritual essence draws very close to the deity, all religious forms that are established upon the principle of absolute transcendentalism are considered as veils. Niffarī, however, does not seek to replace the Islamic image of a transcendent God by means of his doctrine of *waqfa*. He very frequently emphasizes the attributes of majesty and glory: 'I am the Glorious One Whose neighborhood is insupportable and Whose continuance is not sought', states Niffarī in the first section of his *Kitāb al-mawāqif*.[35] By portraying the experience of *waqfa* as arduous and rarely possible, Niffarī restricts it to a few individuals of the spiritual elite who are able to free

[32] Sarrāj, *Luma'*, 382–383.
[33] Arberry (ed.), *Mawāqif*, 80; Arberry (ed. and trans.), *Mawāqif and Mukhāṭabāt*, 85.
[34] On the different semantic contents of the term in early Sufism, see e.g., Salamah-Qudsi, *Institutionalized mashyakha*, 416–417.
[35] Arberry (ed.), *Mawāqif*, 1; Arberry (ed. and trans.), *Mawāqif and Mukhāṭabāt*, 27.

themselves of everything and everyone except God during the time of *waqfa* while they are being completely absorbed into the divine entity. When this experience is over, man's ties with the world return again, and all religious forms that were considered veils become valid once more in what we can call the post-*waqfa* state.

Dwelling on *Qurʾān*ic verses or particular parts of them for the sake of producing new semantic layers of meaning to support spiritual doctrines was a very common strategy in the writings of the early Sufis. In certain places in his writings, Niffarī appears to have chosen particular parts of *Qurʾān*ic verses in order to emphasize the divine essence that the individual is granted in the midst of the ultimate state of *waqfa*. In the index of the *Qurʾān*ic verses in Saʿīd al-Ghānimī's edition of Niffarī's writings (2007), some verses are missing.[36] Verses that are related to water provide a good example of Niffarī's system of employing the holy text in his works. As for verse 30 of *Sūra* 21, Niffarī in *Mukhāṭaba* 4, erases the verbal form *jaʿalnā* (lit. 'We made') which was explained as 'We created' in *Quraʾān* exegetical literature. Instead of the original complete verse, he quotes the following part of the verse: '*min al-māʾ kull shayʾ ḥayy*' (from water proceeds every living thing) and puts it immediately after the watch word 'O servant' (*yā ʿabd*). The sentence that precedes this statement is also interesting. Niffarī says: 'If thou abidest in the vision of Me, thou shalt say to the water "advance", and "recede"' (*yā ʿabd! la-ʾin aqamta fī ruʾyatī la-taqūlanna li-l-māʾ aqbil wa-adbir*).'[37] The phrase *aqbil wa-adbir* is well known in traditionalists' discussions of ablution and the way in which the Prophet Muḥammad used to perform ablutions in particular. Niffarī probably sought to bring forward the *wāqif*'s ability to control the world of water, the world of living creatures by virtue of his sublime state. By the end of the same address, God appears to have said: 'When thou seest Me, knowledge is part of thy water, so make it flow whither thou wilt, that by it thou mayest establish what thou wilt.'[38]

There are frequent utterances by Niffarī which were considered shocking concerning Islamic rituals. In '*Mawqif* of the Veil' (no. 47), God says: 'I have never appeared in the ending of any ritual prayer.' In the same *Mawqif* God is mentioned to have said: 'These are the countries of the community' (*hādhihi awṭān al-ʿāmma*). The latter statement can very well explain Niffarī's approach towards the Islamic mechanism of worshipping God through the system of traditional rituals. This system

[36] See e.g., Arberry (ed.), *Mawāqif*, 151, 154. [37] Ibid., 151.
[38] Arberry (ed. and trans.), *Mawāqif and Mukhāṭabāt*, 136.

suits the normative Muslims not the selected group in the state of *waqfa*. Niffarī considers divine attributes merely as veils to obtain the ultimate closeness to Him. Niffarī portrays God's attribute of clemency in the following sarcastic scene: 'I am the Clement. And I saw the Lord in the midst of His servants, and every one of them was fastened to His belt.'[39] Recollecting God's name is also a veil: '*Dhikrī ḥijāb*',[40] or on another occasion: 'My recollection is not of My temples' (*fa-laysa dhikrī min buyūtī*).[41]

Recent scholarship has generally indicated that Niffarī's texts do not present any type of continuity for earlier and contemporary Sufi literary tradition. However, many of Niffarī's sayings still imply conventional Sufi ideas and theories. The very concept of *mawqif* as the manifestation of the divine absolute's will to 'make man stay or pause' wherever God wants him to do so reflects Niffarī's unique way of emphasizing the direct and personal mystic experience between man and God. This was in fact the final destination of the path as Sufis frequently emphasized.[42] Niffarī makes use of certain Sufi theories implied in common Sufi terminology for the sake of contradicting those theories. In various passages, the reader feels familiar with Niffarī's Sufi language, but when s/he goes deeply into the process of reading s/he gradually realizes Niffarī's intention to undermine both the Sufi language and the whole institution of theories and practices that lies behind it. Meanwhile, on frequent occasions in Niffarī's writings, strong echoes of Wāsiṭī's teachings come to mind. As for the above-mentioned statements concerning *dhikr*, for instance, the following statement of Wāsiṭī should be mentioned: 'Those who recollect God's name are more unmindful than those who forget to recollect His name, since recollection is *siwā*. '[43]

In addition to his wish to undermine Sufism as an established institution of language and practices, Niffarī offers a serious challenge to the Muslim concept of ritual duties. If we turn back to the *Qur'ān* itself, we note that all the verses in which the derivatives of the root (*wqf*) appear (*wuqifū* and *mawqūfūn*) in their original contexts describe the unbelievers and the punishment they are expected to receive.[44] Themes of fire and burning are frequent in Niffarī's *Mawāqif*.[45] The *Qur'ān*ic act of *wuqūf*

39 Arberry (ed.), *Mawāqif*, 77; Arberry (ed. and trans.), *Mawāqif and Mukhāṭabāt*, 83.

40 Arberry (ed.), *Mawāqif*, 80; Arberry (ed. and trans.), *Mawāqif and Mukhāṭabāt*, 85.

41 Arberry (ed.), *Mawāqif*, 148; Arberry (ed. and trans.), *Mawāqif and Mukhāṭabāt*, 134.

42 On this topic, see e.g., Salamah-Qudsi, *Everlasting Sufi*, 313–338.

43 Sulamī, *Ṭabaqāt*, 306.

44 See verses 27 and 30 in *Sūra* 6 and verse 31 of *Sūra* 34.

45 See e.g., Arberry (ed.), *Mawāqif*, 21–22; 81; 83.

imposed upon the unbelievers obtained a totally different meaning in Niffarī's system: It is a description of the *wāqif*, the perfect man who sees God and does not see other than God. It was Niffarī who wrote on behalf of God: 'If you see the fire, drop yourself in it and do not run away.'[46] On another occasion in his *Mawāqif*, Niffarī states that the '*waqfa* is the pillar of knowledge' (*al-waqfa ʿamūd al-maʿrifa*),[47] a statement that reminds us directly of the well-known prophetic tradition: '*Al-ṣalāt ʿimād al-dīn*' (prayer is the pillar of religion). In another place, Niffarī says that, while the wayfarer (*al-sāʾir*) is proud of his prayers, the prayer itself becomes 'proud' of the *wāqif*.[48] Many shocking statements that refer to the concept of *ṣalāt* appear in Niffarī's texts: 'When knowledge calls thee, with all its conditions, at the time of prayer, and thou answerest it, thou art separated from Me.'[49] In yet another statement, an attempt to contradict the Islamic idea of the manifold reward granted to him who does one good work by saying that 'one good work is ten to him who sees Me not, but evil (*sayyiʾa*) to him who sees Me.'[50] It is not an overstatement then to say that such indications, at least in their plain meaning, offer a serious challenge to the Muslim religious institution with some of its pillars and basic principles. However, I would like to emphasize here that similar challenging statements were not infrequent in Sufi writings of the same period, sayings like those of Abū al-Qāsim al-Jurjānī al-Ṭūsī: 'The ninety-nine names of God turn into the attributes of the Sufi wayfarer while he is still making his way along the path and has not arrived yet to its final destination' or many statements quoted by Qushayrī in his *Risāla*, like that of Abū Ḥafṣ al-Naysābūrī: 'Since I knew God neither truth nor untruth entered my heart'[51] or the statement of Wāsiṭī who states that 'knowledge would not be true if the mystic has a divine dispensation [for people!] (*istighnāʾ bi-llāh*) and has a total dependance on God (*iftiqār ilayhi*).'[52]

[46] Ibid., 81. In his brief reference to Niffarī, Christian Lange indicates that the feeling of superiority over hell as it was voiced by Niffarī demonstrates an extreme challenge of the fixation on paradise and hell characteristics of the earlier renunciants and Sufis. See Lange, *Paradise and Hell*, 230–231.

[47] Arberry (ed.), *Mawāqif*, 13. [48] See ibid., 11.

[49] Arberry (ed. and trans.), *Mawāqif and Mukhāṭabāt*, 60. [50] Ibid., 61.

[51] For the first statement see Suhrawardī, *ʿAwārif*, 189. For the other, see Qushayrī, *Risāla*, 155.

[52] Qushayrī, *Risāla*, 155, lines 16–17. It is worth noting that Sarrāj devoted a separate chapter in his *Lumaʿ* to Wāsiṭī's sayings and the ways in which these statements should be reconcilably interpreted (see Sarrāj, *Ṣuḥuf min kitāb al-lumaʿ*, '*bāb fī bayān mā qāla al-Wāsiṭī*,' 12–16. Although this chapter includes only two 'problematic' sayings of Wāsiṭī,

One of the basic features in Niffarī's discourse lies in his systematic attempts to marginalize the position of religious symbols in favour of a sincere relationship between man and God. Recitation of the holy *Qur'ān*, for instance, is not recommended at nights because nights belong to God, 'not to the scriptures that are recited [...] not to the lauds and praises [...] not to invocation'.[53] Obedience (*ṭā'a*) and seeking God's contentment (*ṭalab riḍāhu*) are also negatively indicated: 'And I departed, and saw that to seek after His approval was to disobey Him.'[54]

The imperative form *uktub* (write down) which appears frequently in the *Mawāqif* manifests a parallel to the divine order *iqra'* addressed to the Prophet Muḥammad, implying the very beginning of God's revelation. Niffarī's text reads: 'Write down the manner of My self-revelation to thee by means of the gnosis of revealed certainty, and write down how I caused thee to witness.'[55]

In the text of *Mukhāṭabāt*, we come across several implications for the Prophet. In *Mukhāṭaba* 9, for instance, Niffarī makes use of the traditional idea according to which prayer is described as *qurrat 'ayn* (delight) for the Prophet while referring to the mystic. God says: 'Pray to Me with thy heart, and I will reveal to thee its delight in prayer.'[56] Terms such as *ḥabīb* and *amīn*, traditional titles of the Prophet Muḥammad, are introduced by Niffarī to describe the mystic whom God asks to witness that which He causes none to witness, save *ḥabīb* and *amīn*.[57]

If we separate Niffarī's extremist statements and distribute them in other famous Sufi textbooks of the fourth/tenth and fifth/eleventh centuries, those statements will certainly be absorbed into the general fabric of what is regarded as reconciliatory or even moderate Sufi textbooks, and they will not have the same shocking influence on the reader that they aroused when concentrated in Niffarī's texts. When all these statements are gathered into one fabric, their shocking identity becomes affirmed, and that is why the whole text of *Mawāqif* becomes a strange creature of Niffarī's time. The extremist sayings of Dhū al-Nūn al-Miṣrī and Abū Yazīd al-Basṭāmī, for example, could have shocked more than Niffarī's if they had been compiled in one complete literary product. Were the works

Sarrāj insisted by the end of the chapter that the way in which he interpreted Wāsiṭī's two sayings should be applied to his other statements (see idem, *Luma'*, 409).

53 Arberry (ed.), *Mawāqif*, 71. 54 Ibid., 79. 55 Ibid., 100. 56 Ibid., 140.

57 Arberry (ed.), *Mawāqif* (the text of *Mukhāṭabāt*), 160 (*mukhāṭaba* 12). Cf. Arberry (ed. and trans), *Mawāqif and Mukhāṭabāt*, 142 (*Address* 12, statement no. 4).

of Niffarī published and known in his lifetime, they would have been combined with his individual mode of piety and they would probably have succeeded in gaining the recognition of his contemporaries.

I agree with the notion that 'the first and major audience of the *mawāqif* was an audience of the one who experienced the suspension of time and place which is the world of the *mawqif*.'[58] Still, I would add another relevant suggestion: This 'world of *mawqif*' would have reflected Niffarī's controversial approach towards his Sufi contemporaries, basically, their increasing interest in the status of the sheikh, the spiritual guide who in the course of the fourth/tenth century became a major pillar of the Sufi system of thoughts.[59] Sufi sheikhs occupied more and more the very centre of the Sufi life and praxis, and substantial relationships were increasingly connecting them with their disciples. In the course of time, those sheikhs succeeded in obtaining a special type of spiritual authority as the exclusive mediators between the Sufi disciple and God. In light of these occurrences, it would be possible to assume that Niffarī rejected the increasing position of Sufi sheikhs, and, therefore, he established his complete system of thoughts on the principle of *mawqif*. The divine act of making the mystic stay or pause (*īqāf*) might imply Niffarī's fierce war against the whole Sufi system that grants the sheikh this divine authority over the Sufi wayfarers. Niffarī, most probably, had a very strong desire to release himself from all forms of systemized religiosity and all conventional patterns of spirituality. None of these seems to demonstrate the real life with God as Niffarī saw it.

From another perspective, we might wonder whether there is a satisfactory basis to suggest a possible *malāmatī* impact on Niffarī's world views. In order to answer this question we must compare the case of Niffarī with the basic components of *malāmatiyya* known in his time. *Risālat al-malāmatiyya* of Sulamī is most probably the earliest available document for *malāmatī* teachings during the third/ninth and fourth/tenth centuries. Sulamī portrays the *malāmatī* Sufi as the one whose inner life with God is concealed from people's eyes. His full involvement in regular life affairs helps him protect himself against ostentation since all

[58] Kendig, *Niffarī and His Audiences*, 86.

[59] Sufi sheikhs, from the third/ninth century onward, had increasingly gained a direct intervention in their novices' behaviour and lives, gathering into their hands both functions of instruction '*ta'līm*' and training '*tarbiya*' [see Fritz Meier, 'Khurāsān and the End of Classical Sufism', in *Essays on Islamic Piety and Mysticism*, trans. by John O'Kane with editorial assistance of Bernd Radtke (Leiden: Brill, 1999), 195–198].

outward appearances of piety including good deeds lead to self-ostentation.[60] By doing so, pure sincerity in performing religious deeds (*ikhlāṣ al-a'māl)* is attained.

Interestingly, many statements mentioned in *mawqif al-a'māl* in Niffarī's *Mawāqif* might remind the reader of *malāmatī* connotations. The last statement made by Niffarī was that one should 'weigh science in the balance of intention, and weigh works in the balance of sincerity'. The second part of the statement, '*wa-zin al-'amal bi-mīzān al-ikhlāṣ*'[61] is of great importance since it recalls directly the above-mentioned *malāmatī* doctrine of *ikhlāṣ al-a'māl*. In a previous place in the same section of *Mawāqif*, the following statement appears: 'Perform works, but do not regard thy works.'[62] This recalls a saying attributed to Abū Ḥafṣ al-Naysābūrī, one of the first figures of the Khurāsānian *malāmatī* movement in Nishapur:[63] 'I desisted from performing works, then, I turned back to them. Afterwards, the works left me, and I did not turn back to them.'[64] The relationship between *'ilm* and *'amal* is also shown in the sayings of the *malāmatī* figures of this period.[65] In the same *mawqif al-a'māl* we come across several statements in which comparisons between *'ilm* and *'amal* are also presented.[66] The biographies of those considered to be the founders of the *malāmatī* tradition make it clear that those persons preserved a communal form of life. They had contacts with their disciples and made efforts to teach them the *malāmatī* teachings.[67]

Affinities between several statements in Niffarī's texts and particular *malāmatī* doctrines should not necessarily be seen as evidence of any impact of early *malāmatiyya* on Niffarī. However, it could mean that Niffarī practised the *malāmatī* principle of concealing one's spiritual life as well as his tendency towards a life of seclusion. He was probably not committed to the 'official' *malāmatī* call to live a normal life adhering to the requirements of society, at least if by 'society' we mean here the Sufi

60 See Sulamī, *Risālat al-malāmatiyya*, 87–90. Cf. F. De Jong, 'Malāmatiyya,' the first section 'In the Central Islamic Lands,' *Encyclopaedia of Islam*, second edition, ed. by P. Bearman, Th. Bianquis, C. E. Bosworth, E. van Donzel and W. P. Heinrichs, consulted online on 13 October 2017 http://dx.doi.org/10.1163/1573-3912_islam_COM_0643, and the second section written by Hamid Algar ('In Iran and the Eastern Lands') (ibid.).

61 Arberry (ed.), *Mawāqif*, 26; Arberry (ed. and trans.), *Mawāqif and Mukhāṭabāt*, 45.

62 Arberry (ed.), *Mawāqif*, 25; Arberry (ed. and trans.), *Mawāqif and Mukhāṭabāt*, 44.

63 See J. Chabbi, 'Abū Ḥafṣ al-Ḥaddād,' *Encyclopaedia Iranica*, vol. I, 293–294.

64 Sulamī, *Ṭabaqāt*, 109.

65 See e.g., the sayings of Ḥamdūn al-Qaṣṣār in ibid., 115.

66 See Arberry (ed.), *Mawāqif*, 25–26.

67 See e.g., Sulamī, *Risālat al-malāmatiyya*, 87–88; 103.

community in particular. If this is the case, I suggest that Niffarī was a *malāmatī* in his teachings without being a part of the movement and of those who created its official agenda among the *malāmatī* circle of Nishapur. Meanwhile, Niffarī's tendency to live in solitude does not necessarily contradict the declared teaching of the *malāmatī* figures not to be isolated from the world. The following description of Basṭāmī is quoted by Sulamī in his *Risālat al-malāmatiyya*: 'The true knower of God is the one who eats, drinks, jokes with you and sells to you, buys from you, while his heart is located in the kingdom of the eternal holiness.'[68] Niffarī might have practised a conventional family life in addition to his spiritual tendency to perform solitude and roving in particular phases of his life. That is why relying on the conventional idea that Niffarī was a solitary figure in order to exclude him from the official *malāmatī* circle is also not satisfactory or acceptable. Additionally, the texts of Niffarī succeed in portraying a spiritually graced mystic who became both *wāqif* in the text of *Mawāqif* and *mukhāṭab* (the one who is spoken to by God Himself) in the text of *Mukhāṭabāt*. This notion might not conform to the typical *malāmatī* call for avoiding pleasure in any mystic state (*ḥāl*) and accusing one's soul of hypocrisy and conceit.[69] Most probably, *malāmatī* ideas in Niffarī's texts had nothing to do with any formal or institutionalized circle of *malāma* tiyya.

Remarkably, Niffarī did not mention the name of any specific person in his writings. This fact could be seen as an indication of his separation from his contemporaries. He might have attempted to practise a life of solitude and roving, at least in particular phases in his life. He might have practised a life of renunciation, a mode of anti-social piety that could be entitled 'deviant individualism'.[70] Even though he led a type of family life about which we unfortunately have no information, he, by no means, practised the custom of *siyāḥa* in its early Sufi meaning, roving in solitude and without taking any provisions and planning any clear destination.[71]

[68] Ibid., 92. [69] See ibid., 90–91; De Jong, *Malāmatiyya*.

[70] The term 'deviant individualism' was suggested by Ahmet Karamustafa in his treatment of the roots of the anti-social Islamic piety as part of his introductory remarks on his interesting work on *qalandar* dervishes. See Ahmet Karamustafa, *God's Unruly Friends: Dervish Groups in the Islamic Later Middle Period 1200–1550* (Salt Lake City: University of Utah Press, 1994), 31 ff.

[71] It is usually argued that the Sufi custom of *siyāḥa* essentially differs from *riḥla*, the medieval well-known type of travel, because *siyāḥa* leads to 'internal science' (*'ilm bāṭin*) while *riḥla* leads to 'external science' (*'ilm ẓāhir*). Looking for the hidden science by travelling everywhere and nowhere is the basic description of Sufi *siyāḥa* for the most part (see Touati, *Islam and Travel*, 164). Primary data on the Sufi custom of *siyāḥa* could

'Crossing the desert' was an important means for achieving spiritual progress and even a spiritual guide for the mystic seeker in early Sufi doctrines.[72] In both the *mawqif* of *tīh* (straying) and the *mawqif* of *ikhtiyār* (choice), Niffarī alludes to his errant and solitary life; in the first he indicates that 'the mystic must reach God alone, unaccompanied by ordinary men,'[73] while in the second he states God's order: 'Go forth into the empty desert and sit alone until I see thee: For when I see thee, I shall mount with thee from earth to heaven, and shall not be veiled from thee.'[74]

Generally speaking, what had been regarded as the 'shocking' feature of Niffarī's discourse could not, by itself, be a sufficient explanation for his neglect in Sufi sources. There is a set of dynamics that, while combined, brought about this neglect: Niffarī never called himself a Sufi. Meanwhile, early Sufi teachings and themes had been echoed throughout his writings. It seems as Niffarī intended to detach himself from the entire Sufi institution with all its communal and social features as part of his attempts to promote the position of the individual mystic mode of life. Meanwhile, he was eager to form his ideas into two basic frameworks: the state of *mawqif* and the state of *mukhāṭaba*. Writing down these ideas gives the impression that Niffarī thought about introducing various parts of the text to potential readers among the mystics of his times. I would suppose that Niffarī's life of solitude did not contradict his wish to bring about a shift in the spirituality of his contemporaries, and that is why he was eager to document his ideas. If historically Niffarī himself 'did not trouble to make a collection of his own writings',[75] why could we not suggest that he indeed wanted to do so without being successful at last?

Niffarī, very simply, believed in an individual mode of piety, a mode that does not contradict one's family life, but it could not avoid a serious contradiction with the Sufi institution that began to be consolidated in the course of the third/ninth and fourth/tenth centuries. This institution began to hold many features that would be seen as controversial with the nucleus of the intimate mystic experience. Apart from the controversial feature, one can mention the sheikh–disciple relationship, the collective codes of behaviour consolidated in Sufi manuals of the fourth/tenth and

be sought in: Makkī, *Qūt*, vol. 2, 430, and an anonymous author, *Adab al-mulūk*, 58–60. For a detailed discussion of the use of the concepts *siyāḥa* and *safar* in early Sufi literature, see: Salamah-Qudsi, *Crossing the Desert*, 129–147.

72 See an anonymous author, *Adab al-mulūk*, 173; 174.

73 Arberry (ed. and trans.), *Mawāqif and Mukhāṭabāt*, 230.

74 Ibid., 86.

75 Arberry (ed. and trans.), *Mawāqif and Mukhāṭabāt, introduction*, 7.

fifth/eleventh centuries and the increasing importance of Sufi external codes and rituals, clothes, rules of ethics and detailed regulations of initiation into the Sufi way of life. While Sufi figures who provoked the criticism of Sufi theoreticians and authors aligned themselves with Sufism and claimed to be the representatives of the ideal Sufi thought, Niffarī chose to detach himself from Sufism and its followers. People did not know about him in his lifetime, and when his writings became published, no one troubled himself to say a word about an ambiguous person who doubtfully existed. The relationship between the Sufi disciple and his authoritative master increasingly occupied the very core of the institutionalized Sufi system. While the focus of Sufi writings shifted to a collective discourse of Sufi communal life within the *ribāṭ*-based Sufism, a mere confidential, personal and completely individual tone like that of Niffarī, in spite of its literary value, had, in fact, nothing to do with its contemporary Sufi reality.

BETWEEN NIFFARĪ AND OTHER CONTROVERSIAL FIGURES IN SUFI HISTORY

If we compare Niffarī's case to that of al-Ḥakīm al-Tirmidhī, for instance, a few remarks should be made. It is remarkable that the Sufi handbooks of the fourth/tenth and fifth/eleventh centuries paid scant attention to Tirmidhī.[76] Attempts to exclude Tirmidhī from the Sufi circles were well known, especially among the Sufis of Baghdad, such as Jaʿfar al-Khuldī, who was quoted as saying that Tirmidhī did not belong to *ṣūfiyya*.[77] However, it should be noted that Tirmidhī was privileged to be granted a separate biography in Sulamī's *Ṭabaqāt*,[78] as well as in later Sufi textbooks, such as Qushayrī's *Risāla*[79] and Hujwīrī's *Kashf al-maḥjūb*.[80]

Probably like Tirmidhī, Niffarī did not mention the word *ṣūfī* or any of its derivatives in his writings. In his unique autobiographical work, *Buduww sha'n Abī ʿAbd Allāh al-Ḥakīm al-Tirmidhī* (The Beginning of the Career of al-Ḥakīm al-Tirmidhī), Tirmidhī was eager to describe his own experiences of persecution when his enemies reported to the governor of Balkh that he 'was engaged in heretical innovation and claimed

[76] Al-Ḥakīm al-Tirmidhī, *The Concept of Sainthood in Early Islamic Mysticism: Two Works by al-Ḥakīm al-Tirmidhī*, trans. by Bernd Radtke and John O'Kane (Richmond, Surrey: Curzon Press, 1996), 5.

[77] Sulamī, *Ṭabaqāt*, 454. [78] See ibid., 212–215. [79] See Qushayrī, *Risāla*, 24.

[80] See Jullābī Hujwīrī, *Kashf al-maḥjūb*, 177–178.

to be a Prophet'.[81] Later in his autobiography, Tirmidhī narrates with much pride that after a short time, 'the people gathered before my door, among them certain shaikhs of the city [...] and my words grasped their hearts so firmly that they were taken prisoners'.[82] The latter notion might explain why Tirmidhī's enemies felt the crucial need to exclude him from their circles. He, in fact, was an influential figure whose involvement in the religious and social arenas of his period was clear from his own writings. He used to reveal his spiritual experiences to his fellow men during nightly sessions[83] and succeeded in becoming a public sheikh with many followers.[84] It might be said, then, that Tirmidhī's autobiography 'demonstrates a period in which the mystic was in need of his fellow men in order to share with them his deepest experiences of spiritual revelation'.[85] However, it would be necessary here to add to the previous notion the idea that the same period could witness different cases, in which individual experiences and solitary modes of life should have existed side by side with the general tendency towards a communal Sufi experience like that demonstrated in Tirmidhī's *Buduww shaʾn.*

For Tirmidhī, re-writing the basic lines of his life as well as the mystical visions of himself, of his wife and even of some of his companions, seemed to have been effective instruments to establish his own authority as a Sufi master and to develop his high position within Islamic religiosity of that time. Even if Tirmidhī's name was rarely mentioned in the Sufi handbooks known to us, his figure and teachings were, undoubtedly, present in the consciousness of the authors of these handbooks. The case of Niffarī was different, however. In a social-religious context, he seems to have isolated himself from the wider community. He never claimed to be a mystic, nor had any disciples to tell about as did Tirmidhī.

Tirmidhī, who was eager in his writings to emphasize his association with the Sufi system of transmitting Sufi conduct by means of the sheikh–disciple relationship, motivated his enemies to explicitly reject him. Niffarī, on the other hand, attempts to disavow the Sufi system, and that

[81] Al-Ḥakīm al-Tirmidhī, *The Concept of Sainthood*, 20. [82] Ibid., 23.

[83] See Ibid., 20; 21–22 ('At night, it was our practice to gather and to confer with one another, engaging in discussions'; 'we gathered as guests of one of our brethren to perform *dhikr* recitations'); Cf. Muḥammad b. ʿAlī al-Ḥakīm al-Tirmidhī, *Buduww shaʾn al-Ḥakīm al-Tirmidhī*, in al-Ḥakīm al-Tirmidhī, *Kitāb khatm al-awliyāʾ*, ed. by ʿUthmān Yaḥyā (Beirut: al-Maṭbaʿa al-Khāthūlīkiyya, 1965), Arabic text, 17, 19.

[84] See Tirmidhī, *Buduww shaʾn*, 20–21.

[85] Salamah-Qudsi, *The Will to Be Unveiled*, 205.

is why his case did not seem worthy of any efforts by the *ṣūfiyya* of that time to exclude him.

The comparison with Basṭāmī is also interesting. The idea that God raises the Sufi and stops him in a particular stopping place was employed earlier by Basṭāmī: '*Rafaʿanī marra fa-aqāmanī bayn yadayhi*' (He once raised me, and stopped me in front of Him).[86] It should be noted, meanwhile, that the ecstatic utterances (*shaṭaḥāt*) of Basṭāmī, even the more extremist among them, were, in fact, discrete utterances that could not provide any complete theoretical framework similar to that provided by Niffarī. What could be seen as a demonstration of intensive emotional experiences of Basṭāmī became in Niffarī's work the result of an intellectual and well-calculated act of writing. While Basṭāmī's *shaṭaḥāt* were an expression of living the emotional mystic state, the texts of Niffarī could be seen as a deep study of the mystic state. This study was highly calculated and cognitive, and it usually followed the spiritual experience itself. It is not surprising then to say that Abū Yazīd al-Basṭāmī was not seriously excluded from the Sufi institution of his time and that he succeeded in protecting his own position within its walls. The biography of Basṭāmī was introduced to the basic Sufi textbooks of the fourth/tenth and fifth/eleventh centuries.[87] Sulamī's portrayal of Basṭāmī in his *Ṭabaqāt* is distinguished by the tendency to preserve regular Islamic rituals. In one anecdote mentioned by Sulamī, for instance, Basṭāmī calls for prayer once, and when he finishes, he sees a man who suffered from the effects of travel. When Basṭāmī moves forward to speak with him, the man leaves the mosque immediately. Afterward, when this man was asked why he acted in that way, he answered that when Basṭāmī addressed him, he remembered that one day while travelling he had performed *tayammum* (the Islamic ritual of washing with sand or earth where water is unavailable) instead of making regular ablution (*wuḍūʾ*) while being in a civilized region (*fī al-ḥaḍar*), and that was what caused Basṭāmī to scold him.[88] More than Sulamī, Qushayrī seemed to have been eager to portray the biography of Basṭāmī in a very definite orthodox frame that draws upon Basṭāmī's full commitment to the Muslim law.[89] Jullābī Hujwīrī quotes the following statement of Junayd who states that 'Abū Yazīd holds the same rank among us as Gabriel among the angels.' Hujwīrī himself indicates that

[86] Sarrāj, *Lumaʿ*, 382.

[87] See Sulamī, *Ṭabaqāt*, 60–67; Jullābī Hujwīrī, *Kashf al-maḥjūb*, 132–134; Qushayrī, *Risāla*, 14–15.

[88] See the anecdote in Sulamī, *Ṭabaqāt*, 62–63.

[89] See Qushayrī, *Risāla*, 14–15.

Basṭāmī 'was a lover of theology and a venerator of the *sharī'a* notwithstanding the spurious doctrine which has been foisted on him by some persons with the object of supporting their own heresies'.[90]

The ecstatic utterances of Basṭāmī were privileged with moderate interpretations of none other than the renowned master of Baghdad, Junayd. It was Sarrāj who preserved in his *Kitāb al-luma'* Junayd's interpretations of Basṭāmī's *shaṭḥiyyāt* and, further, added to them his own.[91] The latter fact leaves the impression that Basṭāmī was, as well as or even in spite of his teachings on *sukr* (intoxication) and *'ishq* (passionate love), an accepted figure among the makers of the Sufi institution of his time, that is, the authors of the Sufi textbooks and biographies. Basṭāmī was indeed a part of this institution, while reportedly having several disciples[92] and being in touch with the Sufis of his day by holding teaching sessions and discussing Sufi topics with visitors.[93] The hagiographical work, *Kitāb al-nūr min kalimāt Abī Ṭayfūr* by Abū al-Faḍl Muḥammad b. 'Alī al-Sahlajī (d. 476/1082–1083) on the virtues (*manāqib*) of Basṭāmī, which is the largest collection of Basṭāmī's sayings, displays Basṭāmī as a guide for his fellow men and as a theoretician of the communal ethics among the *ikhwān* (Sufi brothers).[94]

Unlike Basṭāmī, Niffarī seems not to have been involved at all in the Sufi institution of his time. Most probably, he had a critical approach towards his Sufi contemporaries. The claim that he neglected the holy text while rarely quoting from it is not convincing. Niffarī's unique way of quoting from the *Qur'ān* should be treated as one of the components of his individual system of thought in which the state of *waqfa* plays the most fundamental role.

90 Jullābī Hujwīrī, *Kashf al-maḥjūb*, 132. The English translation here is of R. Nicholson [Jullābī Hujwīrī, *The Kashf al-Maḥjūb: The Oldest Persian Treatise on Sufism*, trans. by Reynold A. Nicholson (London: Luzac and Company Ltd., 1976), 106].

91 See Sarrāj, *Luma'*, 380–394. Remarkably, 'Abd al-Raḥmān Badawī indicates that among the Sufi masters involved in interpreting those statements, it was Junayd whose interpretations seem to have been the closest to the original meaning intended by Basṭāmī himself. In Badawī's view, the interpretations made by Sarrāj were, in fact, arbitrary (see Badawī, *Shaṭaḥāt al-ṣūfiyya*, 32–33). See also Carl Ernst, *Words of Ecstasy in Sufism* (Albany: State University of New York Press, 1985), 11–14.

92 See e.g., Sulamī, *Ṭabaqāt*, 65 ('*qāla ba'ḍ talāmidhat Abī Yazīd*").

93 See Gerhard Böwering, 'Besṭāmī (Basṭāmī), Bāyazīd,' *Encylopaedia Iranica*, vol. 4, 184. One of the interesting stories about his teaching sessions refers to Umm 'Alī Fāṭima, the wife of the famous Sufi Aḥmad b. Khiḍrūya. See the reference to this story in Chapter 2.

94 See Sahlajī, *Nūr*, 103, 112–113, 133.

Affinities between certain sayings of Niffarī and others of Abū Bakr al-Wāsiṭī have been mentioned throughout the present chapter. Many of Wāsiṭī's utterances preserved in later Sufi texts are abstruse, and that is why whenever they were quoted they often had to be followed by explanations. Meanwhile, Wāsiṭī was known for being the author of one of the earliest collections of Sufi oral glosses of the *Qur'ān*. He was surrounded by a large community of students and a group of intimate companions.[95] Wāsiṭī represents a particular Sufi mode of thought that was basically founded on a collection of provocative and even ambiguous expressions in which the divine–human relationship was underlined. He was one of the early Sufi figures who were used as targets for anti-Sufi attacks. In comparison with Niffarī, Wāsiṭī was entirely involved in the process of establishing the Sufi doctrinal system. His inclination towards *Qur'ān* exegesis manifests his loyalty to the very essence of formal Islam and orthodox religiosity. Niffarī, on the other hand, had a different approach towards the codes and mechanisms of the formal religion. His system of thought was founded entirely on the non-instrumental state of *waqfa*, and that is why his approach towards both formal Islam and formal Sufism was critical. His case demonstrates a unique mode of piety in which the focus is put on the inward form of devotion by a small group of the elite pious dedicated to the state of *waqfa*. This mode of thought differs from the technical institutionalism of Sufism which came to be known in Niffarī's days. His spirituality aimed at achieving a type of an inner experience which sought to be abstract, more universal, and totally free of all formal and practical instruments emphasized by organized religious traditions. For Niffarī, organized Sufism was nothing but a new veil for his pious aspirations. He, most probably, sought to formulate his linguistic-spiritual discourse in the most sophisticated-intellectual framework. His highly intellectually oriented texts might have served his desire to reject the sheikh–disciple-based Sufism known at his time. The very state of *waqfa* grants the individual devotee a great spiritual power and authority. It could lead him to the state of union with the word of creation '*kun*' (be), as Niffarī reports frequently in his *Mawāqif*. At this point, no more controversies were witnessed. Both power and authority constitute the alternative spiritual solution that Niffarī proposes to man in his individual path towards God, and both of them, rather, might make the role of any mediator such as the Sufi sheikh unnecessary and completely superfluous.

[95] See his biography in: Sulamī, *Ṭabaqāt*, 302–307; Qushayrī, *Risāla*, 26. See also Silvers, *Theoretical Sufism*, 73, 75.

The intellect has been regarded by many early Sufis as one of the major faculties that are involved in the process of receiving divine revelations.[96] Niffarī, most probably, attempted to describe the spiritual states he had during his solitude after experiencing them. While trying to describe in writing what he had experienced in the inner state of *waqfa*, Niffarī found himself combining a group of contradictions at the level of his text. One example of such contradictions is the existence of two opposite divine commands in the same text of *Mawāqif*: 'write down' and 'do not write down'. From another perspective, meanwhile, one should pay attention to the idea that the state of *waqfa* lies, after all, above all contradictions that the human intellect could conceive in the world of *siwā*. In the general outcome, we could suggest that Niffarī's texts demonstrate the victory of the word, the intellect and the act of writing itself. The state of *waqfa* is still in need of the intellect in order to be transmitted to the world of the words through the act of writing.

Though Niffarī stresses the principle of man's obedience to a transcendent deity, the idea of communion with an immanent deity lies at the very basis of his discourse.[97] It would be difficult and even superficial to adopt the classification made by the sociologists of religion according to which 'communion with an immanent deity' distinguishes mysticism while obedience to a transcendent deity distinguishes asceticism in order to distinguish Niffarī's piety as being more mystic than ascetic.[98] Niffarī's devotion is not populist. This inward type of devotion which has no demonstrative aspect is intended for a very special group of devotees. Niffarī practised a solitary roving pattern of life and was not interested in discussing it theoretically, while for Sufi authors, establishing the theoretical background of a roving life was almost a matter of writing about a common ethos.

It appears that at this point of time, the Muslim landscape witnessed other 'men of letters' for whom the Sufi institution was not exactly ideal

[96] See e.g., al-Ḥārith al-Muḥāsibi, *Mā'iyat al-'aql*, ed. by Ḥusayn al-Quwwatlī (Damascus: Dār al-Fikr, 1971), 205 ('The intellect is an instinct, *gharīza*, and knowledge of God flows out from it'). Cf. ibid., 210, 220. Later, this doctrine became confirmed in the works of Abū Ḥāmid al-Ghazālī.

[97] See Melchert, *Origins and Early Sufism*, 14.

[98] On this classification, see e.g., Gert Mueller, 'Asceticism and Mysticism: A Contribution Towards the Sociology of Faith', in *International Yearbook for the Sociology of Religion 8: Sociological Theories of Religion and Language*, ed. by Günter Dux, Thomas Luckmann and Joachim Matthes (Opladen: Westdeutscher Verlag, 1973), 68–132.

or pure. In his writings, Abū Ḥayyān al-Tawḥīdī frequently criticizes the Sufis.[99] In his *al-Ishārāt al-Ilāhiyya*, Abū Ḥayyān refers critically to the institution of *taṣawwuf*. He writes: 'The meaning of *ṭasawwuf* is wider than his name, and his truth is nobler than his outward appearance (*rasm*).' He goes on to indicate that the pure spiritual experience that he looks forward to obtaining should completely avoid such *rusūm* (plural of *rasm*).[100] I argue that Tawḥīdī refers here to the Sufi masters of his days. On another occasion of *al-Ishārāt al-Ilāhiyya*, Tawḥīdī criticizes those who guide their disciples while their inner spirituality is totally decadent. Tawḥīdī uses many cruel expressions here to rebuke both them and those who grant them the authority.[101]

This is not the place to consider the question of whether Abū Ḥayyān al-Tawḥīdī knew about Niffarī's writings or whether he had come across them, though this is an interesting question. Yet, the cases of Tawḥīdī and Niffarī reflect two modes of medieval spirituality that differ essentially from what can be seen as the mainstream of Sufi spirituality which was anchored in the institution of *taṣawwuf*. In every way, regardless of the differences between their cases, Tawḥīdī and Niffarī manifest to a great extent how critical voices against strong and influential institutions of piety could remain only marginal.

[99] See e.g., Tawḥīdī, *Kitāb al-imtā' wa-l-mu'ānasa*, 349. Interestingly, in the introduction to this book, Tawḥīdī accuses himself of *fusūla*, that is, lowness, because of his association with the Sufis and the beggars! (See ibid., 13.) See also his story with Burhān al-Ṣūfī in: Abū Ḥayyān al-Tawḥīdī, *al-Ṣadāqa wa-l-ṣadīq*, ed. by Ibrāhīm al-Kīlānī (Beirut: Dār al-Fikr al-Mu'āṣir, 1996), 232–233.

[100] Abū Ḥayyān al-Tawḥīdī, *al-Ishārāt al-Ilāhiyya*, ed. by 'Abd al-Raḥmān Badawī (Cairo: Maṭba'at Jāmi'at Fu'ād al-Awwal, 1950), vol. 1, 163–164.

[101] See ibid., 207–208.

7

Controversies and Quarrels

Besides the representatives of the Sufi ethos on the one hand and those who chose to detach themselves completely from the communal life of the institutionalized *taṣawwuf* on the other, the current chapter seeks to examine individual tendencies and personal views that generated controversy and constant conflict among the Sufis themselves. The act of observing one's fellow men, and scolding those whose behaviour or sayings seemed not to agree with the known codes or with the personal views of the critic himself, was common among the Sufis as the following discussion will show. The necessity of closing one's eyes to his companions' faults is an important code of behaviour that frequently appears in the writings on Sufi rules for novices as well as sections on Sufi ethics.[1] The frequent need of the authors to repeat this idea implies the existence of a cultural climate fraught with mutual observation and critique. This chapter is founded on the argument that disagreements and debates on Sufi theories and conceptions known among early Sufis could, in many cases, take different forms of actual disputes, tensions or enmities and thereby affect Sufis' interpersonal relationships as well as their practices and codes of behaviour.

Beside – or perhaps behind – the pure and oh-so-brotherly portrait created by the authors of the great Sufi compendia, a large body of delicate interrelationships and personal controversies existed among early Sufis. I intend to examine here individual tendencies and personal views

[1] See e.g., Ibn al-Jawzī, *Ṣifat al-ṣafwa*, vol. 2, 248 (in the biography of ʿAmr b. ʿUthmān al-Makkī); Abū ʿAbd al-Raḥmān al-Sulamī, *Ādāb al-ṣuḥba wa-ḥusn al-ʿishra*, ed. by M. J. Kister (Jerusalem: n.p., 1954), 28.

that generated controversy and conflicts between the Sufis themselves as far as those could be deduced from the sources.

BETWEEN COMPANIONSHIP, FRIENDSHIP AND MUTUAL ENVY AND RANCOUR: SUFI INTERPERSONAL RELATIONSHIPS CONTESTED

The detailed chapters devoted to the concept of companionship (*ṣuḥba*) in Sufi writings, and the frequent references to the essential need for solidarity and brotherly behaviour among early Sufis might leave the elementary impression that, on the level of interpersonal relationships, many Sufis were not exactly 'brothers of the path'. Abū ʿAbd al-Raḥmān al-Sulamī's works provide us with rich data on this matter. In his *Ādāb al-ṣuḥba wa-ḥ usn al-ʿishra*, Sulamī refers very frequently to situations of mutual envy, rebuke, competition and even hatred between the Sufis. On almost every single page of his work, he refers to the crucial need of the Sufis to abstain from rebuke (*taʾnīb*), envy (*ḥiqd*), arrogance (*takabbur*), mutual hatred (*tabāghuḍ*) and backbiting (*waqīʿa*) against their brothers.[2] On one occurrence, for instance, Sulamī writes:

Among the rules of conduct, *ādāb*, that Sufi *ṣuḥba* demands are the condonation of one's brothers' faults (*al-ṣafḥ ʿan ʿatharāt al-ikhwān*), and the avoidance of rebuking with them for those faults (*wa-tark taʾnībihim ʿalayhā*).[3]

On another occurrence, he writes:

And among its [i.e., that of *ṣuḥba*!] rules of conduct, the need to keep good relationships with one's brothers even if a situation of reluctance and disinclination (*waḥsha aw nafra*) occurred between them. The Sufi, in this case, should not forget the former intimate relationships, and he should not reveal the secrets that could reach him on the days of brotherhood (*fī ayyām ukhuwwatihi*).[4]

The reader of Sulamī's *Ādāb al-ṣuḥba* could easily conclude that the main concern of the author was to examine the problematic aspects of his contemporary Sufis' interpersonal relationships as well as to show them the way of living together in solidarity and harmony. This work leaves a strong impression that early Sufis at Sulamī's days used to very frequently experience controversies that motivated some of them to backbite their

[2] Sulamī, *Ādāb al-ṣuḥba*, 30, 31, 33, 38, 41–43, 47–50, 56, 60, 64–66. [3] Ibid., 29.
[4] Ibid., 65; idem, *Majmūʿa-yi āthār-i Abū ʿAbd al-Raḥmān Sulamī: Bakhsh-hā-i az ḥaqāyiq al-tafsīr va-rasāʾil-i dīgar*, ed. by Naṣrullah Pūrjavādī (Tehran: Markaz-i Nashr-i Dānishgāhī, 1369–1372 *Shamsī*), vol. 2, 105.

fellows. In several places, Sulamī insists that each Sufi should avoid criticizing his brothers and abstain from defaming them (*tark al-inkār ʿalayhim*).[5] Yūsuf b. al-Ḥusayn's anecdote with Dhū al-Nūn al-Miṣrī, as narrated in the historical works of Ibn Manẓūr and Ibn ʿAsākir, is particularly interesting. In a clearly arrogant tone, Ibn al-Ḥusayn indicates his seniority in theology upon his Egyptian master. Dhū al-Nūn was said to set a trap for his impatient and haughty disciple who came to him after one year of companionship and asked him to teach him the secret name of God as he would not find a better disciple than him to reveal that secret to.[6]

In a separate section of his *Lumaʿ*, Sarrāj discusses the term *mujārāt al-ʿilm*. He chooses to introduce the following title for this section: 'A Section on Sufis' Ethics during Discussing Sufi Science' (*bāb fī dhikr ādābihim ʿind mujārāt al-ʿilm*).[7] It is here that the creators of the Sufi ethos approach the differences in opinion among early Sufis in a positive manner. This feature is found both in the work of Sarrāj and that of his contemporary, the anonymous author of *Adab al-mulūk*. In both of them, we come across painstaking attempts to 'beautify' a reality that most likely saw frequent controversies among the Sufis and consequently promoted many critical voices that accused the Sufis of creating schisms and being disruptive. The appearance of distinctive theoretical agendas and disparate or even contradicting Sufi teachings stood out as the main factors or this reality. It might be suggested, however, that certain Sufis were accused of seeking social fame (*jāh*) and leadership (*riʾāsa*) by criticizing their fellows and challenging common practices known among them, and that is why Sufi authors attempted to highlight the idea that such contradictions and such critique were the essential instruments to obtain truths and deep knowledge of the Sufi science. The eighteenth chapter of *Adab al-mulūk* was devoted to Sufis' controversies and mutual criticism (*munāqarāt*) as well as to Sufis' debates (*munāẓarāt*).[8] The author opens that chapter by stating that *munāqara* occurs when Sufis need to discuss their science and thereby seek to derive insight from the

[5] Ibid., 43.

[6] See Ibn ʿAsākir, *Taʾrīkh madīnat dimashq*, vol. 74, 224; Ibn Manẓūr, *Mukhtaṣar taʾrīkh dimashq*, vol. 28, 73–74.

[7] See Sarrāj, *Lumaʿ*, 179–182.

[8] Bernd Radtke, the editor of *Adab al-mulūk*, chose to translate the original Arabic title into the German as follows: 'Diskussion über die inneren Erlebnisse und ihre Klassifikation' (anonymous author, *Adab al-mulūk*, the German *introduction*, 29) putting thereby the focus on the different spiritual experiences of the Sufis that, according to the original author of the work, were the major cause for debates and disputes.

different opinions that each of them can offer. Treating this issue in this early text can tell us that Sufi authors felt the need to justify the existence of controversies and mutual criticism among the Sufis while defining and practising Sufi doctrines. Those controversies could, in many cases, turn into serious conflicts and even into situations of rancour and enmity. The author of *Adab al-mulūk* was one among few early authors who chose to shed light on the concept of *munāqara* by treating it in the framework of a separate chapter. According to him, *munāqarat al-ṣūfiyya* is caused by what he considers legitimate differences between the Sufis in the paths that each chose towards God, as well as in their own situations and spiritual characteristics. In the third section of this chapter, a detailed discussion of *munāqara* will be presented.

In one section of his testament to the Sufis at the end of his *Risāla*, Qushayrī refers to the emotions of envy that were known among the Sufi brothers (*al-ḥasad li-l-ikhwān*). When one's companion is granted high states of grace while he himself is underprivileged and stripped of those states, envy enters the heart and threatens one's spiritual stability.[9]

In the course of the sixth/twelfth century, Sufi compendia continued to support the so-called realistic portrait made by the early authors for Sufi interrelationships. Suhrawardī, the author of *ʿAwārif al-maʿārif*, refers in detail to the rules of conduct that the Sufi residents of *ribāṭ* should keep. In one reference, he writes:

> In a case that the Sufi's lower soul (*nafs*) causes anger and quarrel (*khuṣūma*) with his brother, then the latter is required to confront the lower soul by his own heart, since if one's lower soul is confronted by another's lower soul, then a disturbance (*fitna*) will certainly become stirred up (*thārat al-fitna*), and the situation of safeguarding becomes disrupted (*dhahabat al-ʿiṣma*).[10]

Self-conceit, envy, arrogance and competitive relationships are also documented in Sufi sources of the period that followed the seventh/thirteenth century. In Junayd Shīrāzī's *Shadd al-izār*, for instance, the famous Sufi master and one of ʿUmar al-Suhrawardī's disciples, Najīb al-Dīn ʿAlī b. Buzghush (d. 678/1279–1280) says that he once had a debate (*munāẓara*) with the sheikh Jamāl al-Dīn Lūrī on the question who of them was graced with a higher spiritual degree. The narrated conversation between the two personalities is summed up by the sheikh Najīb al-Dīn, who states that his opponent remained in his state and was not able to go beyond it and that while he himself succeeded to ascend to higher

[9] See Qushayrī, *Risāla*, 202. [10] Suhrawardī, *ʿAwārif*, 120.

states of grace, his opponent was only able to be a *majdhūb abtar*. The latter is a term that also appears in ʿIzz al-Dīn Kāshānī's (d. after 735/1335) *Miṣbāḥ al-hidāya* and echoes the Arabic *majdhūb mujarrad* in Suhrawardī's *ʿAwārif*.[11] *Miṣbāḥ al-hidāya* is an attempt to translate Suhrawardī's *ʿAwārif* into Persian; however, its author Kāshānī adds his own annotations and contributes, thereby, to provide us with the way that the original notions and doctrines of Suhrawardī became to be conceived in Kāshānī's days. Kāshānī relies on the original discussion of Suhrawardī for the categories of Sufis who could be qualified for sheikh-status to point out that *majdhūb abtar*, which is the synonym for *majdhūb mujarrad* in Suhrawardī's original discussion, is a Sufi whom God chose to attract. *Jadhb* is an early Sufi term that designates the effortless attraction of the mystic by the divine will.[12] According to Suhrawardī and later on Kāshānī, the one who could be attracted by God without wayfaring through the Sufi path of hardships and difficulties is not allowed to become a guide for other wayfarers. The reference made by ʿAlī b. Buzghush to his counterpart sheikh Lūrī as a *majdhūb abtar* was, in fact, nothing but a clear attempt to discredit him and to deprive him his authoritative position as a Sufi master.

CHALLENGING SUFIS' SOLIDARITY: THE CASES OF RUWAYM, IBN YAZDĀNYĀR AND OTHERS

Daylamī describes Abū ʿAmr al-Zajjājī, who was one of Junayd's companions, as follows: 'Abū ʿAmr al-Zajjājī was a hasty and quick-tempered man (*mutasarriʿ wa-ghaḍūb fī ghāyat al-ḥidda*), and therefore, he ceased to associate with the Sufi sheikhs of his time and even abandoned their company.'[13] Challenging Sufis' solidarity through different ways of action and reaction ascribed to certain personalities in the history of early Sufism is a field that holds interesting findings.

As I mentioned before, our available sources rarely provide us with historical parameters to examine our Sufis' relationships. In the

[11] See Junayd Shīrāzī, *Shadd al-izār*, 336–337.

[12] On *jadhb* and the different phases in its development see A. Salamah-Qudsi, 'The Concept of *Jadhb* and the Image of *Majdhūb* in Sufi Teachings and Life in the Period between the Fourth/Tenth and the Tenth/Sixteenth Centuries', *Journal of the Royal Asiatic Society*, Series 3, 1–17 (published online 19 October 2017 https://doi.org/10.1017/S1356186317000530).

[13] Daylamī, *Sīra*, 141.

Introduction to this book, I referred to the problematic feature of idealized images of key Sufi figures, as such images were formulated by the near contemporaries of these figures and the authors of their hagiographies. Meanwhile, I argued that in certain cases, when unrepeated or unparadigmatic flashes of particular stories appear important, insights about individual tendencies and approaches could be sought. In other cases, what seems like a typical paradigmatic anecdote that appears frequently in the biographies of several Sufi figures at once could offer some social or interpersonal clues regarding the life of one of these figures in particular. When a piece of biographical data appears in the biographies of different Sufi personalities, it is highly likely that this piece of data refers to the actual life of one of these personalities and entered the biographies of the other personalities later. The following discussion is an attempt to further this argument.

An instructive Sufi figure in this regard is Ruwaym b. Aḥmad. His case shows that different dynamics and circumstances stood behind his famous controversy with the Sufis of his time. Ruwaym, as many sources tell us, had no problem with being involved in what his Sufi associates considered 'dusty worldly affairs' while filling the position of deputy of the *qāḍī* of Baghdad. He was ascribed to the *ẓāhiriyya* school of jurisprudence. Accepting this position with all its material demands could be added to Ruwaym's declared commitment to family duties and the way he understood the principle of *tawakkul*. Here, clear lines of conjunction can be seen between personal and communal boundaries in Ruwaym's life.

According to Daylamī's *Sīra*, when the renowned sheikh of Shīrāz Ibn Khafīf met Ruwaym in Iraq, the latter said to him: 'I know that certain Sufi masters warned you of visiting me, and that they said to you that Ruwaym turned away from the way of the hereafter by choosing the way of this world.' When Ibn Khafīf confirmed that he had indeed heard such utterances Ruwaym, as the text of *Sīra* reads, called his daughter and seated her close to him, then commented:

> My brothers want me to be completely committed to the principle of *tawakkul*, and to avoid taking care of my daughter and raising her. I swear to God who does not die that if I found someone who can be responsible for my daughter, and can carry the concerns of raising her instead of me, I would tell you what exalted spiritual states I actually have experienced through fifty years and what sublime ranks God have bestowed upon me.[14]

[14] Ibid., 152. Cf. a similar story about Fatḥ al-Mawṣilī (d. 220/835) and his daughter in Kharkūshī, *Tahdhīb al-asrār*, 353.

This quotation comes to illustrate one aspect of Ruwaym's approach towards his fellow Sufis. We find him here both accusing the Sufis of his time of not taking on the responsibility of caring for children and families and praising himself for taking care of familial responsibilities and commitments while having a more intensive spiritual life than his fellow men, who have relinquished such commitments.

References to Ruwaym in the Sufi sources bring us to another interesting argument: Ruwaym himself was critical towards his fellow Sufis, and Sufi biographies leave a strong impression that he even quarrelled with his associates over certain controversial Sufi practices like *tawakkul* and renunciation. In another part of Daylamī's *Sīra*, Ibn Khafīf tells that, one day when he was in Ruwaym's company, a dervish entered the session and said to Ruwaym: 'My companions send their regards to you and tell you that time is a sword (*al-waqt sayf*), and there is no one who can take care of us.' It appears probably that this dervish was a messenger that was sent to Ruwayn by a group of Sufis to ask him for financial support. Ruwaym's severe reply came immediately: 'Those companions that you are their messenger are not my companions.'[15]

Ruwaym's image in Sarrāj's *Luma*ʿ is portrayed in terms of absolute solidarity with the general Sufi ethos. Except for his famous statement in which he consults someone to sacrifice his spirit as the first step in initiating the Sufi path and to keep himself from being occupied by the 'nonsense trifles of the Sufis' (*turrahāt al-ṣūfiyya*), which is also cited by Sulamī and Anṣārī Haravī, no references to his controversies with his contemporary Sufis are mentioned.[16] On another occasion, furthermore, Ruwaym is cited to have described some of the Sufi sheikhs of his time during *samā*ʿ as a flock of goats.[17] Despite the sardonic imagery, this statement could also be seen as Ruwaym's way to praise the deep spiritual effect of *samā*ʿ on the Sufis.

The anti-Sufi approach of Tanūkhī in his *Nishwār al-muḥāḍara* refers to Ruwaym in addition to other Sufi personalities. Tanūkhī criticizes Ruwaym for concealing his love of this world for forty years. It was Jaʿfar al-Khuldī whose name is mentioned here by Tanūkhī as the representative of the Baghdad-centred movement of *ṣūfiyya*. He was the most famous disciple of Junayd and a prolific biographer and author of Sufi history. Khuldī frequently appears in the sources as the one who had

[15] Daylamī, *Sīra*, 153.
[16] See Sarrāj, *Luma*ʿ, 263; Cf. Sulamī, *Ṭabaqāt*, 173; Anṣārī Haravī, *Ṭabaqāt al-ṣūfiyya*, 77.
[17] See Sarrāj, *Luma*ʿ, 288.

attempted to exclude certain Sufi personalities from the group of *ṣūfiyya*. His statement against Tirmidhī '*mā ʿadadtuhu fī al-ṣūfiyya*' was previously discussed in Chapter 2.[18] The reference made by Jaʿfar al-Khuldī to Ruwaym as it appears in the text of *Nishwār al-muḥāḍara* goes as follows:

I heard Jaʿfar al-Khuldī saying: 'It is the best for the one who seeks to confide a secret to someone to confide it to Ruwaym, since the latter succeeded to conceal his love to the world for forty years.' When he [Jaʿfar al-Khuldī!] was asked how, he answered: 'Ruwaym practised *taṣawwuf* for forty years, and when Ismāʿīl b. Isḥāq,[19] who had at that time a close relationship with Ruwaym, was appointed to the position of the *qāḍī* of Baghdad, he joined Ruwaym to him and made him his deputy, causing Ruwaym to abandon *taṣawwuf* and *tawakkul*, and to wear silk and linen clothes [. . .], to ride on donkeys and mules, to eat delicacies, and to build gorgeous houses.' [Most likely the following sentence is a comment made by Tanūkhī himself!] This means that Ruwaym used to conceal his love to this world at times when he was not able to obtain worldly pleasures; however, when he succeeded to do that, he revealed that love which he had previously concealed.[20]

This critique addressed to Ruwaym by Jaʿfar al-Khuldī differs from another statement ascribed to Ruwaym by Khuldī himself in *Taʾrīkh baghdād*. The latter goes as follows: 'Jaʿfar al-Khuldī told us in his book [most probably his lost *Ḥikāyāt al-mashāyikh*] that he heard Ruwaym saying: [. . .] *Futuwwa* means that you excuse your brothers for making faults, and treat them in a way that does not require from you an apology to them.'[21] The same statement is mentioned by Sulamī in the biography of Ruwaym without any reference made to Jaʿfar al-Khuldī.[22]

Besides the aforementioned statement of Ruwaym where he consults someone to keep himself away from the 'nonsense trifles' of the Sufis, Ruwaym is quoted by Sulamī as praising the *ṣūfiyya* since, unlike other sorts of people who seek outward rituals and worships, they choose to seek the truths of devotion.[23]

Ruwaym's critical approach towards his contemporary Sufis could be deduced from other statements attributed to him in both Sufi and non-Sufi sources. In *Taʾrīkh baghdād*, Ruwaym is quoted to have indicated that

18 This statement appears in Sulamī, *Ṭabaqāt*, 454.

19 Ismāʿīl b. Isḥāq al-Ḥammādī (d. 282/896) was the Mālikī judge who appears in the sources to have questioned the Sufis, especially Nūrī, about prayer and ritual purity after these were taken to the Abbasid *khalīfa* as a result of Ghulām Khalīl's denunciation. See his biography in: Ibn Kathīr, *Bidāya*, vol. 11, 72.

20 Tanūkhī, *Nishwār al-muḥāḍara*, vol. 3, 120.

21 Baghdādī, *Taʾrīkh baghdād*, vol. 9, 429–430.

22 See Sulamī, *Ṭabaqāt*, 171–172.

23 See ibid., 173.

the sincere state of poverty, that is, of being a Sufi, requires concealing poverty from people's eyes and that, thereby, the one who reveals his poverty could not be regarded a true poor or a true Sufi.[24] This approach could be combined with Ruwaym's own way of understanding the meaning of initiating the Sufi path and the complete body of commitments and engagements that this imposed upon the Sufi's personal life as well as his religious work under the influential impact of the Sufi community and its ethos. It might be possible, accordingly, to suggest that Ruwaym intended to criticize his contemporary Sufis, those who appeared to attack him for being a family-oriented Sufi, for their inclination to show off their Sufi mode of life in public as a vehicle to obtain people's admiration and praise. It is Hujwīrī who later on indicates that Ruwaym b. Aḥmad wrote a critical work entitled *Ghalaṭ al-wājidīn* ('The Error of Ecstatic Persons').[25]

Ruwaym's relationships with the Baghdadi Sufi master Junayd gains a particular significance. In order to establish Ruwaym's high position in early Sufism, Anṣārī Haravī asserts that Ruwaym was not a disciple of Junayd, as he was usually considered, but rather his companion. However, it seems like Anṣārī Haravī was not satisfied with portraying Ruwaym as equal to the great master of Baghdad, and that is why he went on to emphasize the higher spiritual rank of Ruwaym upon that of Junayd by indicating that one hair of Ruwaym is better than a hundred Junayds.[26] Later on, in Haravī's biography of Ruwaym, there is an interesting anecdote that involves Ruwaym, Abū ʿAmr al-Zajjājī and Junayd. This anecdote is echoed later in *Taʾrīkh baghdād*. The character of Zajjājī was previously mentioned in this chapter. He was one of Junayd's disciples and was portrayed as a quick-tempered man who sometimes quarrelled with his fellow Sufis. Another reference to his critique of Ibn Khafīf whose mother accompanied him in pilgrimage was already made in Chapter 2. According to Haravī's anecdote, Junayd used to warn his disciples against visiting Ruwaym. When Zajjājī came to Baghdad, he intended to meet Ruwaym in spite of Junayd's instructions not to do that. Their conversation was set off by the entrance of Ruwaym's daughter, and the Sufi father started to dispute, in Zajjājī's presence, the negative approaches of his contemporaries towards him. Those, as Haravī's text reads, criticized Ruwaym for his preoccupation (*shughl*) with his children and his family engagements. Ruwaym is quoted

24 See *Taʾrīkh baghdād*, vol. 9, 429.
25 See Jullābī Hujwīrī, *Kashf al-maḥjūb*, 170.
26 See Anṣārī Haravī, *Ṭabaqāt al-ṣūfiyya*, 76.

to have said that he is the one who can tell those what *ʿilm al-tawḥīd* (the science of unity) is. When Zajjājī arrived at Junayd's place, someone among the latter's companions spoke to him against Zajjājī and informed him of his secret visit. Junayd called Zajjājī immediately and asked him how he found Ruwaym. Zajjājī then replied: 'Hard with himself, great and glorious!' (*sakht, buzūrgavār va-muḥtasham*). Junayd's reply, as both Haravī's and Baghdādī's texts assert, indicates that his behaviour was not meant to censure Ruwaym but to prevent Sufi initiates from censuring Ruwaym (while watching his worldly engagements) and, thus, to fall victims of consulting the friends of God, as Haravī's text reads. Junayd thanked God for protecting his disciple Zajjājī from the temptation and for allowing him to behold the good image of Ruwaym.[27]

Taʾrīkh baghdād's version of the anecdote is slightly different. Junayd's motivation to isolate Ruwaym and marginalize his position as an authority for Sufi conduct is pointed out plainly: Ruwaym 'became involved in some of the politic authority's affairs' (*dakhala fī shayʾ min umūr al-sulṭān*). While Zajjājī was conversing with Ruwaym, Junayd himself entered the place suddenly and noticed his disciple there doing what he ordered him not to do. When both of them left the place, Junayd asked his disciple: 'How did you find Ruwaym?' Zajjājī replied: 'I don't know.' In the last part of the anecdote, the great master of Baghdad asserts that 'people misunderstand Ruwaym's involvement in the politic authority's affairs and think this diminishes his spiritual state.' Paradoxically speaking, Junayd tells his disciple that Ruwaym's Sufi state at the time of his involvement in such affairs is, in fact, higher than his former state when he was completely uninvolved and that his share of poverty is better than it has been ever before. In other words, Junayd's statement came to insinuate that neither Ruwaym's worldly attachments nor his material wealth disrupted his deep state of renunciation.[28] Different from this attempt to positively depict Junayd's attitude towards Ruwaym, there is a statement in the biography of Junayd in Abū Nuʿaym al-Iṣfahānī's *Ḥilyat al-awliyāʾ* that pushes towards another angle in the story. Junayd is quoted as saying when he noticed that Ruwaym had obtained the religious position: 'Whoever wants to look at someone who hides his love of this world (*khabbaʾa fī sirrihi ḥubb al-dunyā*) for twenty years should look at this man [Ruwaym!].' What was then Junayd's motivation to forbid his disciples from visiting Ruwaym? It might be said that he sought

[27] See ibid., 76–77. The story appears later in Jāmī's *Nafaḥāt al-uns*, 95.
[28] Baghdadi, *Taʾrīkh Baghdād*, vol. 9, 430.

to prevent Sufi novices from seeking worldly affairs at the beginning of their spiritual careers since this would leave a negative impact on their spiritual progress. Regardless of the disparate approaches towards his character and mode of life, Ruwaym was conceived in the eyes of Baghdadi Sufis as a Sufi who combined worldly attachments and material wealth and well-being with *taṣawwuf*.

If we compare the short biography of Ruwaym in Qushayrī's *Risāla* with the biographies of other figures in the same work, we come to note that Ruwaym's includes more statements that relate to the Sufi's ethics with his brothers than we find in the others' biographies. Due to the positive tone of all of those statements in Ruwaym's biography, the above-mentioned reference to *turrahāt al-ṣūfiyya*, which is repeated also by Qushayrī, could easily be conceived positively. And when Qushayrī is eager to follow this statement with another statement that conveys a strong positive tone, then no critical voice is felt. The statement that followed the *turrahāt* 's one in Qushayrī's text reads:

> Your association with each group of people is safer than your association with the *ṣūfiyya*, since all people are committed to the outwards (*rusūm*), while the *ṣūfiyya* are committed to the inner truths (*ḥaqāʾiq*). It is also that all people demand from themselves the outwards of religious duties, while the *ṣūfiyya* demand from themselves the truth of devotion. The one that associates with them while disagreeing with them in the meantime is expected to be deprived of the light of faith by God.[29]

In a later non-Sufi source, Ibn Kathīr's *al-Bidāya wa-l-nihāya*, Ruwaym's so-called deep inclination to material world is traced back to the forty years of practising Sufism before his appointment to his official position. Ibn Kathīr, most probably, relies on Tanūkhī's work to tell that Ruwaym abandoned his Sufi life entirely and did not deny himself the pleasure of wearing silk and enjoying other worldly delights: '*Fa-taraka al-taṣawwuf wa-labisa al-khazz* [...] *wa-akala al-ṭayyibāt wa-banā al-dūr* ' ('he abandoned *taṣawwuf*, and weared silk [...] and ate delicacies and built houses').[30] Regardless of its historical reliability, this reference helps in realizing that the controversy around Ruwaym's way of life went beyond the boundaries of Sufi circles. It also remained relevant and became even more poignant during later centuries. It seems most likely to suggest, moreover, that Ruwaym's involvement in the governmental administrative system was the major reason behind the criticism addressed to him by

[29] Qushayrī, *Risāla*, 22. [30] Ibn Kathīr, *Bidāya*, vol. 11, 125.

his Sufi contemporaries and later on by other Muslim thinkers. His family-oriented Sufism, hence, would not have been a focus for any critique if his career had not been interrupted by that appointment.

Abū Bakr al-Ḥusayn b. ʿAlī b. Yazdānyār was an early mystic of Urmiya in the western north of Persia. If we exclude the separate chapter that Sarrāj devotes to Ibn Yazdānyār and his problematic relationships with the Sufis of his day, we come across only one occasion in *Kitāb al-Lumaʿ* where Sarrāj mentions his name: in the aforementioned chapter on the rules of conduct during discussing Sufi science (*mujārāt al-ʿilm*). Interestingly, Ibn Yazdānyār's character is portrayed here as the one who has difficulty in understanding certain Sufi ideas. Sarrāj tells that Abū ʿAbd Allāh al-Ḥuṣrī (d. 371/981), one of the renowned Baghdadi masters of the end of the fourth/tenth century,[31] made an ambiguous statement to Ibn Yazdānyār during discussing Sufi science with him that the latter was not able to understand. When Ibn Yazdānyār asked Ḥuṣrī to repeat the statement, the latter refused to do so.[32] This occasion is another example of Sarrāj's negative approach towards Ibn Yazdānyār. Whether Sarrāj himself was the one who phrased this short anecdote or the one who heard it and chose to include it in this particular place of his work, it is important to note that in both cases the structure of the anecdote was expected to offend Ibn Yazdānyār.

Ḥuṣrī, according to Sufi sources, was one of the renowned Sufi masters of Iraq. He also associated with Abū Bakr al-Shiblī, the mystic who was portrayed in the sources as a disturbed man with frequent states of ecstasy and bewilderment. Sulamī introduces Ḥuṣrī as 'the great master of Iraqi Sufis' (*ustādh al-ʿirāqiyyīn*) and a Sufi who was singled out by a unique doctrine on Sufi unity (*tawḥīd*): '*Lahu lisān fī al-tawḥīd yakhtaṣṣu huwa bihi.*'[33]

Choosing this man as the hero of this anecdote and the one who insulted Ibn Yazdānyār's lack of Sufi knowledge seems not to be arbitrary. Sarrāj intended to show how far this personality was from the knowledge of the great Sufi masters of his day and to what extent his attempts to contest their theories were motivated by his covetousness of leadership and social fame. Sarrāj, as many scholars like Karamustafa Knysh and Avery noted, was more an early observer of Sufism than an

[31] For his detailed biography, see Sulamī, *Ṭabaqāt*, 516–522.
[32] See Sarrāj, *Lumaʿ*, 180. [33] Sulamī, *Ṭabaqāt*, 516.

active Sufi master. His work thereby should be seen as a genuine document of the Sufi climate of the early fourth/tenth century.[34] Sarrāj, who could bear the ecstatic utterances of Basṭāmī, Shiblī and Abū Ḥamza al-Ṣūfī, was unable to bear the personalities of Ghulām Khalīl and Ibn Yazdānyār, who were known for their attempts to backbite and defame the Sufis of Baghdad. I agree with Karamustafa, who argues that the general discourse of *Kitāb al-Luma*ʿ is biased towards the Iraqi version of early Sufism. He was able to defend the most problematic sayings of *shaṭaḥāt* as well as criticize certain doctrines known among different Sufi groups of his time without referring to particular names at the last section of his work, while he could not bear those who chose to slander the Sufis. In the separate section devoted to Ibn Yazdānyār, the author of *Luma*ʿ tells that:

> Abū Bakr b. Yazdānyār used to associate with the Sufi masters as well as travel with them. He conducted Sufi doctrines and replied to hard inquiries on the sciences of Sufi knowledge, states and situations. It was after a short period that Ibn Yazdānyār returned back to his homeland and his own family and worldly inclinations (*ahwā*ʾ). When he became inclined to leadership (*māla ilā al-riʾāsa*), and started to be fascinated by people's gatherings around him, he started slandering his Sufi masters and accusing them of religious innovation (*nasabahum ilā al-bidʿa*), going astray (*ḍalāla*), committing faults (*ghalaṭ*), and of lack of knowledge (*jahāla*).[35]

According to the above quotation, it was only when Ibn Yazdānyār left Baghdad and abandoned the association with the Baghdadi masters that his 'worldly inclinations' appeared, and he started defaming those who were his former close fellows. He is, in Sarrāj's eyes, a traitor who broke the trustworthiness of the Sufis. Ibn Yazdānyār, as the text of *Luma*ʿ reads, attempted to correspond with certain people in different parts of the Muslim lands in order to warn them of the Sufis and to accuse the latter of heresy (*kataba ilā al-bilād yuḥadhdhir minhum al-ʿibād*). Among the Baghdadi Sufis who were targets of his accusations, Sarrāj mentions Junayd, Nūrī, Sumnūn b. Ḥamza (d. 298/910–911), Dhū al-Nūn al-Miṣrī and Jaʿfar al-Khuldī.[36]

Towards the end of Sarrāj's section on Ibn Yazdānyār, an attempt is made to show that even when this man was in Baghdad associating with the great masters, his Sufi knowledge was primitive, an idea that integrates very well with the above reference to his story with Ḥuṣrī. In a

[34] See Karamustafa, *Sufism*, 68–69; Knysh, *Islamic Mysticism*, 120.
[35] Sarrāj, *Ṣuḥuf min kitāb al-luma*ʿ, 10. [36] See ibid., 11.

sarcastic tone, Sarrāj tells that Shiblī used to call Ibn Yazdānyār as the 'bull of Urmiya' (*thawr al-urmanī*). The last paragraph goes as follows:

> [Abū Bakr al-Fārisī tells that] I entered Ibn Yazdānyār's place, and attended his teaching gathering. When he finished, he came close to me and asked me: 'What do you think about those Iraqis referring to Junayd, Nūrī and Shiblī?' I answered him: 'Those are the people of unity' (*arbāb al-tawḥīd*). He [Ibn Yazdānyār!] became angry at my words. One of those who heard our conversation said to me then: 'Oh Man, fear God! Get out of this place and of this town, and do not spend you night here because if you do, a misfortune will happen to you, and you should be responsible for your destiny' (*nālaka makrūh wa-yakūn damuk fī ʿunuqik*).[37]

Ibn Yazdānyār's biography in Sulamī's *Ṭabaqāt* is very informative on the nature of his relationship with his Sufi contemporaries. The first question that comes to mind here is: If this person had such problematic relationships with the Sufis of his day, then why did Sulamī choose to purify his image by devoting a separate biography to him that serves as an influential platform to justify his hostility and slander?

At the very beginning of Ibn Yazdānyār's biography, Sulamī states that this mystic had a special Sufi method and that he used to criticize the sayings of certain Sufis of Iraq (*kāna yunkir ʿalā baʿḍ mashāyikh al-ʿIrāq aqāwīlahum*).[38] At another place in this biography, Sulamī quotes Abū ʿAbd al-Raḥmān al-Mawṣilī, who says that he saw Ibn Yazdānyār after his death in his dream, and that he related a story that happened to him on the Day of Judgment. The story goes as follows:

> When I reached the Day of Judgment, I noticed Adam, peace be upon him, while people greeting him and shaking hands with him. I approached him in order to shake his hands too but he said to me then: 'Move away from me! You are the one who censured my dear Sufis. I became delighted of them' (*anta alladhī waqaʿta fī awlādī al-ṣūfiyya, la-qad qurrat ʿaynāya bihim*). At that moment, a group of people came and steered me away from him.[39]

According to the story and the above reference at the beginning of his biography in Sulamī's work, Ibn Yazdānyār used to blame his Sufi fellows and even to backbite them. Sulamī goes on to point out the reason behind that behaviour, and that is why he quotes the following statement of Ibn Yazdānyār himself:

> Do you think that what motivated me to say what I said is the will to slander *taṣawwuf* and *ṣūfiyya*? I swear to God that I said that only out of jealousy of them

[37] Ibid., 11–12. [38] Sulamī, *Ṭabaqāt*, 423. [39] Ibid., 424.

when they began to reveal God's secrets and to display them before those who are not eligible to be acquainted with them (*afshaw asrār al-Ḥaqq wa-abdawhā ilā ghayr ahlihā*). This behaviour made me jealous of them and motivated me to blame them (*al-kalām fīhim*). Had they not done that, they could have been great leaders (*wa-illā fa-hum al-sāda*), and I should have sought their love for the sake of finding God.[40]

Unlike Sarrāj, Sulamī wanted to defend Ibn Yazdānyār as well as improve his reputation. He chose, thereby, to put the emphasis on the good intentions that motivated him to blame his fellow Sufis and went on to praise his sayings on different Sufi themes. Qushayrī, influenced by Sulamī, did not refrain from praising Ibn Yazdānyār in the short biography he devotes to him. The sentence 'he had a special Sufi method' (*lahu ṭarīqa yakhtaṣṣu bihā*) appears here again. However, while Sulamī's text refers to 'certain Baghdadi Sufis', those who were the victims of Ibn Yazdānyār's slander, Qushayrī's text refers to some men of knowledge in general (*ba'ḍ al-'ārifīn*).[41] No attempt is made to restrict the conflict between Ibn Yazdānyār and the Sufis of Baghdad particularly in *Risāla*. Qushayrī, rather, described very briefly the background of that conflict: 'He used to criticise some of the famed Sufis for certain statements and expressions' (*kāna yunkir 'alā ba'ḍ al-'ārifīn fī iṭlāqāt wa-alfāẓ lahum*).[42] It is most likely that Abū Bakr al-Shiblī was one of the main Sufi figures that were criticized by Ibn Yazdānyār.[43] Notably, Ibn Yazdānyār's biography in Sulamī's *Ṭabaqāt* looks different from other biographies included in the same work: There is no reference to any one of his companions, masters or disciples. Sulamī, as Jawid Mojaddedi noticed, devoted the longest biography in his work to Shiblī.[44] His interest in Shiblī is explained in different ways by recent scholars of early Sufism.[45] There is no doubt that Sulamī had a great respect for Shiblī's intoxicated mode of piety besides his respect for the sober and socially conformist school of Junayd.[46] It is worth noting, then, that Sulamī did not refrain from giving the probable opponent of Shiblī, that is, Ibn Yazdānyār, a credit by introducing his biography in the last part of the fourth generation (*ṭabaqa*) in his work. It should be noted that, in spite of his controversies with certain Baghdadi Sufis, most probably due to their ecstatic utterances that shocked Muslim traditionalists, Ibn Yazdānyār

[40] Ibid., 424–425. [41] Qushayrī, *Risāla*, 30. [42] Ibid.
[43] See Yadu-Allāh Naṣru-Allāhī, '*Rawḍat al-murīdīn-i* Abū Ja'far Ibn Yazdānyār', *'Allāmih: Dū Faṣl-nāmih-yi 'Ilmī*, vol. 12, no. 34 (1391 *Shamsī*), 143.
[44] See Mojaddedi, *The Biographical Tradition in Sufism*, 15.
[45] See Avery, *Shiblī*, 31–33. [46] See Karamustafa, *Sufism*, 63.

was generally seen as one of the prominent Sufi figures of eastern Islam. It might be said that Sulamī, who aimed to integrate Khurāsānian and Baghdadi Sufism into one full scaled scene and to emphasize the diversity of early Sufism and of its representative personalities in his *Ṭabaqāt*, was not able to avoid Ibn Yazdānyār. Additionally, Ibn Yazdānyār developed a unique method of practising Sufism (*ṭarīqa yakhtaṣṣu bihā*) as emphasized by Sulamī and Qushayrī. But what was the real meaning of this unique method? What made it so unique in the eyes of Sufi authors?

Interestingly, Ibn Yazdānyār, the one whose quarrels with the Sufis of Iraq are best known, was not the author of *Rawḍat al-murīdīn*, an interesting and little-known manual on Sufi theories and practicum from the early fifth/eleventh century. The author of this work was, most likely, Abū Jaʿfar al-Saʿīdī Ibn Yazdānyār al-Hamadhānī who was born in 380/990 as Dhahabī indicates; that is a long time after Abū Bakr b. Yazdānār's death.[47] Moreover, *Rawḍat al-murīdīn* does not mirror any controversies with the key figures of Iraqi Sufism during the author's time. Those figures were frequently quoted and even celebrated throughout the work. Besides other reasons, this work could not be attributed to the early figure of Ibn Yazdānyār;[48] however, it does include sayings attributed to him, and those might be added to others in different sources in order to hint to one aspect of his so-called 'unique method'.

On one occasion in *Rawḍat al-murīdīn*'s manuscript, the author quotes the early Ibn Yazdānyār saying that 'the one who abandons good manners (*adab*) with God will be deprived of *sunna* as a punishment, and the one who abandons *sunna* will be deprived of religious duties, and the one who abandons religious duties will be deprived of Sufi knowledge (*ḥirmān al-maʿrifa*).'[49] One basic element in Ibn Yazdānyār's doctrinal system relates to his insistence on the Sufi's need to conceal his inner states of revelation and avoid publicly expressing those states in full. This idea was also emphasized in his biography of Sulamī's *Ṭabaqāt*.

47 See Dhahabī, *Tārīkh al-islām*, vol. 10, 344.

48 Among those reasons, Naṣru-Allāhī indicates the very fact that the author of *Rawḍat al-murīdīn* quotes sayings of Abū Bakr b. Yazdānyār and the fact that Sulamī died almost one hundred years after Abū Bakr b. Yazdānyār. The author quotes from Sulamī's work and that means that he lived and composed after Sulamī. Besides, it was Abū Jaʿfar b. Yazdānyār and not the earlier homonym who was known in the sources as aligned to the Sufis of Iraq as the main body of *Rawḍa* evidences. (See Naṣru-Allāhī, *Rawḍat al-murīdīn*, 142–143.)

49 Abū Jaʿfar b. Yazdānyār, *Rawḍat al-murīdīn*, Princeton MS. 968, fol. 4b.

Unfortunately, there are no satisfying references in neither the Arabic nor Persian sources available to us for questions such as 'what made Ibn Yazdānyār's Sufism different and unique?' and 'in what ways were his Sufi teachings distinguished, and with respect to whom were they distinguished?' It is possible, meanwhile, that, in referring to the practice of keeping Sufi states away from people's eyes, this man was not alone. Many other Sufis of the Iraqi camp urged their companions and fellows to do that.

Certain components of Ibn Yazdānyār's Sufi theory should have likely distinguished this figure from the doctrinal system of the Baghdadi members of *ṣūfiyya* and of their successors. While the above-mentioned Ḥuṣrī was known for his unique teachings on the principle of *tawḥīd*, as Sulamī points out, as well as Junayd who was one of the greatest Sufis that treated this principle, Ibn Yazdānyār did not have any respect for the Baghdadi masters of *tawḥīd* as the previously mentioned story from *Lumaʿ* indicates.

A careful investigation of Sulamī's different ways to introduce the pious personalities in his *Ṭabaqāt* reveals that the way he introduced Ibn Yazdānyār was interestingly unique. Frequently enough throughout this work, Sulamī opens the biographical account with expressions like 'He was unique in his Sufi method of dropping social esteem' (*kāna wāḥidan fī ṭarīqatihi fī isqāṭ al-jāh*),[50] or 'he had a distinctive language on *tawḥīd* that distinguished him' (*lahu lisān fī al-tawḥīd yakhtaṣṣu huwa bihi*)[51] or 'he had a special language in interpreting the *Qurʾān* due to which he was distinguished' (*lahu lisān fī fahm al-Qurʾān yakhtaṣṣu bihi*).[52] Certain key personalities were described as having a unique method in keeping Sufi time (*ṣawn al-waqt*), as was in the case of Sulamī's grandfather and master Abū ʿAmr b. Nujayd.[53] It is to say, therefore, that in all such introductory openings, Sulamī connects each Sufi figure with a certain aspect of the Sufi system of thoughts and practicum. In the case of Ibn Yazdānyār, however, the introductory opening seems to be slightly different: It is more general, and it is not related to any specific aspect. While Sulamī usually adds the particular aspect that makes each of his personalities unique in a straightforward manner, after making the statement of uniqueness and distinction in the case of Ibn Yazdānyār, he simply refers to the latter's serious controversy with the Sufis of Iraq. The latter notion leaves the impression that what made Ibn Yazdānyār

[50] Sulamī, *Ṭabaqāt*, 175. [51] Ibid., 516. [52] Ibid., 260. [53] See ibid., 476.

unique was different from that of Sulamī's other figures. His uniqueness was an outcome of more essential differences, both theoretical and practical, from Baghdadi *ṣūfiyya*, the group Sulamī himself often liked to call 'this *ṭāʾifa*' in his works. Ibn Yazdānyār, who associated with the Sufis of Baghdad for a determined course of time, could not bear the thought that certain figures of the *ṣūfiyya* ignored good manners and modesty (*ḥayāʾ*) in their intoxicated behaviour and, more particularly, in their *shaṭaḥāt*. I consider more likely that Sulamī's reference to Ibn Yazdānyār's *ṭarīqa fī al-taṣawwuf* was barely intended to make a statement about his Sufi doctrines and teachings. It differs, for that reason, from other introductory openings in the same work. The Zoroastrian tone that might be deduced from one of Ibn Yazdānyār's most quoted statements where he uses a dual language of good (*khayr*) versus evil (*sharr*) in describing the spiritual interrelationships between spirit, body, lower soul, heart and intellect,[54] has a little to do with the tendency to ascribe to him a distinctive Sufi method in Sufi sources. If Sulamī wanted to point out a different doctrinal system by his indication that Ibn Yazdānyār had a *ṭarīqa fī al-taṣawwuf* of his own, then he had with greater reason to use such an introductory opening for figures like Ḥallāj and al-Ḥakīm al-Tirmidhī, but he does not actually do that. In light of these remarks, I would suggest understanding the uniqueness in the case of Ibn Yazdānyār as a notion that puts forward two pieces of information: The first relates to Ibn Yazdānyār's choice to exclude himself from the *ṣūfiyyā*, and the other relates to his tendency to emphasize the outward (*ẓāhir*) at the expense of the inward in the eyes of the creators of Sufi compendia.

Anṣārī Haravī, whose Persian *Ṭabaqāt al-ṣūfiyya* follows to a certain degree that of Sulamī, tells at the beginning of the biography that some Sufi masters like Shiblī were those who criticized Ibn Yazdānyār.[55] The later Persian biographer Jāmī repeats this idea and adds to it the same version of the relationships that was provided originally by Sarrāj and Sulamī (that Ibn Yazdānyār attacked the Sufis also).[56] Anṣārī Haravī goes on to tell a story according to which God told Ibn Yazdānyār in a dream that He granted him the best thing that He could give a human being: He released him from the Sufis' chain (*band-i ṣūfiyān*). When people asked Ibn Yazdānyār what 'Sufis' chain' meant, he explained that it meant 'the

[54] See ibid., 425. It is interesting to note that this statement was not brought up in the biography of Ibn Yazdānyār in Anṣārī Haravī's *Ṭabaqāt al-ṣūfiyya*.

[55] See Anṣārī Haravī, *Ṭabaqāt al-ṣūfiyya*, 123.

[56] See Jāmī, *Nafaḥāt al-uns*, 183.

inconceivable state and the untrue signs' (*al-ḥāl al-muḥāl wa-l-ishārāt al-bāṭila*). This man, accordingly, had a strong belief that his Baghdadi fellows did not do anything but show off their inner states in order to attain people's praise. Both Anṣārī Haravī and Jāmī indicate that Ibn Yazdānyār had a long story to tell with the *ṣūfiyya* when the latter criticized him and that this story implied a strong controversy (*dar ān ishkāl ast*) without leaving us clearer information.[57] In his *Sharḥ-i shaṭḥiyyāt*, Rūzbihān Baqlī refers very briefly to Ibn Yazdānyār's controversy with the 'sheikhs of Iraq' (*mashāyikh-i* ʿIrāq), which led at last to Shiblī's admission to the hospital of Baghdad.[58] This controversy appears in the following comparative statement attributed to Ibn Yazdānyār in Ibn al-Mulaqqin's *Ṭabaqāt al-awliyāʾ*: 'Sufism of Khurāsān is practice and no talk; Sufism of Baghdad is talk and no practice; Sufism of Baṣra is talk as well as practice; and Sufism of Egypt is no talk and no practice.'[59]

I referred in Chapter 2 to the figure of Abū al-Qāsim al-Naṣrābādhī who was quoted by Sulamī as attacking the custom of associating with women in the work of *Ṭabaqāt* while he himself was the male personality most often mentioned in Sulamī's biographical work on female Sufis. I argue that this was a well-known strategy in early Sufi writings: to choose the personality whose image in the sources demonstrates the anti-thesis of a particular doctrine or situation and to introduce it for the sake of creating a cover of legitimacy. Making use of this personality, in such cases, serves as the best strategy in the hands of the authors to establish a strong theoretical basis of the doctrine under consideration. Paradoxically, while the figure of Ibn Yazdānyār was usually combined with the custom of backbiting the Sufis (*al-wuqūʿ/al-waqīʿa fī al-ṣūfiyya*), both Sulamī and the author of *Rawḍat al-murīdīn* ascribe an additional statement to him where he himself warns against backbiting the Sufis. This statement goes as follows:

> Aḥmad b. ʿAbd Allāh al-Sharwīnī narrated that he saw Abū Bakr b. Yazdānyār al-Urmawī in his dream and that he [that is Sharwīnī!] asked Ibn Yazdānyār: 'What is the most beneficial act in your view Ibn Yazdānyār replied: 'After unification, nothing is more beneficial than the association with the poor

[57] See Anṣārī Haravī, *Ṭabaqāt al-ṣūfiyya*, 123–124; Jāmī, *Nafaḥāt al-uns*, 183.

[58] See Rūzbihān Baqlī Shīrāzī, *Sharḥ-i shaṭḥiyyāt*, ed. by Henry Corbin (Tehran and Paris: Department d'Iranologie de l'Institut Franco-Iranien and Librairie d'Amerique et d'Orient Adrien-Maisonneuve, 1966), 25.

[59] Ibn al-Mulaqqin, *Ṭabaqāt al-awliyāʾ*, 335. The English translation is of Karamustafa (Karamustafa, *Sufism*, 51).

(*ṣuḥbat al-fuqarāʾ*).' It was at this moment that I asked him: 'Which act is the most harmful?.' He replied: 'backbiting the *ṣūfiyya*.'[60]

It is the same technique also evidenced in the reference to Ruwaym b. Aḥmad in the work of *Rawḍa* while discussing the principle of compassion towards one's brothers (*al-shafaqa ʿalā al-ikhwān*).[61]

Though the cases of Ruwaym and Ibn Yazdānyār are discussed under the same section of this chapter, it is still important to indicate that they are different. Each of these two cases implies a different attempt to challenge the ethos that had been created by the Sufi authors in accordance with the teachings of the Baghdadi *ṣūfiyya* and to destabilize the latter's position as the ultimate façade of early Sufism. The case of Ruwaym could be seen as an attempt to question principles like *tawakkul* and seclusion. This was done from inside the boundaries of Baghdadi *ṣūfiyya*. The case of Ibn Yazdānyār demonstrates an attempt from outside those boundaries to question other principles, practices and customs. The story of each personality, it should be noted, was narrated through different personal perspectives in Sufi and non-Sufi writings. Ruwaym suggested a different manner to integrate a full normative life with *tawakkul*, criticized *ṣūfiyya* and became a target for their attacks; however, his honourable image in Sufi sources was preserved at last. His position as a member of *ṣūfiyya* by himself was not affected by his critique and tense relationships with his contemporary Sufis. As for Ibn Yazdānyār, except for Sarrāj, the majority of Sufi authors agree that he is one of the great Sufi masters of the early phase of Sufism in spite of his severe critique against the Sufis of Baghdad. If Junayd is documented to have adopted the strategy of corresponding with his fellows for the sake of providing them with his guidance, Ruwaym is documented to have written a certain work on the mistakes of the Sufis; while for Ibn Yazdānyār, the preferable strategy seemed to be a direct severe critique that was most likely shared with traditionalists and men of authority.

Sufi authors like Sulamī and Qushayrī were interested in presenting a diversified portrait of early Sufism. Critical voices were integrated into one solid, still colourful, scene, and their controversies had to be absorbed into a general discourse. Only when this discourse is read very carefully can the faint voice of controversy be overheard. The aforementioned story

[60] Abū Jaʿfar b. Yazdānyār, *Rawḍat al-murīdīn*, Princeton MS. 968, fols. 43b–44a; Cf. Sulamī, *al-Muqaddima fi al-taṣawwuf wa-ḥaqīqatihi*, ed. by Ḥusayn Amīn, in *Majmūʿa-yi āthār-i Sulamī*, vol. 2, 464.

[61] Abū Jaʿfar b. Yazdānyār, *Rawḍat al-murīdīn*, Princeton MS. 968, fol. 74a.

about Abū Ḥamza al-Ṣūfī who appears to have criticized the wealthy lifestyle of the great master of the Baghdadi Sufis, al-Ḥārith al-Muḥāsibī, provides another example of how voices of controversy were naturally unavoidable within the solid portrait of the Baghdadi group of *ṣūfiyya*.[62]

ENCOUNTERING CONTROVERSIES AND QUARRELS: THE CONCEPTS OF *MUNĀQARA* AND *NIQĀR*

A famous statement is attributed to Ruwaym: '*Lā yazāl al-ṣūfiyya bi-khayr mā tanāqarū fa-idhā iṣṭalaḥū halakū*' ('the Sufis still prosper inasmuch as they are committed to *munāqara*, but if they become reconciled they will be totally wiped out').[63] In another version of this statement the verb *tanāqarū* is replaced by *tanāfarū* which literally means 'they became disagreeing'. This appears, for instance, in Qushayrī's *Risāla*.[64] Ibn Manẓūr indicates that both *munāqara* and *niqār* mean dispute (*munāzaʿa*).[65] Edward Lane in his *Arabic-English Lexicon* does not refer to *munāqara* at all and discusses the word *munāfara* only.[66]

Carl Ernst refers to *munāqara* in his discussion of the sort of *shaṭḥiyyāt* that are expressed through actions in Sufi literature. He indicates that the shocking and audacious acts of certain Sufis through which they lose their consciousness turn into surprising acts and sayings of wrangling. Ernst suggests comparing this custom with pride and boasting (*iftikhār*) in ancient Arabic poetry. He relies on the influential Sufi manual of Abū al-Najīb al-Suhrawardī in order to explain the dynamics between the basis of *shaṭḥ* and boasting. Suhrawardī refers to boasting (*al-iftikhār wa-iẓhār al-daʿwā*) in the last chapter of his *Ādāb al-murīdīn*, which he dedicates to dispensations (*rukhaṣ*), or the permissible deviations from the rules as Ernst defines it.[67] Boasting, according to Suhrawardī, is considered *rukhṣa*. It is a code of behaviour that is permitted to beginner Sufis since those who succeeded to achieve the high destination of the path

[62] See Sarrāj, *Ṣuḥuf min kitāb al-lumaʿ*, 6–7. See the detailed reference to this story at the beginning of the Introduction.

[63] Sulamī, *Jawāmiʿ ādāb al-ṣūfiyya*, 41. The author of *Adab al-mulūk* formulated the second part of this statement quite differently: '*Fa-in tarakū al-munāqara tarakū al-mudhākara*' (anonymous author, *Adab al-mulūk*, 54).

[64] See Qushayrī, *Risāla*, 139.

[65] See Ibn Manẓūr, *Lisān al-ʿarab*, vol. 5, 229.

[66] See Edward Lane, *Arabic-English Lexicon* (Beirut: Librairie Du Liban, 1968), vol. 1/8, 2824.

[67] See Ernst, *Words of Ecstasy*, 38–39. On *rukhaṣ* see the detailed footnote in Chapter 2.

are not allowed to undertake *rukhaṣ* anymore, and they are required to stay committed to the state of *ʿazīma*.[68]

I argue here that both *munāqara* and *niqār* refer to the strategy that early Sufis developed and used in their attempts to confront a reality that witnessed disputes and quarrels between many Sufi personalities. Neither were meant to carry the meaning of the disputes or the boasting themselves, but the reaction and the way of encountering those disputes through developing manners of conduct (*ādāb*) and integrating the ways of treating internal controversies under them. The terms *munāfara* and *nifār*, meanwhile, designate the act of disputing. In one occasion of *Nafaḥāt al-uns*, Jāmī makes an interesting reference to Anṣārī Haravī's definition of *niqār*: *Niqār* does not mean fighting or quarrelling with each other. It instead means the custom of ordering each other to do what is in harmony with their methods and teachings and prohibiting them of doing what is not. This custom helps the Sufis comply with the values that the principle of Sufi companionship (*ṣuḥba*) imposes upon them.[69]

One of the Shīrāzian contemporaries of Junayd was Abū Muzāḥim (d. 345/956). Jāmī wrote that this man disputed (*munāfara kardan*) both Junayd and Shiblī when he heard them talking about Sufi knowledge. It seems very likely that the way that Abū Muzāḥim chose to dispute them was severe and audacious, and that explains why Jāmī continued to tell that 'Sufi sheikhs used to fear him'.[70]

Sulamī refers to 'the etiquette of *munāqara* among the Sufis' (*ādāb al-munāqara*) in a short section of his *Jawāmiʿ ādāb al-ṣūfiyya*. Sulamī seems to be eager to emphasize the crucial need of the Sufis to experience *munāqara* as well as conciliation. He states: 'Among the Sufi rules of conduct lay Sufis' *munāqara* as well as their conciliation (*muṣālaḥatuhum*), and their aspiration to safeguard their brothers against losing their inner states.'[71] This reference leaves a strong impression that *munāqara* as Sulamī conceived it refers to Sufis' way to confront tensions that could go beyond the regular forms of controversy and reach the point of quarrels marked by a temporary or permanent break in the relationships between the Sufi companions. Locating the concept of conciliation beside the concept of *munāqara* itself as two aspects of Sufi *ādāb* in

68 See Abū al-Najīb al-Suhrawardī, *Ādāb al-murīdīn*, 96.

69 See Jāmī, *Nafaḥāt al-uns*, 75.

70 See ibid., 59.

71 Sulamī, *Jawāmiʿ ādāb al-ṣūfiyya*, 41; idem, *Tisʿat kutub fī uṣūl al-zuhd wa-al-taṣawwuf li-Abī ʿAbd al-Raḥmān Muḥammad b. al-Ḥusayn b. Mūsā al-Sulamī*, ed. by Sulaymān Ibrāhīm Ātesh (N.p.: al-Nāshir, 1995), 250.

Sulamī's text serves as the author's strategy to show that *munāqara* was simply needed to protect one's brother from a probable situation of deviation from the path of truth which was believed to have been caused by his lower soul.

According to early Sufi teachings, the lower soul maintains its influence on the Sufi until he succeeds to purify it completely and turn it into a positive spiritual faculty in his path towards the divine beloved. Sufi authors such as Sulamī and later on ʿUmar al-Suhrawardī confirm that disputing one's brothers is nothing but an effective instrument to fight against the negative influence of their lower souls. Being a domain for the urgent need to help one's brothers, *munāqara* is considered nothing but a call of duty. The same idea appears in Suhrawardī's *ʿAwārif* while referring to the aforementioned statement of Ruwaym. Disputes and quarrels, according to Suhrawardī's work, are motivated by the aspiration of the Sufis to watch over their fellow men as to ascertain the latter's sincerity in practising the Sufi mode of life (*ḥusn tafaqqud baʿḍihim aḥwāl baʿḍ*).[72] While Sulamī mentions the need for conciliation initiated by those who were involved in *niqār*, Suhrawardī, after two centuries, emphasizes the role of the senior disciple of the Sufi sheikh (*khādim*) in solving such disputes. The text of Suhrawardī is more informative in reference to the nature of the disputes that require the intervention of the *ribāṭ*'s leadership. Suhrawardī uses the terms *muʿtadī* (attacker) and *muʿtadā ʿalayhi* (attacked) in this context. This implies a climate of severe quarrels that went far beyond differences in understanding and explaining the mere theories of the Sufis.

Two styles of initiating conciliation after *niqār* are conveyed in the two works of Sulamī and Suhrawardī: the first, which is less formal and closer to the well-known social-ethical code of behaviour, in the text of Sulamī, and the more institutionalized custom within the boundaries of *ribāṭ*-based Sufi life, in the text of Suhrawardī. The existence of such quarrels in early medieval Sufi realities justifies the very existence of such references.

The concepts 'objection' (*iʿtirāḍ*) and 'argumentation' (*munāqasha*) frequently appear in early Sufi sources to indicate controversies on Sufi theories and practices.[73] On one occasion in his *Ṭabaqāt*, Sulamī uses the term *mufāwaḍāt* (lit. negotiations) to indicate differences in opinions and

[72] Suhrawardī, *ʿAwārif*, 120.

[73] See e.g., Daylamī, *Sīra*, 158–159, 169–170; Cf. Ibn al-Qaysarānī, *Ṣafwat al-taṣawwuf*, 218.

method between the two mystics of Shīrāz, Bundār b. al-Ḥusayn (d. 353/964) and Ibn Khafīf.[74] Beside the concepts of *niqār* and *munāqara*, the verbal forms that are derived from them appear in different contexts in those sources. According to classical Arabic lexicons, both *niqār* and *munāqara* mean a verbal controversy and a competition in discussing one particular topic for the sake of confuting the opponent (*al-munāqara murāja'at al-kalām*).[75]

Interestingly, the biography of Bundār in Sulamī's *Ṭabaqāt* includes several references to Sufis' disparity and disagreement. He is quoted by Sulamī to have urged the Sufi not to quarrel with anyone since by doing so he is expected to satisfy his own lower soul (*lā tukhāṣim li-nafsik*). On the same occasion, Bundār states that Sufis agree on the principle of unity, but they disagree on the ways to practise unity.[76] The use of the word *khuṣūma* comes to indicate an actual form of quarrel, not only a difference in opinions concerning Sufi theories. Even though this combination came to be explicitly documented in the writings of later authors, as the following discussion will show, the broad category of *niqār* existing in earlier Sufi works could frequently designate one instrument in the hands of early Sufis to confront differences in opinions. In addition to being an indication of the way of confronting controversies since its earliest appearances, *niqār* referred not only to a plain kind of verbal controversy but also to different forms of tension and conflict that left their prints on the actual lives of the Sufis.

Later Sufi manuals which were written to regulate the communal lives of the Sufis inside their fully established centres could refer to the combination between serious tensions and quarrels from one side and the act of initiating *niqār* in order to confront those tensions from the other side, more explicitly than their ancestors.

Verbal confrontations that are fundamentally evidenced in the sections that were devoted to *mukātabāt* (correspondence) of the early Sufis in the major Sufi collections could be seen as more than just indications of differences in opinions. In the texts of *mukātabāt* it is common to come across pieces of advice and apparent statements of counsel addressed by the Sufi sheikhs to their associates and contemporaries. In certain cases, these point to probable interpersonal controversies between the

[74] See Sulamī, *Ṭabaqāt*, 491.
[75] See Ibn Manẓūr, *Lisān al-'arab*, vol. 5, 229.
[76] See Sulamī, *Ṭabaqāt*, 493.

corresponding parties. In other cases, verbal confrontations that are evidenced in this type of Sufi writing might constitute a way of documenting processes of persecution and exclusion, which were initiated in reality by certain Sufi figures towards those who were not exactly members of the 'mainstream'. In other cases, such confrontations could lead to threats and accusations of treason or going astray. The aforementioned case of Ibn Yazdānyār is one example of such situations. The fourth/tenth century author ʿAbd al-Malik b. Muḥammad al-Naysābūrī al-Kharkūshī devotes one of the last chapters in his *Tahdhīb al-asrār* to Sufis' correspondence ('*bāb fī dhikr mukātabātihim*'). The last paragraph in this chapter is interesting for our discussion. It goes as follows:

> Ibn ʿAṭāʾ[77] wrote to Kharrāz, God has mercy upon both of them, telling him: 'Our companions became committed to *munāqara* of each other after you (*baʿdaka ṣārū yunāqir baʿḍuhum baʿḍan*).' Kharrāz wrote to him as an answer that this [behaviour!] is caused by God's vigilant concern (*ghayra min al-Ḥaqq ʿalayhim*) that seeks to prevent them from having confidence in each other.[78]

God's sincere love towards the Sufis, according to Kharrāz's reply, is the reason for *niqār*. It seems God intends to keep the Sufis disputing each other as means to urge them to keep their eyes on their fellow men and criticize any unacceptable behaviour or saying and causing them, thereby, to set aside their confidence in each other.

It is evidenced that Junayd had several critical approaches towards his fellow Sufis. These could be deduced from his own *Rasāʾil* as well as from his correspondence with certain Sufi figures as they were preserved in early Sufi compendia. Junayd reprimanded Shiblī, for instance, for revealing his overwhelming mystical states that restrained his intellect and drove him to a situation akin to madness. Sarrāj tells that Shiblī sent a letter to Junayd describing one of his mystical states that blotted his tongue and intellect and caused him to feel a deep loneliness among people. Junayd, according to the anecdote, did not write his reply until a whole week had passed. This reply includes Junayd's typical criticism on

[77] Aḥmad b. Muḥammad b. Sahl Abū al-ʿAbbās b. ʿAṭāʾ, one of Junayd's companions. He died in 309/922 or 311/923. See his biography in Sulamī, *Ṭabaqāt*, 260–268; Ibn al-Jawzī, *Ṣifat al-ṣafwa*, vol. 2, 250–251; Baghdādī, *Taʾrīkh baghdād*, vol. 6, 164–170. See also the comprehensive work of Richard Gramlich on Ibn ʿAṭāʾ and his legacy: Richard Gramlich, *Abū l-ʿAbbās b. ʿAṭāʾ: Sufi und Koranausleger* (Stuttgart: Deutsche Morgenländische Gesellschaft, Franz Steiner, 1995). Ibn ʿAṭāʾ's life is referred to in detail in ibid., 1–10.

[78] Kharkūshī, *Tahdhīb al-asrār*, 541.

his Sufi contemporaries: Sufi states should be kept secret, and words of ecstasy 'should be discussed in cellars' (*sarādīb*).[79] Junayd refers to Shiblī in a sarcastic tone in the section devoted to Shiblī's words of ecstasy in *Luma'*. It is according to Junayd that 'Shiblī, God has mercy upon him, was suspended at his [spiritual!] place, and he could not go far. Had he been able to go far, he would have been turned into a great *imām*' (*ūqifa al-Shiblī raḥimahu Allāh fī makānihi fa-mā ba'uda, wa-law ba'uda la-jā'a minhu imām*).[80] Shiblī was considered in Junayd's eyes a Sufi who could not reach the high states of stability and sobriety that help the Sufi to be qualified for guiding others through the path. Junayd, as is usually portrayed in early Sufi sources, ignores Shiblī's inquiries and notions and expresses his, namely Junayd's, compassion towards his recklessness and impetuosity.[81] References to the interesting correspondence between Junayd and Yūsuf b. al-Ḥusayn were made and thoroughly discussed in Chapter 5. The fifth/eleventh century Sufi author and scholar of *ḥadīth* Ibn al-Qaysarānī devotes one section of his *Ṣafwat al-taṣawwuf* to 'the lawfulness of *mujāzā* that the Sufis call *niqār*'.[82] It was the term *mujārā* not *mujāzā* that appeared in Sarrāj's *Luma'* and referred to the custom of discussing Sufi sciences, as I previously noted. *Mujāzā*, on the other hand, indicates the act of calling to account one's brothers for committing unaccepted actions and, moreover and most probably, the act of punishing them.[83] In the Fātiḥ manuscript of *Ṣafwat al-taṣawwuf*, the title of Ibn al-Qaysarānī's chapter appears slightly different: 'chapter on the cause of *mujāzā* and *muṭālaba* of the brothers'.[84] *Muṭālaba* carries the meaning of demanding something from someone, and it thus relates to calling to account Sufis who were involved in quarrels. The word *niqār*, which is the Sufi term that covers both *mujāzā* and *muṭālaba* in Ibn al-Qaysarān's work, designates the Sufis' method for confronting quarrels among their brothers. One's being at fault or involved in a quarrel could make the Sufis impose a particular punishment on him. This punishment, as the following references show, could take the form of paying fines or presenting alms to one's companions.

This supports evidence that the Sufis in Ibn al-Qaysarānī's day were criticized for having quarrels that were even noticed in public. In order to

[79] See Sarrāj, *Luma'*, 233–234.

[80] Ibid., 404. Cf. ibid., 307 (a different version of Junayd's statement). Junayd's criticism of Shilbī's behaviour and statements is also presented in ibid., 233–234.

[81] See e.g., ibid., 404.

[82] Ibn al-Qaysarānī, *Ṣafwat al-taṣawwuf*, 362–363.

[83] See Lane, *Arabic-English Lexicon*, vol. 1/2, 422.

[84] See Ibn al-Qaysarānī, *Ṣafwat al-taṣawwuf*, 362, footnote 1.

defend the phenomenon and to emphasize its necessity, Ibn al-Qaysarānī indicates two prophetic traditions, in one of which a dispute is said to have occurred even between God's prophets Adam and Moses.[85] It is interesting to note that the editor of *Ṣafwat al-taṣawwuf* Ghāda al-Muqaddim ʿUdra refers to Ruwaym's famous statement on *niqār* that Ibn al-Qaysarānī quotes, and she indicates that the word *mā* in the phrase *mā tanāqarū* should be understood as a negative particle, and that the meaning of the sentence should be 'the Sufis are still in goodness, [and!] they did not dispute.'[86] The conditional form in the latter part of the sentence, where the opposite verbal form *iṣṭalaḥū* (became reconciled) appears, shows without a doubt that the editor's suggestion is not convincing. Furthermore, the very content of the traditions that the author included in this section praises the value of disputes since they could help the members of any group to keep following and sincerely practising the group's fundamentals.

Later on in his work, Ibn al-Qaysarānī refers to additional aspects of the tensions between the Sufis; however, he does so through presenting the titles and gathering traditions and *akhbār* of the early generation of Muslims under them. Though no real discussions of the topics are provided here, the data that the author chose to gather under each title are rather informative. Ibn al-Qaysarānī chose, for instance, to collect traditions on issues like the need to apologize to one's brothers (the word 'brothers' here carries the Sufi sense, but its general reference to all members of the Muslim community should also be considered) or the need to accept the apology of someone who expresses regret after making certain mistakes. The author's main intention was to show that all these topics had strong origins in the Prophet and his successors' records of sayings and deeds (*sunna*).[87] He was committed to this goal while bringing to the fore customs that were most likely known during his day, such as the custom according to which the one that committed a fault and needs to apologize is said to give alms to his companions or another custom according to which the one whose companions imposed a fine on him that he did not pay is required to pay a greater sum.[88]

With the establishment of the *ribāṭ*-based Sufism such quarrels seem to have been an integral part of the communal life within the walls of the Sufi centres. This was the reason that motivated certain Sufi theoreticians to regulate such quarrels by accentuating the position of the Sufi sheikh and

[85] Ibid. [86] Ibid., 363, footnote 4. [87] See ibid., 379–383. [88] See ibid., 384–386.

his senior disciple in preserving community harmony and mediating between those who are engaged in quarrels.[89] The above-mentioned reference to Suhrawardī's *ʿAwārif* supports this notion. One of the famous contemporaries of Suhrawardī was Najm al-Dīn Dāya, the author of *Mirṣād al-ʿibād*.[90] In his chapter on the attributes of the Sufi disciple, Dāya records the need to avoid harsh disputes and quarrels (*khuṣūmāt*, *munāzaʿāt*) and to keep himself away from condemning his companions.[91]

The process of establishing a theoretical discourse around *munāqara* in the Sufi writings, by itself, was intended to highlight the crucial necessity that Sufi authors felt to create a homogeneous and solid Sufi ethos according to which all differences in thoughts, controversies and even harsh quarrels and conflicts reflected in the interpersonal relationships between the Sufis in reality could be filtered and justified through the mechanism of *munāqara*. At the basis of this mechanism, *munāqara* acted as one of the ultimate instruments that enabled those authors to portray the Sufi community as a solid unit in spite of individual tendencies and emotions of envy and rancour of which even the Sufi brothers were not exempt.

89 See Salamah-Qudsi, *Idea of Tashabbuh*, 193.

90 Dāya was a disciple of the renowned master of Khawārazm, Najm al-Dīn al-Kubrā (d. 618/1221). See Dāya's biography in: Ṣafadī, *Wāfī bi-l-wafayāt*, vol. 17, 312–313; Jāmī, *Nafaḥāt al-uns*, 435.

91 See Abū Bakr ʿAbd Allāh b. Muḥammad b. Shāhawr Najm al-Dīn Rāzī, *Mirṣād al-ʿibād min al-mabdaʾ ilā al-maʿād*, ed. by Ḥusayn al-Ḥusaynī al-Niʿmatu-Allāhī (N.p.: Maṭbaʿah-yi Majlis, 1312 *Shamsī*), 146.

8

Companionship with Youth (*Ṣuḥbat al-Aḥdāth*)

Companionship with youth or, as it is known in Sufi writings of the period between the fourth/tenth and seventh/thirteenth centuries, *ṣuḥbat al-aḥdāth*, is considered here as one of the lesser-known facets of the relationship between the mystic as an individual and his wider community. In this chapter, I will attempt to place Sufi companionship (*ṣuḥba*) in general and companionship with youth in particular within a wider socio-historical ambit as well as to discuss certain historiographical and theoretical aspects of these customs. I came across this topic after exploring the different types of relationships between Sufi individuals and their wider communal environments from examples of the so-called consensually acclaimed Sufis through those who, on the contrary, chose to leave the general fabric of mainstream Sufism, to the disputes and quarrels that were apparently an integral part of communal life within the Sufi centres of the period under consideration here. As I will show, *ṣuḥbat al-aḥdāth* was often linked with controversial figures in the history of Sufism. However, these figures were by no means marginal in the eyes of the creators of the accepted Sufi ethos – that is, the authors of the great Sufi compendia – from the fourth/tenth century and onwards. Through a broad topical and literary field of inquiry, I seek to present here an insight into an additional sphere for individual-communal dynamics in early Sufism. Examining this topic could enrich our understanding of the diverse ways in which Sufis, particularly those whose names were associated with *ṣuḥbat al-aḥdāth*, as well as Sufi authors used to accommodate certain personal patterns of behaviour with a general system of thought and norms constituting the collective Sufi identity of their time.

ṢUḤBAT AL-AḤDĀTH: INTRODUCTION

Male attraction to youths was a recognized phenomenon in early medieval Muslim societies.[1] Pederasty became a much-discussed theme among Muslim moralists and jurists in the later Abbasid era. Textual evidence of this period leaves no doubt that aristocratic men used to own slaves for sexual intercourse. Yet in the *Qurʾān*, homosexual acts are clearly condemned, although no reference exists to their punishment. As such, an increasing number of *ḥadīth* traditions were fabricated and attributed to the Prophet in order to condemn the custom and warn Muslims against it.[2] Some of the *ḥadīth* traditions emerged in response to the appearance of pederasty as an open theme in early Abbasid poetry. Evidence seems to suggest that actual cases of sodomy (*liwāṭ*) and pederasty were not as popular as the literary theme itself.[3] While medieval Islamic literature seemed to have a free hand in praising the high ideal of masculine beauty, homosexuality was excluded from the general Islamic social and religious norms.

Recent scholarship has differentiated between sodomy, which was harshly condemned in Islamic law, and homoerotic sentiment, which was considered natural and very common.[4] This differentiation explains why pederasty and homoerotic sentiments towards boys could not harm the social status of the adult man. Since Islamic culture is thoroughly phallocratic, the respectability of perpetrators of pederasty remained untouched and their sexual behaviour confidential. The boy in this type of relationship did not purportedly lose his masculinity through his passive role since he was not yet virile and therefore had no masculinity to lose.[5]

[1] See e.g., Khaled el-Rouayheb, *Before Homosexuality in the Arab-Islamic world, 1500–1800* (Chicago: The University of Chicago Press, 2005), 139. Cf. E. K. Rowson, 'Homosexuality', *Encyclopaedia Iranica*, vol. XII, Fasc. 4, section (ii), 'In Islamic Law', 441–445; Bouhdiba, *Sexuality in Islam*, 118–119. For examples of the homoerotic tendencies among poets and bureaucrats in elite Abbasid society, see: Everett Rowson, 'The Traffic in Boys: Slavery and Homoerotic Liaisons in Elite ʿAbbāsid Society', *Middle Eastern Literatures*, vol. 11, no. 2 (2008), 193–204.

[2] See Scott Kugle's profound discussion of the body of forged traditions in reference to homosexuality in Islam in: Scott Kugle, *Homosexuality in Islam: Critical Reflection on Gay, Lesbian, and Transgender Muslims* (Oxford: Oneworld, 2010), 73–127.

[3] See James Bellamy, 'Sex and Society in Islamic Popular Literature', in *Society and the Sexes in Medieval Islam*, ed. by Afaf Lutfi al-Sayyid-Marsot (Malibu, Calif.: Undena Publications, 1979), 40.

[4] See el-Rouayheb, *Before Homosexuality*, 6, 79.

[5] See Sabine Schmidtke, 'Homoeroticism and Homosexuality in Islam: A Review Article', *Bulletin of the School of Oriental and African Studies*, vol. 62, no. 2 (1999), 260–261.

Beside the sexual act itself in both pederasty and sodomy, the 'evil thoughts' that gazing (*naẓar*) at beardless boys (pl. *murdān*, sing. *amrad*) and associating with them could evoke comprised a common, fundamental topic in Muslim disputes on *fitna* (temptation). The Shāfiʿī scholar of the fourth/tenth century Abū Bakr al-Ājurrī (d. 360/970), for instance, warned the readers of his treatise against sodomy (*Dhamm al-liwāṭ*) of associating with those who associate with youth commonly identified with debauchery (*al-ghilmān al-ladhīna yushār ilyahim bi-l-fisq*).[6]

Abū Bakr al-ʿĀmirī (d. 530/1136), commonly known as Ibn al-Khabbāz, was one of the traditionalists under whom Ibn al-Jawzī studied *ḥadīth* and jurisprudence. He authored a short treatise on the religious juridical provisions of gazing at the forbidden *Aḥkām al-naẓar ilā al-muḥarramāt*. In this work, he debates those who permit gazing at women and beardless youths with no legal justification for this gazing (such as the need to teach youths and women or to supply them with medical treatment), claiming that they are protected (*maʿṣūmūn*) from committing sins while doing so.[7]

In the Sufi spheres, references to the much-criticized practice of *ṣuḥbat al-aḥdāth* emerged in the Sufi writings of the fourth/tenth century. Many Sufi masters apparently warned their disciples against falling prey to this epidemic (*āfa*). Qushayrī, for instance, considers *ṣuḥbat al-aḥdāth* as evidence of God's will to humiliate and desert the mystic.[8] His references to the topic will be discussed in detail below. Hujwīrī refers to gazing at youth in his chapter on Sufi dance. His attitude to this issue is more severe than that of Qushayrī as he explicitly states that 'anyone who declares this to be allowable is an unbeliever (*kāfir*)'.[9]

6 See Abū Bakr al-Ājurrī, *Dhamm al-liwāṭ*, ed. by Majdī al-Sayyid Ibrāhīm (Cairo: Maktabat al-Qurʾān, n.d.), 29. See a detailed discussion of the psychological background for this consideration in Arno Schmitt, 'Different Approaches to Male–Male Sexuality/Eroticism from Morocco to Uzbekistan', in *Sexuality and Eroticism among Males in Moslem Societies*, ed. by Arno Schmitt and Jehoeda Sofer (Binghamton, N.Y.: Harrington Park Press, 1992), 2–3. On the relationship between manhood and beards in traditional Muslim societies, see Afsaneh Najmabadi, *Women with Mustaches and Men without Beards: Gender and Sexual Anxieties of Iranian Modernity* (Berkeley: University of California Press, 2005), 15–18.

7 See Muḥammad b. Ḥabīb al-ʿĀmirī, *Aḥkām al-naẓar ilā al-muḥarramāt wa-mā fīhi min al-khaṭar wa-l-āfāt*, ed. by Mashhūr Salmān (Beirut: Dār Ibn Ḥazm, 1995), 33, 42.

8 See Qushayrī, *Risāla*, 201.

9 Jullābī Hujwīrī, *Kashf al-maḥjūb*, 542. Cf. Hellmut Ritter, *The Ocean of the Soul: Man, the World and God in the Stories of Farīd al-Dīn ʿAṭṭār*, trans. by John O'Kane with editorial assistance of Bernd Radtke (Leiden and Boston: Brill, 2003), 471, 556.

In addition to the references to pederasty made by the early Sufi authors such as Hujwīrī and Qushayrī, critics of Sufism widely used the custom in their arguments against the movement. These critics included Ibn al-Khabbāz al-ʿĀmirī, Ibn al-Jawzī, Jawbarī (the first half of the seventh/thirteenth century),[10] Ibn Baydakīn al-Turkmānī (d. the seventh/thirteenth century),[11] ʿIzz al-Dīn b. ʿAbd al-Salām (d. 660/1262),[12] Ḍiyāʾ al-Dīn al-Qurṭubī (d. 656/1258)[13] and later Muslim traditionalists like al-Ghamrī al-Wāsiṭī (d. 849/1445) and Ibn Ḥajar al-Haythamī (d. 974/1567).

In addition to his aforementioned critique against illegal *naẓar* in the last section of his *Aḥkām al-naẓar,* Ibn al-Khabbāz al-ʿĀmirī warned Muslim rulers and governors against allowing those engaged in false renunciation and *taṣawwuf* (*al-muddaʿīn li-l-zuhd wa-madhhab al-taṣawwuf*) to deceive youths and women by associating with them in *samāʿ* gatherings. Ibn al-Khabbāz adds that those who claim to be completely protected from temptation are like the one who drinks wine and claims that wine has no negative effect on him as it does on common people (*al-ʿawāmm*). Ibn al-Khabbāz claims that the group of people of this creed had gone astray, as they had isolated themselves from the Muslim law (*hādhihi al-ṭāʾifa al-ḍālla fī daʿwāhā al-māriqa ʿan al-sharīʿa*); therefore, this group deserved to be cursed and rebuked.[14]

Ibn al-Jawzī's accusations, like those of Ibn al-Khabbāz, came in opposition to certain Sufi authors who permitted both gazing at an *amrad* and associating with him under certain conditions. Muḥammad b. Ṭāhir Ibn al-Qaysarānī, the aforementioned *ḥadīth* scholar of the *ẓāhirī* school of law, is one of those whom Ibn al-Jawzī severely criticizes. Ibn al-Jawzī, followed later by Dhahabī, attributes to Ibn al-Qaysarānī a treatise that permits gazing at beardless youth.[15]

The Ḥanafī scholar of the seventh/thirteenth century Idrīs b. Baydakīn al-Turkmānī associated companionship with youth (*muʿāsharat al-aḥdāth*)

[10] See ʿAbd al-Raḥmān b. ʿUmar al-Jawbarī, *al-Mukhtār fī kashf al-asrār wa-hatk al-astār*, ed. by ʿIṣām Shubbārū (Beirut: Dār al-Taḍāmun, 1992).

[11] See Idrīs b. Baydakīn al-Turkmānī, *Kitāb al-lumaʿ fī al-ḥawādith wa-l-bidaʿ*, ed. by Ṣubḥī Labīb (Cairo: n.p., 1986).

[12] See Izz al-Dīn Ibn ʿAbd al-Salām, *al-Fatāwā al-mawṣiliyya*, ed. by Iyād al-Ṭabbāʿ (Damascus: Dār al-Fikr, 1999), 84–85, 95–97.

[13] See Aḥmad b. ʿUmar al-Anṣārī al-Qurṭubī known as Ibn al-Muzayyin, *Kashf al-qināʿ ʿan ḥukm al-wajd wa-l-samāʿ* (Ṭanṭā: Dār al-Ṣaḥāba, 1992). See also the detailed reference to this work later in this chapter.

[14] See ʿĀmirī, *Aḥkām al-naẓar*, 81–83.

[15] See Ibn al-Jawzī, *Talbīs Iblīs*, 217; Dhahabī, *Siyar*, vol. 19, 364.

with *samāʿ* gatherings. He denounced those who claim that looking at *murdān* is an instrument to contemplate God's majesty in creating the world of beauty. The author sought refuge with God from both 'brotherhood with women' (*ukhuwwat al-niswān*) and association with youths (*ṣuḥbat al-murdān*).[16]

In several instances in his *Kashf al-qināʿ ʿan ḥukm al-wajd wa-l-samāʿ* (*Unveiling the Sufi Ecstasy and Listening to Music*), Ḍiyāʾ al-Dīn Aḥmad b. ʿUmar al-Qurṭubī known as Ibn al-Muzayyin mentioned the erotic behaviour of some mature Sufis during *samāʿ* gatherings. In one instance, bn al-Muzayyin refers to masters who associate with boys (*yakhtaliṭ al-shuyūkh wa-l-ṣighār*) and notes that this association comprises a major element of the Sufi rituals firmly rejected by *sunnī* Islam.[17] Elsewhere he stated:

> One is likely to see a mature man, who is highly respected for his social status, merits, intelligence, and religious gravity and reverence, abandoning all his gravity and modesty aside during *samāʿ*. He is likely to turn yellow, and [in an intense ecstatic state!] touches with his hands (*yaʿbath bi-yadayhi*) [his sexual organs!], leans towards his companion and draws him close to him (*yajurruhu ilayhi*), beats by his legs and shakes his shoulders. [This state is maintained!] until *samāʿ* totally overwhelms this man, and, consequently, he begins to dance like shameless people (*mujjān*) and move like effeminates (*makhānīth*) and women.[18]

According to Ibn al-Muzayyin, during *samāʿ*, many old Sufis would rub their cheeks and white hair on the feet of the effeminate singer and in their ecstasy often took off their garments that they then gave him.[19] The Egyptian Sufi scholar of the ninth/fifteenth century, Muḥammad b. ʿUmar al-Ghamrī al-Wāsiṭī, considers gazing at the *amrad* and associating with him very dangerous, sometimes even more so than gazing at women and associating with them: 'Gazing at *amrad* is a poisoned arrow.'[20] The author devotes one chapter of his work *al-Ḥukm al-maḍbūṭ fī taḥrīm fiʿl qawm Lūṭ* (*The Accurate Provision in Prohibiting the Act of the People of Lot*) to what he calls the epidemics that affect the Sufis as a result of associating with youth (*bāb fī al-āfāt al-dākhila ʿalā al-fuqarāʾ min mukhālaṭat al-aḥdāth*). He also severely criticizes the *ḥadīth* traditions that Sufis used in order to legitimize the custom of gazing at

16 See Ibn Baydakīn, *Kitāb al-lumaʿ*, vol. 1, 84–87.

17 See Ibn al-Muzayyin, *Kashf al-qināʿ*, 19. 18 Ibid., 48.

19 See ibid., 84. On the erotic customs during *samāʿ* see Fritz Meier, 'The Dervish Dance', in *Essays on Islamic Piety and Mysticism*, 38.

20 Shams al-Dīn Muḥammad b. ʿUmar al-Ghamrī al-Wāsiṭī, *al-Ḥukm al-maḍbūṭ fī taḥrīm fiʿl qawm Lūṭ*, ed. by ʿUbayd Allāh al-Miṣrī (Ṭanṭā: Dār al-Ṣaḥāba, 1988), 53.

beautiful faces and bodies. Ghamrī warns the Sufi masters of his time of outburst of erotic tendencies towards their beautiful boy disciples, saying that 'one who claims that his sexual desire does not spring up when he gazes at beautiful beardless is a liar.'[21]

Ghamrī was one of the earliest authors who criticized the sexual rituals of *muṭāwiʿa,* an antinomian sect of the early Ottoman period which celebrated, in addition to other erotic rituals, the practice of *naẓar* towards beardless youths.[22]

Khaled el-Rouayheb points out that this group must have flourished in Egypt between the fifteenth and eighteenth centuries since critical references to it by Egyptian religious scholars are widely available from this period. After Ghamrī, Muḥammad al-Dajjānī (d. 1070/1660) and ʿAlī al-ʿAdawī al-Ṣaʿīdī (d. 1188/1775) wrote tracts condemning the group.[23] ʿAbd al-Wahhāb al-Shaʿrānī urged readers not to denounce all *muṭāwiʿa*'s followers since, like other groups, it could include both 'the good and the bad'.[24]

Ibn Ḥajar al-Haythamī, the prolific Shāfiʿī author of the tenth/sixteenth century, considers lustful gazing at *amrad*, touching him and associating with him in solitude all as great sins (*kabāʾir*) since 'the seduction by

[21] See ibid., 60–62.

[22] Ghamrī calls this group *jamāʿa min al-muslimīn*. See Ghamrī, *al-Ḥukm al-maḍbūṭ*, 108. Ghamrī wrote also a special treatise against them which is entitled *al-ʿUnwān fī taḥrīm muʿāsharat al-shabāb wa-l-niswān* (MS Maktabat al-Malik ʿAbd Allāh b. ʿAbd al-ʿAzīz, 928, 6 fols.). Cf. Michael Winter's discussion of ʿAbd al-Wahhāb al-Shaʿrānī's approach towards this group in Egypt of the tenth/sixteenth century in: Michael Winter, *Society and Religion in Early Ottoman Egypt: Studies in the Writings of ʿAbd al-Wahhāb al-Shaʿrānī* (New Brunswick, N.J.: Transaction Books, 1982), 104–105. Interestingly, Masʿūd al-Qināwī (d. after 1205/1790) makes a reference to this group in his *Sharḥ lāmiyyat Ibn al-Wardī*. He indicates that, in the earlier stages of Sufism, the Sufi masters of *muṭāwiʿa* used to company *murdān*, and called them *bidāyāt* (lit. beginnings) for the sake of educating them in the same way that they did with their sons. They used to teach the *amrad* without gazing at him or touching him. The *muṭāwiʿa* of Qināwī's days, however, go totally astray because, contrary to their ancestors, they 'sleep with *murdān*, associating with them as they do with women, and even order them to massage their bodies and embracing them with their breast and backs [...] embracing *murdān* is known among them as 'the relaxation of the poor' (*wa-yusammūnahā rāḥat al-fuqarāʾ*).' Masʿūd b. Ḥasan al-Qināwī, *Sharḥ lāmiyyat Ibn al-Wardī al-musammāh fatḥ al-raḥīm al-raḥmān sharḥ naṣīḥat al-ikhwān wa-murshidat al-khullān*, ed. by Bū Jumʿa ʿAbd al-Qādir Mikrī (Jeddah: Dār al-Minhāj, 2008), 70–72.

[23] See Khaled el-Rouayheb, 'Heresy and Sufism in the Arabic-Islamic World, 1550–1775: Some Preliminary Observations', *Bulletin of the School of Oriental and African Studies*, vol. 73 (2010), 361; Cf. idem, *Before Homosexuality*, 36–37; 170, footnote 111.

[24] ʿAbd al-Wahhāb al-Shaʿrānī, *Laṭāʾif al-minan wa-l-akhlāq fī bayān wujūb al-taḥadduth bi-niʿmat Allāh ʿalā al-iṭlāq* (Cairo: ʿAbd al-Ḥamīd al-Ḥanafī, 1357/1938–9), vol. 2, 18.

beautiful beardless youth is more frequent and more shameful [than the seduction by women!]' (*li-anna al-fitna bi-l-murd aqrab wa-aqbaḥ*).[25]

Critical voices against this custom among Sufis followed early references to it in Sufi writings of the fourth/tenth century. Those voices benefitted from both early works devoted to the condemnation of sodomy (*dhamm al-liwāṭ*) in Muslim society in general[26] and the criticisms made by Sufi authors in Sufi literature in particular.

The doctrine according to which the divine beauty is manifested in beautiful human faces and bodies was well-known among early Sufis, as evidenced in certain sources of the fourth/tenth century and later on.[27] This doctrine could make more sense in light of recent socio-religious theories about the position of the human body in our life. In his fascinating book on saints' bodies (2007), Scott Kugle says what is now known among sociologists of religion – that the human body 'is a means of thinking rather than simply the object of thought'.[28] Contemplating phenomenal beauty through looking and touching the world of bodies is not only permissible but also necessary in order to 'transcend the phenomenal world [. . .] and experience the omnipresence of God'.[29]

The different strategies used by Sufi authors and theoreticians to deal with *ṣuḥbat al-aḥdāth* are of great significance. In many occasions of the early Sufi compendia, Sufi authors condemn what they termed as an abiding epidemic (*āfa*) from which only a few Sufis were able to protect themselves.[30] Abū Saʿīd al-Kharrāz was reported to have seen the devil in

[25] Aḥmad b. Muḥammad b. ʿAlī b. Ḥajar al-Haytamī, *Kitāb al-zawājir ʿan iqtirāf al-kabāʾir* (Cairo: al-Maktaba al-Khayriyya, 1284 A.H.), vol. 2, 4.

[26] One of the earliest works of this kind is the aforementioned tenth century's work of Muḥammad b. al-Ḥusayn al-Ājurrī, *Dhamm al-liwāṭ*.

[27] See the early work of ʿAlī b. Muḥammad al-Daylamī, *ʿAṭf al-alif al-maʾlūf ʿalā al-lām al-maʿṭūf*, ed. by Joseph Norment Bell and Maḥmūd al-Shāfiʿī (Beirut and Cairo: Dār al-Kitāb al-Lubnānī and Dār al-Kitāb al-Miṣrī, 2007), 203–205; and the English translation of this work, *A Treatise on Mystical Love*, 163–165. According to Ibn al-Dabbāgh (d. 696/1297), observing human beauty could be a type of worshipping God as long as this is done for the sake of reasoning the divine power of creation [see ʿAbd al-Raḥmān b. Muḥammad al-Anṣārī Ibn al-Dabbāgh, *Kitāb mashāriq anwār al-qulūb wa-mafātiḥ asrār al-ghuyūb*, ed. by Hellmut Ritter (Beirut: Dār Ṣādir and Dār Bayrūt, 1959), 120]. For the development of this doctrine and the critique on it in the circles of traditionalists, see e.g., J. N. Bell, *Love Theory in Later Ḥanbalite Islam* (Albany: State University of New York Press, 1979), 139–144; Ritter, *The Ocean of the Soul*, 484–501.

[28] See Scott Kugle, *Sufis and Saints' Bodies: Mysticism, Corporeality, and Sacred Power in Islam* (Chapel Hill: The University of North Carolina Press, 2007), 13.

[29] El-Rouayheb, *Before Homosexuality*, 101.

[30] See e.g., Sulamī, *Ṭabaqāt*, 179; Qushayrī, *Risāla*, 201. See additional textual references later in this chapter.

his dream, and that devil allegedly informed him that he had left among the Sufis only one 'Satanic behaviour', which is *ṣuḥbat al-aḥdāth*. The immediate comment of Kharrāz was that 'only few Sufis were able to avoid that behaviour'.[31] Beyond such references, we do not come across a systematic discourse of condemnation against the practice of *ṣuḥbat al-aḥdāth* in early Sufi compendia. While Sarrāj, for instance, devoted full chapters in the last section of his *Luma*ʿ to treat what he considered misunderstandings of the accepted Sufi teachings and ethos among the Sufis of his time, he does not refer as such to *ṣuḥbat al-aḥdāth*. When a particular homoerotic behaviour of a specific Sufi becomes flagrant, then the controversy in the writings of his attackers becomes clearly apparent.[32] The case of Awḥad al-Dīn Kirmānī (d. 635/1237–1238) will be described in great detail hereinafter.

A variety of medieval sources (works of *adab*, legal works, poetry, studies of medicine, historical works, *riḥla* and others) portrays a reality in which homoerotic relationships were widely practised by many and even by those who occupied high social, religious and intellectual positions. This differed totally from the humiliating attitude towards the *maʾbūn*, that is, the passive partner in homosexual relationships between two adults.[33]

Consideration of the pervasive homoerotic notions in Arabic sources as evidence for actual sexual mores of medieval Islamic society does not always seem to be correct.[34] The contributors of *Homoeroticism in Classical Arabic Literature* (edited by Wright Jr. and Rowson, 1997) show that many of the homoerotic notions and male motifs in early Abbasid literature, both poetry and prose, served as sophisticated symbols and metaphors of social, political and moral themes. Homoeroticism is presented here as 'a reflection of sublime and often subversive ideals'.[35] Based on this argument, it is possible that the use of *ṣuḥbat al-aḥdādh*'s theme beside other homoerotic images among certain Sufis, like Yūsuf

[31] Sulamī, *Ṭabaqāt*, 227. Cf. Bell, *Love Theory*, 142.

[32] Cf. el-Rouayheb, *Heresy and Sufism*, 373.

[33] See Franz Rosenthal, 'Fiction and Reality: Sources for the Role of Sex in Medieval Muslim Society', in *Society and the Sexes*, 3. See a detailed survey of the scholarly works in this field in Schmidtke, *Homoeroticism*, 261–265.

[34] See el-Rouayheb, *Before Homosexuality*, 75–85.

[35] J. W. Wright Jr. and Everett K. Rowson, *Homoeroticism in Classical Arabic Literature*, ed. by J. W. Wright Jr. and Everett K. Rowson (New York: Columbia University Press, 1997), the editors' *introduction*, xv. A.

b. al-Ḥusayn as the following discussion will show, was a tool utilized by certain Sufi figures to confront the Sufi institution itself.

Besides exploring the aforementioned issues, in the following pages I wish to place early Sufism within the wider medieval scene of Islamic homoeroticism by examining early Sufi usages of homoerotic notions as well as by investigating the different strategies employed by the authors of early Sufi collections to treat homoerotic tendencies among the Sufis of that early period. Examining these two aspects together is expected to shed light onto the forms of correlation between the personal lives and behaviours of the Sufis involved and the ways they engaged in the life within the community of Sufis. In addition, this investigation might widen our understanding of the structural and thematical elements of the discourse that treated homoeroticism in Sufi compendia of that period in general.

Before moving on to our discussion, it is worth indicating that, due to lack of space, links between the texts that are brought up here, and those provided in classical Arabic works on profane love theory will not be addressed. For certain Sufis of the early sixth/twelfth century, the most prominent of whom is Aḥmad al-Ghazālī, the rules of love are the same whether the object of love is human or superhuman (the divine).[36] References to parallel points between sacred love and earthly love in the

[36] See Aḥmad Ghazālī, *Sawāniḥ*, bā taṣḥīḥāt-i jadīd va-muqaddame va-tawzīḥāt-i Naṣrullāh Pūrjavādī (Tehran: Intishārāt-i Bunyād-i Farhang-i Irān, 1359 *Shamsī*), 2; for a detailed discussion of Aḥmad Ghazālī's doctrine of the oneness of love in the recent work of Joseph Lumbard, *Aḥmad al-Ghazālī, Remembrance, and the Metaphysics of Love* (Albany: State University of New York Press, 2016), 151–184; idem, 'Aḥmad al-Ghazālī', *The Oxford Encyclopedia of Islam and Philosophy, Science and Technology* (Oxford: Oxford University Press, 2014), 270–274. A thorough treatment of the affinities between the doctrinal systems and terminology of earthy love tradition and divine love tradition is best provided in: Ritter, *Ocean of the Soul*, 382–447. Notably, only a few attempts were made in modern scholarship to investigate those affinities and the impacts that each of the two traditions left on the other, a field which still in need of more scholarly endeavours. On divine and human love in Islam, see William Chittick, 'Divine and Human Love in Islam', in *Divine Love: Perspectives from the World's Religious Traditions*, ed. by Jeff Levin and Stephen G. Post (West Conshohocken, Pa.: Templeton Press, 2010), 163–200. On love and its position in early Sufism, extensive studies have been written, the most recent of which: William Chittick, *Divine Love: Islamic Literature and the Path to God* (New Haven: Yale University Press, 2013) which focuses on sources, primarily Persian, up to the sixth/twelfth century; Leonard Lewisohn, 'Sufism's Religion of Love, from Rābiʿa to Ibn ʿArabī', in *The Cambridge Companion to Sufism*, 150–180; Joseph Lumbard, 'From *Ḥubb* to *ʿIshq*: The Development of Love in Early Sufism', *Journal of Islamic Studies*, vol. 18, no. 3 (2007), 345–385 (with a survey of the major contributions on love theories and development especially in the footnotes).

following pages are restricted to our attempt to analyse Sufi theories on earthly beauty as a manifestation of God's absolute beauty. This attempt may allow us a glance into the ways of the Sufi institution in its formative stage presented by the authors of the most influential Sufi manuals to treat individual and distinctive voices of homoerotic tones.

MAJOR INQUIRIES

If we simply adopt the English translation of *ṣuḥba* as general 'friendship', it seems quite evident that the friendship cult among the Sufis, from the very beginnings of the Sufi movement in the course of the third/ninth and fourth/tenth centuries, was very often coloured in highly erotic terms, which made it difficult to assess its real content. The erotic content of the *ṣuḥbat al-aḥdāth* tradition and the relationship between this often-criticized tradition and the so-called male–male sexual trends in the wider range of Islamic medieval society had rarely, if ever, been examined.[37] The task of distinguishing the Sufi doctrines of friendship from overt erotic relations as demonstrated in the textual references to *ṣuḥbat al-aḥdāth* is, in itself, of great scholarly significance. When the different meanings of the term *ṣuḥba* are treated in scholarly works, we rarely find references to *ṣuḥbat al-aḥdāth*.[38] Some scholars make the general assumption that sexual activities among males occurred within Sufi teaching circles and ritual gatherings without providing any definite evidence of the early sources.[39]

The following questions may arise: What was the exact meaning of the term *ṣuḥbat al-aḥdāth*, and what types of relationships did it involve? Who were the Sufi personalities whose names were associated with this

[37] It is quite well known that male–male sexual trends in medieval Islamic culture differ from the modern concept of homosexuality. The concept 'homosexuality' itself was not known until 1869. See el-Rouayheb, *Before Homosexuality*, *introduction*, 1. Stephen Murrat and Will Roscoe suggest the plural form of the modern term, that is 'homosexualities', in order to signify the multicultural diversity of this trend. [See Stephen Murrat and Will Roscoe, *Islamic Homosexualities: Culture, History, and Literature* (New York: New York University Press, 1997), *introduction*, 4–6.] Cf. Arno Schmitt, *Bio-Bibliography of Male–Male Sexuality and Eroticism in Muslim Societies* (Berlin: Verlag Rosa Winkel, 1995), 24; *Sexuality and Eroticism*, Jeffrey Weeks' Foreword, ix.

[38] See e.g., Laury Silvers, 'The Teaching Relationship in Early Sufism: Reassessment of Fritz Meier's Definition of the *shaykh al-tarbiya* and the *shaykh al-ta'līm*', *The Muslim World*, vol. 93 (2003), 77–78.

[39] See e.g., Bouhdiba, *Sexuality in Islam*, 119.

custom in Sufi biographies? To what extent does this custom imply individual tendencies attributed to particular Sufis only despite its frequent description as an epidemic among the Sufis? By what means do references to *ṣuḥbat al-aḥdāth* in Sufi works, in addition to general discussions of *ṣuḥba*, provide us with new insights of the interpersonal relations among early Sufis? What were the strategies that Sufi authors employed to tackle the whole range of thoughts, fears and expectations implied in the tradition of *ṣuḥbat al-aḥdāth*? Would it be possible to suggest an indirect effect of *ṣuḥbat al-aḥdāth*, as one of the common social features of Sufi communities, on the process of establishing a collective identity that embraced the entire Sufi community?

In the actual reality of the early Sufi communities, the practice of keeping company with youths contributed, in the course of time, to the collective identity of the Sufis in the eyes of their enemies. From another point of view, dealing with the idea of companionship with youths should benefit from a wider discussion of the role that young affiliates played in the process of spreading the Sufi systems of thought and its practical modes of life. However, in scholarly works that deal with the 'eros' in Sufi life and literature, there is no discussion of the role played by these young affiliates. *Ṣuḥbat al-aḥdāth* is presented in those works as only one facet of that 'eros' and not as a reflection of the relations between the individual and the wider society or community. The works of Annemarie Schimmel, Abdelwahab Bouhdiba and Khālid al-Rouayheb are the most outspoken in this regard.[40]

In addition to the well-known problems of sources in Sufi studies in general, dealing with the erotic facet of Sufism involves another serious problem.[41] Works like those of Ibn ʿArabī and Farīd al-Dīn ʿAṭṭār and from the later period of ʿAbd al-Ghanī al-Nābulsī (d. 1143/1730), are usually regarded by scholars as the greatest literary manifestations of the erotic aspect of Sufism.[42] Jalāl al-Dīn Rūmī's (d. 672/1273) *Mathnavī*, for

40 In addition to the above-mentioned works of Bouhdiba and el-Rouayheb, the most outspoken work of Annemarie Schimmel on this topic is her article 'Eros-Heavenly and Not So Heavenly in Sufi Literature and Life', in *Society and Sexes*, 119–142.

41 On the meaning of 'the erotic' in religious studies see Jonah Winters, 'Themes of the Erotic in Sufi Mysticism', first posted online in 1997: http://bahai-library.com/?file=winters_themes_erotic_sufism.html, and updated and reloaded in 2016 (http://bahai-library.com/pdf/w/winters_erotic_mysticism.pdf), *introduction*, 1–3.

42 What frames Ibn ʿArabī's erotic depictions and their role in the process of knowing the divine was his heterosexual conception of sexuality. According to him, God is most perfectly witnessed in women [On Ibn ʿArabī's theories on the divine feminine and his

instance, contains a lot of references to explicit sexual imagery and acts, including pederasty and fornication.[43] As for the earlier period we lack such erotic references. Besides, only a few texts that carry a sympathetic approach towards the Sufi teachings on gazing at beautiful human beings have survived.[44]

On the methodological level, if our knowledge of medieval Muslim society could hardly be 'gleaned from some genres of literature' as Franz Rosenthal says,[45] the metaphorical language and shocking images frequently found in the statements and stories of the early mystics just make life more difficult for the researcher. Data referring to *ṣuḥbat al-aḥdāth* gathered from Sufi-oriented works should be cross-referenced with parallel data supported by anti-Sufi and non-Sufi works. A careful process of cross-checking the available sources should be undertaken, which includes searching for each relevant anecdote or statement found in one Sufi source with all its variations and modifications in other Sufi sources as well as in non-Sufi biographies. Each version of the same anecdote implies a specific way of perception and understanding. Sometimes, the omission of an anecdote reveals the author's personal attitude in different socio-religious contexts. It is interesting, for instance, to compare the different references to the early mystic Yūsuf b. al-Ḥusayn, whose name

cosmological heterosexual conceptions, see e.g., Saʿdiyya Shaikh, *Sufi Narratives of Intimacy: Ibn ʿArabī, Gender, and Sexuality* (Chapel Hill: The University of North Carolina Press, 2012), 173–202]. Different from Ibn ʿArabī's conception, the erotic depictions of ʿAbd al-Ghanī al-Nābulsī from later period were basically homoerotic. Nābulsī brought to the fore the Sufi tradition of companionship with youth and gazing at them in his *Ghāyat al-maṭlūb fī maḥabbat al-maḥbūb* ('The Furthest of Desires in the Love for the Beloved'). Nābulsī sought to defend the idea of what he considered as pure brotherly love among the Sufis as well as boldly consolidate the doctrine according to which divine beauty is manifested in beautiful human faces and bodies. In order to establish his basic idea that love addressed to the *murd* is devoid of any lustful desires, Nābulsī draws attention to the Prophet's love towards Zayd b. Ḥāritha, to the latter's son Usāma and to his love towards all of his companions (*ṣaḥāba*), the majority of whom were beautiful. [See ʿAbd al-Ghanī b. Ismāʿīl al-Nābulsī, *Ghāyat al-maṭlūb fī maḥabbat al-maḥbūb*, MS. 134 [1388], Daiber Collection, Institute of Oriental Culture, University of Tokyo, 32 folios. I noticed that this work came to publication in an Italian translation in 1995 [see ibid., translated by Samuela Pagani (Rome: Bardi, 1995). Most recently, ʿAlāʾ al-Dīn Bakrī and Shīrīn Qūrī published an edited version of Nābulsī's text in Damascus: Dār Shahrazād al-Shām, 2007. For further discussion of ʿAbd al-Ghanī al-Nābulsī's defence of the practice of contemplating human beauty in both his poetry and prose, see el-Rouayheb, *Before Homosexuality*, 100–110.]

43 On the erotic aspects in Rūmī's *Mathnavī*, see Mahdi Tourage, *Rūmī and the Hermeneutics of Eroticism* (Leiden and Boston: Brill, 2007).

44 See Bell, *Love Theory*, 253–254, footnote no. 69 and the references mentioned there.

45 Rosenthal, *Fiction and Reality*, 3.

is associated with *ṣuḥbat al-aḥdāth*, in the works of Ibn al-Jawzī. As I will show later on, the critical approach of Ibn al-Jawzī against *ṣuḥbat al-aḥdāth* and the choices he made at different points throughout his writings to either mention the problematic sayings of Ibn al-Ḥusayn or ignore them just demonstrate how crucial the need for a careful and critical utilization of such sources is.

The data referring to *ṣuḥbat al-aḥdāth* gathered from Sufi-oriented works should be cross-referenced with parallel data supported by anti-Sufi and non-Sufi works. Works of proper *adab*, like those of al-Jāḥiẓ, al-Muḥsin al-Tanūkhī and Abū Ḥayyān al-Tawḥīdī, as well as Arabic works on the theory of love, contain references to Sufis or famous scholars who did not refrain from expressing their erotic inclination towards beardless boys. Such references should be viewed as part of the overarching concern with sexual morality in medieval Muslim society.[46] In certain cases, fathers prevented their boys from associating with Sufi masters, like in the story about the renowned early mystic ʿAmr b. ʿUthmān al-Makkī and the boy who associated with him in Iṣfahān.[47]

I should refer here to the work of Tanūkhī dated from the fourth/tenth century. Preceding Ibn al-Jawzī's systematic critique of Sufi teachings and practices in the sixth/twelfth century, the work of Tanūkhī provides a significant picture of anti-Sufi views. He mentions in his work Sufi gatherings of *samāʿ* where beardless boys used to recite the *Qurʾān*.[48] Among the Sufis attacked by Tanūkhī were Ḥallāj, Ibn Khafīf, Shiblī and Ruwaym b. Aḥmad. Later in the following discussion I will draw the attention to Tanūkhī's denunciation of his contemporary Sufis' heterosexual practices during their gatherings.

Moreover, we should keep in mind that references to male-to-male relationships throughout Sufi works in particular could be implied in different contexts and not only whenever the specific term of *ṣuḥbat al-aḥdāth* appears. Therefore, we should carefully seek out such references.

[46] See e.g., Tawḥīdī, *Baṣāʾir*, vol. 2, 105–106; Tanūkhī, *Nishwār al-muḥāḍara*, vol. 4, 276 [See this story also in Jaʿfar b. Aḥmad Abū Muḥammad al-Qāriʾ al-Sarrāj, *Maṣāriʿ al-ʿushshāq* (Beirut: Dār Ṣādir, 1958), vol. 2, 292]. Sarrāj's *Maṣāriʿ*, for instance, provides a great number of stories about Sufis who gaze at beautiful youths and associated with them while exposing themselves to hard ascetic tests in order to avoid any sensual feelings and forbidden acts. One of the early Sufis who appears very frequently in the text of *Maṣāriʿ* narrating such stories is the aforementioned Abū Ḥamza al-Ṣūfī. See Ritter's discussion of these stories in Ritter, *Ocean of the Soul*, 474–484.

[47] See Jāmī, *Nafaḥāt al-uns*, 84–85.

[48] See Tanūkhī, *Nishwār al-muḥāḍara*, vol. 2, 356.

While focusing on masculine allusions and homoerotic literature in early Abbasid period, J. W. Wright Jr. draws largely upon Jaroslav Stetkevych's pioneering discussion of paradox and Arabic hermeneutical terminology (1989) to suggest considering homoerotic imagery in early Abbasid poetry as literary expressions of satire and criticism rather than expressions of actual tendencies and behaviours.[49] The question here is as follows: Is it possible that some of the early Sufis allegedly involved in these acts intended to protest against social norms or, more particularly, the accepted norms and sublime ethos formulated by the authoritative elite of the Sufis of Baghdad? The individual case of Niffarī provides evidence for the existence of distinctive modes of piety whose representatives might have completely detached themselves from the mainstream of the Sufis of Baghdad. These mainstream Sufis appear to have enjoyed a high degree of authority in the process of creating the accepted Sufi ethos and doctrine and an influential position beside other players in the 'drama of authority in urban Muslim communities'.[50] They dictated Sufi norms and even enjoyed a type of monopoly in that period. If this was indeed the case of Niffarī and, as previously shown, of other individuals not generally known as Sufis like Abū Ḥayyān al-Tawḥīdī, then is it possible that the erotic colour of *ṣuḥbat al-aḥdāth* was the way for certain Sufi individuals to register a sort of a protest against the Sufis of Baghdad?

ṢUḤBA IN EARLY SUFI WORKS

To begin, let us draw attention to the different variations of the term *ṣuḥba*, as documented in the early Sufi works and manuals. Remarkably, this term was used flexibly and loosely in a way that allowed for several possible disparate meanings. The Arabic verb *ṣaḥiba* has several meanings: Lane indicates 'associated, kept company, comrade', and refers to *ṣāḥib* as a 'fellow traveller'.[51] Steingass in his *Persian-English Dictionary* provides the following meanings for the nominal form *ṣuḥbat*: 'associating together, society, friendship, companionship, conversation, discourse, intercourse, coition'. Furthermore, the Persian verbal form *ṣuḥbat kardan* is translated as 'to keep company, to converse with' and 'to sit together'.[52] The idea of conversation is not mentioned by Lane. In *Lisān al-ʿarab*, the

[49] See J. W. Wright Jr., *Masculine Allusion*, 1–23. [50] Karamustafa, *Sufism*, 24.
[51] Edward Lane, *Arabic-English Lexicon*, vol. 1/4, 1652.
[52] Francis Joseph Steingass, *A Comprehensive Persian-English Dictionary* (London: Paul, Trench, Trubner, 1947), 728.

basic equivalent of *ṣaḥiba* is *ʿāshara*, a verbal form that accentuates reciprocity by means of an actual contact between the two partners of the relationship (not implying sex).[53] In the *Qurʾān*, different meanings of the root *ṣḥb* and its derivations are displayed. The nominal plural form *aṣḥāb* in most of its *Qurʾān*ic occurrences indicates the neutral meaning of 'the people of'.[54] Furthermore, the singular form *ṣāḥib* frequently indicates the one who differs from his fellow men and even becomes their enemy.[55] In a few verses, however, the singular form means follower and friend.[56]

The concepts of *ṣuḥba* and *ukhuwwa* were well-developed within Sufi circles with a good deal of *ḥadīth* traditions supporting and even encouraging them. Many detailed epistles and long chapters were composed for this purpose.[57] The term supposedly indicates a direct relationship between two people, for instance, between a sheikh and a subordinate, between equal Sufis and between Sufis in general.[58] Besides Sufi guidance that was to be attained through accompanying one's *ṣāḥib* for a determined period of time, *ṣuḥba* should be seen as a clear manifestation of the social intercourse between Sufi brothers. They used to travel together, perform pilgrimage, attend mutual invitations and rove in the deserts practising *siyāḥa* as well as follow other Sufi practices.

Ṣuḥba was frequently combined in Sufi literature with the idea of removing personal reservations (*zawāl/suqūṭ al-ḥishma*) between Sufi brothers. This idea is one of the problematic descriptions of friendship among early Sufis, and it has its deep roots in the Sufi settings. Abū Sulaymān al-Dārānī, for instance, writes that he used to borrow money

[53] See Ibn Manẓūr, *Lisān al-ʿarab*, vol. 1, 519.

[54] E.g., verses (24, 25): *aṣḥāb al-janna* (the people of paradise); (19,57), (8,39), (43,40): *aṣḥāb al-jaḥīm / al-nār* (the people of hell).

[55] Verses (22, 81); (46, 34).

[56] Verses (40, 9); (34, 18). Cf. Ḥasan al-Mālikī, *al-Ṣuḥba wa-l-ṣaḥāba bayn al-iṭlāq al-lughawī wa-l-takhṣīṣ al-sharʿī* (ʿAmmān: Markaz al-Dirāsāt al-Tārīkhiyya, 2004), 14–17.

[57] Among the best known are *Ādāb al-ṣuḥba* of Abū ʿAbd al-Raḥmān al-Sulamī and *Ādāb al-ṣuḥba wa-ḥusn al-ʿishra* of Abū Ḥāmid al-Ghazālī. Hujwīrī mentions many other writings none of which have survived. The word *ṣuḥba*, however, was not included in any of Hujwīrī's titles (see Jullābī Hujwīrī *Kashf al-maḥjūb*, 439). See also Kister's list, based on Ibn al-Nadīm's *Fihrist* in: Sulamī, *Ādāb al-ṣuḥba*, 15. Cf. Fritz Meier, 'A Book of Etiquette for Sufis', in *Essays on Islamic Piety and Mysticism*, 54; footnote 21. Detailed sections on *ṣuḥba* and *ukhuwwa* are found in: Makkī, *Qūt*, vol. 2, 442–489; Qushayrī, *Risāla*, 145–147; Sarrāj, *Lumaʿ*, 176–179. Sarrāj treats *ṣuḥba* in other chapters of his *Lumaʿ*: '*bāb fī ādāb al-mashāyikh wa-rifqatihim*' (ibid., 204–205); and '*bāb fī dhikr ādābihim fī al-ṣadāqa wa-l-mawadda*' (ibid., 208–209).

[58] See Laury Silvers, *Teaching Relationship in Early Sufism*, 77–78.

from a Baghdadi 'brother' until one day this brother asked him: 'How much do you need?' As a result, their brotherhood was no longer possible.[59] Similar anecdotes appear quite frequently in many other writings of that time.[60] Such stories give the impression that the word *ḥishma* in the context of *ṣuḥba* basically implies the firm mutual financial support that early Sufi communities tended to establish. In addition to removing personal reservations as a basic feature of pure friendship, we come across another approach by those who took pains to emphasize the importance of keeping modesty (*iḥtishām*) among brothers and to call Sufi attention to the fact that companionship with those who cause them to discard their reservations is highly dangerous. 'Associate with those whom you feel shy with' (*ʿāshir man taḥtashimuhu*), asserts Sulamī's grandfather, Ismāʿīl b. Nujayd.[61]

Even though Qushayrī does not mention the term of *zawāl al-ḥishma* by itself, he alludes to it in his chapter on *adab* (good manners). While a full commitment to particular ethics among Sufi brothers, as well as between the Sufi and God, is the idea displayed in the majority of the statements gathered by Qushayrī here, several anecdotes imply the need for *tark al-adab* (abandonment of ethical behaviour) as a sign for a pure intimacy and true love. In order to prove this, Qushayrī indicates the story of none other than the Prophet. The story portrays the relationship between the Prophet and both Abū Bakr and ʿUmar as more intimate than the relationship between him and ʿUthmān. It was said that the Prophet never used to cover his thigh until ʿUthmān entered the place where the Prophet used to sit with the two other companions.[62] If this story was not enough, Qushayrī introduced the figure of Junayd to emphasize the idea of *tark al-adab*. Junayd is quoted as saying, 'when one's love is true, the rules of proper behaviour fall away.'[63] This saying stands in contrast to the general tone of Junayd's sayings, in which his

[59] Makkī, *Qūt*, vol. 2, 460.
[60] Statements like 'we used not to company with those who are accustomed to say "my shoes" or "my carriage" (*kunnā la naṣḥab man yaqūl naʿlī wa-rakwatī*)' (Qushayrī, *Risāla*, 146; Sarrāj, *Lumaʿ*, 175).
[61] Sulamī, *Ādāb al-ṣuḥba*, 35.
[62] See Qushayrī, *Risāla*, 142, lines 7–9.
[63] Ibid., 142, line 13. Cf. idem, Knysh's translation of Qushayrī's *Risāla* in: *Al-Qushayrī's Epistle on Sufism*, trans. by Alexander Knysh (Reading UK: Garnet Publishing, 2007), 296.

insistence on commitment to both *sharīʿa* and ethical behaviour is well documented.[64]

In his chapter on *ṣuḥba* and 'brotherly love' (*maḥabbat al-ikhwān*), Abū Ṭālib al-Makkī differentiates between two approaches known among the Sufis of his time. One was the asocial approach that rejects all types of social intercourse, and the other was an approach that considers friends as intercessors (*shufaʿāʾ*): 'In a brotherly relationship, the one who attains a higher spiritual rank promotes his partner towards his own rank.'[65] In another paragraph, Makkī writes that if someone isolates himself and cuts all his social ties by condemning the value of brotherhood, his behaviour implies a hidden desire to gain fame and people's admiration. This behaviour, adds Makkī, includes 'self-conceit and mockery of the ordinary people' (*kibr wa-taṭāwul ʿalā al-ʿāmma*).[66]

Makkī locates *ṣuḥba* in the fourth degree of his 'seven degrees of social acquaintance (*taʿāruf*)'. According to him, a social acquaintance begins with mere acquaintance, which is obtained through seeing and hearing, and reaches at its seventh degree the state of *maḥabba* (love) which could under certain conditions be followed by *khulla* (intimacy) with one's brother. Friendship (*ṣadāqa*) follows *ṣuḥba* and precedes both *ukhuwwa* (brotherhood) and *maḥabba*. The ultimate state of *khulla* is higher than all those degrees. It is interesting to note that, according to Makkī, *ṣuḥba* stresses the idea of following the example of the *maṣḥūb* (the one you accompany), while *ṣadāqa* stresses a closer relationship that includes mutual visits (*muzāwara*), mutual stays overnight (*mubāyata*) and total sociability. As for *ukhuwwa*, *maḥabba* and *khulla*, they could only mark the relationship between equal partners that have similar spiritual states and traits. *Khulla,* which could only happen between peers, as Makkī emphasizes, seems to have been a very rare type of relationship in his time: '*Wa-lā yakūn hādhā illā fī ʿāqilayn ʿālimayn ʿalā miʿyār wa-ṭarīq wāḥid, hādhā aʿazz mawjūd wa-aghrab maʿhūd*' (This could not occur except in [the case of!] two rational, intelligent men whose norms and paths are the same. This is the rarest situation and the queerest custom).[67] The latter notion underlines, in my view, the author's fear that his treatment of *khulla* among the Sufi brothers might be understood as a justification of an intimate relationship between old Sufis and young novices. That is why in his chapter Makkī frequently emphasizes the

[64] See e.g., Sulamī, *Ṭabaqāt*, 143–145 (the biography of Junayd); Iṣfahānī, *Ḥilyat al-awliyāʾ*, vol. 10, 276.
[65] Makkī, *Qūt*, vol. 2, 442–443. [66] Ibid., 480. [67] See ibid., 477–478.

condition of equivalency in *khulla* by having similar states and traits (‘*nuẓarāʾ fī al-ḥāl*’, that is, ‘peers in the spiritual state’) but adds that this supreme state rarely occurs among his contemporaries.

It is evident that Sufi *ṣuḥba* served as a powerful motivation for anti-Sufi criticism. Again, Tanūkhī’s work provided the following anecdote where the hostile attitude towards the principle of *ṣuḥba*, especially between women and men in the Sufi spheres, is explicitly manifested. The great master of Shīrāz Abū ʿAbd Allāh Ibn Khafīf was accused of encouraging his followers to perform collective sexual practices a short time after they consoled the widow of their friend. Tanūkhī’s story, later accepted by Ibn al-Jawzī, relates that after consoling the woman, the Sufi master of Shīrāz asked her to permit a collective sexual intercourse between his fellow men and the women who attended at her home. It was stated that the woman agreed, and the group of men intermixed with the group of women all night (*ikhtalaṭat jamāʿat al-rijāl bi-jamāʿat al-nisāʾ ṭūl laylatihim*). Interestingly, Tanūkhī follows the story with his comment: ‘I heard that such episodes were very common in those times, until the Buwayhī Sultan ʿAḍud al-Dawla [who reigned between 339/951 and 372/983!] knew about these groups and beated them with whips, arrested them and exiled many of them.’[68]

In my opinion, what may actually have happened is that Ibn Khafīf intended to console the widow by holding a *dhikr* ceremony (a Sufi gathering of recalling God’s name) at her home. The critical voices against both the Sufi ritual of *dhikr* and the custom of *ṣuḥba* might have added the sexual act to the original story in order to justify their attacks.[69] At the core of this criticism lies the hostile attitude towards the principle of *ṣuḥba*, especially when it describes gatherings of women and men in Sufi spheres.[70] Ibn Khafīf’s successor, Abū Isḥāq al-Kāzarūnī (d. 426/1033),

68 See Tanūkhī, *Nishwār al-muḥāḍara*, vol. 3, 228–229. Daylamī refers to this story in his *Sīra*; however, he does not indicate the last part which involves the reference to the sexual act. Daylamī’s version ends as follows: ‘The sheikh began to console the widow using the words of the Sufis (*akhadha yuʿazzī al-marʾa bi-kalām al-ṣūfiyya*) until she said: “I became consoled”’ (Daylamī, *Sīra*, 271). See also Ibn al-Jawzī, *Talbīs Iblīs*, 487.

69 The editors of Daylamī’s treatise on love indicate that the core of the story could be true. See Daylamī, *Treatise on Mystical Love*, *introduction*, xli–xliii, and particularly footnote 129.

70 Karamustafa maintains that there are vague signs that the traditionalist preacher who initiated what is known in the early history of Sufism as the inquisition of *ṣūfiyya* (*miḥnat al-ṣūfiyya*), Ghulām Khalīl, ‘was raised by talk of sexual promiscuity at Sufi meetings, possibly caused by intermixing between genders and association of adult males with male adolescents at these gatherings’. For Karamustafa, meanwhile, even though the available

was also accused by his contemporary traditionalists of permitting company with beardless youths in his *khānqāh*.[71]

Daylamī, who composed the famous biography of Ibn Khafīf at the end of the fourth/tenth century, attributes the following saying to Ibn Khafīf: 'Among the divine benefactions, three are the most beautiful: the good odour (*al-rā'iḥa al-ḥasana*), the nice voice (*al-ṣawt al-jamīl*), and gazing (*al-naẓar*).'[72] According to Sufi traditions, Ibn Khafīf lived with his servant alone in his own retreat for thirty-five years.[73] Certain characteristics in the figure of Ibn Khafīf seem to have been controversial in his time and later on as well. According to both Daylamī and Jullābī Hujwīrī, Ibn Khafīf married four hundred women during the course of his lifetime. The biographers insisted that he did so in order to grant those women a type of blessing. Daylamī, Hujwīrī and later even 'Aṭṭār sought to make it clear that the great sheikh of Shirāz did not touch his wives and that he divorced most of them later on or kept some of them at his place to serve him.[74] According to another story, Ibn Khafīf was said to have once passionately desired a woman, and that same night he married the daughter of his servant whom he divorced after seven months.[75] Probably, such anecdotes when combined with many other sayings attributed to Ibn Khafīf in which he celebrates beauty and passionate love,[76] provided the basis for Tanūkhī's story.

Ṣuḥba between male and female mystics was treated leniently in Sulamī's biographical accounts of Sufi women. Women associated with men during learning sessions as well as during travels for the sake to meet Sufi masters. Stories about women who performed *mujāwara* (a certain

data about close relationships between males and females and the references to many Sufi masters who had female disciples did not provide 'a clear departure from the *sunna*', allegations of sexual misconduct among the Sufis were, most probably, among the motivations for Ghulām Khalīl's ire against the Sufis (see Karamustafa, *Sufism*, 23).

71 See Maḥmūd b. 'Uthmān, *Kitāb firdaws al-murshidiyya fī asrār al-ṣamadiyya* (*Die Vita des Scheich Abū Isḥāq al-Kāzarūnī*), in der Persischen Bearbeitung von Maḥmūd b. 'Uthmān, herausgegeben und eingeleitet von Fritz Meier (Leipzig: Brockhaus, 1948), 502. According to Jāmī, Kāzarūnī became a disciple of Abū 'Alī Ḥusayn b. Muḥammad Fīrūzābādī Akkār who was himself a disciple of Ibn Khafīf (see Jāmī, *Nafaḥāt al-uns*, 254).

72 Daylamī, *Sīra*, 259. Cf. idem, *Treatise on Mystical Love, introduction*, xxxix.

73 See Daylamī, *Sīra*, the Arabic translation of the Turkish *introduction* of AnneMarie Schimmel (for the Persian version of *Sīra*, 1955), 34.

74 See Jullābī Hujwīrī, *Kashf al-Maḥjūb*, 318. Cf. 'Aṭṭār, *Tadhkirat al-awliyā'*, vol. 2, 128; Daylamī, *Sīra*, 270.

75 See Daylamī, *Sīra*, 269–270.

76 See e.g., idem, *Treatise on Mystical Love, introduction*, xxxv–xl.

period of time spent in Mecca) in the company of men appeared quite frequently in the sources.[77] The aforementioned story of Umm ʿAlī Fāṭima, the wife of Aḥmad b. Khiḍrūya al-Balkhī, comes to mind here.[78]

Another female figure usually mentioned in this regard is Fāṭima of Nishapur, who was known in Sufi hagiographies through the confession of Dhū al-Nūn al-Miṣrī that this woman was his own master (*ustādh*).[79] Although I have already referred to this woman in Chapter 2, her case is highly relevant here too. This woman spent her life in a long *mujāwara*, and in none of her biographical accounts was her family status clearly stated. Contrary to the devotional tone of Dhū al-Nūn's words, Sulamī posts another anecdote according to which this great Egyptian mystic refused to accept a present that Fāṭima had sent to him. He further said, 'There is humbleness and lowliness in accepting women's support' (*fī qubūl arfāq al-niswān madhalla wa-nuqṣān*).[80] This story, as I see it, has two implications: The first relates to the Sufi systems of relationships, while the other has to do more with the way that such relationships, particularly male-to-female relationships, were perceived by outsiders. From the Sufi point of view, by the frequent references to *arfāq* (those are, as previously stated, goods or food given to the poor for subsistence), we can infer that pious rich women used to financially support Sufi groups and that this custom was very popular in medieval Muslim societies.[81]

From an outsider's point of view, Sufi stories that involved companionship between male and female figures were always an attractive topic for the opponents of the movement. Such stories, whether historically accurate or not, emphasize the role of *ṣuḥba* as an influential system of thought and praxis in early Sufi spheres. Ibn al-Jawzī, for example, talks about another woman of Ubulla in Iraq called Rayḥāna who apparently hosted some of her male contemporary Sufis at her house on a regular basis. Her guests, according to Ibn al-Jawzī, would hear her reciting divine love poetry all through the night.[82] Jāmī mentions another

[77] See e.g., Sulamī, *Dhikr al-niswa*, 143. [78] See Chapter 2.

[79] This word was used by Sulamī to indicate the Sufi tradition of elevating exceptionally pious women to the status of spiritual men. See Sulamī, *Dhikr al-niswa*, Rkia Cornell's *introduction*, 43, footnote 108. For the first editor of Sulamī's book, the Egyptian Maḥmūd al-Ṭanāḥī, this example merely displays a 'linguistic anomaly' (Sulamī, *Dhikr al-niswa*, ed. by Maḥmūd al-Ṭanāḥī, *introduction*, 19).

[80] Sulamī, *Dhikr al-niswa*, 143.

[81] See e.g., Qushayrī, *Risāla*, 203, lines 25–26; Sulamī, *Dhikr al-niswa*, 143.

[82] See Ibn al-Jawzī, *Ṣifat al-ṣafwa*, vol. 4, 39–40.

anonymous Persian woman who used to stay overnight in the home of Najīb b. Buzghush.[83]

Nevertheless, *ṣuḥba* between male and female Sufis was not the focus of the self-critical approach of the early Sufi authors. It is rather *ṣuḥbat al-aḥdāth* that lies behind such a self-critical tone. In his *Ṭabaqāt al-ṣūfiyya*, Sulamī frequently refers to what he calls the shameful custom of *ṣuḥbat al-aḥdāth*.[84] As for his attitude towards women, he barely uses a negative tone. Only in one instance in his work does Sulamī quote what can be considered as a negative view towards women and female behaviour in general.[85] Yet, it is interesting to note that in other pieces of textual evidence, the Sufi critical approach against *ṣuḥbat al-aḥdāth* appears side by side with the critical approach against accepting women's support. According to one statement by Yūsuf b. al-Ḥusayn, the early mystic whose name will frequently appear in discussions of *ṣuḥbat al-aḥdāth* (see hereinafter), there are three 'epidemics' (*āfāt*) of the Sufis: '*ṣuḥbat al-aḥdāth*, *mu'āsharat al-aḍdād* (associating with opponents) and *arfāq al-niswān*'.[86] In the biography of the early Persian mystic of al-Jabal region, Muẓaffar al-Qirmīsīnī, Sulamī quotes Muẓaffar's stance against accepting women's *arfāq* immediately after stating his opposition to *ṣuḥbat al-aḥdāth*.[87]

In other cases, there seems to be a connection between companionship with youths and early Sufi arguments against particular opponent groups such as *qurrā'*. By the third/ninth century, the term *qurrā'* became the title of a distinguished group of specialists in the different legitimate readings of the holy text. In Sufi literature, the term was perceived negatively. For Sufi authors, the image of the *qāri'* (the singular of *qurrā'*) manifests the antithesis of the Sufi's image. Makkī's attack against *qurrā'* in his *Qūt al-qulūb*, for instance, was very aggressive. Makkī quotes al-Fuḍayl b. 'Iyāḍ's statement in which he warns his counterparts from associating with *qurrā'* because they do not hesitate to accuse anyone who disagrees with them of unbelief. Makkī, however, quotes another statement of Bishr b. al-Ḥārith who was said to prefer companionship with a youth (*fatā*) over companionship with a *qāri'*.[88]

83 See Jāmī, *Nafaḥāt al-uns*, 634.

84 See e.g., Sulamī, *Ṭabaqāt*, 179, 197–198, 227, 411–412.

85 See ibid., 291.

86 Ibid., 179.

87 Ibid., 411–412. Cf. Qushayrī, *Risāla*, 29 whereas Muẓaffar's statement on *ṣuḥbat al-aḥdāth* was not indicated.

88 See Makkī, *Qūt*, vol. 1, 350. Nonetheless, in other occasions of this work the term *qurrā'* was used more positively. See e.g., ibid., vol. 2, 422. See also anonymous author, *Adab al-*

THE EROTIC COLOUR OF EARLY *ṢUḤBA*

The above-mentioned *zawāl al-ḥishma* is the basic aspect of love and intimacy in Makkī's classification of relationships among the Sufis. Nonetheless, it is unclear what this aspect actually contained. Some anecdotes, for instance, imply that perfect fraternal intimacy (*uns*) is not achieved unless man feels free to have sexual intercourse at his brother's own place.[89] But if Makkī restricts *zawāl al-ḥishma* to relationships in which equality and parallelism between the partners are preserved, then what can be said about *ṣuḥba* between unequal partners? Contrary to the well-established combination of *ṣuḥba* and *zawāl al-ḥishma* in the Sufi theoretical system of Makkī's time and preceding it, Makkī's attempt to dissociate the two might reflect his intention to confront a reality in which parts of *zawāl al-ḥishma* actually found their way into 'unequal' relationships, that is, relationships between Sufis who were not exactly peers in respect to their spiritual ranks. Inequality might have substantially manifested itself in master–disciple relationships. However, this paragraph of Makkī's work is not a sufficient basis for any conclusions of this type.

Throughout the formative period of Sufism, circles of learning and patterns of discipleship became cornerstones of a collective Sufi life. In the course of time, master–disciple relationships became firmly established, and the 'master of training' (*shaykh al-tarbiya*) stood out as a prominent functioning actor on the Sufi scene.[90] Although they are difficult and daring questions, I believe that the following are still worth asking here: Were there any erotic aspects of master–disciple relationships during the early phase of Sufism? Does the frequent concept of *zawāl al-ḥ ishma* insinuate that something went beyond the mutual material support among the brothers? Does the paean of harmonious relationships and ideal fraternal altruism in the early Sufi works conceal a hidden erotic content?

mulūk, 4 (here, the author indicates that there are very few pious *qurrā'* in reality: '*qalīl minhum*').

89 See Makkī, *Qūt*, vol. 2, 476.

90 Fritz Meier identifies this type of sheikhhood as the one that involves 'the direct intervention of the sheikh in the student's behaviour by means of instructions, the application of which he supervises and the eventual outcome of which he then awaits and criticizes' (Meier, *Khurāsān and the End of Classical Sufism*, 195–196). Cf. the critical notes of Laury Silvers on Meier's argument. The basic problem in Meier's classification, according to Silvers, is his adoption of a later terminological system provided by Ibn ʿAbbād al-Rundī (d. 792/1390) for the early period of Sufism. See Silvers, *Teaching Relationship in Early Sufism*, 70.

A careful study of male-to-male sexuality in medieval Sufi circles (though it was in itself part of male sexuality in early Muslim societies) could shed new light on this hidden facet of the relationship between Sufi mystics as individuals and their wider communities. It would be tempting to agree with the general suggestion according to which male-to-male sexuality in Muslim societies had little to do with sexual intercourse between men and implied more of a type of erotic relationship between men and boys and to apply this assumption to the Sufi domain.

TRACING *ṢUḤBAT AL-AḤDĀTH* IN THE MAJOR SUFI COLLECTIONS OF THE EARLY PERIOD

A textbook by *Shīʿī-Ismāʿīlī* author Jaʿfar b. Manṣūr al-Yaman (late third/ninth-early fourth/tenth century), titled *Kitāb al-ʿālim wa-l-ghulām* (*The Book of the Master and the Disciple*), presents an early spiritual dialogue by means of which the young disciple, the *ghulām*, succeeds in obtaining a high level of spiritual knowledge through dramatic and extremely deep dialogue with his master. It is interesting to note that the word *ghulām* in this context signifies a 'young man [...] who was the youngest of them [his group!] in age, but the one who had the best character of all'.[91] Wisdom and spiritual merits distinguish this young man in the text. This use concurs with the *Qurʾān*ic appearances of the word *ghulām*, which mostly refer to young prophets or their offspring.[92]

It is worth noting that authors of early Islamic literature frequently used the words *ghulām* and *ghilmān* to indicate boys whose beauty inflamed the erotic desire of both married and unmarried adult men.[93] In early Sufi writings in particular, *ḥadath* and its plural form *aḥdāth*, more than *ghulām* or *ghilmān*, carried a negative connotation. *Fatā* and *fityān*, on the other hand, are perceived in Sufi literature as indications of chivalry and total unselfishness in interactions with one's Sufi brothers.[94]

While the first documented critique against the Sufi custom of association with youths goes back to the sixth/twelfth century and not before, as

[91] Jaʿfar b. Manṣūr al-Yaman, *The Master and the Disciple: An Early Islamic Spiritual Dialogue*, a new Arabic edition and English translation of *Kitāb al-ʿālim wa-l-ghulām*, ed. and trans. by James Morris (London and New York: I.B. Tauris in association with The Institute of Ismaili Studies, 2001), English translation, 68, paragraph 27.

[92] See ibid., 175, footnote 22.

[93] See e.g., Ājurrī, *Dhamm al-liwāṭ*, 29; Daylamī, *Sīra*, 188; Ghazālī, *Iḥyāʾ*, vol. 3, 149.

[94] See e.g., Sarrāj, *Lumaʿ*, 129–132; Qushayrī, *Risāla*, 113–115.

I previously indicated, we can assume that such a critique originated at an earlier stage. In one occurrence in Tanūkhī's *Nishwār al-muḥāḍara*, for instance, the term *ṣuḥbat al-aḥdāth* appears with no reference to Sufis.[95] In the following discussion, I would like to examine the process that brought about the negative perception of *aḥdāth* as a deep-rooted notion in the critical discourse against Sufis and Sufism from the sixth/twelfth century and onwards. Meanwhile, I will attempt to develop a detailed argument around the different strategies and techniques that served Sufi authors and theoreticians to treat the problematic custom.

Instead of ignoring their opponents' accusations of going astray, Sufi authors of the period under discussion attempted to develop a sophisticated mechanism of treating the custom which included both confirmation and condemnation. These authors felt completely free to concern themselves with the topic in their works. Sulamī, whose *Ādāb al-ṣuḥba* is a primary source for later Sufi doctrines on brotherly ethics, provides the following interesting themes:

a. In the reference to the servant (*khādim*), the term *ḥusn al-ʿishra* (lit. good association) is used instead of *ṣuḥba*.[96]
b. The word *aḥdāth* is mentioned only once in Sulamī's book, where the author refers to the young members of the Sufi association whose respect towards their masters must be shown by maintaining complete silence in their company.[97]
c. The legitimate act of gazing at one's brethren is conditioned by doing so with pure love. This notion is asserted in one of the most interesting paragraphs of this book. Sulamī indicates that the Sufi should gaze at the most beautiful qualities of his brother and must keep gazing while conversing and communicating with him: '*Wa-yakūn naẓaruhu ilā maḥāsinihi wa-ilā aḥsan shayʾ yabdū minhu*.'[98]

This paragraph deals mostly with 'peer brethren' whose gazing at each other carries no lustful desires. It even demonstrates Sulamī's attempt to condemn the probably common tendency of certain Sufis of his day to search for their fellows' imperfections to justify their blame and criticism. The idea that a true brother (*akh*) rarely exists, to the extent that 'looking

95 See Tanūkhī, *Nishwār al-muḥāḍara*, vol. 3, 173.
96 See Sulamī, *Ādāb al-ṣuḥba*, 52.
97 See ibid., 76.
98 Ibid., 85. Cf. a detailed statement attributed to Abū al-Ḥusayn al-Nūrī on the different degrees of gazing, in Sulamī, *Ṭabaqāt*, 157, lines 6–11.

for the red sulfur is easier than looking for a true brother',[99] is asserted frequently by Sufi authors.

Sulamī devotes a chapter at the end of his *Sunan al-ṣūfiyya* (*The Customs of the Sufis*) to discuss a number of dispensations (*rukhaṣ*) permitted to the Sufis. Among the *rukhaṣ* mentioned by Sulamī, we find dancing, singing and gazing at beautiful faces, and no regard is given to the sex or the social status of the one whose beautiful face 'clarifies the vision' according to the famous tradition usually quoted in this connection.[100] Later, it was the sixth/twelfth century Sufi master of Baghdad, Abū al-Najīb al-Suhrawardī, who is well known for confirming the first and most influential application of the Sufi system of *rukhaṣ* as previously noted. Keeping company with youths becomes one of the forty dispensations applied by Abū al-Najīb in his substantial chapter on *rukhaṣ* at the very end of his *Ādāb al-murīdīn* (*A Sufi Rule for Novices*).[101] However, while informality is recommended among Sufi peers who are equal friends of the path, the author insists on keeping strict formal behaviour with young men.[102]

The term *ṣuḥbat al-aḥdāth* does not appear in Makkī's *Qūt al-qulūb*. Makkī, who distinguishes between the negative impacts of lustful gazing at the *amrad* and regular companionship between the Sufi sheikhs and their young disciples, acknowledges the youths' ability to reach the high ranks of knowledge and even to provide their sheikhs with knowledge they might need.[103]

[99] Sulamī, *Ādāb al-ṣuḥba*, 41.

[100] Permission to gaze at beautiful faces is supported by the following saying which is commonly ascribed to the Prophet: 'Three things clarify the vision: Looking at greenery, looking at water, and looking at beautiful faces.' This English translation was made by Joseph Norment Bell in: Bell, *Love Theory*, 23.

[101] Based on Menahem Milson's translation of the title (see Abū al-Najīb al-Suhrawardī, *Sufi Rule for Novices*). Ian Netton chooses to translate the title to *The Manners of the Novices* [See Ian Netton, 'The Breath of Felicity: *Adab, Aḥwāl, Maqāmāt* and Abū al-Najīb al-Suhrawardī', in *Classical Persian Sufism from Its Origins to Rūmī*, ed. by Leonard Lewisohn (London: Oneworld, 2003), vol. 1, 458]. Abū al-Najīb al-Suhrawardī refers to companionship with youth in two places of his manual: In the first, he regards the matter as 'reprehensible because of the harms involved in it', and then he conditions it on self-discipline and ethical training and urges his fellowmen to 'avoid informal behaviour with them' (Abū al-Najīb al-Suhrawardī, *Sufi Rule for Novices*, Milson's translation, 47–48, section 87). In the other place, Abū al-Najīb mentions companionship with youth as part of his system of dispensations, making reference to the previous conditions of this custom (see ibid., 79, section 198).

[102] Cf. ibid., 46, Section 79.

[103] See Makkī, *Qūt*, vol. 2, 457.

Qushayrī devotes one section to *ṣuḥbat al-aḥdāth* in his spiritual advice for Sufi novices (*al-waṣiyya li-l-murīdīn*) at the very end of his *Risāla*.[104] He considers this custom as a sign of a mystic whom God humiliated and deserted (*ʿabd ahānahu Allāh* [...] *wa-khadhalahu*). This act of humiliation, according to Qushayrī, has nothing to do with a situation in which the mystic whom God humiliated by *ṣuḥbat al-aḥdāth* is granted extraordinary deeds and marvels. Qushayrī writes: '*wa-law bi-alf karāma ahhalahu*' (in spite of the fact that He granted him a thousand marvels). This sentence can be interpreted in two ways:

1. Association with youths in itself ought not to hinder the mystic from reaching the state of being granted the ability to perform marvels (*karāmāt*).
2. Association with youths might attract great Sufi masters who had already reached the high spiritual ranks in the path and who had been granted the ability to perform *karāmāt*.

Qushayrī uses many infinitive forms to describe what he considers as one of the most severe epidemics in Sufi communities (*aṣʿab al-āfāt fī hādhihi al-ṭarīqa*): *ṣuḥba, muʿāshara* (lit. association with) and *mujālasa* (lit. sitting with). In contrast with the words *ṣuḥba*, *muṣāḥaba* and *mujālasa* that imply a neutral and, in many cases, unstable and inconstant type of relationships among the Sufi fellow men, the word *muʿāshara* might have implied a stronger and more prolonged relationship.[105] What might support this assumption is that Qushayrī refers to the probable situation of debauchery (*fisq*) and depravity while using the term *muʿāsharat al-aḥdāth*. Qushayrī then quotes Fatḥ al-Mawṣilī's statement, 'stay away from the company of youths and do not mingle with them', and

[104] Qushayrī mentions the idea of *ṣuḥbat al-aḥdāth* in his *waṣiyya* four times in two subdivisions of the last part of his *Risāla:* In one place he uses the same term of *ṣuḥbat al-aḥdāth* (*Risāla*, 201, line 31); in the second place he uses *muʿāsharat al-aḥdāth wa-mukhālaṭatuhum* (associating with youth and intermixing with them, ibid., 202, line 3); in the third place, the term *mujālasat al-aḥdāth wa-mukhālaṭatahum* (sitting with youth and associating with them, ibid., 202, line 6) appears. In the last place, which appears in a separate subdivision, the phrase *ṣuḥbat ḥadath* is included among the customs that prevent the aspirant from advancing in the Sufi path. Those customs, according to Qushayrī, are successively: seeking social fame and constant real estate (The Arabic word *maʿlūm* indicates a predetermined amount of income. Having such a financial source of livelihood might contradict the very ideal of absolute trust of God), companionship with youth and sexual desire for women (see ibid., 202, line 32).

[105] See Lane, *Arabic-English Lexicon*, vol. 1/5, 2051 ('*ʿāsharahu* [...] held social or familiar intercourse [...] or became intimate with him').

comments: 'There are, however, those who claim to have overcome the depravity pertaining to this issue.'[106]

It appears that the problem with *ṣuḥbat al-aḥdāth*, according to Qushayrī, is that it involves the heart being occupied by a human being instead of being completely occupied by the divine creator. However, there is a different approach to this problem, one probably known in Qushayrī's days: According to this approach, association with youths was not seen exactly as a catastrophic phenomenon (*'tahwīn dhālik ʿalā l-qalb'* which means considering this [custom!] as easy and trivial in the heart's eyes). Interestingly, Qushayrī makes use of the word *tahwīn* here to combine it with the Qurʾānic word *hayyin* (easy) and with *hawān* which is taken from the same root to signify humiliation.[107] In addition to the two statements of Abū Bakr al-Wāsiṭī and Fatḥ al-Mawṣilī that Qushayrī quotes to warn the Sufis against associating with youths, he clearly refers to a group of Sufis who considered association with youths as a means for testing their souls (*balāʾ al-arwāḥ*) while exposing themselves to the possibility of sliding into depravity. In order to justify the custom, some of them made use of the doctrine of *shāhid* (lit. witness) and even referred to certain renowned masters who had not refrained from using this doctrine to justify their own custom of associating with youths.[108]

Most probably, Qushayrī does not only refer to Wāsiṭī's clear condemnation of *ṣuḥbat al-aḥdāth* but also alludes to an additional component of Wāsiṭī's system of thought, which is the sophisticated doctrine on God's manifestations in His creation and the place of gazing within it. Wāsiṭī says that God makes Himself known through His world of creation. Creatures demonstrate God's order and absolute beauty. Nonetheless, the world of creation veils God from being known because what becomes known is the object instead of God.[109] Based on this thesis, God alone is the true reality, and everything else is nothing,[110] and therefore the above doctrine of observing earthly manifestations of beauty, like boyish

106 Based on the English translation of Alexander Knysh in: Qushayrī, *Qushayrī's Epistle,* 411.

107 See Qushayrī, *Risāla*, 201.

108 According to the doctrine of *shāhid* a young boy is considered to be a reflection of divine beauty.

109 See the detailed discussion of Wāsiṭī's teachings in Silvers, *Theoretical Sufism*, 71–94, and particularly 81.

110 See e.g., Sulamī, *Ḥaqāʾiq al-tafsīr*, vol. 2, 385. ʿImrān's edition, however, is not critical and that is why Silvers uses the manuscript of the British Museum (Oriental 9433) instead. See Silvers, *Theoretical Sufism*, 80.

beauty, as merely a channel to divine beauty, is to be considered *shirk* (associating others with God) and even *kufr* (infidelity).[111] Turning back to Qushayrī's text, we find him mentioning these two terms without referring to Wāsiṭī.[112]

As noted before, *ṣuḥbat al-aḥdāth* was frequently compared with other maladies that often appeared among early Sufis. In another section of Qushayrī's testament, the author refers again to *ṣuḥbat ḥadath* among other deficiencies that might frustrate the Sufi in the path of his purification:

> When the aspirant is tested by [worldly!] renown, a secure and abundant livelihood, friendship with a youth, attraction to a woman, or the belief in an assured source of sustenance, and there is no master next to him who would suggest to him how to rid himself of this, then he should travel and move away.[113]

Qushayrī's references to another group of youth, those whom he calls *shubbān* (the plural form of *shābb*) in his final section of *Risāla* leave the impression that this group is different from that of *aḥdāth*. The words *shābb* and *shubbān* in Qushayrī's text refer to the young beginner aspirants of the Sufi path, those who usually served the spiritually matured aspirants of the Sufi community, the *fuqarāʾ*. These young aspirants were allowed, unlike their mature fellow Sufis, to travel in order to avoid any type of temptation that could be caused by staying among their fellow men. *Shubbān* and *aḥdāth* were two separate groups of youths engaged in Sufi spheres. The latter were not engaged in the Sufi sphere of their own free will but merely by being the young companions of actual Sufi aspirants. They were not considered men. The *shubbān*, on the other hand, were young, independent men who looked forward to becoming mature disciples. As for those *shubbān*, Qushayrī does not explain what he means by referring to the problematic and still ambiguous term *fitna* while discussing the most harmful outcome of the long stay of the young aspirant, the *shābb*, with his mature fellow men, the *fuqarāʾ*, instead of travelling: 'For if a young man (*al-shābb*) enjoys rest and idleness, he enters the arena of temptation (*fitna*).'[114] Although there is no clear explanation of what *fitna* means in this context, one might suggest that

[111] In Sulamī's *Ṭabaqāt*, Wāsiṭī is quoted to have said that the mystic who remains prisoner of his glance or is occupied by the manifestations of the divine beauty through His creatures (*shawāhid*), is considered among *fussāq* (dissolute people), and he is expected to be veiled from truth and certainty. See Sulamī, *Ṭabaqāt*, 303.

[112] See Qushayrī, *Risāla*, 202. [113] Ibid.

[114] Ibid., 200; Knysh's translation in idem, *Qushayrī's Epistle*, 408.

it refers to the somewhat erotic relationships between peer males, namely between men and men and not only between men and boys, in Sufi communities of that period

For most of its appearances in the text of *Risāla*, the word *ghulām* comes to designate a certain type of youth whose spiritual insight and Sufi wisdom seem to have predominated that of the celebrated Sufi masters.

This usage of the word appears in other Sufi manuals that were composed both before Qushayrī's time and after it.[115] The figure of the wise *ghulām* in the above-mentioned *Shīʿī-Ismāʿīlī* dialogue of Jaʿfar al-Yaman might have been the theoretical prototype of the wise young aspirant in early Sufi manuals.

Cultivating the textual references and contexts of *ghilmān* and *shubbān*, each one separately, helps us recognize that the *aḥdāth* is commonly the title combined with the critical references to erotic content of male-to-male relationships in Sufi spheres.[116] Thus, the approach towards youth as a general notion was ambivalent. On the theoretical level at least, the virtues of wise young men might symbolize the purest form of intensive love, self-sacrifice and deep religious passion. Youthful vigor in Sufi spheres manifests the very principle of *futuwwa* (chivalry), in which total surrender to the beloved and pure altruism are best manifested. The early figure, ʿUtba b. Abān b. Ṣamʿa al-Baṣrī, known as ʿUtba al-Ghulām,[117] who led a renunciatory life from the time he was a boy, might be a clear example of youthful vigor. Like his fellow *zuhhād* of Baṣra, his biography was not presented in the biographical sections of the works of Sulamī, Qushayrī or Hujwīrī. Abū Nuʿaym al-Iṣfahānī's *Ḥilyat al-awliyāʾ* provides the earliest biography for ʿUtba. Later, he was mentioned by Ibn al-Jawzī, ʿAṭṭār and Shaʿrānī.[118] His title *ghulām* was

[115] For the theme of the youth whose spiritual wisdom overcomes that of the masters, see e.g., Qushayrī, *Risāla*, 92, lines 5–10; 13–15. Cf. the use of *ghilmān* with the negative meaning of *aḥdāth* in: Daylamī, *Sīra*, 139 (*al-naẓar ilā l-ghilmān*).

[116] The other Arabic words for 'young man' or 'boy' could have been used in stories about a type of an attraction of Sufi or non-Sufi figures to youth in more neutral contexts without any critical tone. See for example the story of Junayd with the Sheikh and the boy (*ṣabiyy*) who was beating him in Sulamī, *Muqaddima fī al-taṣawwuf*, ed. by Yūsuf Zaydān, 23–24; and the story of the old blind man with his *ghulām*: Ibid., 27–28.

[117] He fell fighting against the Byzantines. No date of death is provided in his biography.

[118] For ʿUtba al-Ghulām's biography, see e.g., Dhahabī, *Siyar*, vol. 7, 62–63; Ibn al-Jawzī, *Ṣifat al-ṣafwa*, vol. 3, 281–285; Iṣfahānī, *Ḥilyat al-awliyāʾ*, vol. 6, 244–257; ʿAṭṭār, *Tadhkira*, vol. 1, 57–59; ʿAbd al-Wahhāb al-Shaʿrānī, *Tanbīh al-mughtarrīn*, ed. by ʿAbd al-Jalīl al-ʿAṭā al-Bakrī (Damascus: Dār al-Bashāʾir, 1990), 312; and idem, *Ṭabaqāt*, vol. 1, 40.

generally attributed to his young age. Sha'rānī asserts that this refers to his sincerity in worship in a way that resembles the pure worship of the young Christian monks. There are no previous references to 'Utba's sinful life prior to his repentance that precede Sha'rānī's mention of the subject in his work. Interestingly, Abū Ḥāmid al-Ghazālī mentions the prayer of 'Utba al-Ghulām as one of the transmitted prayers (*ad'iya ma'thūra*) that are to be recited in the morning and evening and after every ritual prayer. In addition to the prayers of the Prophet Muḥammad, Adam, Abraham, 'Īsā, al-Khiḍr and 'Alī, Abū al-Dardā', Ghazālī mentions the prayers of 'Utba al-Ghulām, Ibrāhīm b. Adham and Ma'rūf al-Karkhī.[119]

As for *fatā* (pl. *fityān*), from its very beginning Sufism sought to absorb the concept of *futuwwa*, which was, on the actual level, one part of the social structure of Muslim society and, on the religious and theoretical level, a basic principle of *Shī'ī* Islam. The figure of 'Alī b. Abī Ṭālib (d. 40/661) supported, naturally, the Sufi image of the faithful *fatā*.[120] One should also bear in mind that the majority of the later Sufi *ṭarīqa*s chose to trace their spiritual lineage back to 'Alī. 'Alī's approach towards gazing, in its basic meaning, seems to have been manipulated by later Ḥanbalī critics of the Sufi custom of gazing. At the end of Abū Naṣr al-Sarrāj's section on 'Alī b. Abī Ṭālib, the following saying is ascribed to 'Alī: 'In four things, goodness is to be sought: in silence, in saying, in gazing, and in moving [...] If gazing is not performed for the sake of learning (*'ibra*), it is considered inadvertence (*ghafla*).'[121] Here, the implied attitude towards the act of *naẓar* – no matter what its object is – is positive. While the figure of 'Alī is brought in Sarrāj's text to legitimate *naẓar*, it is used by Ibn al-Jawzī in his *Dhamm al-hawā* as part of the many traditions in which the Prophet Muḥammad is reported to have warned his cousin 'Alī against the 'second glance'. This idea was among the strategies used by Ibn al-Jawzī to attack not only the Sufi practices but also the views of many other non-Sufi theoreticians who allow *naẓar*.[122]

Abū Ḥāmid al-Ghazālī opens the chapter on brotherhood and companionship of his *Iḥyā'* by stating that the brotherly bond is like the bond of marriage. Both impose particular rights and duties. Interestingly,

[119] See Ghazālī, *Iḥyā'*, vol. 1, 513–519.

[120] 'Alī b. Abī Ṭālib was the cousin and son-in-law of the Prophet Muḥammad and the fourth *khalīfa* who was murdered in the year 40/661.

[121] Sarrāj, *Luma'*, 132, lines 11–14.

[122] Ibn al-Jawzī, *Dhamm al-hawā*, ed. by Muṣṭafā 'Abd al-Wāḥid (Cairo: Dār al-Kutub al-Ḥadītha, 1962), 90. Cf. Bell, *Love Theory*, 19–20.

Ghazālī makes use of the term *munāsaba* (agreement) in his discussion of brotherhood for the sake of God (*al-ukhuwwa fī Allāh*) as well as in his discussion of *ṣuḥba* to indicate that companions are attracted to each other due to a primordial harmony between their souls. This was the same concept that Ghazālī used to describe the supreme motivation for divine love later.[123] The above-mentioned idea of removing the modesty between the brethren appears here as well.[124] In his Persian *Kimyāy-i sa'ādat*, Ghazālī criticizes the doctrine of *shāhid* which is practised through gazing at youth using the terms *shūr* (passion), *savād* (blackness) and *liwāṭ* (sodomy) to describe the custom. Notwithstanding, in the same place, Ghazālī refers to a different, still very rare state in which the divine beauty manifests itself in the image of a human being. This was the case when the Prophet, according to the well-known *ḥadīth*, beheld God in a dream in the form of a beardless youth. Ghazālī explains that what is seen in the dream is only a symbol or a likeness of God. The angel Gabriel is also reported in another tradition to have appeared to the Prophet Muḥammad in the form of Diḥya al-Kalbī (d. circa 50/670), one of the Prophet's companions, who was known in those days for his extraordinary beauty.[125]

'Umar al-Suhrawardī describes in detail the norms of living within the Sufi community of *ribāṭ* in his *'Awārif al-ma'ārif*. In a previous occasion,[126] I have shown that the broad category of *khādim* in Suhrawardī's writings seems to have included various types of affiliation and functions that go beyond the common assumption that a *khādim* was the senior disciple of a particular Sufi sheikh. It is important to note here that, while the *khādim* enjoyed a high-ranking position inside the *ribāṭ*, another category named by Suhrawardī and Kāshānī as *aṣḥāb al-khidma* (lit. companions of service) was also meant to designate those who serve the

[123] See Ghazālī's discussion of *munāsaba* in the context of brotherly love in Ghazālī, *Iḥyā'*, vol. 2, 241–242, 245. Cf. Ghazālī's discussion of *munāsaba* in the context of divine love: Ibid., vol. 4, 434. The common term that appears in the early Sufi discussions of *ṣuḥba* was, differentially, *muwāfaqa* (see e.g., Sulamī, *Muqaddima*, 22).

[124] See Ghazālī, *Iḥyā'*, vol. 2, 281.

[125] See Abū Ḥāmid Muḥammad b. Muḥammad al-Ghazālī, *Kīmyā-i sa'ādat* (Tehran: Kitābkhānih va-Chāpkhānih-yi Markazī, 1967), 379–380. See an interesting discussion of the different doctrines that relate to God's ability to appear to man in any form He wishes (*tamaththul*) in early medieval Islam in Ritter, *Ocean of the Soul*, 461–463. Rūzbihān Baqlī's visionary autobiography *Kashf al-asrār*, for instance, is full of references to occasions in which Rūzbihān was reported to have seen God in different forms such as a Turk or a beardless boy (see e.g., Rūzbihān Baqlī, *Unveiling of Secrets*, the Arabic text, 41, section 82; 56, section 114; 99, section 176).

[126] See Chapter 2.

residents of the *ribāṭ* in daily life and mundane affairs.[127] Such service, according to Suhrawardī, might have lead particular members of this group in the course of time to attain the status of disciplined Sufis. Based on early Sufi notions, serving the Sufis is simply one facet of *ṣuḥba* with those who are of a higher degree.[128] In Suhrawardī's writings, as far as I know, the term *ṣuḥbat al-aḥdāth* appears very occasionally.[129] Nonetheless, Suhrawardī writes in detail on the practical daily life of *shubbān* in the framework of the *ribāṭ*-based Sufi system. He uses the two plural forms, *shubbān* and *shabāb,* to indicate the young generation among the disciplined affiliates to the Sufi community (*jamāʿa*).[130] Suhrawardī urges the young disciples to live together with their peers in what he calls *bayt al-jamāʿa* (house of the community), as this can create a situation in which their behaviour is monitored and beneficially controlled by their masters. Another sphere for reclusive existence is the *zāwiya*, which offers old men and masters a place for individual training and retreat (*khalwa*). Suhrawardī makes two interesting points here:

1. The Sufi master should impose a period of reclusion upon one disciple who seems to have been offended by the communal sphere of the *ribāṭ*. In order to carry out this decision, the Sufi master grants the disciple his own *zāwiya*.
2. In the same paragraph, Suhrawardī declares that the Sufis of *ribāṭ* are actually 'human beings and, therefore, some acts which are disposed by human nature come out of them' (*ahl al-ribāṭ bashar, wa-tabdū minhum umūr bi-muqtaḍā ṭabʿ al-bashar*). As a result, companionship of those Sufis would become very harmful for 'the one who does not like their way' (*man lā yuḥibb ṭarīqahum*).[131] In fact, the last sentence is quite ambiguous. Elsewhere, Suhrawardī insists on the crucial need to be faithful to the commands of the Sufi sheikhs even when their apparent behaviour seems unexpected and unusual.[132]

Based on the assumption that the first point designates the young disciplined affiliate of the *ribāṭ* while the second designates the *khādim*,

[127] See Suhrawardī, *ʿAwārif*, 239; Salamah-Qudsi, *Idea of Tashabbuh*, 189–195.
[128] See e.g., Qushayrī, *Risāla*, 145.
[129] See Abū Ḥafṣ al-Suhrawardī, *Waṣiyya ilā aḥad al-fuqarāʾ*, MS Jagiellońska, 3991, fol. 66a.
[130] The word *shabāb* which appears sometimes as a synonym of *ḥadātha*, that is, youth (see Ibn Manẓūr, *Lisān al-ʿarab*, vol. 1, 480) designates frequently the opposite form for senescence.
[131] See Suhrawardī, *ʿAwārif*, 118.
[132] See ibid., 286.

whatever the specific content of this category may be, the text implies a connection between the two points. Some of the youth mentioned in the first point are probably *khādims* who served their fellow men and at the same time received Sufi training under their sheikhs; they are thus also related to in the second point.[133] Would it then be possible to assume that the 'acts that are disposed by human nature' include, among other meanings, certain erotically oriented behaviour of Sufi masters? This remains an unanswered inquiry throughout Suhrawardī's works.

In other occasions of his writings, Suhrawardī criticizes his contemporaries' *samāʿ* gatherings in which a beardless singer (*qawwāl amrad*) and a marriageable woman *(imraʾa ghayr muḥarrama*) become obvious instruments for seduction: 'The people of the brothels (*ahl al-mawākhīr*), then, are in better situation than that of such Sufis.'[134] Yet, he also makes it clear that attacking the Sufi *samāʿ*, regardless of the different types of listeners and their different situations, is not fair.[135] This might be a good example of the author's ambivalent attitude towards such a problematic topic in classical Sufism. On another occasion in Suhrawardī's *ʿAwārif*, he clarifies that love for one's wife is likely to occupy the place of divine love in the heart of a Sufi. Love for illegal purposes (*fī bāb ghayr mashrūʿ*), which most likely refers to the love of boys and youth in Sufi spheres, is more dangerous. No matter whether the real content of this love includes sodomy or just a type of brotherly or even fatherly relationship according to Suhrawardī, the one who claims that this is his way to obtain *mushāhada*; contemplating the creator's omnipotence and absolute heavenly beauty through human beauty, is a liar and pretender (*kadhdhāb muddaʿī*).[136]

Introducing *amrad* singers to *samāʿ*, close association of the male disciples with servant boys and young peers along with different erotic practices to which the early Sufi manuals infrequently alluded, are the most controversial customs which became closely affiliated with *samāʿ*, as Najm al-Dīn Kubrā, Suhrawardī's contemporary, indicates.[137]

133 In the same place in the text of *ʿAwārif*, the author states that 'if the young aspirant serves the people of God [...]' (ibid., 118). I argue that the term *khādim* during Suhrawardī's time was not particularly institutionalized, and, therefore, it had not been restricted to *khādim*'s position as a senior disciple of the sheikh. This term could include different functions in *ribāṭ*-based Sufism at that time. See Salamah-Qudsi, *Idea of Tashabbuh*, 189–195.

134 Suhrawardī, *ʿAwārif*, 157. 135 Ibid., 159. 136 See ibid., 152.

137 See e.g., Najm al-Dīn Kubrā, *Ādāb al-murīdīn*, ed. by Husein Badr al-Dīn (Tehran: Ṣafā, 1362 *Shamsī*), 327.

One of the famous contemporaries of Suhrawardī was the renowned Persian Sufi Awḥad al-Dīn Kirmānī. Although Kirmānī's spiritual lineage turns back to Suhrawardī's uncle and master, Abū al-Najīb al-Suhrawardī, and although Kirmānī even received *khirqa* from ʿUmar al-Suhrawardī himself, he demonstrates a very different spirituality than that of Suhrawardī. Jāmī tells us that Kirmānī believed that 'true witnessing of God' should be sought through 'visionary manifestations', which is why he used to tear the youths' shirts during *samāʿ* parties and press his breast to theirs. This practice is called *shāhid bāzī* (lit. playing the witness) in Persian literature, as systematically advocated in ʿAyn al-Quḍāt Hamadhānī's (d. 526/1131) *Tamhīdāt*.[138] Lloyd Ridgeon provides us with a profound discussion of Kirmānī's controversial practice of *shāhid bāzī*, which apparently involved both gazing at beardless youths and dancing with them during *samāʿ* gatherings.[139] Jāmī states that Suhrawardī criticizes this act and considers it a bad innovation (*ibtidāʿ*) to *sunnī* Islam. According to Jāmī, Suhrawardī was more concerned with the possibility that this strange behaviour, which in itself is not a deficiency in Kirmānī's spirituality, might be imitated by beginner disciples who are not protected from seduction like their masters.[140] Jāmī sounds eager to show that the attacks against Kirmānī's behaviour were not due to the behaviour itself since his actions

[138] In ʿAyn al-Quḍāt Hamadhānī's *Tamhīdāt* the term *shāhid bāzān* refers to those who gaze at the beautiful witness, that is, the beautiful beardless, and they become able to discover the true meaning of life and death through the witness and the witnessed (= God). In one occasion of *Tamhīdāt*, for instance, the Prophet Muḥammad is quoted to have said: 'On the night of the ascension I saw my lord as a young man. [. . .] Beware of the beardless youth as those have a complexion like that of God (*iyyākum wa-l-murd fa-inna lahum lawnan ka-lawn Allāh*).' (ʿAyn al-Quḍāt Hamadhānī, *Tamhīdāt*, 321). On the term *shāhid bāzān* and its position in Hamadhānī's teachings, see Firoozeh Papan-Matin, *Beyond Death: The Mystical Teachings of ʿAyn al-Quḍāt al-Hamadhānī* (Leiden and Boston: Brill, 2010), 82–88.

[139] See Lloyd Ridgeon, 'The Controversy of Shaykh Awḥad al-Dīn Kirmānī and Handsome, Moon-Faced Youths: A Case Study of *Shāhid-Bāzī* in Medieval Sufism', *Journal of Sufi Studies*, vol. 1 (2012), 2. See also Nasrollah Pourjavady, 'Stories of Aḥmad al-Ghazālī "Playing the Witness" in Tabrīz (Shams-i Tabrīzī's Interest in *shāhid-bāzī*)', in *Reason and Inspiration in Islam: Theology, Philosophy and Mysticism in Muslim Thought, Essays in Honour of Hermann Landolt*, ed. by Todd Lawson (London and New York: Tauris, 2005), 212.

[140] See Jāmī, *Nafaḥāt al-uns*, 591. From another perspective, Najīb Māyil Haravī, the editor of another work of Suhrawardī, uses Suhrawardī's critical attitude towards Kirmānī to accuse him that is Suhrawardī of narrow mindedness and ignorance of his contemporaries' teachings on divine love [See ʿUmar al-Suhrawardī, *Rashf al-naṣāʾiḥ al-īmāniyya wa-kashf al-faḍāʾiḥ al-yūnāniyya*, trans. to Persian by Muʿīn al-Dīn Jamāl b. Jalāl al-Dīn known as Muʿallim Yazdī (d. 789/1387), ed. by Najīb Haravī (N.p.: Chāp va-Nashr-i Bunyād, 1986), Haravī's *introduction*, 5–8].

could be performed by mature Sufis without negatively affecting their purity and chastity, but due to its negative influence on immature Sufis. I consider most probably that Suhrawardī's criticism of Kirmānī was more severe than what Jāmī describes. In a quick reference in the text of *'Awārif*, Suhrawardī mentions different groups of people who ascribe themselves to the *ṣūfiyya* although they do not belong to them. Among such groups, he describes those who believe that God could be embodied in certain human bodies and therefore permit beholding beautiful human beings: '*Minhum man yastabīḥ al-naẓar ilā al-mustaḥsanāt.*' Unexpectedly, Suhrawardī mentions Ḥallāj here to negate the resemblance between his case and such theories.[141] It is difficult not to associate Kirmānī with this critical paragraph in Suhrawardī's work. Most probably, the relationship between the two Sufis was delicate and tense, among other things, because of Kirmānī's doctrine and behaviour. According to historical sources, it was Kirmānī who replaced Suhrawardī in the prestigious position of *sheikh al-Marzubāniyya* of Baghdad, the Sufi *ribāṭ* that the Abbasid ruler al-Nāṣir li-Dīn Allāh (reigned between 575/1180 and 622/1225) had previously awarded to Suhrawardī.[142] Kirmānī's case indeed demonstrates how a controversial Sufi with homoerotic behaviour succeeded in becoming an influential Sufi who used to move in elite Sufi circles and, even to occupy a prestigious position in the religious institution of the Abbasid rule. In spite of his passionate Sufism and fondness of *shāhid bāzī*, he found time for family life and was married to one of the great-granddaughters of Abū al-Najīb al-Suhrawardī.[143]

Later Sufi writings following the seventh/twelfth century contributed to consolidate the practical position of young *khādim*s in Sufi communal spheres. The eighth/fourteenth century Sufi sheikh 'Abd Allāh b. Khalīl al-Basṭāmī (d. 785/1383 or 794/1392) attributed the following tradition to the Prophet: 'Ill-natured *khādim* is better than a diligent worshipper.' He emphasizes that the servant should not be judged or punished and that he

[141] See Suhrawardī, *'Awārif*, 102.

[142] See 'Abd al-Razzāq b. Aḥmad b. al-Fuwaṭī, *al-Ḥawādith al-jāmi'a wa-l-tajārib al-nāfi'a fī al-mi'a al-sābi'a*, ed. by Mahdī al-Najm (Beirut: Dār al-Kutub al-'Ilmiyya, 2003), 72. This appointment seems to have harmonized with a general policy of conciliating the Ḥanbalī party of Baghdad which had been adopted by al-Nāṣir's successor, al-Mustanṣir. Suhrawardī, who was himself a Shāfi'ī, was deprived of many positions he enjoyed during the former rule of al-Nāṣir. The relationships between Kirmānī and Suhrawardī were thoroughly investigated by Lloyd Ridgeon: See Ridgeon, *Controversy of Shaykh Awḥad al-Dīn Kirmānī*, 12–13, 19–27.

[143] See ibid., 15.

is even qualified to intercede for the Muslim believers. According to Basṭāmī, *khādim* was the only person who is allowed to assist to the Sufi affiliates or masters during their solitude (*khalwa*).[144]

YŪSUF B. AL-ḤUSAYN AL-RĀZĪ (D. 304/916–917) AND OTHER FIGURES

The reader of fourth/tenth century Sufi works cannot overlook the distinguished character of Abū Ya'qūb Yūsuf b. al-Ḥusayn al-Rāzī whose biographical account has come down to us in Sulamī's *Ṭabaqāt al-ṣūfiyya*. In this work, Yūsuf b. al-Ḥusayn advises his fellow men as follows: 'Whatever you see me do, do the like, except associating with youth for that is the most terrible of temptations' (*kullamā ra'aytumūnī af'aluhu fa-if'alūhu illā ṣuḥbat al-aḥdāth fa-innahu aftan al-fitan*).[145] The same mystic is also quoted by Sulamī to have said: 'More than a hundred times have I vowed to my Lord that I would associate with no lad, but the beauty of the cheek, the erectness of the stature, and the languishing of the eyes have caused me to break my vow, yet God has never had to question me concerning any offence committed with them.'[146] Interestingly, al-Ghamrī al-Wāsiṭī does not quote the second statement while preserving the idea of the mystic's covenant with God.[147]

Sarrāj quotes another version of the first statement: 'Imitate every act you see me doing except in two things: Do not incur debts in your relationship with God, and do not hold company with youth (*lā taṣḥabū al-murdān*).'[148] As for the second statement, Sulamī was the only early biographer who mentions it. Other biographers mentioned a more general statement, in which Ibn al-Ḥusayn seems to have warned his disciples

[144] See 'Abd Allāh b. Khalīl al-Basṭāmī, *Mishkāt al-miṣbāḥ fī bayān awrād al-masā' wa-l-ṣ abāḥ*, MS Yahuda collection 1086 (15), fol. 29a; fols. 36b–37a. I would like to thank Prof. Yehoshua Frenkel (University of Haifa) for providing me with a copy of this manuscript.

[145] Sulamī, *Ṭabaqāt*, 179; The English translation is based on Margoliouth's translation of Ibn al-Jawzī's *Talbīs*: Ibn al-Jawzī, *Talbīs Iblīs (Delusion of the Devil)*, trans. by David Samuel Margoliouth (New Delhi, 2011), vol. 2, 82. Cf. Sarrāj, *Luma'*, 264 (here the statement appears differently: 'Follow my example in everything except two things: Do not incur debts in your relationship with God, and do not company beardless youth' (*iqtadū bi-jamī' mā ra'aytum minnī illā shay'ayn, fa-lā tastadīnū 'alā Allāh ta'ālā wa-lā taṣḥabū al-murdān*).

[146] Sulamī, *Ṭabaqāt*, 179. Margoliouth's translation of Ibn al-Jawzī's *Talbīs Iblīs*, vol. 2, 82. Cf. Sarrāj, *Luma'*, 264, lines 1–3.

[147] See Ghamrī, *al-Ḥukm al-maḍbūṭ*, 64. [148] Sarrāj, *Luma'*, 264.

of three epidemics (*āfāt*) known among the *ṣūfiyya*: companionship with youth, associating with opponents (*mu'āsharat al-aḍdād*), and accepting women's presents (*qubūl arfāq al-niswān*).[149] It is possible that in Sulamī's eyes, the personal daring tone implied in the previous two quotations did not appear problematic since it could support the high spirituality of Ibn al-Ḥusayn who was able to fight against his lower soul and to protect himself from the powerful seduction of youthful beauty. This viewpoint, however, is not clearly stated in Sulamī's work. Furthermore, it is plausible that Sulamī intended to put the focus on the extreme degree of sincerity in the guidance given by the Sufi sheikh even when his sincerity with his disciples is at the cost of humbling himself before them, and revealing his 'shame' in public.

In one interesting passage of Sarrāj's chapter on correspondence between early Sufis apart of *Kitāb al-luma'*, Yūsuf b. al-Ḥusayn tells that he wrote a letter to one man of wisdom (*katabtu ilā ba'ḍ al-ḥukamā'*) complaining to him of his inclination to worldly desires and of his 'unacceptable attributes of which he himself is not satisfied' (*al-akhlāq allatī lastu arḍāhā min nafsī li-nafsī*). The anonymous 'man of wisdom' advised Ibn al-Ḥusayn not to seek closeness to those who are not entrusted with the souls of their companions.[150]

Later on, Ibn al-Jawzī refers to the problematic sayings of Yūsuf b. al-Ḥusayn in the detailed chapter he devoted to criticize the Sufi custom of *ṣuḥbat al-aḥdāth* in his *Talbīs*. Ibn al-Jawzī classifies the Sufis who engaged in this custom into seven categories, and the case of Ibn al-Ḥusayn appears in two of them. It appears in the fifth category of 'those who associate with youths while protecting themselves from committing sins, considering that a means to struggle against their lower souls'[151] and in the seventh category, of those 'who are aware that it is unlawful to associate with or gaze at the beardless, only they are unable to abstain therefrom'. In his discussion of the seventh category, Ibn al-Jawzī quotes first the two statements that reveal Ibn al-Ḥusayn's personal inclination to youth in addition to the same three verses of the Abbasid poet Ṣarī' al-Ghawānī (d. 208/823) that Ibn al-Ḥusayn was said to have recited in the

[149] See Qushayrī, *Risāla*, 24. The third epidemic appears in other sources as *rifqat al-niswān* which might signify also associating with women. See Ibn 'Asākir, *Ta'rīkh madīnat dimashq*, vol. 74, 222; Ibn Manẓūr, *Mukhtaṣar ta'rīkh dimashq*, vol. 28, 72. The three epidemics' statement was not mentioned in Ibn Kathīr's *Bidāya* (see Ibn Kathīr, *Bidāya*, vol. 11, 126–127), and Dhahabī's *Siyar* (see Dhahabī, *Siyar*, vol. 14, 248–251).

[150] See Sarrāj, *Luma'*, 236.

[151] Ibn al-Jawzī, *Talbīs Iblīs*, 351.

work of Sulamī. Afterwards, Ibn al-Jawzī explicitly accuses Ibn al-Ḥusayn of ignorance (*jahl*), declaring that:

> This person has exposed a failing which God concealed, letting it be known that each time he saw a tempting object he annulled his repentance. What has become of the Sufic resolve to inure the soul to hardships? Further he foolishly supposes that only a guilty act is a sin; had he possessed any knowledge he would have known that association with them and gazing on them are sinful. Consider then what havoc ignorance effects with its possessors![152]

Meanwhile, it is interesting to note that Ibn al-Jawzī himself does not bring forward any of Ibn al-Ḥusayn's sayings on companionship with youth in his biographical work *Ṣifat al-ṣafwa* but, rather, portrays a very pious image of him. In his *Muntaẓam*, Ibn al-Jawzī even displays a more detailed account of Ibn al-Ḥusayn in which he quotes famous anecdotes and sayings from earlier sources, and avoids any reference to companionship with youth.[153] How, then, can the same figure be portrayed in two contradictory images in the works of the same author? One part of the answer most probably lies in a single piece of data that all biographers were concerned to emphasize, which is the contact between Yūsuf b. al-Ḥusayn and Aḥmad b. Ḥanbal. Allegedly, Ibn al-Ḥusayn sought to learn *ḥadīth* under Ibn Ḥanbal.[154] This discipleship motivated the Ḥanbalite biographer Ibn Abī Yaʿlā to include the biography of Ibn al-Ḥusayn in his *Ṭabaqāt al-ḥanābila*.[155]

Though Ibn al-Jawzī's declared approach towards the Sufi customs in general was critical, his specific reference to the case of Yūsuf b. al-Ḥusayn was ambivalent. The above-mentioned comment of Ibn al-Jawzī on the two sayings of Ibn al-Ḥusayn, in spite of its severity, leaves the impression that Ibn al-Ḥusayn and other Sufis of this group are guiltless of sliding into adultery. The basic problem in their case, according to Ibn al-Jawzī, is that they 'foolishly suppose that only a guilty act is a sin', while gazing at youth and associating with them are in themselves forbidden. It seems that Ibn al-Jawzī could not accuse a prominent mystic like Ibn al-Ḥusayn, who had close relationships with the great mystics of Baghdad,

[152] See ibid., 357; Margoliouth's translation of *Talbīs*, vol. 2, 82.

[153] See Ibn al-Jawzī, *Muntaẓam*, vol. 13, 171–172. Ibn al-Jawzī even mentions Yūsuf b. al-Ḥusayn among the 'famous preachers of *Rayy*' (*aʿyān al-mudhakkirīn bi-l-Rayy*). [Ibn al-Jawzī, *Kitāb al-quṣṣāṣ wa-l-mudhakkirīn*, ed. by Muḥammad al-Ṣabbāgh (Beirut: al-Maktab al-Islāmī, 1988), 272.]

[154] See Baghdādī, *Taʾrīkh baghdād*, vol. 16, 462.

[155] See Muḥammad b. Abī Yaʿlā, *Ṭabaqāt al-ḥanābila*, vol. 2, 561–564.

with illegal sexual practices.[156] Meanwhile, it seems untenable to assert the chaste and pure nature of Ibn al-Ḥusayn's involvement in the practice while his statements imply unavoidable erotic contents.

The Persian Sufi of the late sixth/twelfth century, Rūzbihān Baqlī, uses Ibn al-Ḥusayn's sayings while warning the Sufis of his time against claiming that companionship with women and boys does not affect them.[157]

While early Sufi literature leaves no clear evidence concerning the actual approach of Ibn al-Ḥusayn's contemporaries towards his daring sayings, there is something of interest to note here. Ibn al-Ḥusayn was one of the mystics to whom Junayd chose to address a personal letter. Junayd's letter to him, which is preserved among *Rasā'il al-Junayd*, alludes to an implied personal conflict between the two mystics as I previously noted in Chapter 5. The one who initiated this controversial correspondence was Junayd. Among the people of *Rayy*, it was specifically the group of *zuhhād* who reportedly harboured the most hostile attitude towards Ibn al-Ḥusayn.[158] This hostility was most likely motivated by a particular type of *malāmatī* behaviour held by him.[159] The *malāmatī* mode of piety indicates the need to get rid of the lower human will that seeks to perform goodness in order to gain people's admiration and social fame. Pure sincerity in performing religious deeds (*ikhlāṣ al-a'māl*) is sought, according to one quotation from Ibn al-Ḥusayn, through removing both 'the love of people's praise and the fear of their dispraise'.[160] Ibn al-Ḥusayn was known also for his relationship with Abū

156 This could be compared with a similar consideration in modern scholarship in reference to 'Abd al-Ghanī al-Nābulsī. While J. S. Trimingham considers Nābulsī's defence of the custom of contemplation of beardless boys as a literary convention that had not to be understood literally, el-Rouayheb criticizes Trimingham's notion, telling that what lies behind it, probably, was the researcher's difficulty to believe that a respected Islamic scholar like Nābulsī could condone the problematic practice. See el-Rouayheb, *Before Homosexuality*, 101–102.

157 See Rūzbihān Baqlī, *Sayr al-arwāḥ aw al-miṣbāḥ fī mukāshafat ba'th al-arwāḥ*, ed. by 'Āṣim al-Kayyālī (Beirut: Dār al-Kutub al-'Ilmiyya, 2007), 34. Cf. idem, *L'Itinéraire des Esprits Ruzbehan*, tr. et commente par Paul Ballanfat (Paris: Les Deux Océans, 2001), 158.

158 See Dhahabī, *Siyar*, vol. 14, 250.

159 Qushayrī, Sulamī and Iṣfahānī emphasize the ideas of *ikhlāṣ* and *isqāṭ al-taṣannu'* (lit. leaving out the artificiality) in his account. Jullābī Hujwīrī's biography of him, on the other side, was very brief (see Jullābī Hujwīrī, *Kashf al-maḥjūb*, 171–172). Additional evidence for Ibn al-Ḥusayn's *malāmatī* teachings are provided in his aforementioned letter to Junayd (see Muṣṭafā, *Tāj al-'ārifīn*, 345 as well as the detailed discussion of this letter in Chapter 5).

160 Iṣfahānī, *Ḥilya*, vol. 10, 260.

Turāb al-Nakhshabī whose unique teaching on *tawakkul* and his roving life led to his legendary tragic death in the desert, as noted before. Abū Turāb was particularly famous for his impact on the Khurāsānian founders of *malāmatiyya*.[161] Both ʿAbd Allāh Anṣārī Haravī and, later on, Jāmī indicate that Ibn al-Ḥusayn intended to adopt *malāmatī* behaviour in order to alienate people from him and cause them to insult him (*darīn kār talibīsī ṭarīq-i malāmat dāshtih mardumān bar khīshtan shūrānīdan va-qabūl-i īshān bi-khīshtan vīrān-kardan*).[162]

It was Ibn al-Ḥusayn's mode of religious life which was based on certain codes of *malāmati* behaviour, including practising companionship with youth, that most probably brought about the critical attitude of both Junayd and the renunciants of *Rayy* towards him.[163] He himself tells us that Dhū al-Nūn ignored him because of his ugly appearance the first time he met him in Egypt.[164]

It is interesting to note that other Sufis who were involved in stories about gazing at beautiful youths according to the sources were themselves controversial figures who provoked traditionalists' ire and accusations of heresy. Abū Ḥamza al-Ṣūfī, for instance, appears frequently in Jaʿfar b. Aḥmad al-Qāriʾ al-Sarrāj's *Maṣāriʿ al-ʿushshāq* telling stories about Sufis who were involved in gazing. Abū al-Ḥusayn al-Nūrī tells a story in which he himself was involved in gazing at a beautiful youth in Baghdad.[165] Both Abū Ḥamza and Nūrī were accused of heresy due to their problematic utterances and provocative behaviour. Abū Ḥamza, for instance, was accused of *ḥulūl* as Sarrāj tells in his *Lumaʿ*.[166] Again, in these two cases, neither *naẓar* nor *ṣuḥbat al-aḥdāth* seem to have been the actual motivation for the traditionalists' accusations.

The omission of these statements in the works of Sufi and non-Sufi biographers in the period between the fourth/tenth century (when Sulamī composed his work) and the sixth/twelfth century (when Ibn al-Jawzī composed his work) might indicate an increasingly negative perception

161 See Sulamī, *Ṭabaqāt*, 114.

162 Anṣārī Haravī, *Ṭabaqāt al-ṣūfiyya*, 77; Jāmī, *Nafaḥāt al-uns*, 97.

163 According to his biography in Ibn ʿAsākir's *Taʾrīkh madīnat dimashq* someone said to Ibn al-Ḥusayn: '*Law tajammalta qalīlan*' (why haven't you adorned yourself?). This request might have implied controversial behaviour by Ibn al-Ḥusayn that motivated his contemporaries to ask him to be committed to more socially and religiously acceptable behaviour. Interestingly, the reply given by him was: 'People do not cease visiting our place with their jugs seeking to receive our benediction and prayers, and you call me to adorn myself?' (Ibn ʿAsākir, *Taʾrīkh madīnat dimashq*, vol. 74, 227).

164 See Ibn Manẓūr, *Mukhtaṣar taʾrīkh dimashq*, vol. 28, 76.

165 See Sulamī, *Ṭabaqāt*, 154–155.

166 See Sarrāj, *Ṣuḥuf min kitāb al-lumaʿ*, 5–7.

of the notion of *ṣuḥbat al-aḥdāth* in Muslim society. However, accusations of infidelity lingered without any detailed explanations. What possibly concerned Junayd in his letter to Ibn al-Ḥusayn was the latter's attempt to distinguish between his own behaviour in practising *ṣuḥbat al-aḥdāth* and other problematic customs by virtue of his *malāmatī* doctrines and fortified position as a master on one hand, and his decisive prohibition to his disciples from behaving so, on the other. Some statements in Ibn al-Ḥusayn's biography relate that the latter used to blame himself for not being committed to the same behaviour that he called his fellows to preserve.[167]

The individual case of Yūsuf b. al-Ḥusayn is interesting for many reasons. The references to him by Sufi and non-Sufi authors leave the impression that examining one character can reveal so many aspects related to early Sufi life and thought. Controversial behaviour by Ibn al-Ḥusayn stands at the basis of the criticism against him. This behaviour includes his open homoerotic practices which he probably carried out as a way of challenging the Baghdadi Sufi institution in both literary form, through the statements themselves, and through actual behaviour as well. His frequent use of the first pronoun and individual tone while referring to his own experiences, his impure repentance and spiritual weakness make it tangible that behind the literary image of this character there may be different components of the actual settings of the Sufis in his days. His relevance to companionship with youth is only the entrance point to a wider array of notions, interpersonal ties and individual tendencies.

Now, I would like to draw attention to an additional early figure, Abū ʿAbd Allāh Aḥmad b. Yaḥyā b. al-Jallāʾ. Sulamī is his *Ṭabaqāt* quotes his grandfather telling him that Ibn al-Jallāʾ in the region of *Shām*, Junayd in Baghdad and Abū ʿUthmān al-Ḥīrī in Nishapur were three peerless Sufi masters.[168] Ibn al-Jallāʾ was mentioned in one anecdote about a Syrian Sufi who had become implicated in what seemed like an erotic gaze at a Christian boy. According to the anecdote in Makkī's *Qūt*, Ibn al-Jallāʾ the great master of *Bilād al-Shām* rebuked this behaviour and even told the Sufi that he would be punished sooner or later.[169] Interestingly, according

[167] See Ibn ʿAsākir, *Taʾrīkh madīnat dimashq*, vol. 74, 229.

[168] See Sulamī, *Ṭabaqāt*, 166; Qushayrī, *Risāla*, 22; See also Ibn al-Jallāʾ's extensive biography in Ibn ʿAsākir's *Taʾrīkh madīnat dimashq*, vol. 6, 81–93. A detailed reference to the sources of Ibn al-Jallāʾ's life and teachings is provided by Daphna Ephrat in her *Spiritual Wayfarers, Leaders in Piety: Sufis and the Dissemination of Islam in Medieval Palestine* (Cambridge, Mass. and London: Harvard University Press, 2008), 64–65, footnote 69. See also ibid., 39–47.

[169] See Makki, *Qūt*, vol. 1, 377.

to another version of the anecdote mentioned by Jullābī Hujwīrī, the one who gazed at the Christian boy was Ibn al-Jallāʾ himself, while the person who rebuked his behaviour and informed him that divine punishment would not spare him for this misdeed was Junayd. When the Baghdadi master noticed the suspicious behaviour of his young fellow Sufi, he told him that his act was motivated by his lower soul and not by his purported wish to observe the divine glory manifested in God's creatures.[170] Junayd was replaced in other versions by Abū ʿAbd Allāh al-Balkhī (d. 319/931).[171] A serious punishment that follows a forbidden glance is a well-known idea that has its roots in literary works on the theory of profane love.[172] The story of Ibn al-Jallāʾ was born in the spirit of this idea, and that is why its actual historical accuracy is somewhat doubtful. Even if the general framework of the story is literary, Ibn al-Jallāʾ should have been included in one group of Sufis whose names most often appear in discussions of problematic *naẓar*.

Another early figure is Abū al-ʿAbbās Aḥmad b. Yaḥyā al-Shīrāzī, one of Ibn Khafīf's companions.[173] In *Sīrat Ibn Khafīf* and *Nafaḥāt al-uns*, Aḥmad b. Yaḥyā was said to have engaged in ecstatic movements during *samāʿ* gatherings. One day, he became so totally submerged in a deep state of ecstasy (*wajd*) during *samāʿ* that he caught two firebrands in his hand and covered them by a piece of his sleeve. Afterwards, he asked a boy who attended the gathering to accompany him.[174]

Junayd is frequently mentioned in similar anecdotes as the great master whose role reflects what we can call the communal Sufi ethos of that time. Junayd prayed on behalf of Abū ʿAmr b. ʿUlwān[175] from *Rayy* after the latter craved for a woman during the recital of a ritual prayer, and as a

[170] See Jullābī Hujwīrī, *Kashf al-maḥjūb*, 169–170.

[171] See Ibn ʿAsākir, *Taʾrīkh madīnat dimashq*, vol. 6, 84; Ibn al-Jawzī, *Dhamm al-hawā*, 127. The reference here is to Muḥammad b. al-Faḍl b. al-ʿAbbās of Balkh. See his biography in Sulamī, *Ṭabaqāt*, 206–211; Jāmī, *Nafaḥāt al-uns*, 116–117.

[172] See e.g., Ibn al-Jawzī, *Dhamm al-hawā*, 126–130 (*dhikr ithm al-naẓar wa-ʿuqūbatihi*).

[173] The majority of early Sufi and non-Sufi biographers did not provide a separate biography to Aḥmad b. Yaḥyā al-Shīrāzī. His name appears commonly as one of those who transmitted Ibn Khafīf's sayings in the latter's biography. See e.g., Dhahabī, *Siyar*, vol. 16, 343. Junayd Shīrāzī during the late eighth/fourteenth century, however, provides us with a separate biography in his *Shadd al-izār* telling there that Aḥmad b. Yaḥyā was the first Sufi that Ibn Khafīf accompanied (see Junayd Shīrāzī, *Shadd al-izār*, 137–138). Aḥmad b. Yaḥyā's date of death is not provided in the sources, including Junayd Shīrāzī's work and Jāmī's *Nafaḥāt al-uns*.

[174] See Daylamī, *Sīra*, 188; Jāmī, *Nafaḥāt al-uns*, 144–145.

[175] This person appears in the sources as a transmitter of Junayd. See e.g., Dhahabī, *Siyar*, vol. 12, 512.

result his whole body turned black.[176] Referring again to the above-mentioned anecdotes of Ibn al-Jallāʾ, it seems most probable that Hujwīrī's version was more authentic than that of Makkī and that the latter preferred to replace the original 'hero' of the story with an anonymous Syrian Sufi while granting Ibn al-Jallāʾ the position of the critical denouncer. Makkī, elsewhere, indicates that those Sufis who use verse 99 of *Sūra* 6 ('Look at their fruits when they begin to bear') to allow gazing at beautiful boys should abstain from doing so by virtue of verse 30 of *Sūra* 24 ('Tell the believing men to lower their gaze'). In accordance with this idea, Makkī emphasizes the importance of keeping a good opinion of one's companions besides the need for concealing their bad behaviour (*al-satr ʿan al-ikhwān*).[177] As for Jullābī Hujwīrī, we should note that he mentions the problematic story of Ibn al-Jallāʾ in the biography of the latter. This is specifically the place where he should have emphasized the statements and anecdotes that offered praise of the great Syrian master. Hujwīrī, likely, did not feel that his reference to the anecdote in the biographical account would contradict his clear statement of condemnation of *ṣuḥbat al-aḥdāth* in the last section of his work. Just the opposite, the anecdote serves him to emphasize Ibn al-Jallāʾ's deep repentance and to show the beginner aspirants in Sufi communities that even renowned masters are not fully exempt from the temptations of the lower soul. If we do not read this text with the question on *ṣuḥbat al-aḥdāth* in mind, then we will most probably be unaware of any contradictions between the two paragraphs in Hujwīrī's work.

CULTIVATING THE DATA: A PROPOSED ANALYSIS

Generally speaking, love for boys demonstrates one aspect of the sexual mores in medieval Muslim societies. Different types of medieval sources support the idea that many men 'would fall in love with boys. Many would desire sex with them, and some would do so', as Arno Schmitt puts it. Schmitt indicates that being a married man and a father who has one or more beloved boys for sexual intercourse besides his relationship with women seems to have been considered 'perfectly normal'.[178] Such an assertion, however, should be made very cautiously. Normality as implied in the statement 'perfectly normal' here does not mean that the majority

176 See Makkī, *Qūt*, vol. 1, 378–379. 177 Ibid., vol. 1, 163.
178 Schmitt, *Different Approaches*, 5–6.

of the population accepted or adopted this type of relationship.[179] Marriage was highly institutionalized and even sanctified in Islam. The best way to obey God and to perfect one's faith is to get married. Fear of gazing at beardless boys developed parallel to the fear of gazing at women in Islamic legal literature and even came to be seen as more dangerous. 'The sodomites (*al-lūṭiyya*) are of three kinds: those who gaze, those who touch the hands, and those who commit that act' is a statement that appears frequently in this regard.[180]

Authors of Sufi works generally condemned erotic company with youth even though they do not provide any detailed and elaborate discussion of the practice. Sulamī, for instance, quotes the following statement of Muẓaffar al-Qirmīsīnī: 'The one who associates with youth while being committed to charity and purity is expected to fall into impurity, how much more for the one who associates with them without being committed to charity?'[181] However, when it became connected with renowned Sufi figures, erotic attraction to boys does not seem to have been considered a serious reason for denunciation.

Makkī, for instance, points out five categories of people whose company is prohibited. There is no clear indication to youth here.[182] On the contrary, it is probable that the tendency of certain Sufis to associate with boys led particular Sufi authors to praise such figures by emphasizing that their sexual chastity remained even when the temptation was so strong. Ibn al-Jawzī asserted this idea in his critical discussion of *ṣuḥbat al-aḥdāth*.[183] In Qushayrī's chapter on *samā'*, Mumshād al-Dīnawarī (d. 299/911) is quoted as saying that he is protected from being affected by all amusing aspects of this world including those known in *samā'* gatherings.[184]

In certain occasions, Sufi authors exploited companionship with youth as a vehicle to deal with other problematic customs known among their

179 See S. D. Goitein, 'The Sexual Mores of the Common People', in *Society and the Sexes*, 48. Goitein claims here that while what he calls the 'cult of the ephebes, or attractive male youths' became a style of life for the entire community after being the exclusive privilege of men in power, for the majority of the population sexual satisfaction was still to be sought through marriage.

180 This statement was originally attributed to Abū Sahl by Ibn al-Jawzī, *Dhamm al-hawā*, 116. Cf. Bell, *Love Theory*, 21. The statement appears also in Dhahabī, *al-Kabā'ir* (Damascus and Beirut: al-Maktaba al-Umawiyya, 1971), 57–58. See also Suharawardī, *'Awārif*, 163.

181 Sulamī, *Ṭabaqāt*, 411–412.

182 See Makkī, *Qūt*, vol. 2, 484. Furthermore, Makkī shows that gazing at beautiful human beings is considered a small sin (*ṣaghā'ir al-dhunūb*) (ibid., vol. 1, 391).

183 See Ibn al-Jawzī, *Talbīs Iblīs*, 351.

184 See Qushayrī, *Risāla*, 172.

fellow men like associating with women and accepting their presents and donations.

Youth were a vital element in the life of the increasingly institutionalized Sufi communities. Boys and young men used to attend Sufi gatherings and circles of instruction and training. They became the basic hard-core instrument of disseminating Sufi knowledge and training. Being followed by numerous young affiliates and even lay affiliates[185] gradually became an indication of the Sufi master's charisma and socio-religious authority in a period in which spirituality was centred on charismatic sheikhs more than on theories and abstract doctrines.

The many dynamics that brought about the cohesion of *ṣuḥbat al-aḥdāth* with Sufism in the eyes of its attackers are varied: the growing number of voices that sought to portray the legitimate boundaries of worshipping God through contemplating human beauty, like those of Kirmānī, ʿAyn al-Quḍāt Hamadhānī and Aḥmad al-Ghazālī;[186] the engagement of certain early Sufis with *ṣuḥbat al-aḥdāth* besides other *malāmatī* behaviour and the lack of a systematic discourse of condemnation in the works of the great Sufi theoreticians.

Writing against *ṣuḥbat al-aḥdāth* attracted many authors of late medieval times. A treatise entitled *Salwat al-aḥzān li-l-ijtināb ʿan mujālasat al-aḥdāth wa-l-niswān* (*Forgetfulness of All Sorrows in Avoiding Association with Youth and Women*) was apparently composed by Muḥammad b. Ḥamīd al-Mashtūlī (d. after 1167/1753) in the course of the twelfth/eighteenth century.[187] More recently, the Saudi ʿAbd al-Karīm b. Ṣāliḥ al-Ḥamīd published his *Aḥdāth ṣuḥbat al-aḥdāth* (*The Episodes of Companionship with Youth*) (1999). In our day, the critique against *ṣuḥbat al-aḥdāth* is provided essentially by numerous *sunnī-salafī* network websites.[188]

[185] This term was presented by Erik Ohlander to designate a group of undisciplined affiliates to Sufi communities. Although those affiliates participated in the religiosity of the *ribāṭ*, their affiliation was weak and exempt from any commitment to Sufi institutionalized methods of gaining instruction. See Ohlander, *Sufism in an Age of Transition*, 243–246.

[186] See Ridgeon, *Controversy of Shaykh Awḥad al-Dīn Kirmānī*, 3.

[187] This author was confused with the early Abū Bakr al-Mubārak b. Kāmil al-Khaffāf (d. 543/1148). See the Cairo edition of *Salwat al-aḥzān* which was edited by Ṭāriq al-Ṭanṭāwī (Cairo: Maktabat Ibn Sīnā, 1991).

[188] Visit e.g., the website of 'Saḥāb Salafī Network': www.sahab.net/forums/index.php?app=forums&module=forums&controller=topic&id=37448 whereas the entry *taḥdhīr al-ikhwān min muṣāḥabat al-murdān* (forewarning brothers from association with beardless youth) contains many traditions directed against the Sufi custom (accessed 27 October 2017).

The basis for this chapter is the primary suggestion that singling out such a marginal topic like *ṣuḥbat al-aḥdāth* and shedding light on it would effectively help us Investigate a hidden domain, one that lies between communal and individual spheres of the early Sufi scene. The earliest Sufi manuals indicate that Sufis were divided into two groups: those who preferred total seclusion from society and those whose followers chose to be socially associated since their Sufi companions were expected to elevate them to higher spiritual ranks. For this reason, Makkī compared companionship and brotherhood to childbirth (*al-ukhuwwa ʿamal ka-l-wilāda*).[189] Sources of the period provide the impression that most early Sufis were social and that, over the course of time, *ṣuḥba* became a venerated principle within the very core of Sufi ethos. Individual modes and distinct tendencies in reference to Sufis' ways of practising *ṣuḥba* were evident.

As for *ṣuḥbat al-aḥdāth* in particular, I argued that it should be examined through considering both the general-communal Sufi ethos which finds its best expression in Sufi literature and the more personal tone that comes through, despite not being explicitly expressed. Sensitivity to the aspects of the interpenetration between the individual and communal domains is essential while discussing different conceptions and customs among early Sufis.

Ṣuḥbat al-aḥdāth is, by all means, one part of the general system of Sufi *ṣuḥba*. If companionship can bring to mind different aspects of the *eros*, companionship with youth was by its very essence seen as an embodiment of the *eros* in Sufi Islam. Theoretically speaking, youth could be a symbol of deep love and uncompromising sincerity, yet it could bring to mind prohibited beauty and dangerous temptation. On the practical level, companionship with youth – in the primary sense of the term without the erotic connotation – was unavoidable in the communal life of the Sufis. Preaching assemblies held around renowned Sufi masters gathered massive audiences of youth and women. Anecdotes abound of youth who fainted upon hearing the intense words of Sufi masters. Such anecdotes, besides other data, establish a portrait in which youth played a fundamental role in the life of early Sufis. Boys were encouraged to associate with Sufi masters and to join their circles of training. A reference to Abū Saʿīd b. Abī al-Khayr whose mother encouraged him, when he was a child, to accompany his father to a gathering of dervishes was previously made.[190]

[189] Makkī, *Qūt*, vol. 2, 442–443.
[190] See Ebn-e Monavvar, *The Secrets of God's Mystical Oneness*, 76.

The erotic content of *ṣuḥbat al-aḥdāth* cannot be ignored even for the period in which a clear textual evidence is lacking. However, this erotic content was not the motivation behind the current chapter. What did interest me here was the need to delve into the different strategies used by early Sufis to treat what seemed to be an individual matter that progressively transformed into a collective Sufi issue as well as an identifying feature of the whole body of Sufism in the eyes of its enemies.

Abdelwahab Bouhdiba says that 'homosexuality was widespread in the student communities and especially in the confraternities.'[191] Other modern scholars like el-Rouayheb bring to the fore the sexual acts of certain antinomian Sufi sects of the later premodern period like the *Khawāmīs* of seventeenth-century Egypt.[192] As for the earlier stages in the history of Sufism, less obvious clues are available. However, what should concern us more is not to point out such clues but rather to arrive at a deeper understanding of how a delicate topic like *ṣuḥbat al-aḥdāth* could become a rich domain for diverse patterns of relationships between individual Sufis and the communal ethos under which they lived and acted.

There is no systematic discourse of treating the homoerotic aspect of *ṣuḥba* and criticizing it in the influential works of early Sufi authors. The topic was touched on accidentally and frequently as an incidental part of other issues. Meanwhile, by nominating it as one of the common *āfāt* of the Sufis, the makers of Sufi ethos contributed, like their attackers, to transforming the individual frame of *ṣuḥbat al-aḥdāth* into a more communal one by insisting on the idea that this was a widespread epidemic among Sufis.

In the course of the sixth/twelfth and seventh/thirteenth centuries, famous Sufi manuals like that of *Ādāb al-murīdīn* and *ʿAwārif al-maʿārif* seemed incapable of bearing the aggressive attacks on the custom. The elusive and evasive approach of the authors of those manuals towards *ṣuḥbat al-aḥdāth* helped strengthen a part of the critical discourse against Sufism.

191 Bouhdiba, *Sexuality in Islam*, 119. Cf. al-Qināwī, *Sharḥ lāmiyyat Ibn al-Wardī*, 62–76. Cf. Qamar ul-Huda, *Striving for Divine Union: Spiritual Exercises for Suhrawardī Ṣūfīs* (London and New York: Routledge Curzon, 2003), 29. The accusation of practising sodomy among *futuwwa* groups is attributed to the work of the seventh/thirteenth century author Ibn Baydakīn al-Turkmānī (though an exact reference is missing here). Cf. Turkmānī, *Kitāb al-lumaʿ*, vol. 1, 507.

192 See el-Rouayheb, *Heresy and Sufism*, 375–376.

Concluding Remarks

From the very beginning of my acquaintance with Sufi material, the personal lives of early Sufis engaged my interest. For quite a few years now, I have, so to speak, been wandering in the wide spaces of early Sufi writings which, while they were produced in the course of the early centuries of the development of the Sufi tradition in Islamic culture, they contributed to create the high and consensually accepted ethos of the Sufis around the world of Islam. Works such as Sarrāj's *Kitāb al-luma'*, Sulamī's *Ṭabaqāt al-ṣūfiyya* and *Dhikr al-niswa*, 'Abd Allāh Anṣārī Haravī's *Ṭabaqāt al-ṣūfiyya*, Makkī's *Qūt al-qulūb*, Kalābādhī's *Ta'arruf*, Qushayrī's *Risāla*, Hujwīrī's *Kashf al-maḥjūb* and 'Ayn al-Quḍāt Hamadhānī's *Tamhīdāt* in addition to many others, could, in my view, provide more than the basic elements of the general and dramatic story of the development of early Sufism. Minor and less dramatic stories could also be found. You simply need to get closer to the sources and let them whisper to you. Early Sufi personalities were portrayed both in the sources as well as in the scholarly works more as actors who operated in complete accordance with a predetermined scenario and had neither private spaces of their own nor interpersonal relationships and human conflicts between them and their contemporary counterparts.

I agree with the accepted convention that the image of a particular Sufi figure as portrayed by his near contemporaries can provide a more useful means to sketch the components of his unique piety than his real life and that the idealized images of the hagiographies' heroes contain very little historical truth. However, while trying to sketch the methodological basis of this project, I became convinced that, in certain cases, whenever singular and unique appearances of particular stories occur, certain historical and individual conclusions could be deduced. Sometimes, what may seem like a typical paradigmatic anecdote in different Sufi sources could imply social or interpersonal allusions. For instance, Abū al-Qāsim al-Junayd's letter to Yūsuf b. al-Ḥusayn, while typically constructed in Junayd's style, may have alluded to a personal conflict between the two mystics. The attempt to reconstruct the personal atmosphere behind the correspondence between the two figures on the basis of the fragments that are preserved in different sources is particularly interesting.

Approaching personal spaces does not involve only the Sufi's own family life and personal engagements. It also concerns one's own way of operating between the two axis points: his own way of practising Sufism on the one hand and the general expected discipline sketched and imposed by his close community and the authorized makers of its ethos, on the other. It was very interesting for me to note that the Sufi lexicon could, in certain cases, express the dynamic relationships between those two points. One interesting example relates to early Sufi theories on *waqt*, that is, the mystic moment. The statement 'he was the one of his *waqt*' is introduced by Sulamī, Qushayrī and others to indicate the high spiritual positions of their heroes in the eyes of their contemporaries. The word *waqt*, which refers on many occasions to the distinct personal experience of the mystic state (*ḥāl*), could imply on other occasions the unique position the Sufi enjoyed in his large community or even carry the two meanings at the same time.

My efforts to extract certain aspects of Sufi family engagements and interpersonal conflicts from the available texts were monitored by the twofold division that I chose for the main argument: the personal realm and the communal realm. I made a clear statement at the beginning of the book that this division was not intended to present any presupposed dichotomy between the two realms. In all the chapters, connections between the two realms had a strong presence. Throughout the two major sections of this book, I tried to show that the establishment of the Sufi communal identity and the formation of early Sufis as a clear and distinct religious group, which was in fact a progressive and a long process, could be witnessed earlier than originally thought. In the first section, Sufi family ties were discussed as a mirror for communal interests and collective articulations of the Sufis as a group, while the communal aspects of the latter in the second section were discussed as a mirror for personal dimensions of certain Sufi personalities. Sufis' personal lives could, by all means, reflect one of the most remarkable facets of tension that Sufism brought about in normative Islamic life: the essential tension between the renunciatory mode of life originated in the pre-Islamic and early Islamic traditions of *zuhd*, at least during Sufism' formative period, on the one hand, and the religious-social structure of Islam itself, which is a communal-familial-based institution *par excellence*, on the other. Notably, due to many changes that occurred in later Sufism, the renunciatory mode of life became redefined by the Sufis, and the tension between those two modes moved to other domains and took other forms.

The renunciatory practices of *zuhhād* (the early ascetics of Islam) could include, among many others, coldness towards one's wife and offspring. Such approaches usually tended to consider women as well as sexual activities as social attachments that were believed to distract men from a completely pure devotional life. This, indeed, was the major reason for the disparagement of women in the second/eighth and early third/ninth-century books of renunciation (*kutub al-zuhd*). Celebrating coldness both toward women and familial commitments became documented also in the writings of certain early Sufis. This theoretical tendency went side by side with the familial and marital relationships conducted in reality. Afterwards, in the course of the fourth/tenth and fifth/eleventh centuries, this renunciatory tone turned into clear declarations of the disadvantages of marital relationships for one's spiritual life. Sufi authors provide detailed discussions on this concern while some of them could even tell us their own personal experience as in the case of Jullābī Hujwīrī. Even when a certain author attempted to prove that a comprehensive family life in accordance with the high Islamic communal ideal did not contradict the Sufi inner life with God, the tension between the two aspects of life was still implied and could not be ignored, at least on the theoretical level.

However, Sufis' actual lives in the framework of their particular communities started witnessing the appearance of the female actors. A growing number of women succeeded in integrating into the general fabric of Sufi piety as the outstanding biographical work of Sulamī indicates. Women started to undertake an increasingly fashionable method of associating Sufi spheres through the influential system of financial support (*arfāq*). The increasing female involvement in Sufi circles and associations, besides other dynamics, contributed to changing the very principles on which the Sufi system of thought in its earlier stage had relied. After the fifth/eleventh century, Sufi writings gave way to theories on the symbolic feminine element in spiritual life. Works such as those of Ibn ʿArabī and Bahāʾ al-Dīn Walad are the most outspoken among the positive and symbolic images of femininity in medieval

Muslim spirituality. Female beauty could be seen as a manifestation of the absolute divine beauty. However, the positive approaches towards women were not restricted to this symbolic realm. In parallel, a new comprehensive system of thought appeared in the writings of the great Sufi authors of this period where marriage itself came to be considered one of the clear proofs of God's ultimate state of grace. This means that in the exalted rank of *intihāʾ* (reaching the final destination of the Sufi path), the mystic becomes allowed to practise everything he had not been allowed to practise as a beginner because he is believed to be completely protected by God against being occupied by his earthly life at the expense of his heavenly life. The idea was not unknown in early Sufi writings. However, in later Sufi manuals it gained a central position in the Sufi doctrinal system. Sufi sheikhs, accordingly, were given permission to enjoy various acts of relaxation and ease, such as having many wives and enslaved women and possessing property.

Studying the distinctive cases of Sufi mothers by means of integrating the personal and communal realms was intended to challenge, to the degree that the available data allow, the iconic image of mothers, according to which the idea of a mother as an ultimate support in Sufi domains goes without saying. Mothers who were Sufis themselves as well as mothers of Sufi figures provide us with different narratives of the harmony or even the lack of harmony between diversified maternal identities and Sufi devotional life.

On the other side of the maternal relationship coin, studying the cases of maternal uncles could shed light on additional points of conjunction between the personal and the communal aspects of life on both sides, the Sufi nephews and their Sufi uncles who acted, very frequently, as their Sufi masters and guides. When the Sufi master was none other than the maternal uncle, the boundaries between the family space and the Sufi space where the devotee received his spiritual guidance dissolve to become one integrated unit. Although authors of Sufi hagiographies were not interested in portraying the family background of their heroes, including the latter's ties with their uncles, some items of the existing data provide an interesting portrait of cases such as that of Sahl al-Tustarī and his uncle Muḥammad b. Sawwār and that of Junayd and his uncle Sarī al-Saqaṭī. Following the available fragments relating to Junayd and his uncle, for instance, helps create an image of Junayd different than the image that Sufi and non-Sufi sources usually portrayed of him. Junayd, the man of self-confidence and even arrogance as it appears from the sources, shows a high degree of modesty before his uncle and refuses to carry out his uncle's request to preach because he felt great modesty before people. Such a piece of data, I showed, could be perceived differently. Although the authors who quoted this story sought to highlight Junayd's modesty, the opposite description of a man, one who does not trust others including his own master, his uncle, could be also implied here. It appears that in Jāmī's day, the veneration that Junayd gained among early Sufis started to raise criticism. On one occasion in his biographical work, for instance, Jāmī writes that Ruwaym b. Aḥmad is better than Junayd and that 'one hair taken from Ruwaym is better than one hundred Junayds.'[1] Interestingly, Junayd is quoted by Jāmī to have said: 'People think that I am the disciple of Sarī al-Saqaṭī while [in fact!] I am the disciple of Muḥammad b. ʿAlī al-Qaṣṣāb.'![2]

Few were the documented cases of paternal uncles who acted as influential masters of renowned Sufi personalities. There was a strong impression from the examined material that the influence of maternal uncles on their nephews' careers was, for the most part, more supportive than that of their mothers.

It is clear for us that early Sufis were community oriented. Even those controversial personalities such as al-Ḥakīm al-Tirmidhī and Abū Yazīd al-Basṭāmī had circles of close disciples as they had circles of contemporary opponents and enemies. Each of them had his own distinguished set of interpersonal relationships. Tirmidhī could experience an attempt of exclusion addressed to him by one of the outspoken representatives of Baghdadi Sufism, Jaʿfar al-Khuldī. However, in his autobiography, Tirmidhī states clearly that he was surrounded by many followers and companions. Basṭāmī's case was different. He succeeded in gaining a famed reputation even among pious female Sufis despite his ecstatic utterances. Parallel to the early networks of communal Sufi relationships, one chapter in this book was devoted to certain individual cases whose heroes tended to reject what I called the general ethos of early Sufism and, thereby, detached themselves partly on some occasions and completely on others, from the life and activities of their contemporary Sufi communities. The detailed examination of Niffarī demonstrates an attempt made by one pious man to completely detach himself from the Sufi mainstream institution that succeeded in the course of the third/ninth and fourth/tenth centuries to monopolize the spiritual scene of Iraq, to stand at its very front and to gain the authority to decide who could be a

[1] Jāmī, *Nafaḥāt al-uns*, 95. [2] Ibid., 82.

Sufi and who could not. Though Niffarī's case stood at the most extreme edge of rejecting the monopoly of *ṣūfiyya*, this distinct Baghdad-centred movement that applied to itself exclusively the title and could distinguish itself with particular characteristics at that time, there are also cases of Sufi personalities who had their own ways to negotiate that monopoly and to dispute its representatives. Sufi personalities did not detach themselves from the communal lives of their contemporary Sufis; however, they had to handle their own interpersonal tensions and conflicts. The two final chapters narrate the stories of tensions of the latter type. Within the broad category of *niqār*, which is allegedly perceived as indicating mere differences in opinions and verbal controversies between early Sufis on certain doctrines and practices, many actual tensions, conflicts and enmities were also implied. In Chapter 7 I argued that both *munāqara* and *niqār*, which appear in early Sufi sources, refer to the strategy that early Sufis used in their attempts to confront a reality that witnessed disputes between many Sufi personalities. The two terms were not meant to carry the meaning of the disputes or the boasting themselves, but the reaction and the way of encountering those disputes through developing manners of conduct (*ādāb*) and integrating the ways of treating internal controversies under them. The terms *munāfara* and *nifār*, on the other hand, designate the very act of disputing.

The sections devoted to *mukātabāt* (pieces of correspondence) in the major Sufi compilations could be seen as more than indications of different opinions. In the texts of *mukātabāt* it is not unusual to come across pieces of advice and statements of counsel addressed by the Sufi sheikhs to their associates. In certain cases, these point to probable interpersonal controversies between the corresponding parties. Such verbal confrontations might have documented processes of exclusion initiated in reality by certain Sufi figures towards those who were not exactly members of the mainstream, and those who did not exactly succeed in gaining the sympathy of the consensually acclaimed Sufis whose sayings and acts were the building blocks of the main body of early Sufi ethos and doctrinal system.

The critical voices of Ruwaym b. Aḥmad and of Abū Bakr al-Ḥusayn b. ʿAlī b. Yazdānyār towards their contemporary Sufis, for instance, were crossbred with additional data deduced both from Sufi biographies and non-Sufi historiographies. Thus, some of the obscure constituents of the relationships between each of those figures with his close community came to be seen in a new light. It was Junayd who seems to have warned his fellows against visiting Ruwaym. As for Ibn Yazdānyār, even Sarrāj, the renowned author of *Kitāb al-lumaʿ*, accuses him of treason (*khiyāna*) for the severe critique that he addressed to the Sufis. I have tried to obtain a position to better understand the probable contents of such a critique and the dynamics of relationships that surrounded it and, to a remarkable extent, had to be subordinated to it.

What motivated me to treat *ṣuḥbat al-aḥdāth* in the last chapter was the need to delve into the different strategies used by early Sufis to treat what seemed to be an individual matter that progressively transformed into a collective Sufi issue, as well as an identifying feature of the whole body of Sufism in the eyes of its enemies. How could a delicate topic such as *ṣuḥbat al-aḥdāth* become a rich domain for diverse patterns of relationships between individual Sufis and the communal ethos? By nominating it as one of the common *āfāt* of the Sufis, the makers of Sufi ethos contributed, like their attackers, to transforming the individual frame of *ṣuḥbat al-aḥdāth* into a more communal one by insisting on the idea that this was a widespread epidemic among Sufis. The daring statements of controversial personalities such as Yūsuf b. al-Ḥusayn al-Rāzī and Abū Ḥamza al-Ṣūfī reveal one instrument for challenging the Baghdadi Sufi institution both in literary form (through the statements themselves) and through actual behaviour. Examining Ibn al-Ḥusayn's fragments in the sources revealed a frequent use of the first pronoun and a clear individual tone while describing his impure repentance and spiritual weakness. To add to this his inclination to *malāmatī* behaviour and his correspondence with Junayd in which mutual accusations were delivered, I concluded that the literary image of Ibn al-Ḥusayn and his relevance to companionship with youth should be seen as an entrance point to a wider array of notions, interpersonal ties and individual tendencies where many other personalities could play their own and distinctive roles.

Appendix: A Survery of Sulamī's accounts of Pious Women in His *Dhikr al-niswa* (Rkia Cornell's edition, 1999)

Women introduced as wives	Women introduced as mothers	Women introduced as sisters	Women introduced as companions / servants or/disciples of other women	Women introduced as *ustādh* (teacher) of other pious women	Women introduced as companions/associates of male pious or women whom great pious men used to consult	Women introduced as residents of different places only
Nusiyya bint Salmān, 93	Umm ʿAbd Allāh (mother of Ismāʿīl b. ʿAyyāsh), 101	Saʿīda bint Zayd (sister of Ḥammād b. Zayd), 109	Maryam of Baṣra (companion and servant of Rābiʿa al-ʿAdawiyya), 85	Ḥukayma al-Dimashqiyya (*ustādh* of Rābiʿa bint Ismāʿīl), 127	Rābiʿa al-ʿAdawiyya, 75–81	Lubāba al-Mutaʿabbida of Jerusalem, 83
Rābiʿa bint Ismāʿīl, (wife of Aḥmad b. Abī al-Ḥawārī), 139	Fāṭima bint Aḥmad (mother of Abū ʿAbd Allāh al-Rūdhbārī), 215	Ḥafṣa bint Sīrīn (sister of Muḥammad b. Sīrīn), 123	Muʿādha al-ʿAdawiyya (companion of Rābiʿa al-ʿAdawiyya) (this piece of data could not be true. Muʿādha lived a hundred years before Rābiʿa)., 89		Shabaka al-Baṣriyya (companion of her brother), 91	Muʾmina bint Buhlūl, 87
ʿĀʾisha, wife of Abū Ḥafṣ al-Naysābūrī, 157	Ziyāda bint al-Khaṭṭāb (mother of Ismāʿīl b. Ibrāhīm al-Quhistānī), 231	Zubda and Muḍgha (sisters of Bishr al-Ḥāfī), 193	Ghufayra al-ʿĀbida (companion of Muʿādha al-ʿAdawiyya), 97		Rābiʿa al-Azdiyya ('ʿAbd al-Wāḥid b. Zayd was her companion and transmitted reports about her'), 129.	Rayḥāna al-Wāliha of Baṣra (reported to be a contemporary of Ṣāliḥ al-Murrī too), 95
Ṣafrāʾ of Rayy (wife of Abū Ḥafṣ al-Naysābūrī)	Umm al-Ḥusayn (mother of Abū Bishr al-Ḥalāwī), 239	ʿAbda and Āmina (sisters of Abū Sulaymān al-Dārānī), 195	Unaysa bint ʿAmr al-ʿAdawiyya (*tilmīdha*, disciple) of Rābiʿa al-ʿAdawiyya		Fāṭima al-Naysābūriyya ('Dhū al-Nūn al-Miṣrī sought her advice'), 143	ʿĀfiya al-Mushtāqa of Baṣra, 99
Umm ʿAlī (wife of Aḥmad b. Khiḍrūya), 169		Maymūna (sister of Ibrāhīm al-Khawwāṣ), 217	Kurdiyya bint ʿAmr (servant of Shaʿwāna), 117			Shaʿwāna of Ubulla, 107

Fakhrawayh bint ʿAlī (wife of Abū ʿAmr b. Nujayd, Sulamī's grandfather)		Ḥasnā bint Fayrūz of Yemen, 121
Fāṭima Umm al-Yumn (wife of Abū ʿAlī al-Rūdhbārī), 187	Baḥriyya (companion of Shaqīq al-Balkhī), 149	Lubāba al-ʿĀbida of Syria, 125
ʿĀʾisha of Merv (wife of Aḥmad b. al-Sarī), 197	Amat al-Ḥamīd bint al-Qāsim (companion of Abū Saʿīd al-Kharrāz), 155	Umm Sālim al-Rāsibiyya of Baṣra, 133
Umm ʿAbd Allāh (wife of ʿAbd Allāh al-Sijzī), 201	Fāṭima bint ʿAbd Allāh (companion of Abū Saʿīd al-Kharrāz), 173	ʿUbayda bint Abī Kilāb of Baṣra, 135
Fuṭayma (wife of Ḥamdūn al-Qaṣṣār), 207	Fāṭima bint Aḥmad al-Ḥijāfiyya (companion of Zakariyyā al-Sukhtanī), 181	Hind bint al-Muhallab of Baṣra, 127
Amat Allāh al-Jabaliyya (wife of ʿAbd Allāh al-Jabalī), 209	Fāṭima bint Aḥmad b. Hāniʾ (companion of Abū ʿUthmān al-Ḥīrī), 199	Umm Hārūn of Damascus, 147
Qusayma (wife of Yaʿqūb of Tinnīs), 211	Marhāʾ of Nisibis (associated with many pious men of her time), 213	Fāṭima al-Bardaʿiyya of Ardabīl, 151
Malika bint Aḥmad (wife of al-Ḥasan b. Ḥayyawayh), 233	Al-Wahaṭiyya Umm al-Faḍl (associated with Ibn Khafīf and many others), 227	ʿĀʾisha of Dīnawar, 153
ʿĀʾisha bint Aḥmad of Merv (wife of ʿAbd al-Wāḥid al-Sayyārī), 259	Fāṭima bint ʿImrān (associated with Abū ʿAbd Allāh al-Zāhid), 235	Muʾnisa of Syria, 175

(*cont.*)

Women introduced as wives	Women introduced as mothers	Women introduced as sisters	Women introduced as companions / servants or/disciples of other women	Women introduced as *ustādh* (teacher) of other pious women	Women introduced as companions/associates of male pious or women whom great pious men used to consult	Women introduced as residents of different places only
					Umm Kulthūm (associated with Naṣrābādhī and ʿAbd Allāh b. Munāzil), 241	ʿAmra of Farghāna, 191
					ʿAzīza al-Harawiyya, 243	Ḥabība of Baṣra, 203
					Umm ʿAlī bint ʿAbd Allāh b. Ḥamshādh (companion of Naṣrābādhī), 245	Fāṭima of Damascus, 205
					Surayra al-Sharqiyya (companion of Abū Bakr al-Fārisī), 247	ʿAwna of Nishapur, 221
					Jumʿa bint Aḥmad known as Umm al-Ḥusayn al-Qurashiyya (companion of Naṣrābādhī and Khiḍrī and others), 251	Qurashiyya of Nasā, 225
						ʿAbdūsa bint al-Ḥārith of Dāmaghān, 237
						ʿUnayza of Baghdad, 249
						Umm al-Ḥusayn al-Warrāqa from Iraq, 253
15	4	7	5	1	19	22

Bibliography

PRIMARY SOURCES

ʿAbd al-Ghāfir b. Ismāʿīl al-Fārisī, Abū al-Ḥasan, *al-Muntakhab min al-siyāq li-taʾrīkh naysābūr*, selected by Ibrāhīm b. Muḥammad al-Ṣarīfīnī, ed. by Muḥammad ʿAbd al-ʿAzīz (Beirut: Dār al-Kutub al-ʿIlmiyya, 1989).

ʿAbd Allāh Anṣārī Haravī, *Ṭabaqāt al-ṣūfiyya*, ed. by Akram Shifāʾī (Tehran: N.p., n.d.).

ʿAbd Allāh Anṣārī Haravī, *Manāzil al-sāʾirīn* (Beirut: Dār al-Kutub al-ʿIlmiyya, 1988).

ʿAbd Allāh b. al-Mubārak, *Kitāb al-zuhd wa-l-raqāʾiq*, ed. by Ḥabīb al-Raḥmān al-Aʿẓamī (Mālkūn, India: Majlis Iḥyāʾ al-Maʿārif, 1971).

al-Ājurrī, Abū Bakr, *Dhamm al-liwāṭ*, ed. by Majdī al-Sayyid Ibrāhīm (Cairo: Maktabat al-Qurʾān, n.d.).

al-ʿĀmirī, Muḥammad b. Ḥabīb, *Aḥkām al-naẓar ilā al-muḥarramāt wa-mā fīhi min al-khaṭar wa-l-āfāt*, ed. by Mashhūr Salmān (Beirut: Dār Ibn Ḥazm, 1995).

Anonymous author, *Adab al-mulūk*, ed. by Bernd Radtke (Beirut: Beiruter Texte und Studien Herausgegeben vom Orient-Istitut der Deutschen Morgenländischen Gesellschaft in Kommission bei Franz Steiner Verlag Stuttgart, 1991).

ʿAṭṭār, Farīd-al-Dīn, *Tadhkirat al-awliyāʾ*, ed. by R. A. Nicholson (Leiden: Brill, 1905).

Muslim Saints and Mystics: Episodes from the Tadhkirat al-awliyāʾ (Memorial of the Saints), trans. by A. J. Arberry (London: Routledge & Kegan Paul, 1966).

Augustine (Saint), *Confessions*, trans. by Henry Chadwick (Oxford: Oxford University Press, 1998).

ʿAyn al-Quḍāt Hamadhānī, Abū al-Maʿālī ʿAbd Allāh b. Muḥammad, *Tamhīdāt*, ed. by ʿAfīf ʿUsayrān (Tehran: Kitābkhānih-yi Manūchihrī, 1341 *Shamsī*/1962).

al-Basṭāmī, ʿAbd Allāh b. Khalīl, *Mishkāt al-miṣbāḥ fī bayān awrād al-masāʾ wa-l-ṣabāḥ*, MS Yahuda collection 1086 (15), fols. 21a–50a.

al-Bāʿūniyya, ʿĀʾisha, *al-Muntakhab fī uṣūl al-rutab fī ʿilm al-taṣawwuf* (*The Principles of Sufism*), ed. and trans. by Emil Homerin (New York and London: New York University Press, 2014).

al-Bidlīsī, ʿAmmār, *Ṣawm al-qalb*, in *Zwei Mystische Schriften des ʿAmmār Al-Bidlīsī*, ed. by Edward Badeen (Beirut: Orient Institut in Kommission bei Franz Steiner Verlag Stuttgart, 1999).

al-Bukhārī, Muḥammad b. Ismāʿīl, *Ṣaḥīḥ al-Bukhārī* (Beirut: Dār al-Kutub al-ʿIlmiyya, 2001).

al-Daylamī, Abū al-Ḥasan ʿAlī b. Muḥammad, *Sīrat al-Shaykh al-Kabīr Abī ʿAbd Allāh Muḥammad ibn Khafīf al-Shīrāzī*, trans. from the Persian into Arabic (after the original Arabic had been lost) by Ibrāhīm al-Dusūqī Shatā (Cairo: Al-Hayʾa al-ʿĀmma li-Shuʾūn al-Maṭābiʿ al-Amīriyya, 1977).

A Treatise on Mystical Love, trans. by Joseph Norment Bell and Hassan Maḥmūd al-Shāfiʿī (Edinburgh: Edinburgh University Press, 2005).

ʿAṭf al-alif al-maʾlūf ʿalā al-lām al-maʿṭūf, ed. by Joseph Norment Bell and Maḥmūd al-Shāfiʿī (Beirut and Cairo: Dār al-Kitāb al-Lubnānī and Dār al-Kitāb al-Miṣrī, 2007).

al-Dhahabī, Muḥammad b. Aḥmad, *al-ʿIbar fī khabar man ghabar*, ed. by Ṣalāḥ al-Dīn al-Munajjid and Sayyid Fuʾād (Kuwait: Dāʾirat al-Maṭbūʿāt, 1960–1966).

al-Kabāʾir (Damascus and Beirut: Al-Maktaba al-Umawiyya, 1971).

Siyar aʿlām al-nubalāʾ, ed. by Shuʿayb al-Arnāʾūṭ et al. (Beirut: Dār al-Risāla, 1982–1988).

Tadhkirat al-ḥuffāẓ (Beirut: Dār al-Kutub al-ʿIlmiyya, n.d.).

Tārīkh al-islām wa-wafayāt al-mashāhīr wa-l-aʿlām, ed. by Bashshār Maʿrūf (Beirut: Dār al-Gharb al-Islāmī, 2003).

Ebn-e Monavvar, Moḥammad, *The Secrets of God's Mystical Oneness or the Spiritual Stations of Shaikh Abu Sa'id [Asrār al-towḥid fi maqāmāt al-Šeyḵ Abi Sa'id]*, trans. with notes and introduction by John O'Kane (Costa Mesa, Calif. and New York: Mazda Publishers, 1992).

al-Ghamrī al-Wāsiṭī, Shams al-Dīn Muḥammad b. ʿUmar, *al-Ḥukm al-maḍbūṭ fī taḥrīm fiʿl qawm Lūṭ*, ed. by ʿUbayd Allāh al-Miṣrī (Ṭanṭā: Dār al-Ṣaḥāba, 1988).

al-ʿUnwān fī taḥrīm muʿāsharat al-shabāb wa-l-niswān, MS Maktabat al-Malik ʿAbd Allāh b. ʿAbd al-ʿAzīz (928, 6 fols.)

al-Ghazālī, Abū Ḥāmid Muḥammad, *Iḥyāʾ ʿulūm al-dīn*, ed. by Muḥammad ʿAbd al-Malik al-Zughbī (Cairo: Dār al-Manār, n.d.).

al-Ghazālī, Abū Ḥāmid Muḥammad, *al-Maʿārif al-ʿaqliyya*, ed. by ʿAbd al-Karīm al-ʿUthmān (Damascus: Dār al-Fikr, 1963).

Kīmyā-i saʿādat (Tehran: Kitābkhānih va-Chāpkhānih-yi Markazī, 1967).

al-Ghazālī, Aḥmad, *Tracts on Listening to Music Being Dhamm al-Malāhī and Bawāriq al-Ilmāʿ*, ed. by James Robson (London: Printed and published under the patronage of the Royal Asiatic Society, 1938).

Sawāniḥ, bā taṣḥīḥāt-i jadīd va-muqaddame va-tawzīḥāt-i Naṣrullāh Pūrjavādī (Tehran: Intishārāt-i Bunyād-i Farhang-i Irān, 1359 *Shamsī*).

al-Ḥakīm al-Tirmidhī, Muḥammad b. ʿAlī, *Buduww shaʾn al-Ḥakīm al-Tirmidhī*, in al-Ḥakīm al-Tirmidhī, *Kitāb khatm al-awliyāʾ*, ed. by ʿUthmān Yaḥyā (Beirut: Al-Maṭbaʿa al-Khāthūlīkiyya, 1965).

The Concept of Sainthood in Early Islamic Mysticism: Two Works by al-Ḥakīm al-Tirmidhī, trans. by Bernd Radtke and John O'Kane (Richmond, Surrey: Curzon Press, 1996).

al-Ḥallāj, al-Ḥusayn b. Manṣūr, *Kitāb al-ṭawāsīn*, ed. by Louis Massignon (Paris: Geuthner, 1913).

al-Haytamī, Aḥmad b. Muḥammad b. ʿAlī b. Ḥajar, *Kitāb al-zawājir ʿan iqtirāf al-kabāʾir* (Cairo: al-Maktaba al-Khayriyya, 1284 A.H.).

Ḥunayn b. Isḥāq, *Jawāmiʿ kitāb ṭīmāwus*, in *Aflāṭūn fī al-Islām*, ed. by ʿAbd al-Raḥmān Badawī (Tehran: Muʾassasat-i Muṭālaʿāt-i Islāmī-i Dānishgāh-i Mak-Gīl, 1974), 85–119.

Ibn Abī Yaʿlā, Abū al-Ḥusayn Muḥammad, *Ṭabaqāt al-ḥanābila*, ed. by ʿAbd al-Raḥmān al-ʿUthaymīn (Makka: Al-Amāna al-ʿĀmma li-l-Iḥtifāl bi-Murūr Miʾat ʿĀm ʿalā Taʾsīs al-Mamlaka, 1999).

Ibn al-ʿAdīm, Kamāl al-Dīn ʿUmar b. Aḥmad, *Bughyat al-ṭalab fī tārīkh ḥalab*, ed. by Suhayl Zakkār (Beirut: Dār al-Fikr, 1988).

Ibn ʿArabī, Muḥyī al-Dīn, *ʿUqlat al-mustawfiz*, in Ibn ʿArabī, *Kleinere Schriften des Ibn Al-ʿArabī*, ed. by H. S. Nyberg (Leiden: Brill, 1919).

al-Futūḥāt al-makkiyya (Cairo: *Al-Bābī al-Ḥalabī*, 1293/1876).

Ibn ʿAsākir, ʿAlī b. al-Ḥasan, *Taʾrīkh madīnat dimashq: tarājim al-nisāʾ*, ed. by Sukayna al-Shihābī (Damascus: Dār al-Fikr, 1981).

Ibn ʿAṭāʾ Allāh al-Sikandarī, *Tartīb al-sulūk*, ed. by Khālid Zuhrī (Beirut: Dār al-Kutub al-ʿIlmiyya, 2004).

Ibn al-Athīr al-Jazrī, *Usd al-ghāba fī maʿrifat al-ṣaḥāba*, ed. by Muḥammad al-Bannā and Muḥammad ʿĀshūr (Cairo: Dār al-Shaʿb, 1970).

Ibn Baṭṭūṭa, *Riḥlat Ibn Baṭṭūṭa, tuḥfat al-nuẓẓār fī gharāʾib al-amṣār wa-ʿajāʾib al-asfār*, ed. by Muḥammad al-ʿAryān and Muṣṭafā al-Qaṣṣāṣ (Beirut: Dār Iḥyāʾ al-ʿUlūm, 1987).

Ibn al-Dabbāgh, ʿAbd al-Raḥmān b. Muḥammad al-Anṣārī, *Kitāb mashāriq anwār al-qulūb wa-mafātīḥ asrār al-ghuyūb*, ed. by Hellmut Ritter (Beirut: Dār Ṣādir and Dār Bayrūt, 1959).

Ibn al-Fuwaṭī, ʿAbd al-Razzāq b. Aḥmad, *al-Ḥawādith al-jāmiʿa wa-l-tajārib al-nāfiʿa fī al-miʾa al-sābiʿa*, ed. by Mahdī al-Najm (Beirut: Dār al-Kutub al-ʿIlmiyya, 2003).

Ibn al-ʿImād, ʿAbd al-Ḥayy b. Aḥmad, *Shadharāt al-dhahab fī akhbār man dhahab*, ed. by ʿAbd al-Qādir al-Arnāʾūṭ and Maḥmūd al-Arnāʾūṭ (Damascus: Dār Ibn Kathīr, 1988).

Ibn al-Jawzī, Jamāl al-Dīn Abū al-Faraj, *Dhamm al-hawā*, ed. by Muṣṭafā ʿAbd al-Wāḥid (Cairo: Dār al-Kutub al-Ḥadītha, 1962).

Ṣifat al-ṣafwa (Ḥaydarābād al-Dukn, India: Maṭbaʿat Dāʾirat al-Maʿārif al-ʿUthmāniyya, 1936).

Birr al-wālidayn, ed. by Muḥammad ʿAbd al-Qādir ʿAṭā (Beirut: Muʾassasat al-Kutub al-Thaqāfiyya, 1988).

Kitāb al-quṣṣāṣ wa-l-mudhakkirīn, ed. by Muḥammad al-Ṣabbāgh (Beirut: Al-Maktab al-Islāmī, 1988).

Talbīs Iblīs, ed. by ʿIṣām al-Ḥarastānī and Muḥammad al-Zughlī (Beirut: al-Maktab al-Islāmī, 1994).

Akhbār al-nisā' (incorrectly attributed to Ibn Qayyim al-Jawziyya), ed. by Aḥmad b. 'Alī (Cairo: Dār al-Manār, 1998).

al-Muntaẓam fī tārīkh al-mulūk wa-l-umam, ed. by Muḥammad 'Abd al-Qādir 'Aṭā and Muṣṭafā 'Abd al-Qādir 'Aṭā (Beirut: Dār al-Kutub al-'Ilmiyya, n.d.).

Talbīs Iblīs (Delusion of the Devil), trans. by David Samuel Margoliouth (New Delhi, 2011).

Ibn al-Jazrī, *al-Zahr al-fā'iḥ fī dhikr man tanazzaha 'an al-dhunūb wa-l-makārih* (Cairo: Al-Maṭba'a al-Milījiyya, 1906).

Ibn Kathīr, Ismā'īl b. 'Umar Abū al-Fidā', *al-Bidāya wa-l-nihāya* (Beirut: Maktabat al-Ma'ārif, 1991).

Ibn Khafīf, Abū 'Abd Allāh, *Kitāb al-iqtiṣād*, in Florian Sobieroj, Ibn Ḫafīf aš-Šīrāzī und seine Schrift zur Novizenerziehung (*Kitāb al-Iqtiṣād*): Biographische Studien, Edition und Übersetzung, Inaugural-Dissertation zur Erlangung der Doktorwürde der Philosophischen Fakultäten der Albert-Ludwigs-Universität zur Freiburg, 1992.

Ibn Khamīs al-Mawṣilī, Al-Ḥusayn b. Naṣr, *Manāqib al-abrār wa-maḥāsin al-akhyār fī ṭabaqāt al-ṣūfiyya*, ed. by Sa'īd 'Abd al-Fattāḥ (Beirut: Dār al-Kutub al-'Ilmiyya, 2006).

Ibn Khillikān, Aḥmad b. Muḥammad Shams al-Dīn, *Wafayāt al-a'yān wa-anbā' abnā' al-zamān*, ed. by Iḥsān 'Abbās (Beirut: Dār Ṣādir, 1968–1972).

Ibn Manẓūr, Muḥammad b. Mukarram, *Mukhtaṣar ta'rīkh dimashq*, ed. by Rūḥiyya al-Naḥḥās, Riyāḍ 'Abd al-Ḥamīd Murād and Muḥammad Muṭī' al-Ḥāfiẓ (Damascus: Dār al-Fikr, 1984–1988).

Lisān al-'arab (Beirut: Dār Ṣādir, 1994).

Ibn al-Mulaqqin, Abū Ḥafṣ 'Umar b. 'Alī, *Ṭabaqāt al-awliyā'*, ed. by Nūr al-Dīn Sharība (Beirut: Dār al-Ma'rifa, 1986).

Ibn al-Muzayyin, Aḥmad b. 'Umar al-Anṣārī al-Qurṭubī, *Kashf al-qinā' 'an ḥukm al-wajd wa-l-samā'* (Ṭanṭā: Dār al-Ṣaḥāba, 1992).

Ibn al-Nadīm, *al-Fihrist* (Beirut: Dār al-Ma'rifa, n.d.).

Ibn al-Qaysarānī, Muḥammad b. Ṭāhir al-Maqdisī, *Ṣafwat al-taṣawwuf*, ed. by Ghāda al-Muqaddim 'Udra (Beirut: Dār al-Muntakhab, 1995).

Ibn Sa'd, Muḥammad, *Kitāb al-ṭabaqāt al-kabīr*, ed. by 'Alī Muḥammad 'Umar (Cairo: Maktabat al-Khānjī, 2001).

Ibn al-Sā'ī, 'Alī b. Anjab, *Akhbār al-Ḥallāj aw munājayāt al-Ḥallāj*, ed. by L. Massignon and B. Kraus (Paris: Maktabat Laroze, 1936).

Ibn Yazdānyār, Abū Ja'far, *Rawḍat al-murīdīn*, Princeton MS. 968, fols. 2a–98a.

Ibn al-Zayyāt, Abū Ya'qūb Yūsuf b. Yaḥyā al-Tādilī, *al-Tashawwuf ilā rijāl al-taṣawwuf wa-akhbār Abī al-'Abbās al-Sabtī*, ed. by Aḥmad al-Tawfīq (Casa Blanca: Manshūrāt Kulliyyat al-Ādāb, 1997).

Ikhwān al-Ṣafā', *Rasā'il ikhwān al-ṣafā' wa-khullān al-wafā'*, ed. by Khayr-al-Dīn al-Ziriklī (Cairo: Al-Maktaba al-Tijāriyya, 1928).

al-Iṣfahānī, Abū Nu'aym, *Ḥilyat al-awliyā' wa-ṭabaqāt al-aṣfiyā'*, ed. by Muṣṭafā 'Abd al-Qādir 'Aṭā (Beirut: Dār al-Kutub al-'Ilmiyya, 1997).

Izz al-Dīn Ibn 'Abd al-Salām, *al-Fatāwā al-mawṣiliyya*, ed. by Iyād al-Ṭabbā' (Damascus: Dār al-Fikr, 1999).

Ja'far b. Manṣūr al-Yaman, *The Master and the Disciple: An Early Islamic Spiritual Dialogue*, a new Arabic edition and English translation of *Kitāb al-'Ālim wa-l-Ghulām*, ed. and trans. by James Morris (London and New-York: I.B. Tauris in association with The Institute of Ismaili Studies, 2001).
al-Jāḥiẓ, 'Amr b. Baḥr, *Kitāb al-ḥayawān*, ed. by 'Abd al-Salām Hārūn (Cairo: Al-Bābī al-Ḥalabī, 1938).
al-Bayān wa-l-tabyīn, ed. by 'Abd al-Salām Hārūn (Cairo: Maktabat al-Khānjī, 1968).
Jāmī, 'Abd al-Raḥmān, *Nafaḥāt al-uns*, ed. by Mahdī Pūr (Tehran: Intishārāṭ-i Kitābfurūshī-i Maḥmūdī, 1918).
al-Jawbarī, 'Abd al-Raḥmān b. 'Umar, *al-Mukhtār fī kashf al-asrār wa-hatk al-astār*, ed. by 'Iṣām Shubbārū (Beirut: Dār al-Taḍāmun, 1992).
al-Jullābī al-Hujwīrī, Abū al-Ḥasan 'Alī b. 'Uthmānm, *Kashf al-maḥjūb*, ed. by Valentin Zukovsky (Leningrad: Maṭba'at-i Dār al-'Ulūm-i Ittiḥād-i Jamāhīr-i Shūravī-yi Sūsyālīstī, 1926).
The Kashf al-Maḥjūb: The Oldest Persian Treatise on Sufism, trans. by Reynold A. Nicholson (London: Luzac and Company Ltd., 1976).
Junayd, Abū al-Qāsim, '*Rasā'il wa-rudūd*', in *Tāj al-'ārifīn: Dirāsāt wa-nuṣūṣ manshūra wa-ghayr manshūra*, ed. by Muḥammad Muṣṭafā (Cairo: Dār al-Ṭibā'a al-Muḥammadiyya, 1987).
'Rasā'il al-Junayd', in Ali Hassan Abdel-Kader, *The Life, Personality and Writings of al-Junayd: A Study of a Third/Ninth Century Mystic with an Edition and Translation of His Writings* (London: Luzac & Company, 1962), the Arabic text, 1–62.
Tāj al-'ārifīn al-Junayd al-Baghdādī: al-A'māl al-kāmila, ed. by Su'ād al-Ḥakīm (Cairo: Dār al-Shurūq, 2004).
Junayd Shīrāzī, Mu'īn-al-Dīn, *Shadd al-izār fī ḥaṭṭ al-awzār 'an zuwwār al-mazār*, ed. by Muḥammad Qazvīnī and 'Abbās Iqbāl (Tehran: Chāpkhānih-yi Majlis 1949).
al-Jurjānī, 'Alī b. Muḥammad, *Kitāb al-ta'rīfāt* (Beirut: Maktabat Lubnān, 1969).
al-Kalābādhī, Abū Bakr, *Kitāb al-ta'arruf li-madhhab ahl al-taṣawwuf*, ed. by 'Abd al-Ḥalīm Maḥmūd and Ṭāha Srūr (Cairo: 'Īsā al-Bābī al-Ḥalabī, 1960).
Kāshānī, 'Izz-al-Dīn Maḥmūd, *Miṣbāḥ al-hidāya wa-miftāḥ al-kifāya*, ed. by Jalāl-al-Dīn Humāyī (Tehran, 1381 *Shamsī*/2002).
al-Kharkūshī, 'Abd al-Malik b. Muḥammad al-Naysābūrī, *Tahdhīb al-asrār*, ed. by Bassām Bārūd (Abū Ẓabī: Al-Majma' al-Thaqāfī, 1999).
al-Kharrāz, Aḥmad b. 'Īsā Abū Sa'īd, *Rasā'il al-Kharrāz*, ed. by Qāsim al-Sāmirrā'ī (Baghdad: Maṭba'at al-Majma' al-'Ilmī al-'Irāqī, 1967).
al-Khaṭīb al-Baghdādī, Aḥmad b. 'Alī, *Ta'rīkh baghdād*, ed. by Bashshār Ma'rūf (Beirut: Dār al-Gharb al-Islāmī, 2001).
al-Kubrā, Najm al-Dīn, *Fawā'iḥ al-jamāl wa-fawātiḥ al-jalāl*, ed. by Ftitz Meier (Wiesbaden: F. Steiner, 1957).
Ādāb al-murīdīn, ed. by Husein Badr al-Dīn (Tehran: Ṣafā, 1362 *Shamsī*).
Maḥmūd b. 'Uthmān, *Kitāb firdaws al-murshidiyya fī asrār al-ṣamadiyya* (*Die Vita des Scheich Abū Isḥāq al-Kāzarūnī*), herausgegeben und eingeleitet von Fritz Meier (Leipzig: Brockhaus, 1948).

Majd-al-Dīn al-Baghdādī, *Tuḥfat al-barara*, partially quoted in Najm al-Dīn al-Kubrā, *Fawā'iḥ al-jamāl wa-fawātiḥ al-jalāl*, ed. by Fritz Meier (Wiesbaden: F. Steiner, 1957), appendix, 279–281, 286–289, 294–295.

al-Makkī, Abū Ṭālib, *Qūt al-qulūb fī mu'āmalat al-maḥbūb wa-waṣf ṭarīq al-murīd ilā maqām al-tawḥīd* (Cairo: Al-Bābī al-Ḥalabī, 1961).

al-Malaṭī, Abū al-Ḥusayn Muḥammad b. Aḥmad, *al-Tanbīh wa-l-radd 'alā ahl al-ahwā' wa-l-bida'*, ed. by Muḥammad al-Kawtharī (Baghdad and Beirut: Maktabat al-Muthannā and Maktabat al-Ma'ārif, 1968).

al-Mālikī, 'Abd Allāh b. Muḥammad Abū Bakr, *Riyāḍ al-nufūs fī ṭabaqāt 'ulamā' al-qayrawān wa-afrīqiyya wa-zuhhādihim wa-nussākihim wa-siyar min akhbārihim wa-faḍā'ilihim wa-awṣāfihim*, ed. by Bashīr al-Bakkūsh (Beirut: Dār al-Gharb al-Islāmī, 1983).

al-Mashtūlī, Muḥammad b. Ḥamīd, *Salwat al-aḥzān li-l-ijtināb 'an mujālasat al-aḥdāth wa-l-niswān*, ed. by Ṭāriq al-Ṭanṭāwī (Cairo: Maktabat Ibn Sīnā, 1991).

al-Mizzī, Yūsuf b. 'Abd al-Raḥmān, *Tahdhīb al-kamāl fī asmā' al-rijāl*, ed. by Bashshār Ma'rūf (Beirut: Mu'assasat al-Risāla, 1983).

al-Mu'āfā b. 'Imrān, *Kitāb al-zuhd*, ed. by 'Āmir Ṣabrī (Beirut: Dār al-Bashā'ir al-Islāmiyya, 1999).

al-Muḥāsibī, al-Ḥārith, '*Risāla fī l-maḥabba*', in Iṣfahānī, *Ḥilyat al-awliyā' wa-ṭ abaqāt al-aṣfiyā'*, ed. by Muṣṭafā 'Abd al-Qādir 'Aṭā (Beirut: Dār al-Kutub al-'Ilmiyya, 1997), vol. 10, 82–112.

Mā'iyat al-'aql, ed. by Ḥusayn al-Quwwatlī (Damascus: Dār al-Fikr, 1971).

al-Muqaddasī, Muḥammad b. Aḥmad, *Aḥsan al-taqāsīm fī ma'rifat al-aqālīm* (Beirut: Dār Iḥyā' al-Turāth al-'Arabī, 1987).

Muslim b. al-Ḥajjāj, Abū al-Ḥusayn, *Ṣaḥīḥ Muslim*, ed. by Muḥammad Fu'ād 'Abd al-Bāqī (Cairo and Beirut: Dār Iḥyā' al-Kutub al-'Arabiyya and Dār al-Kutub al-'Ilmiyya, 1991).

al-Mustamlī al-Bukhārī, Abū Ibrāhīm Ismā'īl b. Muḥammad b. 'Abd Allāh, *Sharḥ kitāb al-ta'arruf li-madhhab al-taṣawwuf* (Tehran: Chāpkhānih-yi Dānishgāh-i Tehrān, 1346 *Shamsī*).

al-Muttaqī al-Hindī, 'Alā' al-Dīn, *Kanz al-'ummāl fī sunan al-aqwāl wa-l-af'āl* (Ḥaydarābād al-Dukn: Dār al-Ma'ārif al-'Uthmāniyya, 1945–1974).

al-Nābulsī, 'Abd al-Ghanī b. Ismā'īl, *Ghāyat al-maṭlūb fī maḥabbat al-maḥbūb*, MS. 134 [1388], Daiber Collection, Institute of Oriental Culture, University of Tokyo, 32 folios.

Ghāyat al-maṭlūb fī maḥabbat al-maḥbūb, trans. by Samuela Pagani (Rome: Bardi, 1995).

Ghāyat al-maṭlūb fī maḥabbat al-maḥbūb, ed. by 'Alā' al-Dīn Bakrī and Shīrīn Qūrī (Damascus: Dār Shahrazād al-Shām, 2007).

Najm al-Dīn Rāzī, Abū Bakr 'Abd Allāh b. Muḥammad b. Shāhawr, *Mirṣād al-'ibād min al-mabda' ilā al-ma'ād*, ed. by Ḥusayn al-Ḥusaynī al-Ni'matu-Allāhī (N.p.: Maṭba'ah-yi Majlis, 1312 *Shamsī*).

al-Nawawī, Yaḥyā b. Sharaf al-Dīn, *Riyāḍ al-ṣāliḥīn min kalām sayyid al-mursalīn* (Cairo: Maktabat Maṣr, 1995).

al-Niffarī, Muḥammad b. ʿAbd al-Jabbār b. Ḥasan, *The Mawāqif and Mukhāṭabāt*, ed. and trans. by A. J. Arberry (London: J. W. Gibb Memorial Series, 1935).

Kitāb al-mawāqif wa-yalīhi kitāb al-mukhāṭabāt, ed. by Arthur J. Arberry (Cologne: Manshūrāt al-Jamal, 1996).

al-Qāriʾ al-Sarrāj, Jaʿfar b. Aḥmad Abū Muḥammad, *Maṣāriʿ al-ʿushshāq* (Beirut: Dār Ṣādir, 1958).

al-Qināwī, Masʿūd b. Ḥasan, *Sharḥ lāmiyyat Ibn al-Wardī al-musammā fatḥ al-raḥīm al-raḥmān sharḥ naṣīḥat al-ikhwān wa-murshidat al-khullān*, ed. by Bū Jumʿa ʿAbd al-Qādir Mikrī (Jeddah: Dār al-Minhāj, 2008).

al-Qurṭubī, Muḥammad b. Aḥmad, *al-Jāmiʿ li-aḥkām al-Qurʾān* (Beirut: Dār al-Fikr, 1993).

al-Qushayrī, Abū al-Qāsim ʿAbd al-Karīm, *al-Risāla al-qushayriyya* (Cairo: Al-Bābī al-Ḥalabī, 1940).

Al-Qushayrī's Epistle on Sufism, trans. by Alexander Knysh (Reading U.K.: Garnet Publishing, 2007).

Rūzbihān Baqlī Shīrāzī, *Sharḥ-i shaṭḥiyyāt*, ed. by Henry Corbin (Tehran and Paris: Department d'Iranologie de l'Institut Franco-Iranien and Librairie d'Amerique et d'Orient Adrien-Maisonneuve, 1966).

The Unveiling of Secrets Kashf al-Asrār: The Visionary Autobiography of Rūzbihān al-Baqlī (1128–1209 A.D.), ed. by Firoozeh Papan-Matin in collaboration with Michael Fishbein (Leiden: Brill, 2006).

Sayr al-arwāḥ aw al-miṣbāḥ fī mukāshafat baʿth al-arwāḥ, ed. by ʿĀṣim al-Kayyālī (Beirut: Dār al-Kutub al-ʿIlmiyya, 2007).

L'Itinéraire des Esprits Ruzbehan, tr. et commente par Paul Ballanfat (Paris: Les Deux Océans, 2001).

al-Ṣafadī, Ṣalāḥ al-Dīn Khalīl b. Aybak, *al-Wāfī bi-l-wafayāt*, ed. by Aḥmad al-Arnāʾūṭ and Turkī Muṣṭafā (Beirut: Dār Iḥyāʾ al-Turāth al-ʿArabī, 2000).

al-Sahlajī, Abū al-Faḍl Muḥammad b. ʿAlī, *al-Nūr min kalimāt Abī Ṭayfūr*, in *Shaṭaḥāt al-ṣūfiyya*, ed. by ʿAbd al-Raḥmān Badawī (Kuwait: Wikālat al-Maṭbūʿāt, 1976).

al-Sakhāwī, Shams al-Dīn Muḥammad b. ʿAbd al-Raḥmān, *al-Ḍawʾ al-lāmiʿ li-ahl al-qarn al-tāsiʿ* (Beirut: Dār Maktabat al-Ḥayā, n.d.).

al-Samʿānī, ʿAbd al-Karīm b. Muḥammad, *Kitāb al-ansāb*, ed. by ʿAbd al-Raḥmān al-Yamānī (Ḥaydarābād al-Dukn, India: Maṭbaʿat Dāʾirat al-Maʿārif al-ʿUthmāniyya, 1977).

al-Sarrāj al-Ṭūsī, Abū Naṣr, *Kitāb al-lumaʿ fī al-taṣawwuf*, ed. by Reynold A. Nicholson (Leiden: Brill, 1914),

Ṣuḥuf min kitāb al-lumaʿ, ed. by A. J. Arberry (London: Luzac, 1947).

Shaqīq al-Balkhī, *Ādāb al-ʿibādāt*, in *Nuṣūṣ ṣūfiyya ghayr manshūra*, ed. by Paul Nwyia (Beirut: Dār al-Mashriq, 1973), 17–22.

al-Shaʿrānī, ʿAbd al-Wahhāb b. Aḥmad, *al-Ṭabaqāt al-kubrā* (Cairo: Al-Maṭbaʿa al-Azhariyya, 1925).

Laṭāʾif al-minan wa-l-akhlāq fī bayān wujūb al-taḥadduth bi-niʿmat Allāh ʿalā al-iṭlāq (Cairo: ʿAbd al-Ḥamīd al-Ḥanafī, 1357/1938–9).

Tanbīh al-mughtarrīn, ed. by ʿAbd al-Jalīl al-ʿAṭā al-Bakrī (Damascus: Dār al-Bashāʾir, 1990).
al-Anwār al-qudsiyya fī bayān qawāʿid al-ṣūfiyya (Beirut: Dār Ṣādir, 1999).
al-Shiblī, Abū Bakr, *Dīwān Abī Bakr al-Shiblī Jaʿfar b. Yūnus*, ed. by Kāmil Muṣṭafā al-Shaybī (Baghdad: Dār al-Taḍāmun, 1967).
al-Subkī, Tāj al-Dīn, *Ṭabaqāt al-shāfiʿiyya al-kubrā*, ed. by ʿAbd al-Fattāḥ al-Ḥilū and Maḥmūd al-Ṭanāḥī (Cairo: Dār Iḥyāʾ al-Kutub al-ʿArabiyya, n.d.).
al-Suhrawardī, ʿAbd al-Qāhir b. ʿAbd Allāh Abū al-Najīb, *A Sufi Rule for Novices*, an abridged translation and introduction by Menahem Milson (Cambridge, Mass.: Harvard University Press, 1975).
Ādāb al-murīdīn, ed. by Menahem Milson (Jerusalem: Institute of Asian and African Studies, Hebrew University of Jerusalem, 1977).
al-Suhrawardī, Abū Ḥafṣ ʿUmar, *ʿAwārif al-maʿārif*, in Abū Ḥāmid al-Ghazālī, *Iḥyāʾ ʿulūm al-dīn* (Cairo: Al-Bābī al-Ḥalabī, 1967).
Die Gaben der Erkenntnisse des ʿUmar as-Suhrawardī (ʿAwārif al-Maʿārif), ubersetzt und eingeleitet von Richard Gramlich (Wiesbaden: Steiner, 1978).
Rashf al-naṣāʾiḥ al-īmāniyya wa-kashf al-faḍāʾiḥ al-yūnāniyya, trans. to Persian by Muʿīn al-Dīn Jamāl b. Jalāl al-Dīn known as Muʿallim Yazdī (d. 789/1387), ed. by Najīb Haravī (N.p.: Chāp va-Nashr-i Bunyād, 1986).
al-Ajwiba al-Suhrawardiyya, MS. Jagiellońska, 3476, fols. 16b–21a.
Untitled treatise, MS. Jagiellońska, 3994, fols. 25b–58b.
Waṣiyya ilā aḥad al-fuqarāʾ, MS. Jagiellońska, 3991, fols. 65a–68b.
al-Sulamī, Abū ʿAbd al-Raḥmān, '*Risālat al-malāmatiyya*', in Abū al-ʿAlāʾ ʿAfīfī, *al-Malāmatiyya wa-l-ṣūfiyya wa-ahl al-futuwwa* (Cairo: Dār Iḥyāʾ al-Kutub al-ʿArabiyya, 1945).
Ādāb al-ṣuḥba wa-ḥusn al-ʿishra, ed. by M. J. Kister (Jerusalem: n.p., 1954).
Ṭabaqāt al-ṣūfiyya, ed. by Johannes Pedersen (Leiden: Brill, 1960).
Kitāb al-arbaʿīn fī al-taṣawwuf (Ḥaydarābād al-Dukn, India: Maṭbaʿat Dāʾirat al-Maʿārif al-ʿUthmāniyya, 1950).
Jawāmiʿ ādāb al-ṣūfiyya and ʿuyūb al-nafs wa-mudāwātuhā, ed. by Etan Kohlberg (Jerusalem: Jerusalem Academic Press, 1976).
al-Muqaddima fī al-taṣawwuf wa-ḥaqīqatihi, ed. by Yūsuf Zaydān (Cairo: Maktabat al-Kulliyāt al-Azhariyya, 1987).
Majmūʿa-yi āthār-i Abū ʿAbd al-Raḥmān Sulamī: Bakhsh-hā-i az ḥaqāyiq al-tafsīr va-rasāʾil-i dīgar, ed. by Naṣrullah Pūrjavādī (Tehran: Markaz-i Nashr-i Dānishgāhī, 1369–1372 *Shamsī*).
al-Sulamī, Abū ʿAbd al-Raḥmān, *al-Muqaddima fī al-taṣawwuf wa-ḥaqīqatihi*, ed. by Ḥusayn Amīn, in *Majmūʿa-yi āthār-i Abū ʿAbd al-Raḥmān Sulamī: Bakhsh-hā-i az ḥaqāyiq al-tafsīr va-rasāʾil-i dīgar*, ed. by Naṣrullah Pūrjavādī (Tehran: Markaz-i Nashr-i Dānishgāhī, 1369–1372 *Shamsī*), vol. 2, 457–532.
Dhikr al-niswa al-mutaʿabbidāt al-ṣūfiyyāt, ed. by Maḥmūd al-Ṭanāḥī (Cairo: Maktabat al-Khānjī, 1993).
Tisʿat kutub fī uṣūl al-zuhd wa-al-taṣawwuf li-Abī ʿAbd al-Raḥmān Muḥammad b. al-Ḥusayn b. Mūsā al-Sulamī, ed. by Sulaymān Ibrāhīm Ātesh (N.p.: Al-Nāshir, 1995).

Early Sufi Women: Dhikr an-niswa al-muta'abbidāt aṣ-ṣūfiyyāt, ed. and trans. by Rkia Elaroui-Cornell (Louisville: Fons Vitae, 1999).
Ḥaqā'iq al-tafsīr: Tafsīr al-Qur'ān al-'azīz, ed. by Sayyid b. 'Imrān (Beirut: Dār al-Kutub al-'Ilmiyya, 2001).
al-Suyūṭī, Jalāl al-Dīn 'Abd al-Raḥmān, *Ṭabaqāt al-mufassirīn*, ed. by 'Alī Muḥammad 'Umar (Cairo: Maktabat Wahba, 1976).
al-Ṭabarī, Abū Khalaf Muḥammad b. 'Abd al-Malik, *Salwat al-'ārifīn wa-uns al-mushtāqīn*, in Gerhard Böwering and Bilal Orfali, *The Confort of the Mystics: A Manual and Anthology of Early Sufism* (Leiden and Boston: Brill, 2013).
al-Tamīmī al-Fāsī, Abū 'Abd Allāh Muḥammad b. 'Abd al-Karīm, *al-Mustafād fī manāqib al-'ubbād bi-madīnat fās wa-mā yalīhā min al-bilād*, ed. by Muḥammad al-Sharīf (Taṭwān: Kulliyyat al-Ādāb wa-l-'Ulūm al-Insāniyya, 2002).
al-Tanūkhī, al-Muḥsin b. 'Alī, *Nishwār al-muḥāḍara wa-akhbār al-mudhākara*, ed. by 'Abbūd al-Shāljī (Beirut: Dār Ṣāḍir, 1995).
al-Ṭarṭūshī, Abū Bakr Muḥammad b. al-Walīd, *Birr al-wālidayn: Mā yajib 'alā l-wālid li-waladihi wa-mā yajib 'alā al-walad li-wālidihi*, ed. by Muḥammad 'Abd al-Karīm al-Qāḍī (Beirut: Mu'assasat al-Kutub al-Thaqāfiyya, 1986).
al-Tawḥīdī, Abū Ḥayyān, *al-Ishārāt al-Ilāhiyya*, ed. by 'Abd al-Raḥmān Badawī (Cairo: Maṭba'at Jāmi'at Fu'ād al-Awwal, 1950).
al-Ṣadāqa wa-l-ṣadīq, ed. by Ibrāhīm al-Kīlānī (Beirut: Dār al-Fikr al-Mu'āṣir, 1996).
Kitāb al-imtā' wa-l-mu'ānasa, ed. by Muḥammad al-Fāḍilī (Algeria: Dār al-Abḥāth, 2007).
al-Tilimsānī, 'Afīf al-Dīn, *Sharḥ mawāqif al-Niffarī*, ed. by Jamāl al-Marzūqī (Cairo: Al-Hay'a al-Miṣriyya al-'Āmma li-l-Kitāb, 2000).
Sharḥ mawāqif al-Niffarī: Muḥammad b. 'Abd al-Jabbār b. al-Ḥasan, ed. by 'Āṣim Ibrāhīm al-Kayyālī (Beirut: Dār al-Kutub al-'Ilmiyya, 2007).
al-Tirmidhī, Muḥammad b. 'Īsā, *al-Jāmi' al-kabīr*, ed. by Bashshār Ma'rūf (Beirut: Dār al-Gharb al-Islāmī, 1998).
al-Turkmānī, Idrīs b. Baydakīn, *Kitāb al-luma' fī al-ḥawādith wa-l-bida'*, ed. by Ṣubḥī Labīb (Cairo: n.p., 1986).
Yāqūt b. 'Abd Allāh al-Ḥamawī, *Mu'jam al-buldān* (Beirut: Dār Ṣādir, 1977).

SECONDARY SOURCES

Abdal-Rehim, Abdal-Rehim, 'The Family and Gender Laws in Egypt during the Ottoman Period', in *Women, the Family, and Divorce Laws in Islamic History*, ed. by Amira El-Azhary Sonbol with a foreword by Elizabeth Warnock Fernea (Syracuse, N.Y.: Syracuse University Press, 1996), 96–111.
Abdel-Kader, Ali Hassan, *The Life, Personality and Writings of al-Junayd: A Study of a Third/Ninth Century Mystic with an Edition and Translation of His Writings* (London: Luzac & Company, 1962).

Ahmed, Leila, 'Early Islam and the Position of Women: The Problem of Interpretation', in *Women in Middle Eastern History: Shifting Boundaries in Sex and Gender*, ed. by Keddie and Baron (New Haven: Yale University Press, 1991), 58–73.

Algar, Hamid, *Jami* (New Delhi: Oxford University Press, 2013).

'Malāmatiyya: in Iran and the Eastern Lands', *Encyclopaedia of Islam*, second edition, ed. by P. Bearman, Th. Bianquis, C. E. Bosworth, E. van Donzel and W. P. Heinrichs. Online: http://dx.doi.org/10.1163/1573-3912_islam_COM_0643 (accessed 13 October 2017).

Amri, Nelly, and Laroussi Amri, *Les Femmes Soufies ou la Passion de Dieu* (St. Jean de Braye: Éd Dangles, 1992).

Andrae, Tor, *In the Garden of Myrtles: Studies in Early Islamic Mysticism*, trans. from the Swedish by Birgitta Sharpe (Albany, N.Y.: State University of New York Press, 1987).

Anjum, Tanvir, *Chishtī Sufis in the Sultanate of Delhi 1190–1400: From Restrained Indifference to Calculated Defiance* (Karachi: Oxford University Press, 2011).

Arberry, A. J., 'al-Djunayd', *Encyclopaedia of Islam*, second edition, ed. by P. Bearman, Th. Bianquis, C. E. Bosworth, E. van Donzel and W. P. Heinrichs. Online: http://dx.doi.org/10.1163/1573-3912_islam_SIM_2117 (accessed 9 October 2017).

Avery, Kenneth, *A Psychology of Early Sufi Samāʿ: Listening and Altered States* (London and New York: Routledge Curzon, 2004).

Shiblī: His Life and Thought in the Sufi Tradition (Albany, N.Y.: State University of New York Press, 2014).

Badawī, ʿAbd al-Raḥmān, *Shaṭaḥāt al-ṣūfiyya* (Kuwait: Wikālat al-Maṭbūʿāt, 1976).

Bell, J. N., *Love Theory in Later Ḥanbalite Islam* (Albany, N.Y.: State University of New York Press, 1979).

Bellamy, James, 'Sex and Society in Islamic Popular Literature', in *Society and the Sexes in Medieval Islam*, ed. by Afaf Lutfi al-Sayyid-Marsot (Malibu, California: Undena Publications, 1979), 23–42.

Belqāsim, Khālid, *al-Ṣūfiyya wa-l-farāgh: Al-Kitāba ʿind al-Niffarī* (Beirut: Al-Markaz al-Thaqāfī al-ʿArabī, 2012).

Bori, Caterina, 'A New Source for the Biography of Ibn Taymiyya', *Bulletin of the School of Oriental and African Studies*, vol. 67, no. 3 (2004), 321–348.

Bosworth, C. E., 'Rifāʿiyya', *Encyclopaedia of Islam*, second edition, ed. by P. Bearman, Th. Bianquis, C. E. Bosworth, E. van Donzel and W. P. Heinrichs. Online: http://dx.doi.org/10.1163/1573-3912_islam_SIM_6296 (accessed 9 October 2017).

Bouhdiba, Abdelwahab, *Sexuality in Islam*, trans. from the French by Alan Sheridan (London: Routledge & Kegan Paul, 1985).

Böwering, Gerhard, 'Ideas of Time in Persian Sufism', *Iran*, vol. 30 (1992), 77–89.

'Early Sufism between Persecution and Heresy', in *Islamic Mysticism Contested: Thirteen Centuries of Controversies and Polemics*, ed. by Frederick de Jong and Bernd Radtke (Leiden: Brill, 1999), 45–67.

'Besṭāmī (Basṭāmī), Bāyazīd,' *Encylopaedia Iranica*, vol. 4, fasc. 2, 183–186.

Briffault, Robert, *The Mothers: A Study of the Origins of Sentiments and Institutions* (New York: The Macmillan, 1927).

Cahen, Cl., and L. Gardet, 'Kasb', *Encyclopaedia of Islam*, second edition, ed. by P. Bearman, Th. Bianquis, C. E. Bosworth, E. van Donzel and W. P. Heinrichs. Online: http://dx.doi.org/10.1163/1573-3912_islam_COM_0457 (accessed 1 October 2017).

Chabbi, J., 'Abū Ḥafṣ al-Ḥaddād,' *Encyclopaedia Iranica*, vol. I, 293–294.

Chittick, William, *Sufism: A Short Introduction* (Oxford: One World, 2000).

'Divine and Human Love in Islam', in *Divine Love: Perspectives from the World's Religious Traditions*, ed. by Jeff Levin and Stephen G. Post (West Conshohocken, Pa.: Templeton Press, 2010), 163–200.

Divine Love: Islamic Literature and the Path to God (New Haven: Yale University Press, 2013).

Clements, Forrest, 'Use of Cluster Analysis with Anthropological Data', *American Anthropologist*, vol. 56, no. 2 (2009), 180–199.

Cooperson, Michael, 'Ibn Ḥanbal and Bishr al-Ḥāfī: A Case Study in Biographical Traditions', *Studia Islamica*, vol. 86 (1997), 71–101.

Crone, Patricia, and Martin Hinds, *God's Caliph: Religious Authority in the First Centuries of Islam* (Cambridge: Cambridge University Press, 1986).

De Jong, F., 'Malāmatiyya: in the Central Islamic Lands,' *Encyclopaedia of Islam*, second edition, ed. by P. Bearman, Th. Bianquis, C. E. Bosworth, E. van Donzel and W .P. Heinrichs. Online: http://dx.doi.org/10.1163/1573-3912_islam_COM_0643 (accessed 13 October 2017).

Dieterici, F., *Die Philosophie bei den Arabern im IX-ten Jahrhünderten* n.Chr.: *Gesamtdarstellung und Quellenwerke* (Leipzig: J.C. Hinrichs,1858–1895).

Digby, Simon, 'The Sufi Shaikh as a Source of Authority in Mediaeval India', in *Islam et Société en Asie du Sud*, ed. by Marc Gaborieau (Paris: Editions de l'École des Hautes Études en Sciences Sociales, 1986), 57–77.

Dreher, Josef, 'Comment un Homme Peut-il Perdre plus qu'il ne Possède? Essais d'Explication d'une Sentence Énigmatique d'al-Junayd (m. 298/910) Concernant les Progrès et les Dangers sur le Chemin vers Dieu', *Institut Dominicain d'Études Orientales du Caire: Mélanges (MIDEO)*, vol. 27 (2008), 413–422.

Dwyer, Daisy, 'Women, Sufism, and Decision-Making in Moroccan Islam', in *Women in the Muslim World*, ed. by Lois Beck and Nikki Keddie (Cambridge, Mass.: Harvard University Press, 1978), 585–598.

El-Cheikh, Nadia Maria, 'Women's History: A Study of al-Tanūkhī', in *Writing the Feminine: Women in Arab Sources*, ed. by Manuela Marín and Randi Deguilhem (London and New York: I.B. Tauris Publishers, 2002), 129–148.

El-Rouayheb, Khaled, *Before Homosexuality in the Arab-Islamic World, 1500–1800* (Chicago: The University of Chicago Press, 2005).

'Heresy and Sufism in the Arabic-Islamic World, 1550–1775: Some Preliminary Observations', *Bulletin of the School of Oriental and African Studies*, vol. 73 (2010), 357–380.

Ephrat, Daphna, *Wayfarers, Leaders in Piety: Sufis and the Dissemination of Islam in Medieval Palestine* (Cambridge, Mass. and London: Harvard University Press, 2008).

Ernst, Carl, *Words of Ecstasy in Sufism* (Albany, N.Y.: State University of New York Press, 1985).

Giladi, Avner, 'Herlihy's Thesis Revisited: Some Notes on Investment in Children in Medieval Muslim Societies', *Journal of Family History*, vol. 36, no. 3 (2011), 235–247.

'Sex, Marriage and the Family in al-Ghazālī's Thought: Some Preliminary Notes', in *Islam and Rationality: The Impact of al-Ghazālī, Papers Collected on His 900th Anniversary*, ed. by Georges Tamer (Leiden and Boston: Brill, 2015), vol. 1, 165–185.

Muslim Midwives: The Craft of Birthing in the Premodern Middle East (New York: Cambridge University Press, 2015).

Goitein, S. D., 'The Sexual Mores of the Common People', in *Society and the Sexes in Medieval Islam*, ed. by Afaf Lutfi al-Sayyid-Marsot (Malibu, Calif.: Undena Publications, 1979), 43–61.

Goldziher, Ignaz, *Die Richtungen der Islamischen Koranauslegung* (Leiden: Brill, 1920).

Muhammedanische Studien (Halle A. S.: Max Niemeyer, 1890).

Introduction to Islamic Theology and Law, trans. by Andras Hamori and Ruth Hamori, with an introduction and additional notes by Bernard Lewis (Princeton, N.J.: Princeton University Press, 1981).

Gramlich, Richard. *Die Schiitischen Derwischorden Persiens* (Wiesbaden: Franz Steiner, 1976).

Abū l-ʿAbbās b. ʿAṭāʾ: Sufi und Koranausleger (Stuttgart: Deutsche Morgenländische Gesellschaft, Franz Steiner, 1995).

Alte Vorbilder des Sufitums (Wiesbaden: Otto Harrassowitz Verlag, 1996).

Herlihy, David, *Medieval Households* (Cambridge, Mass.: Harvard University Press, 1985).

Hofer, Nathan, *The Popularisation of Sufism in Ayyubid and Mamluk Egypt* (The Tun: Edinburgh University Press, 2015), 1173–1325.

Horovitz, J., 'Djuraydj', *Encyclopaedia of Islam*, second edition, ed. by P. Bearman, Th. Bianquis, C. E. Bosworth, E. van Donzel and W. P. Heinrichs. Online: http://dx.doi.org/10.1163/1573-3912_islam_SIM_2122 (accessed 5 October 2017).

Hussaini, S. Sh. Kh., 'Abū ʿAbd-Al-Raḥmān Solamī,' *Encyclopædia Iranica*, vol. I, no. 3, 249–250. Online: www.iranicaonline.org/articles/abu-abd-al-rahman-solami-mohammad-b (updated 19 July 2011).

Karamustafa, Ahmet T., *God's Unruly Friends: Dervish Groups in the Islamic Later Middle Period 1200–1550* (Salt Lake City: University of Utah Press, 1994).

'*Walāya* According to al-Junayd (d. 298/910)', in *Reason and Inspiration in Islam: Theology, Philosophy and Mysticism in Muslim Thought: Essays in Honour of Hermann Landolt*, ed. by Todd Lawson (London: Tauris, 2005), 64–70.

Sufism: The Formative Period (Berkeley and Los Angeles: University of California Press, 2007).

'The Ghazālī Brothers and Their Institutions', in *Ötekilerin Peşinde: Ahmet Yaşar Ocak'a Armağan* (Festschrift in Honor of Ahmet Yaşar Ocak), ed. by Mehmet Öz and Fatih Yeşil (Istanbul: Timaş Yayınları, 2015), 265–275.

Karmi, Ghada, 'Women, Islam and Patriarchalism', in *Women and Islam: Critical Concepts in Sociology*, ed. by Haideh Moghissi (London and New York: Routledge, 2005), vol. 1: *Images and Realities*, 165–179.

Kendig, Elizabeth, 'Niffarī and His Audiences: The *Mawāqif* of Muḥammad Ibn 'Abdi 'l-Jabbār al-Niffarī (d. ca. 359/970)', M.A. thesis, University of Toronto, 2006.

Knysh, Alexander, *Islamic Mysticism: A Short History* (Leiden, Boston, Koln: Brill, 2000).

Kueny, Kathryn, *Conceiving Identities: Maternity in Medieval Muslim Discourse and Practice* (Albany, N.Y.: State University of New York Press, 2013).

Kugle, Scott, *Sufis and Saints' Bodies: Mysticism, Corporeality, and Sacred Power in Islam* (Chapel Hill: The University of North Carolina Press, 2007).

Homosexuality in Islam: Critical Reflection on Gay, Lesbian, and Transgender Muslims (Oxford: Oneworld, 2010), 73–127.

Lane, Edward, *Arabic-English Lexicon* (Beirut: Librairie Du Liban, 1968).

Lange, Christian, *Paradise and Hell in Islamic Traditions* (New York: Cambridge University Press, 2016).

Lewisohn, Leonard, 'Sufism's Religion of Love, from Rābiʿa to Ibn ʿArabī', in *The Cambridge Companion to Sufism*, ed. by Lloyd Ridgeon (New York: Cambridge University Press), 150–180.

Lings, Martin, 'The *Qurʾan*ic Symbolism of Water', *Studies in Comparative Religion*, vol. 2, no. 3 (1968), 6 pp. Online: www.studiesincomparativereligion.com/uploads/articlepdfs/62.pdf (accessed 24 March 2015).

Longhurst, Robyn, *Maternities: Gender, Bodies and Space* (New York: Routledge, 2008).

Lumbard, Joseph, 'Aḥmad al-Ghazālī (d. 517/1123 or 520–1126) and the Metaphysics of Love,' Dissertation, Yale University, 2003).

'From *Ḥubb* to *ʿIshq*: The Development of Love in Early Sufism', *Journal of Islamic Studies*, vol. 18, no. 3 (2007), 345–385.

'*Aḥmad al-Ghazālī*', *The Oxford Encyclopedia of Islam and Philosophy, Science and Technology* (Oxford: Oxford University Press, 2014), 270–274.

Aḥmad al-Ghazālī, Remembrance, and the Metaphysics of Love (Albany, N.Y.: State University of New York Press, 2016).

Malamud, Margaret, 'The Politics of Heresy in Medieval Khurāsān: The Karrāmiyya in Nishapur', *Iranian Studies*, Religion and Society in Islamic Iran during the Pre-Modern Era, vol. 27, no. 1/4 (1994), 37–51.

al-Mālikī, Ḥasan, *al-Ṣuḥba wa-l-ṣaḥāba bayn al-iṭlāq al-lughawī wa-l-takhṣīṣ al-sharʿī* (ʿAmmān: Markaz al-Dirāsāt al-Tārīkhiyya, 2004).

Martin, David L., 'An Account of Ruwaym b. Aḥmad from al-Sulamī's *Ṭabaqā al-Ṣūfiyya*', *Al-ʿArabiyya*, vol. 16, no. 1/2 (1983), 27–55.

al-Marzūqī, Jamāl, *Falsafat al-taṣawwuf: Muḥammad b. ʿAbd al-Jabbār al-Niffarī* (Beirut: Dār al-Tanwīr, 2007).

Massignon, Louis, *Recueil de Textes Inédits* (Paris: P. Geuthner, 1929).

'Le Temps dans la Pensée Islamique', in *Opera Minora: Texte Recuellis, Classes et Presentes avec une Bibliographie par Y. Moubarac* (Beirut: Dār al-Maʿārif, 1963), vol. 2, 606–612.

The Passion of al-Ḥallāj, Mystic and Martyr of Islam, trans. from the French with a biographical foreword by Herbert Mason (Princeton, N.J.: Princeton University Press, 1982).

Essay on the Origins of the Technical Language of Islamic Mysticism (Notre Dame, Ind.: University of Notre Dame Press, 1997).

Meier, Fritz, *Die Vita des Scheich Abū Isḥāq al-Kāzarūnī*, in der Persischen Bearbeitung von Maḥmūd b. ʿUthmān (Leipzig: Brockhaus, 1948).

'Khurāsān and the End of Classical Sufism', in *Essays on Islamic Piety and Mysticism*, trans. by John O'Kane with editorial assistance of Bernd Radtke (Leiden: Brill, 1999), 189–219.

'The Dervish Dance: An Attempt at an Overview', in *Essays on Islamic Piety and Mysticism*, trans. by John O'Kane with editorial assistance of Bernd Radtke (Leiden: Brill, 1999), 23–48.

'A Book of Etiquette for Sufis', in *Essays on Islamic Piety and Mysticism*, trans. by John O'Kane with editorial assistance of Bernd Radtke (Leiden: Brill, 1999), 49–92.

Melchert, Christopher, 'The Transition from Asceticism to Mysticism at the Middle of the Ninth Century C.E.', *Studia Islamica*, vol. 83 (1996), 51–70.

'Early Renunciants as *Ḥadīth* Transmitters', *The Muslim World*, vol. 92 (2002), 407–418.

'Origins and Early Sufism', in *The Cambridge Companion to Sufism*, ed. by Lloyd Ridgeon (New York: Cambridge University Press, 2015), 3–23.

Mernissi, Fatima, 'Women in Muslim History: Traditional Perspectives and New Strategies', in *Women and Islam: Critical Concepts in Sociology*, ed. by Haideh Moghissi (London: Routledge, 2005), vol. 1, 37–52.

Mojaddedi, Jawid A., 'Legitimizing Sufism in al-Qushayri's Risāla', *Studia Islamica*, vol. 90 (2000), 37–50.

The Biographical Tradition in Sufism: The Ṭabaqāt genre from al-Sulamī to Jāmī (Richmond, Surrey: Curzon Press, 2001).

'Getting Drunk with Abū Yazīd or Staying Sober with Junayd: The Creation of a Popular Typology of Sufism', in *Sufism, Volume I: Origins and Development*, ed. by Lloyd Ridgeon (London: Routledge, 2008), 171–187.

'Junayd in the *Ḥilyat al-awliyāʾ* and the *Nafaḥāt al-uns*', in *Tales of God's Friends: Islamic Hagiography in Translation*, ed. by John Renard (Berkeley: University of California Press, 2009), 79–91.

Mourad, Suleiman Ali, *Early Islam between Myth and History: Al-Ḥasan al-Baṣrī (d. 110H/728CE) and the Formation of His Legacy in Classical Islamic Scholarship* (Leiden and Boston: Brill, 2006).

Mueller, Gert, 'Asceticism and Mysticism: A Contribution towards the Sociology of Faith', in *International Yearbook for the Sociology of Religion 8: Sociological Theories of Religion and Language*, ed. by Günter Dux, Thomas Luckmann and Joachim Matthes (Opladen: Westdeutscher Verlag, 1973), 68–132.

Murrat, Stephen, and Will Roscoe, *Islamic Homosexualities: Culture, History, and Literature* (New York: New York University Press, 1997).

Najmabadi, Afsaneh, *Women with Mustaches and Men without Beards: Gender and Sexual Anxieties of Iranian Modernity* (Berkeley: University of California Press, 2005).

Nallino, Carlo A., *Raccolta di Scritti Editi e Inediti, a Cura di Maria Nallino* (Rome: Istituto per l'Oriente, 1940).

Naṣru-Allāhī, Yadu-Allāh, '*Rawḍat al-murīdīn-i* Abū Jaʿfar Ibn Yazdānyār', *ʿAllāmih: Dū Faṣl-nāmih-yi ʿIlmī*, vol. 12, no. 34 (1391 *Shamsī*), 141–154.

Netton, Ian, 'The Breath of Felicity: *Adab, Aḥwāl, Maqāmāt* and Abū al-Najīb al-Suhrawardī', in *Classical Persian Sufism from Its Origins to Rūmī*, ed. by Leonard Lewisohn (London: Oneworld, 2003), vol. 1, 457–482.

Nguyen, Martin, *Sufi Master and Qur'an Scholar: Abū'L-Qāsim al-Qushayrī and the Laṭāʾif al-Ishārāt* (London: The Institute of Ismaili Studies, 2012).

Nizami, Khaliq Ahmad, 'Muslim Mystic Ideology and Contribution to Indian Culture', in *Sufism and Society in Medieval India*, ed. by Raziuddin Aquil (New Delhi: Oxford University Press, 2010), 1–30.

Nwyia, P., 'Textes Mystiques Inédits d'Abū al-Ḥasan al-Nūrī', *Mélanges de L'Universitat St-Joseph*, vol. 44 (1968), 117–120.

Ohlander, Erik, *Sufism in an Age of Transition: ʿUmar al-Suhrawardī and the Rise of the Islamic Mystical Brotherhoods* (Leiden and Boston: Brill, 2008).

Papan-Matin, Firoozeh, *Beyond Death: The Mystical Teachings of ʿAyn al-Quḍāt al-Hamadhānī* (Leiden and Boston: Brill, 2010).

Pourjavady, Nasrollah. 'Stories of Aḥmad al-Ghazālī 'Playing the Witness' in Tabrīz (Shams-i Tabrīzī's Interest in *shāhid-bāzī*)', in *Reason and Inspiration in Islam: Theology, Philosophy and Mysticism in Muslim Thought, Essays in Honour of Hermann Landolt*, ed. by Todd Lawson (London and New York: Tauris, 2005), 200–220.

Qamar ul-Huda, *Striving for Divine Union: Spiritual Exercises for Suhrawardī Ṣūfīs* (London and New York: Routledge Curzon, 2003).

Rapoport, Yossef, *Marriage, Money and Divorce in Medieval Islamic Society* (New York: Cambridge University Press, 2005).

Renard, John, *Knowledge of God in Classical Sufism: Foundations of Islamic Mystical Theology* (Mahwah, N.J.: Paulist Press, 2004).

Historical Dictionary of Sufism (Historical Dictionaries of Religions, Philosophies, and Movements, No. 58) (Lanham, Md., Toronto and Oxford: The Scarecrow Press, 2005).

Ridgeon, Lloyd, 'Javanmardi: Origins and Development until the 13th Century and its Connection to Sufism', *Annals of Japan Association for Middle East Studies*, vol. 21, no. 2 (2006), 49–74.

Morals and Mysticism in Persian Sufism: A History of Sufi-futuwwat in Iran (London and New York: Routledge, 2010).

Jawanmardi: A Sufi Code of Honour (Edinburgh: Edinburgh University Press, 2011).

'The Controversy of Shaykh Awḥad al-Dīn Kirmānī and Handsome, Moon-Faced Youths: A Case Study of *Shāhid-Bāzī* in Medieval Sufism', *Journal of Sufi Studies*, vol. 1 (2012), 1–28.

Ritter, Hellmut, 'Muslim Mystic's Strife with God', *Oriens*, vol. 5 (1952), 1–16.
The Ocean of the Soul: Man, the World and God in the Stories of Farīd al-Dīn ʿAṭṭār, trans. by John O'Kane with editorial assistance of Bernd Radtke (Leiden and Boston: Brill, 2003).
Roded, Ruth, *Women in Islamic Biographical Collections from Ibn Saʿd to Who's Who* (Boulder: Colorado and London, 1994).
Rokach, Lior, and Oded Maimon, 'A Survey of Clustering Algorithms', in *Data Mining and Knowledge Discovery Handbook*, eds. Lior Rokach and Oded Maimon (New York: Springer, 2005), 269–298.
Rosenthal, Franz, 'Fiction and Reality: Sources for the Role of Sex in Medieval Muslim Society', in *Society and the Sexes in Medieval Islam*, ed. by Afaf Lutfi al-Sayyid-Marsot (Malibu, Calif.: Undena Publications, 1979), 3–22.
Rowson, Everett, 'The Traffic in Boys: Slavery and Homoerotic Liaisons in Elite ʿAbbāsid Society', *Middle Eastern Literatures*, vol. 11, no. 2 (2008), 193–204.
'Homosexuality', *Encyclopaedia Iranica*, vol. XII, fasc. 4, section (ii), 'In Islamic Law', 441–445.
Runyan, Wm. McKinley, 'Idiographic Goals and Methods in the Study of Lives', *Journal of Personality*, vol. 51, no. 3 (1983), 413–437.
Saʿb, Nada, Ṣūfī Theory and Language in the Writings of Abū Saʿīd Aḥmad ibn Īsā al-Kharrāz (d. 286/899), Dissertation, Yale University, December 2003.
Salamah Qudsi, Arin, 'Institutionalized *Mashyakha* in the Twelfth Century Sufism of ʿUmar al-Suhrawardī', *Jerusalem Studies in Arabic and Islam*, vol. 36 (2009), 381–424.
'A Lightning Trigger or a Stumbling Block: Mother Images and Roles in Classical Sufism', *Oriens*, vol. 39, no. 2, 2011, 199–226.
'The Everlasting Sufi: Achieving the Final Destination of the Path (*Intihāʾ*) in the Sufi Teachings of ʿUmar al-Suhrawardī (d. 632/1234)', *Journal of Islamic Studies*, vol. 22, no. 3 (2011), 313–338.
'The Idea of *Tashabbuh* in Sufi Communities and Literature of the Late 6th/12th and Early 7th/13th Century in Baghdad', *Revista al-Qantara*, vol. XXXII, no. 1 (January–June 2011), 175–197.
'The Will to Be Unveiled: Sufi Autobiographies in Classical Sufism', *Al-Masaq: Islam and the Medieval Mediterranean*, vol. 24, no. 2 (2012), 199–207.
Bayn sayr wa-ṭayr: Al-Tanẓīr, ḥayāt al-jamāʿa, wa-bunā al-muʾassasa fī taṣawwuf Abī Ḥafṣ al-Suhrawardī (Beirut: Dār al-Kutub al-ʿIlmiyya, 2012).
'Crossing the Desert: *Siyāḥa* and *Safar* as Key Concepts in Early Sufi Literature and Life', *Journal of Sufi Studies*, vol. 2 (2013), 129–147.
'Remarks of al-Niffarī's Neglect in Early Sufi Literature', *British Journal of Middle Eastern Studies*, vol. 41, no. 4 (2014), 406–418.
'The Concept of *jadhb* and the Image of *majdhūb* in Sufi Teachings and Life in the Period between the Fourth/Tenth and the Tenth/Sixteenth Centuries', *Journal of the Royal Asiatic Society*, Series 3, 1–17. Online: https://doi.org/10.1017/S1356186317000530 (published 19 October 2017).
Salem, Feryal, *The Emergence of Early Sufi Piety and Sunnī Scholasticism: ʿAbdallāh b. al-Mubārak and the Formation of Sunnī Identity in the Second Islamic Century* (Leiden and Boston: Brill, 2016).

Schimmel, Annemarie, *Mystical Dimensions of Islam* (Chapel Hill: University of North Carolina Press, 1975).

'The Feminine Element in Sufism', in Annemarie Schimmel, *Mystical Dimensions of Islam* (Chapel Hill: University of North Carolina Press, 1975), 426–435.

'Women in Mystical Islam', in *Women and Islam*, ed. by Aziza al-Hibri (Oxford: Pergamon Press, 1982), 145–151.

'Eros-Heavenly and Not So Heavenly in Sufi Literature and Life', in *Society and the Sexes in Medieval Islam*, ed. by Afaf Lutfi al-Sayyid-Marsot (Malibu, Calif.: Undena Publications, 1979), 119–142.

Schmidtke, Sabine, 'Homoeroticism and Homosexuality in Islam: A Review Article', *Bulletin of the School of Oriental and African Studies*, vol. 62, no. 2 (1999), 260–266.

Schmitt, Arno, 'Different Approaches to Male-Male Sexuality/Eroticism from Morocco to Uzbekistan', in *Sexuality and Eroticism among Males in Moslem Societies*, ed. by Arno Schmitt and Jehoeda Sofer (Binghamton, N.Y.: Harrington Park Press, 1992), 1–24.

Bio-Bibliography of Male-Male Sexuality and Eroticism in Muslim Societies (Berlin: Verlag Rosa Winkel, 1995).

Sered, Susan, 'Mothers and Icons', *Nashim: A Journal of Jewish Women's Studies and Gender Issues*, vol. 3 (2000), 5–14.

Shaikh, Saʿdiyya, *Sufi Narratives of Intimacy: Ibn ʿArabī, Gender, and Sexuality* (Chapel Hill: The University of North Carolina Press, 2012).

Silvers, Laury, 'The Teaching Relationship in Early Sufism: Reassessment of Fritz Meier's Definition of the *shaykh al-tarbiya* and the *shaykh al-taʿlīm*', *The Muslim World*, vol. 93 (2003), 69–97.

'Theoretical Sufism in the Early Period: With an Introduction to the Thought of Abū Bakr al-Wāsiṭī (d. ca. 320/928) on the Interrelationship between Theoretical and the Practical Sufism', *Studia Islamica*, vol. 98, no. 99 (2004), 71–94.

A Soaring Minaret: Abū Bakr al-Wāsiṭī and the Rise of Baghdadi Sufism (Albany, N.Y.: State University of New York Press, 2010).

'Early Pious, Mystic Sufi Women', in *The Cambridge Companion to Sufism*, ed. by Lloyd Ridgeon (New York: Cambridge University Press, 2015), 24–52.

Smith, Margaret, *Muslim Women Mystics: The Life and Work of Rābiʿa and Other Women Mystics in Islam* (Oxford: Oneworld, 2001).

Smith, W. Robertson, *Kinship and Marriage in Early Arabia*, new edition with additional notes by the author and by Ignaz Goldziher (Oosterhout N.B.: Anthropological Publications, 1966).

Steingass, Francis Joseph, *A Comprehensive Persian-English Dictionary* (London: Paul, Trench, Trubner, 1947).

Stern, Gertrude, *Marriage in Early Islam* (London: Royal Asiatic Society, 1939).

Stewart, David, 'The Structure of the *Fihrist*: Ibn al-Nadīm as Historian of Islamic Legal and Theological Schools', *International Journal of Middle East Studies*, vol. 39, no. 3 (2007), 369–387.

Sublet, Jacqueline, 'Nisba', *Encyclopaedia of Islam*, second edition. Online: http://dx.doi.org/10.1163/1573-3912_islam_COM_0866 (accessed 7 August 2016).

Sviri, Sara, '*Wa-Rahbānīyatan Ibtada'ūhā*: An Analysis of Traditions Concerning the Origin and Evaluation of Christian Monasticism', *Jerusalem Studies in Arabic and Islam*, vol. 13 (1990), 195–208.

Thibon, Jean-Jacques, *L'oeuvre d'Abū ʿAbd al-Raḥmān al-Sulamī (325/937–412/1021) et la Formation du Soufisme* (Damas: Institut Français du Proche-Orient, 2009).

Tor, D. G., 'God's Cleric: al-Fuḍayl b. ʿIyāḍ and the Transition from Caliphal to Prophetic Sunna', in *Islamic Cultures, Islamic Contexts: Essays in Honor of Professor Patricia Crone*, ed. by Behnam Sadeghi, Asad Ahmed, Adam Silverstein and Robert Hoyland (Leiden and Boston: Brill, 2015), 195–228.

Touati, Houari, *Islam and Travel in the Middle Ages*, trans. from the original French edition (*Islam et Voyage au Moyen Âge: Histoire et Anthropologie d'une Pratique Lettrée* (Paris: Le Seuil, L'univers historique, 2000) by Lydia Cochrane (Chicago and London: The University of Chicago Press, 2012).

Tourage, Mahdi, *Rūmī and the Hermeneutics of Eroticism* (Leiden and Boston: Brill, 2007).

Van Ess, Joseph, *Ungenützte Texte zur Karrāmiyya: Eine Materialsammlung* (Heidelberg: C. Winter-Universitaetsverlag, 1980).

Watt, Montgomery, 'Some Mystics of the Later Third/Ninth Century', *Islamic Studies*, vol. 7, no. 4 (1968), 309–316.

Wensinck, A. J., *Concordance et Indices de la Tradition Musulmane* (Leiden: Brill, 1992).

Winter, Michael, *Society and Religion in Early Ottoman Egypt: Studies in the Writings of ʿAbd al-Wahhāb al-Shaʿrānī* (New Brunswick, N.J.: Transaction Books, 1982).

Winters, Jonah, 'Themes of the Erotic in Sufi Mysticism'. Online: http://bahai-library.com/?file=winters_themes_erotic_sufism.html (posted 1997); http://bahai-library.com/pdf/w/winters_erotic_mysticism.pdf (updated and reloaded 2016).

Wright Jr., J. W., and Everett K. Rowson, *Homoeroticism in Classical Arabic Literature*, ed. by J. W. Wright Jr. and Everett K. Rowson (New York: Columbia University Press, 1997).

Wright Jr., J. W., 'Masculine Allusion and Structure of Satire in Early ʿAbbāsid Poetry', in *Homoeroticism in Classical Arabic Literature*, ed. by J. W. Wright Jr. and Everett K. Rowson (New York: Columbia University Press, 1997), 1–23.

Yazaki, Saeko, *Islamic Mysticism and Abū Ṭālib al-Makkī: The Role of the Heart* (London and New York: Routledge, 2013).

al-Yūsuf, Yūsuf Sāmī, *Muqaddima li-l-Niffarī* (Damascus: Muʾassasat ʿAlāʾ al-Dīn, 2004).

Zysow, Aron, 'Karrāmiya', *Encyclopaedia Iranica*, vol. xv, fasc. 6, 590–601.

Index